FORD PERFORMANCE
BY PAT GANAHL

FORD PERFORMANCE

EDITED BY
LARRY SCHREIB

PRODUCTION BY
LARRY ATHERTON

ISBN 0-931472-05-9
PART No. 05-9

S-A DESIGN BOOKS, 515 WEST LAMBERT, BLDG E, BREA, CA 92621-3991

CONTENTS

INTRODUCTION 4
MODERN FORD ENGINE FAMILIES 5
THE 90 V-SMALLBLOCK 6
THE BIG BLOCK "FE" 9
429 & 460, THE "385" FAMILY 12
351 CLEVELAND & 400;
THE "335" FAMILY 14
A CHRONOLOGY OF FORD ENGINES 17

THE 90 V FAMILY; THE SMALLBLOCK 19
INTRODUCTION 19
BLOCKS 20
CRANKSHAFT 21
RODS 22
PISTONS 23
CAMSHAFTS & VALVETRAIN 24
CYLINDER HEADS 27
INDUCTION SYSTEM 31
IGNITION 32
MISCELLANEOUS 33
THE 351 WINDSOR 33
THE BOSS 302 35
BUILDING A 90 V SMALLBLOCK 38

THE "FE" BIG BLOCK 42
INTRODUCTION 43
BLOCKS 46
CRANKSHAFTS 46
PISTONS 48
HEADS 49
HIGH-RISER 50
MEDIUM-RISER 51
TUNNEL-PORT 51
COBRA JET/LOW-RISER 51
ROCKERARMS 52
VALVES 52
CAMSHAFTS 54
INTAKE MANIFOLDS 58
EXHAUST 58
IGNITION 58
BIG-BLOCK BUILDING TIPS 59
THE SINGLE OVERHEAD CAM 427 63
BUILDING AN "FE" BIG BLOCK 68

THE CLEVELAND FAMILY 72
INTRODUCTION 73
CYLINDER BLOCKS 75
CRANKSHAFT 76
RODS & PISTONS 77
CYLINDER HEADS 78
VALVETRAIN 81
CAMSHAFTS 84
INDUCTION SYSTEMS 85
IGNITION 86
HEADERS 88
MISCELLANEOUS 89
BUILDING TIPS 90
THE 400 CID 91
A LOOK AT THE PRO-STOCK 351-C 92
351 CLEVELAND FOR CIRCLE TRACK 98
SHORT BLOCKS 98
HEADS 100
CAMSHAFT 102
OTHER PARTS 103
BUILDING A 351 CLEVELAND 104

THE "385" FAMILY 108
INTRODUCTION 109
CYLINDER BLOCK 109
CRANKSHAFT 110
RODS 111
PISTONS 112
HEADS/ROCKERS 113
INTAKE SYSTEMS 116
CAMS/VALVE SPRINGS 116
EXHAUST 118
OTHER PARTS 118
THE BOSS 429 120
STREET BOSS 429 120
THE NASCAR 429 121
THE CAN-AM BOSS 429 121
BUILDING A "385" ENGINE 122

APPENDIX 126

INTRODUCTION

Ford engines—including the Red Head four-banger (above) and the legendary flathead (above right)—are the cornerstones of hot rodding history. These engines formed the heritage on which modern Ford engines are founded.

INTRODUCTION: MODERN FORD ENGINE FAMILIES

There are two types of Ford engine books. One discusses flathead V-8's, Fronty T's, and Riley 4-port Model C's; the other describes the Ford high performance engines of the 1960's and early 70's, telling how to modify such engines with factory Off Highway Only (OHO) or Muscle parts. Both are history books. This volume is for the racer, off-roader, boater, or street rodder who wants to build more performance into his modern Ford engine using current, available parts and up-to-date modification techniques. Hopefully, it will fill a void that has persisted in this area for several years.

One of the major reasons why modern Ford performance engine building has been largely overlooked by writers is that the subject appears quite complex. Indeed, it does take some sorting out. Rather than a basic small block and a basic big block, with unilateral parts interchangeability within each family, Fords of recent vintage come in all sizes, shapes, and configurations. Some small blocks are bigger than big blocks. Some engines of exactly the same size are completely different. Some parts interchange between engine families, and some families contain engines with different blocks and heads than other members of the same family.

You can't tell the players without a scorecard. So let's begin by narrowing down the field to four engine families, and then we will take a chronological look at the various offerings within each related group.

Ford engines of recent history (post-flathead) can be categorized into six general families: (1) the Y-block, which was introduced in 1954 as a 239-incher, reached its peak as a supercharged 312 in '57, and was carried in production as a 292-incher through 1962; (2) the MEL family, which was primarily known for the huge (especially for the time) 430-inch Lincoln and Mercury Marauder engines of the mid-50's, and which continued production through 1968 in Lincolns and Mercuries as a 462; (3) the FE or "big block" family, which has been the longest running and most varied of the overhead valve Ford engines; (4) the 90°V family, or "small block," made famous by the Mustang and at Indianapolis; (5) the "335" family, which includes the 351-Cleveland and 400 cid; and (6) the "385" family comprised of the 429 and 460 big blocks. This book will be concerned only with the last four of these six families, since these are the Ford engines that are readily available today and the ones for which at least some high performance products are available.

The main purpose of this book will be: to cover each of the current Ford V-8 engine types in one publication; to

Ford designed the Mustang to capture the youth market, and the potent pony car still retains its image as the hot rod of today. This small block, modified with contemporary induction, ignition, and headers reflects the state of the art in creative street machinery.

Many Ford enthusiasts covet and seek out the still plentiful Shelby Cobra and Ford Muscle Parts factory hop-up goodies for their small blocks. This roadster runs a 302 with rare triple Holley two-barrel intake.

show the most pertinent performance modifications for each type; to give a rundown on performance/specialty products currently available; and to upgrade the familiar subject of Ford engine parts swapping for the "good" combinations. It will be assumed that the majority of readers are interested primarily in honest, reliable street performance, bracket racing building tips, ski-boat engines, or circle track competition using Ford engines and parts that are readily available. We will also cover the latest full-on racing applications, as well as all the super-trick factory racing ventures of the late 60's and early 70's. However, we realize that many of these highly-touted Cobra, Boss, and OHO factory racing parts are simply no longer available to the common Ford engine builder, and we present them here primarily as historical interest to any Ford enthusiast and as a guide to those who might luckily happen upon such goodies.

When Carroll Shelby slipped a Ford small block into the agile British A.C. roadster he came up with a snake of a race car with a singularly venomous bite. Introduced as a limited-production model in 1963, the first 75 had 260 cid small blocks, the next 580 came with the High-Performance 289 version.

FOUR FAMILIES OF FORD

THE 90°V SMALL BLOCK

Introduced in 1962 in a 221 cubic inch version for their new "intermediate sized" Fairlane, the 90°V engine was the first true Ford small block, designed for weight-saving "thinwall" iron casting techniques. The new little motor was long and narrow. It weighed just over 450 pounds (considerable additional weight was saved by eliminating the crankcase "skirt" of previous OHV Fords). The basic two-barrel, 8.7:1 compression version was rated at a very optimistic 216 horsepower. At first it didn't cause a lot of excitement among hot rodders. By late '62, however, Ford management was getting ready to mount one of the most comprehensive and energetic factory racing programs in Detroit history, and decided to kick it off with a shot at the Indianapolis 500—with their brand new little V-8, in basically stock form. Meanwhile they had increased the bore of the production engine 0.300-inch, for a 260 inch total displacement, and offered it as an option in "Sprint" Falcons as well as in the Fairlanes. The Indy engine used a cast iron block (sleeved down to 255 cubic inches) and heads, but otherwise it was identical to the production design. With Weber carburetors the engine produced 375 horsepower on gasoline. This was good enough to place second and seventh (Clark and Gurney) in the '63 Memorial Day Classic and to secure the publicity and image that Ford was seeking.

The next year (1964) Ford launched a new era of automotive design, marketing, and performance with the Mustang—the first "Pony Car," and predecessor of the Muscle Machines. With it came the small block punched out to four inches (4.0 inches by 2.87 inches) for 289 cubic inches in a very obviously oversquare, short-stroke arrangement. At the same time Carroll Shelby was stuffing small Ford V-8's and four-speeds into A.C. Bristol roadsters with Ford factory approval, and the Cobra mystique was born. Eventually a special package consisting of a four-barrel manifold and carb, solid-lifter cam, 10½:1 compression, and finned aluminum valve covers was offered for the factory Mustang. Yielding an advertised 271 horsepower, this High Performance 289 Mustang posed the first real threat to Chevrolet's long-standing small block supremacy.

In the middle of the '65 production year Ford changed from a smaller five-bolt bellhousing configuration to the larger current six-bolt design. All 221, 260 and early 289 engines have the smaller bellhousing flange (which might be an advantage in some engine-swapping situations where floorboard or firewall clearance is tight), but there is little problem of transmission interchangeability since the bellhousing portion of automatic transmissions (C-4) unbolts and can be swapped. The 289 remained in production virtually un-

Undoubtedly the best known performance machine of all time—the reputation of the original Shelby GT-350 Mustang was known around the world. By modern standards the GT-350 is still a remarkable machine.

So lovely to look at, so exhilarating to drive and so expensive to own—only six Daytona Cobra Coupes were built to compete in international closed-coupe competition. It is among the rarest of all Fords ever built.

When Ford went racing, they went with style. The spectrum of all-out racing Ford engines is awesome—including: 1-3) the dual overhead cam small block, proven at the Indy Brickyard (beneath the four gear-driven camshafts, 32 valves, and direct-port injection, dwells the same 90° V-8 offered in the fourth-generation Mustang and, hopefully, for years to come); 4) after driving a rockerarm small block in the '63 Indy race, Dan Gurney built the Gurney-Weslake heads and added slide-valve injectors to crank out 600 horses; 5) another Gurney project, the rare Gurney-Eagle has three valves per cylinder (two intake, one exhaust) and was designed by John Miller of All American Racers; 6)after racing fervor was squelched at Ford, the DOHC was turned over to A.J. Foyt, who continued the bloodline in Championship cars as the turbocharged Coyote engine; 7)and, an even rarer Weslake head conversion intended for DeTomaso Mangustas and Panteras (the engine below the heads and Weber carbs is a production Ford 302).

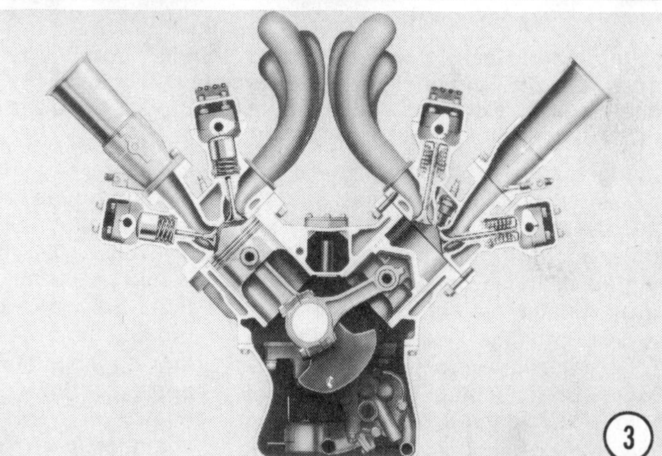

Young enthusiasts don't call good things "boss" any more. But the Ford engine by that name is still boss of the small blocks. For a showroom production model, the Boss 302 Mustang was an outright factory hot rod.

The Mustang name lives today and the "muscle" image of the original Cobras and Shelbys continues to have tremendous sales appeal, despite the modest power levels.

changed from 1965 through 1968.

After Ford's surprising success with the stock rockerarm small block at Indianapolis in '63, they turned their engineers loose on one of the most sophisticated projects ever concocted at Dearborn, the Dual Overhead Cam Ford engine. Using the same basic 90°V, 255-inch block (cast of aluminum), they added a pair of aluminum heads with four gear-driven overhead cams, four valves per cylinder, and Hilborn fuel injectors. It was designed strictly for racing at Indy (it has never been offered in a production Ford), and it has been eminently successful.

Dan Gurney, of All-American Racers, still liked the reliability of a pushrod engine, however. By 1967 he had developed his own bolt-on aluminum heads for the Ford small block, known as the Gurney-Weslake head (later as the Gurney-Eagle). Used successfully by Gurney at Indianapolis with four-bolt main cap, cast iron Ford blocks, these heads were also designed to be sold as bolt-on kits for street or racing production cars. For racing, four downdraft Weber carburetors were offered, and a single four-barrel manifold was later produced for street versions. Some of these kits trickle into the swap meet or collector's market even today, but few of them reached the public when first introduced.

In 1968 Ford increased the stroke of the little engine to three inches (4.00 inches by 3.00 inches) to arrive at the current small block production displacement of 302 inches. Still very actively engaged in racing, Ford immediately introduced a set of "Tunnel-Port" heads for 302's used in Trans Am cars. Patterned after the more successful Tunnel-Port heads designed for the Nascar 427 big block engine, this design (which routed the intake pushrods in small tubes through the center of giant round intake ports) didn't produce the expected results on the smaller displacement engine. Consequently, the Tunnel-Port small block heads never reached production. But the next year ('69) Ford refined the big port design for the 302 by moving the pushrods to the side of the ports, canting the valves for a "semi-hemi" (or "poly-angle") combustion chamber, and retaining gigantic oval ports for both intake and exhaust. Known as the Boss 302 engine and offered in '69 and '70 Boss Mustangs and Mercury Cougar Eliminators, it included 10½:1 compression pistons, four-bolt mains, forged rods, and a windage tray, a 290° duration solid-lifter cam, dual-point distributor, and an aluminum intake manifold with a 780-cfm Holley four-barrel carb. In other words, it was an out and out factory hot rod engine, and it acted like one!

The last development in the 90°V small block line came in 1969, and it was a major one. The new engine is known as the 351-Windsor, and it features a different block, different heads, a unique intake manifold, a new crankshaft, and even an altered firing order. Most of the changes were made to handle the half-inch longer 351-W stroke (4.00 inches by 3.50 inches). The new block is not only beefier in the main bearing web area, but is significantly "taller" than the other small blocks, having 1.275-inch higher decks. Thus the cylinder heads are spaced farther apart, meaning the 351-W has a wider intake manifold which will not interchange with any others in the Ford line. The crankshaft is not only stroked half an inch, but also has larger rod journals as well as significantly larger (3.00-inch) main journals to add rigidity. Although the cam is ground in a different firing order (1-3-7-2-6-5-4-8 for the 351-W, 1-5-4-2-6-3-7-8 for other small blocks), cams from other engines in the family can be used in the Windsor if the firing order is rewired at the distributor to match the cam. The 315-W heads are very similar to those on other small blocks, and can be adapted to the smaller engines as we will demonstrate later. Although they have slightly larger head bolts (½-inch as opposed to 7/16-inch), a minor variation in the water passages, and an extra head bolt, the rest of the Windsor head bolt pattern is the same as the 260-289. Valve arrangement on the Windsor is identical to other small blocks (except the Boss 302), but the ports and valves are larger (1.84-inch intakes, 1.54-inch exhausts). The combustion chambers are also larger, yet still of a "quench" rather than an open-chamber design. First introduced in both two-barrel and four-barrel versions with 10½:1 compression (rated 320 and 360hp respectively), by '71 the four-barrel engine was discontinued and the compression dropped to 9:1 (240hp). The Windsor remains in the Ford engine lineup today, basically unchanged except for compression ratios and valve timing, but the horsepower ratings continue to deteriorate—the current output being approximately 140 horsepower.

By 1971 all auto manufacturers were beginning to feel the effects of smog control legislation, and Ford was entering the waning years of the high performance age. The Boss head package was adapted to the new and bigger 351-Cleveland, and the 302 was downgraded to a two-barrel, 9:1 compression engine rated at 210 horsepower (less than the rating of the original 221 small block!). In '72 the compression dropped to 8.5:1 and the rated horsepower to a modest 140. The next year the compression dropped another half a point with a sacrifice of another five horsepower. These specs remained virtually unchanged until '77, when the compression was boosted slightly to 8.4:1, with no advertised increase in power. Don't let the recent numbers discourage you, however, it's still the same good little engine it always has been and parts are plentiful to pep it back up to performance era standards.

THE BIG BLOCK "FE"

The oldest of the modern Ford engines and the most varied is the big block, or the FE family, which began production back in 1958 with two sizes, 332 and 352 cubic inches. The FE is cast in the "Y-block" or extended skirt style and is of the older thick-wall construction; a complete engine weighs over 700 pounds. One of the FE design idiosyncracies, which often frustrates manifold swappers, is the extra wide intake manifold, through which all the pushrods are routed. Changing the intake on one of these engines requires not only removing the distributor and retiming the ignition, but removing the valve covers, all the pushrods, and afterwards resetting all the valves. This minor irritation certainly did not engender enough complaints to hinder the career of the FE, since it remained in production through 1971. The real beauty of this engine family is that, despite several confusing head and manifold combinations, the blocks are all basically the same (except for some changes in oiling or main caps); bearing sizes and bolt patterns remained unchanged; all engines from the 390 to the 428 even maintained the same rod length; and the various heads will bolt onto any given block within the family (although the larger valves fitted in some heads will not clear the small-bore blocks).

In 1961 when Ford eased out of its first short-lived ban on racing, the FE was pumped up to 390 inches, a four-speed was offered in full sized cars, and Super Stock drag racing was born. With three two-barrel carbs on an aluminum manifold, cast iron headers, and 10.6:1 compression, the '61 Super High Performance 390 was rated at a very healthy 401 horsepower. Offered from '61 to '63, the High Performance 390 (with three-twos or a single four-barrel) featured a special block with beefier main bearing webs and caps, a grooved crank for better main bearing oiling, larger "cornerless" oil galleries, and a pressure relief valve in the oil system at the top rear of the block. They (and the Police Interceptor 390) all came with solid-lifter cams and adjustable rockers, and no provision was made in the block to route oil to the lifters (eliminating the possibility of using hydraulic lifters). The High Performance 390 heads had smaller combustion chambers (59.7-62.7cc) than the standard heads (average 69cc), the pistons were flat-tops with eyebrows, and the connecting rods had a stronger bottom end with 13/32-inch bolts rather than the standard 3/8-inch.

Then, in 1962, primarily to compete with the mystique of the "gigantic" (which it was, for the time) 409 Chevy, Ford got the FE into the 400-plus inch category with a seemingly insignificant 0.080-inch overbore—yielding 406 cubic inches. The 406 used the same beefier and better oiling block as the High Performance 390, and a few of the late'63 vintage 406 engines were fitted with "cross-bolted" main bearing caps identical to those later used on the 427. Running 11.4:1 compression, the 406 was offered with a single four-barrel for 385hp, or with the three two-barrel ("6V") setup for 405hp. And yes, it kept right up with the 409 on both the drag strips and the circle tracks.

By 1964 Ford was building racing engines. The 406 bore was opened up another 0.100-inch (4.23 inches by 3.78 inches) to give 427 cubic inches, and with a stout 11.5:1 compression ratio and dual four-barrel carbs it produced an advertised 425 horsepower. This engine appeared in several versions

The muscle-car era began in 1961, when the 390 Fords and 409 Chevys met for the first time at the Winternationals drag races. By '62, the Ford big block was opened up to 406 cubic inches and came with three carburetors, cast iron headers, and a four-speed floor shift—all straight from the factory.

When Ford slightly enlarged their mid-size Fairlane to accept the big block engines in '66, rodders knew they had a potent package. Extremely popular was the "GTA" model, like this one, which came with the 335 horsepower 390 GT engine. The favorite of Stock class drag racers today, however, is the '66 427 Fairlane, of which only 70 were made.

between late 1963 and 1968, some being regular production models (Low-Riser, Medium-Riser) and others being strictly special order or over-the-counter combinations (High-Riser, Tunnel-Port, SOHC). The general 427 nomenclature refers to the type of heads used on the engine (with accompanying manifolds), plus they are further distinguished by block design. Most '63-64 vintage blocks were identical to the High Performance 390 and 406 block design, including large oil galleries with a pressure relief valve, but without oiling to the lifter bores house, since only mechanical camshafts were used in these engines. Only a few '63-64 engines (High-Risers and some 8V Low-Risers) had the cross-bolted main caps. From '65 on, all came with a new "side-oiler" block. Rather than routing the main oil gallery down the center of the block, like all other FE engines, with oil distribution going to the cam journals before getting to the crank, the side-oiler has the main oil gallery low on the left side near the pump outlet. This gallery feeds directly to the mains, then to the cam, and then to the rockers via grooves in the second and fourth cam journals. A grooved camshaft must be used in a side-oiler; other blocks have grooves in the block around the cam bearings to feed the lifters. In 1968 an extra set of passages was added to the side-oiler block to feed the lifter galleries, allowing hydraulic-lifter cams to be used in these engines. A side-oiler 427 can be distinguished externally by noting a bulge running along the left side of the block between the skirt and the freeze plugs.

In '68 the Fairlane was increased in size again and renamed the Torino. The slippery body style was an immediate success on the Grand National super tracks...and Dan Gurney didn't do badly with the big block at his home course, the twisting Riverside Raceway, either.

Headwise, 427 history goes something like this. The Low-Riser was offered in late '63 and '64. It used essentially the same heads as the 390/406 with non-machined combustion chambers, a cast iron crank, Police Interceptor type rods, a solid-lifter cam and adjustable rockers. In 1968 the Low-Riser was again offered, but in a more streetable version with a side-oiler block and a hydraulic cam. In '64 the High-Riser engine was offered in limited production for racing in Nascar Galaxies and Thunderbolt Fairlanes. These heads featured very tall rectangular intake ports, machined combustion chambers, lightweight valves, and a raised-runner intake manifold which placed the carburetor(s) about two to three inches higher than other designs. Since cars fitted with this engine required a special bubble or scoop in the hood to clear the carburetors, they weren't offered as regular production models. The High-riser came with a cast crank, stronger rods, pop-up pistons, and a choice of a single four-barrel or a dual four-barrel, dual-plane aluminum intake manifold.

The Medium-Riser engine was offered from '65 through '67. It featured the side-oiler block, a steel crank, fully machined heads with shorter rectangular ports, and a choice of a regular dual-plane, four-barrel intake, or an equal-runner, four-barrel with offset carb (known as the "sidewinder"), or a dual-plane, dual four-barrel intake. These manifolds placed the carbs three inches lower than High-Risers, so they could be installed under the hoods of production Fords. Also offered for the Medium-Riser was a single-plane, elevated, dual four-barrel intake, known as the "Tunnel-Wedge" (not to be confused with the Tunnel-Port).

The Tunnel-Port 427 heads and manifolds became available as an option in 1968. These heads have huge round "straight shot" intake ports which, rather than bending around the pushrods, required that the pushrods pass through the middle of the port (in the manifold) in a small tube. The Tunnel-Ports have fully machined combustion chambers and bigger 2.25-inch intake valves (others use 2.19-inch intakes). Ford offered a single-plane, single four-barrel intake for the Tunnel-Port, as well as both single-plane and dual-plane, dual four-barrels.

Going back a bit to 1965, the wildest 427 option of all was the SOHC (single overhead cam). Offered only as an over-the-counter package (it was never installed by the factory in a

Only someone who has driven one can describe what it's really like. Undoubtedly the fastest and hairiest production automobile ever sold in America was the 427 Shelby Cobra, offered to the public from '65 through '67.

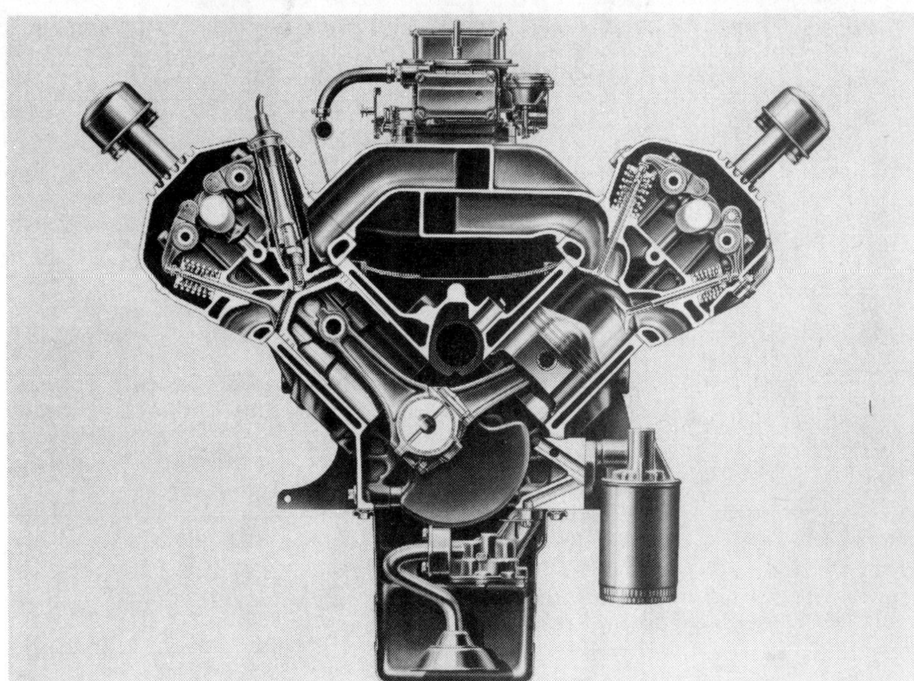

The Single Overhead Cam (SOHC) 427 was a side-oiler big block with a wild set of hemi heads. You bought the complete engine, with dual four-barrels, cast iron headers, and a deep-sump oil pan, in a crate at the dealer's for about $2500. A surprisingly large number were sold, and are cherished by Ford-philes today.

production car), the SOHC applied some of Ford's new-found overhead cam technology (from the little Indy small block) to a big and brutish Nascar and drag racing powerplant. The unique design consisted of a set of aluminum heads with hemispherical combustion chambers and opposed valves actuated by roller rockers riding on a single camshaft located in the center of each head. According to some critics, the one drawback of this engine was the very long chain used to drive the two cams, which could stretch slightly and make degreeing the valve events rather touchy or permit valve timing variations. On the other hand, the SOHC did produce results impressive enough to raise immediate cries of protest from the Nascar and NHRA stock-class competition and the new engine was shortly "factored" out of contention. The "Cammers" were seen in several notable drag combinations during the mid-60's, and a surprising number of these engines are still around and being run today; in fact they seem to be gaining popularity as a prized collector's item. The SOHC block was essentially identical to the side-oiler 427 except that an extra drainback oil passage is cast in the rear of each cylinder bank. The Cammer heads cannot be swapped onto another 427 block unless some provision is made to carry oil from the heads back to the pan.

The 427 was last offered by Ford in production cars in 1968 as a four-barrel, 10.9:1 compression, cast crank, hydraulic-cam engine rated at 390 horsepower. But it will long be remembered by hot rodders as one of Detroit's most direct involvements in the hot rod sport. The 427 was designed from the axiom, "bigger is better," and Ford readily admits that it was an out and out hot rod mill: "...frankly, you can't improve upon (the 427) factory performance like you can with other stock engines...because the 427 was designed and built for high performance. A fact proven by its consistent wins on strips and tracks around the world since its introduction..."[1]

Meanwhile, the immediate successor to the 427, the 428, had been introduced in 1966. What difference does one cubic inch make? The 427 and the 428 are very similar engines (unlike the 429, which belongs to a different family), and both are based on the FE design. The one cubic inch displacement difference was brought about by a fairly substantial change in both bore and stroke—the 427 measuring 4.23 inches by 3.78 inches and the 428 measuring 4.13 inches by 3.98 inches. The "squarer" dimensions of the long-stroke 428 should immediately identify it as a more tractable version of the big block, and so it was. It was designed for more utilitarian use than the full-race 427, and it provides lots of pulling power all through the rpm range. The initial 428, with a single four-barrel and 10.5:1 compression (rated at 345 horses), was fitted with heads and intake similar to the 390 and was installed in the larger passenger cars and station wagons. Although the 428 has the same bore size as the 406, unfortunately it does not share the same improved-oiling block design as the 406 or 427. Like the standard 390, the 428 has a restriction in the oil passage to the rear mains designed to force more oil pressure to the lifter

1. Ford Muscle Parts Catalog, p.61

The Ford SOHC conversion for the 427 engine is a true hemispherical chamber design with huge opposed valves and extremely efficient ports. The single cam on top of each head controls rockerarms that actuate the valves. Except for the long chains used to drive the cams the design proved to be extraordinarily effective and trouble free.

From '68 to '70 Ford took their new drag racing program directly to the people, visiting drag strips and dealer showrooms across the country. For '68 the drivers were Randy Wood and Ed Terry, and the machines were a 428 Cobra Jet Mustang and a 428 CJ Torino.

Sharp eyes will identify a 427 Low-Riser in Wes Johnson's very clean and consistent Shelby Mustang. The '68 GT 500 originally came with a Cobra Jet 428.

To debut the new Cobra Jet 428, Ford built six specially-prepped Mustangs to take full advantage of NHRA Super Stock rules (solid-lifter cams, lighter valves, etc.). The first two were introduced at the '68 Winternationals, driven to 1-2 class finish by Al Joniec and Hubert Platt.

galleries, and the main oil galleries are smaller with sharp bends. A further complicating characteristic of the 428 (a problem also common to the 427) is that it came with thin cylinder walls. Boring one of these engines more than .030-inch is definitely not suggested. And, as you might expect, all of the 428 assemblies feature cast crankshafts and two-bolt mains. In actuality, the 428 is a bored and stroked 390.

When the 427 disappeared from the Ford line with the introduction (in 1968) of the new 428 version, the 428 was immediately spruced up to take over the job of promoting performance. Ford had already introduced a new Mustang design with a bigger engine compartment and a wider front tread than the first model, and the big block was ready to drop in. They called the combination a Cobra Jet, and this name also became identified with the engine. The "CJ 428" package consisted of cast aluminum, dished and eyebrowed pistons, giving a compression ratio of 10.7:1 (a 12.5:1 pop-up was also offered through dealers). It also had stronger "Police Interceptor" rods with 11/32-inch bolts, a cast iron intake manifold with a 735-cfm Holley carb, a choice of two different hydraulic camshafts, and a new set of cylinder heads very similar to the Medium-Riser 427 (but with slightly taller intake ports and non-machined combustion chambers). A special order aluminum "Police-Interceptor" manifold, identical in design to the iron one, was also available. As stated by Ford, the 428 CJ "answers the call for a reliable, streetable high performance engine...(it) is quiet...a docile street performer...low in cost. It is a high volume, regular production engine that can turn in amazing performance right off the showroom floor."[2] The Cobra Jet was marketed as a Mustang option, but some of them were also put in Mercury Cougars, Comet Cyclones, and Ford Torinos. In 1969 the Super Cobra Jet package was offered for 428 Mustangs. Primarily it was an accessory group including an engine oil cooler and lower rear end gears, but the SCJ engines also got a much better capscrew connecting rod (the same rod used in the Medium-Riser 427).

1970 was the last year for the 428 and marked the end of development of the FE engine line. The 390 was offered for one more year as a production car engine, being the last common FE big block powerplant.

2. 1969 Ford Performance Parts Catalog, pp 4,5.

However, it should probably be mentioned that FE engines of various sizes have always been offered in the Ford truck line, some until very recently. Light truck FE engines came in 360 and 390 inches, both being similar to other big blocks except that they were designed for hard work, not high speed. These engines came with compression ratios around 8.5:1. For larger rigs, Ford had the 361 and 391 engines (a 361 FE was also used in '58 and '59 Edsels—it was a regular passenger car engine). The extra cubic inch denotes that these engines are actually "FT" truck engines, the main difference being that they had very low compression ratios (7.4:1), heavy duty parts, and steel cranks. As a point of information, the truck steel cranks are readily available, have the same journal sizes as all FE's (the 361 has the same stroke as the 352; the 391 is the same as the 390 and 427), and need only high-rpm balancing and to have the snout turned down for installation in car engines. However, such a swap is uncommon—probably because the FE cast cranks are plenty tough as is.

429 & 460, THE "385" FAMILY

The average showroom customer was probably beginning to wonder

The cammer proved itself in 1969, winning virtually every major Funny Car event of the season in Mickey Thompson's Mach 1 Mustang. The car was driven by Danny Ongais.

When NHRA instituted the Pro Stock Class in 1970, Ford was participating with Hubert Platt's "Georgia Shaker" SOHC Mustang. With essentially stock body and chassis, it ran high nines, low tens.

what Ford was up to when their engine options for 1968 included the 427, the 428, and the 429. Simple: the 427 was the real high performance member of the FE big block family, the 428 was a tamed down production version of the FE, and the 429 was not an FE at all, but rather a brand new big block of modern design trying out its first innings in the Ford lineup. Actually, the new big block, labeled the "385" family, was introduced in two versions in '68, the 429 (4.36 inches by 3.59 inches) and the giant 460 (4.36 inches by 3.85 inches) for Lincolns and Mercuries. Supposedly the new engine was designed for "big luxury cars," but the design was certainly more up to date than the ten-year-old FE, and it remotely resembled another very competitve big block already in production over in another sector of Detroit. The 429 block is a thinwall casting, it is big and beefy with longer bore centers than the FE, it has huge bearings, and it introduced into the Ford line the canted-valve cylinder head arrangement. This new head design, which was to prove so successful the next year on the Boss 302 small block, canted the intake and exhaust valves at two different angles to form a slightly hemispherical chamber, thus allowing the use of larger valves and gaining a better "unshrouded" intake mixture path into the cylinder. Because of the staggered valve arrangement, this was the first OHV Ford engine that didn't use rocker shafts, each rocker riding on a fulcrum on a separate pedestal.

With the disappearance of the 427 in '68, and possibly because of the SOHC's rejection by both Nascar and NHRA a few years earlier, Ford engineers immediately sketched out a very interesting set of high performance cylinder heads for the new 429. Introduced in 1969 as the Boss 429 and installed in at least 500 Boss 429 Mustangs that year (to make sure it would be legal), this unique design has come to be known either as the "Shotgun 429" or the Semi-Hemi. The aluminum heads were of a modified hemispherical design with one very short and one very long rockerarm per cylinder and one camshaft in the normal location in the middle of the block. The Boss 429 block was of the same basic design as the other family members, but altered enough (stronger main bearing webbing, a different oiling system, four-bolt mains) so that they are not interchangeable. A few all-aluminum Boss 429 blocks were also produced. The huge, round ports of the unique heads and the giant 2.40-inch intake valves made the engine a little empty on mid-range torque, but it dominated the long Nascar superspeedways.

When the FE 428 was phased out in 1970, the 429 became the new Cobra Jet engine. The switchover took place during the '70 model year, so some Cobra Jets that year came with the 428 and others came with the 429. The 429 CJ package included substantially bigger heads (ports and valves), stamped steel rockers, screw-in rocker studs (early '70 models), and guideplates like the Boss 302. Compression was upped to 11.3:1 (from 10.5:1), and the induction was handled by a cast iron intake with a single 700-cfm Rochester four-barrel. Compared to the Boss 429, the 427, and other Ford specialty performance engines, the CJ 429 was a practical performance package that provided plenty of power (rated at 370hp), didn't cost much extra to manufacture, was very livable on the street, and even satisfied impinging emission standards.

Still thinking along these lines, Ford introduced the next "upgrade" of the 385 family in '71, the Super Cobra Jet 429. Rated at only five more horsepower, the SCJ 429 featured the

The 429 big blocks haven't yet attained the popularity, among hot rodders, of other Ford engines...probably because they lacked the factory promoted performance image. But they offer plenty of power (by current standards) in a readily available, low cost package. It's not a bad looking engine, either.

The most exotic engine ever offered by Ford in production line models was the Boss 429 Hemi. This '69 Boss Mustang is completely stock...anyone could buy one off the showroom floor. Unfortunately, the end of the performance era was already in sight when the Hemi was introduced.

One of the few to recognize the potential of the 460 Ford as a brutish, reliable bracket racing powerplant is Don Cumby of Whittier, CA. The 460 in his '70 Torino is relatively mild—Venolia pistons, .700-inch lift/320° duration cam, slightly reworked CJ heads, a much-modified Offy tunnel ram, two Holley carbs, and Hays ignition. With a C-6 automatic, 5.14 gears, and 14 x 32 slicks, it pulls the 3875-pound car to 10.50/130 mph times.

extra insurance of four-bolt main caps, forged aluminum pistons, a bigger oil pump and an external oil cooler, and (like the CJ) a cast crank of a higher nodularity than the base 429. Also included in the SCJ package was a mechanical camshaft with adjustable rockers (the CJ had a juice cam), and a bigger-based intake manifold with a 780 Holley four-barrel carb.

The 429 was dropped from the Ford line after 1973, but the big 460 (same bore, approximately a .250-inch longer stroke), which was introduced along with the 429 in '68, is still in production. Originally rated at 360 horsepower with 10.5:1 compression and a four-barrel carb, it dropped to 212 horses (8.5:1) in '72, and then down to about 200 horses (8.0:1) the next year. However, these later advertised horsepower figures reflect net output, as opposed to earlier flywheel (brake) horsepower ratings. There's no getting around the fact that an engine of this size is going to produce some big power numbers, especially if fitted with some of the earlier factory or modern specialty parts. Obviously all "385" family components are interchangeable (other than the Boss heads/block), since the only difference between the 429 and the 460 is the stroke length. Because of the output, the availability, and the relatively moderate cost, the 460 has become very popular as a muscular powerplant for ski boats and off-road pickups.

351-CLEVELAND & 400; THE "335" FAMILY.

According to official definition the 351-Windsor engine is a small block, while the 351-Cleveland is, well, in between. There is no official definition. In appearance, the 351-C looks very much like a small block with an extra extension cast on the front to house the timing gears and mount the fuel pump. Pulling a valve cover reveals the staggered rockerarm arrangement denoting canted valves as on the Boss 302 and 385 family engines. The Cleveland engine is obviously an outgrowth of the 90°V small block line, but very few parts interchange between the two families.

The 351-Cleveland engine was introduced during the 1970 model year in two versions, the two-barrel (2V) and the four-barrel (4V). The difference entailed more than a manifold switch, however. The early 4V 351-C not only came with a cast iron, dual-plane intake manifold with an Autolite carb and a slightly hotter hydraulic camshaft, but also had completely different cylinder heads than the 2V. Featuring bigger valves, substantially larger intake and exhaust ports, and smaller "quench" combustion chambers (the 2V has large, round, "open" chambers), these heads very closely resemble those on the Boss 302. The 2V engine was rated at 240 horsepower (9.0:1 compression) while the 4V was advertised at 285 horsepower (10.7:1). Obviously the four-barrel 351-C heads are in increasing demand these days. You can still find them in junkyards, but the proprietor generally knows what they are worth (three to four times as much as the low compression types).

In 1971 the 302 small block was offered only in a two-barrel version and the Boss package was shifted to the 351-Cleveland. Unfortunately, this combination was offered only one year; it is the ultimate factory 351-C. The only difference between the 351 Boss heads and the 351-C 4V heads is in the rockerarm pedestals, which are machined to accept 7/16-inch studs and adjustable stamped steel rockers. Both the Boss 351 and the 351-C 4V heads are almost identical to the Boss 302, having canted valves of the same size (2.19-inch intakes and 1.71-inch exhausts) and the same large oval ports. The chambers are slightly larger on the 351—66-67cc as opposed to 57-60cc for the Boss 302. Other components of the Boss 351 are equally impressive. The block came with four-bolt main caps, selected for hardness. The crank is cast, but also selected for minimum 90% nodularity. The rods are 1041-H forged steel, shot-peened, Magnafluxed, and fitted with 180,000 psi, 3/8-inch bolts and nuts. Forged aluminum pop-up pistons give a stout 11.1:1 compression ratio. A mechanical camshaft of 290° duration and 0.477-inch lift was used with hardened and ground pushrods and guide plates. It was topped off with an aluminum, dual-plane manifold and an Autolite 4300-D carb.

But 1971 was the last year for high compression engines from Ford. Smog control legislation was tightening, and high octane pump gasoline was rapidly disappearing. The 351-C was born in a period of increasing restrictions, which meant a period of rapid changes. In mid-'71 (May), a new kind of "performance" engine was assembled around the 351 Cleveland—a package that relied more on association with a previous high performance name than anything else. Christened the 351 Cobra Jet, it retained the 4-bolt bottom end, but came only with a hydraulic cam (of slightly more duration than the 4V 351), and a special set of heads which combined the large valves and ports of the Boss and 4V engines with the large open combustion chambers of the 2V design. With a cast aluminum flat-top piston, the 351 CJ yielded less compression than even the standard 4V 351-C (9.0:1 as opposed to 10.7:1). The CJ also came with a spread-bore Autolite carburetor featuring smaller primaries but larger secondaries than the regular four-barrel, and thus requiring a different mounting flange and bolt pattern on essentially the same cast iron intake manifold.

For 1972 the Cobra Jet was still offered in name, but the engine was identical to the four-barrel 351-C for that year. Both were dropped to 9:1 compression, and the cam timing was retarded four degrees. For '72 the Boss nomenclature was changed to HO, for "High Output," and most of the good Boss 351 hardware was retained. However, the HO engine got the open chamber heads and flat-top forged pistons for a compression of 9.2:1, and the solid-lifter cam was given a little less duration and a little more lift (275°; 0.491-inch).

By 1973 Ford had gone to dish-top pistons and the standard 351-C came only in a two-barrel version rated at about 160 horsepower. The four-barrel model was still called a Cobra Jet, but was dropped to 8.0:1 compression and rated at 266 horses. This was the last production year in the brief history of the 351 Cleveland.

There's no question that the 351-Cleveland is one of Ford's prettiest engines, and for this reason it is prized by builders of early model all-Ford street rods.

Another engine, also of the "335" family, which debuted at the same time as the 351 Cleveland is the Ford 400. It is often referred to as a Cleveland itself, but it is not officially designated as such—probably because it is the only 400 cid engine Ford produces and therefore needs no further identification. It resembles the Cleveland engine in general appearance and in several dimensions but, again, not too many parts interchange. To accommodate the .500-inch longer stroke and 0.800-inch longer connecting rods, the 400 block is cast with approximately one-inch taller cylinders than the 351-C. The difference is similar to that between the standard small block and the 351 Windsor engines. Although the 400 uses the same open-chamber, canted-valve heads as the 2V 351 Clevelands, the raised deck height means that the manifold flanges are spaced farther apart and therefore the engine requires a unique, wider intake manifold. And don't get excited about dropping that half-inch stroker crank into a Cleveland, because it won't fit. The 351-C has 2.799-inch journals, and the 400 has 3.00-inch mains. (This is, however, the same size as the journals in the 351-W, where such a swap could be contemplated...if it were worth the trouble.) So far the 400 has attracted little attention in the way of performance modification, mainly because of the lack of specialty/performance intake manifolds or headers and also because of the availability of the 460.

Another Ford engine that you have probably heard very little about, but which rightfully belongs to this same family, is the 351-M. The "M" stands for Modified—but not in the way most performance enthusiasts use the term. After production ceased on the 351 Cleveland, apparently the Windsor plant was unable to keep up with customer demand for an engine of this displacement, so the Ford engineers "modified" the 400 by installing the 351-W crankshaft in the 400 block.

There is little debate that the Cleveland is the culmination of Ford's aggressive performance engineering throughout the '60's. They learned that cylinder heads make the engine, and these heads were made to *breathe*. Too bad this engine didn't stay in the lineup longer.

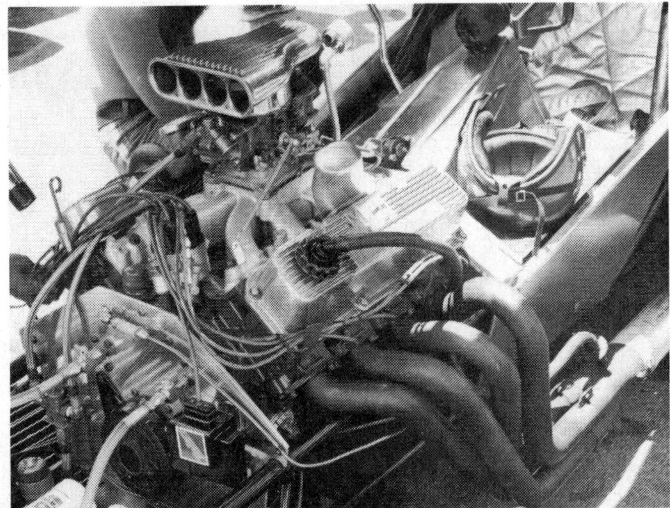

The relative scarcity of engines and speed parts is the major drawback to racing a Cleveland, but the results can be gratifying. It doesn't take much work to make one of these engines fly, especially in the econo bracket classes.

In 1972, NHRA opened Pro Stock to compact bodies, and a highly successful Ford Pro package was born—the 351-C Pinto. As the number on the window attests, the Gapp and Roush entry dominated the class, winning the '73 World Championship.

This gives a 351 cubic inch engine with approximately one-inch taller decks than the Cleveland, and what must be very long connecting rods or very tall pistons (we haven't seen the insides of a 351-M; they aren't popular in performance shops). This engine uses the same intake manifold as the 400, of which only a two-barrel version has been offered. The 351-M has been in production since 1975.

What happened to Ford's unprecedented participation in racing engine development and production? It came to a very unprecedented halt early in 1973 with one of the most unilateral and unbending directives ever to come down from Ford management. We can only speculate about the real reasons behind the move, but the typical statement given was that it had become, "...increasingly important that all company programs be consistent with our intensive efforts to build safer cars and to promote safe driving practices." If you are a Ford performance history fan, you have undoubtedly heard stories about how tons of high performance engine parts were either scrapped or scuttled out back doors in the dead of night, how files were emptied and research and development programs ash canned, and how Ford performance experts suddenly disappeared from Dearborn. Who knows? Most of the specialty performance hardware went to Holman and Moody, and the DOHC Indy engine wound up at A.J. Foyt's shop (to become the Coyote). The subject of high performance or racing was not to be discussed anywhere in the Ford plants or its subsidiaries. A directive dated February 6, 1973 instructed all concerned to "effectively eliminate any financial participation in performance products, parts or events as well as any communication related to performance activities." The same memo also stated that all product development of off-highway and performance parts by Ford was to be discontinued, all promotion of such parts and activities (including Indianapolis and Trans-Am) was to cease, that no new OHO or high performance parts should be added to existing inventories, but that such parts still on the shelves should be phased out through sales.

What all of this means is that in 1973 Ford quit building their own hot rod engines and hop-up parts, and that the job of modifying Ford engines reverted once more to the backyard mechanic and the specialty parts suppliers. Because Ford's involvement in performance engine design and supplies was so pervasive up until this point, most literature—both in book form and in magazine articles—has centered primarily on factory engine combinations and Ford factory parts. There are still plenty of these high performance factory parts around, to be sure, and any Ford enthusiast will want to know how to identify them, how to evaluate them, and how to assemble them in various combinations. For this reason we will present in this book a cataloging of such factory components, especially those that might still be in decent shape after ten years—manifolds, blocks, cylinder heads, etc.—but we realize that many of these parts are now looked on more as coveted collector's items than anything else. Therefore, it is our primary intention to discuss the performance modification of existing and readily available Ford V-8 engines using the many excellent specialty/performance parts now being produced for them, and to keep in mind that "performance" these days means something different than it did ten years ago. We shall presume that the majority of our readers will be building "recreational" engine packages to be used on the street, in bracket racing, in off-road or four-wheel drive vehicles, or in boats. You'll have to live with 90 octane gasoline at best, and you'll have to pay enough for it that you won't forget about fuel economy. You'll probably be running a single four-barrel carb, and you'll spend enough on any engine rebuild that you want to be sure the engine lives and remains reliable once it is put to work. We will touch on the latest developments in more sophisticated Ford engine building—Pro Stock, Nascar, drag boat—to keep you informed of the possibilities and the state of the art. But this book is primarily for the Ford enthusiast who wants to pick up where the factory left off in 1973.

Following Bob Glidden's one year blitz in 1978 with a new Fairmont, most Ford Pro Stock heavies switched from Mustang II's to the "shoebox" for the '79 season. They're still running Clevelands for power, though.

Probably one of the most exotic cars ever produced by American automotive technology, the fabulous Ford GT-40 was designed to win the Le Mans 24-hour endurance race. In stunning fashion, attesting to the strength of the Ford performance heritage, the GT-40 eventually produced a smashing 3-car sweep of the overall championship class.

Since the factory hasn't offered anything to equal them in almost 15 years, muscle cars from the mid-60's dominate NHRA stock classes. Fords still hold their own, one of the prized combinations being the '66-67 427 Fairlanes, such as Greg Foreman's 1977-78 A/S record holder.

A CHRONOLOGY OF FORD ENGINES

YEAR	FAMILY	DISPLACEMENT	BORE X STROKE	COMPRESSION	COMMENTS
58	FE	332	4.00 x 3.30	9.5:1	2-bbl
		352	4.00 x 3.50	10.2:1	4-bbl
59	FE	332	4.00 x 3.30	8.9:1	2-bbl
		352	4.00 x 3.50	9.6:1	4-bbl
60	FE	352	4.00 x 3.50	8.9:1	2-bbl
				9.6:1	4-bbl
61	FE	352	4.00 x 3.50	8.9:1	2-bbl
		390	4.05 x 3.78	9.6:1	4V—300 hp
				10.6:1	4V—375 hp/Hi Perf
				10.6:1	6V—401 hp/Hi Perf
62	90°V	221	3.50 x 2.87	8.7:1	2V—145 hp
		260	3.80 x 2.87	8.7:1	2V—164 hp
	FE	352	4.00 x 3.50	8.9:1	2V
		390	4.05 x 3.78	9.6:1	4V—300 hp
				10.5:1	4V—375 hp/Hi Perf
					6V—T-Bird only
		406	4.13 x 3.78	11.4:1	4V—385 hp
				11.4:1	6V—405 hp
63	90°V	221	3.50 x 2.87	8.7:1	2V—145 hp
		260	3.80 x 2.87	8.7:1	2V—164 hp
		289	4.00 x 2.87	9.0:1	2V—195 hp
				10.5:1	4V—271 hp/Hi Perf
	FE	352	4.00 x 3.50	8.9:1	2V
		390	4.05 x 3.78	9.6:1	4V—300-330 hp
				10.5:1	6V—340 hpT-Bird
		406	4.13 x 3.78	11.4:1	4V—385 hp
					6V—405 hp
		427	4.23 x 3.78	11.5:1	4V—410 hp
					8V—425 hp
64	90°V	260	3.80 x 2.87	8.8:1	2V—200 hp
		289	4.00 x 2.87	9.0:1	4V—271 hp/Hi Perf
	FE	352		10.5:1	4V
		390	4.00 x 3.50	9.3:1	4V—300 hp
		427	4.05 x 3.78	10.0:1	4V—410 hp
			4.23 x 3.78	11.5:1	8V—425 hp
65	90°V	260	3.80 x 2.87	8.8:1	2V—164 hp
		289	4.00 x 2.87	9.3:1	2V—200 hp
				10.0:1	4V—225hp
				10.5:1	4V—271 hp/Hi Perf
	FE	352	4.00 x 3.50	9.3:1	4V
		390	4.05 x 3.78	10.0:1	4V—300-330 hp
		427	4.23 x 3.78	11.2:1	4V—410 hp
					8V—425 hp
66	90°V	289	4.00 x 2.87	9.3:1	2V—200 hp
				10.0:1	4V—225 hp
				10.5:1	4V—271 hp/Hi Perf
	FE	352	4.00 x 3.50	9.3:1	4V
		390	4.05 x 3.78	9.5:1	2V—265 hp
				10.5:1	4V—315 hp
				11.0:1	4V—335 hp
					4V—335 hp GT Fairlane
		410	4.05 x 3.98	10.5:1	4V—330 hp/Merc
		427	4.23 x 3.78	11.0:1	4V—410 hp
					8V—425 hp
		428	4.13 x 3.98	10.5:1	4V—345 hp
67	90°V	289	4.00 x 2.87	9.3:1	2V—200 hp
				10.0:1	4V—225 hp
				10.5:1	4V—271 hp/Hi Perf
	FE	390	4.05 x 3.78	9.5:1	2V—270 hp
				10.5:1	4V—315 hp
				10.5:1	4V—320 hp GT Must.
		410	4.05 x 3.98	10.5:1	4V—330 hp/Merc
		427	4.23 x 3.78	11.0:1	4V—410 hp
					8V—425 hp
		428	4.13 x 3.98	10.5:1	4V—345 hp
68	90°V	289	4.00 x 2.87	8.7:1	2V—195 hp
				10.5:1	4V—271 hp/Hi Perf
		302	4.00 x 3.00	9.0:1	2V—210 hp
				10.0:1	4V—235 hp
	FE	390	4.05 x 3.78		265-335 hp
		427	4.23 x 3.78	10.9:1	4V—390 hp
		428	4.13 x 3.98	10.7:1	4V—335 hp/CJ
				10.5:1	4V—345 hp
	385	429	4.36 x 3.59	10.5:1	4V—360 hp
		460	4.36 x 3.85	10.5:1	4V—365 hp

YEAR	FAMILY	DISPLACEMENT	BORE X STROKE	COMPRESSION	COMMENTS
69	90°V	302	4.00 x 3.00	9.5:1	2V—220 hp
				10.5:1	4V—290 hp/Boss
		351-W	4.00 x 3.50	9.5:1	2V—250 hp
				10.7:1	4V—290 hp
	FE	390	4.05 x 3.78		265-320 hp
		428	4.13 x 3.98	10.5:1	4V—335 hp/CJ
	385	429	4.36 x 3.59	10.5:1	2V—320 hp
					4V—360 hp
					4V—375 hp/Boss
		460	4.36 x 3.85	10.5:1	4V—365 hp
70	90°V	302	4.00 x 3.00	9.5:1	2V—220 hp
				10.5:1	4V—290 hp/Boss
		351-W	4.00 x 3.50	9.5:1	2V—250 hp
				11.0:1	4V—300 hp
	FE	390	4.05 x 3.78	9.5:1	2V—265 hp
		428	4.13 x 3.98	10.5:1	4V—335 hp/CJ
	385	429	4.36 x 3.59	10.5:1	2V—320 hp
					4V—360 hp
				11.3:1	4V—370 hp/CJ
					4V—375 hp SCJ
					4V—375 hp/Boss
		460	4.36 x 3.85	10.5:1	4V—375 hp
71	90°V	302	4.00 x 3.00	9.0:1	2V—210 hp
		351-W	4.00 x 3.50	9.0:1	2V—240 hp
	335	351-C	4.00 x 3.50	9.0:1	2V—240 hp
				10.7:1	4V—285 hp
				11.1:1	4V—330 hp/Boss
		400	4.00 x 4.00	9.0:1	4V—260 hp
	FE	390	4.05 x 3.78	8.6:1	2V—255 hp
	385	429	4.36 x 3.59	10.5:1	2V—320 hp
					4V—360 hp
				11.3:1	4V—370 hp/CJ
					4V—375 hp/SCJ
		460	4.36 x 3.85	10.5:1	4V—365 hp
72	90°V	302	4.00 x 3.00	8.5:1	2V—140 hp
		351-W	4.00 x 3.50	8.3:1	2V—153 hp
	335	351-C	4.00 x 3.50	8.6:1	2V—163-177 hp
					4V—248-266 hpCJ & HO
		400	4.00 x 4.00	8.4:1	2V—172 hp
	385	429	4.36 x 3.59	8.5:1	4V—205-212 hp
		460	4.36 x 3.85	8.5:1	4V—212 hp
73	90°V	302	4.00 x 3.00	8.0:1	2V—138 hp
		351-W	4.00 x 3.50	8.0:1	2V—154 hp
	335	351-C	4.00 x 3.50	8.0:1	2V—156 hp
					4V—246 hp
					4V—266 hp/CJ
		400	4.00 x 4.00	8.0:1	2V—163-171 hp
	385	429	4.36 x 3.59	8.0:1	4V—197 hp
				8.5:1	4V—208 hp
		460	4.36 x 3.85	8.0:1	4V—208 hp
74	90°V	302	4.00 x 3.00	8.0:1	2V—140 hp
		351-W	4.00 x 3.50	8.0:1	2V—162 hp
					4V—255 hp
	335	400	4.00 x 4.00	8.0:1	2V—170 hp
	385	460	4.36 x 3.85	8.0:1	4V—195-275 hp
75	90°V	302	4.00 x 3.00	8.0:1	2V—122-129 hp
		351-W	4.00 x 3.50	8.0:1	2V—140-154 hp
	335	351-M	4.00 x 3.50	8.0:1	2V—148-150 hp
		400	4.00 x 4.00	8.0:1	2V—143-158 hp
	385	460	4.36 x 3.85	8.0:1	4V—217 hp
76	90°V	302	4.00 x 3.00	8.0:1	2V—130-138 hp
		351-W	4.00 x 3.50	8.0:1	2V—140-154 hp
	335	351-M	4.00 x 3.50	8.0:1	2V—152 hp
		400	4.00 x 4.00	8.0:1	2V—180 hp
	385	460	4.36 x 3.58	8.0:1	4V—202 hp
77	90°V	302	4.00 x 3.00	8.1:1	2V—122 hp
				8.4:1	2V—122-137 hp
		351-W	4.00 x 3.50	8.3:1	2V—135-149 hp
	335	351-M	4.00 x 3.50	8.0:1	2V—161 hp
		400	4.00 x 4.00	8.0:1	2V—168-173 hp
	385	460	4.36 x 3.85	8.0:1	4V—197 hp
78	90°V	302	4.00 x 3.00	8.4:1	2V—135 hp
		351-W	4.00 x 3.50	8.3:1	2V—143 hp
	335	351-M	4.00 x 3.50	8.0:1	2V—145-153 hp
		400	4.00 x 4.00	8.0:1	2V—160-167 hp
	385	460	4.36 x 3.85	8.0:1	4V—202 hp

THE 90°V-8 SMALLBLOCK
221,260,289,289-HP,302,302-Boss and 351 WINDSOR ENGINES

THE 90°V FAMILY: THE SMALL BLOCK

Historically speaking, the current Ford small block V-8, introduced in 1962, has been the premier competition powerplant of the modern Ford engine line. It debuted at Indianapolis with Cinderella success and has continued racing at the Brickyard and other major tracks in highly modified forms ever since. Throughout the Sixties it powered machines like the Ford GT-40 and Shelby Cobra roadsters to national and international sports car racing fame. And the most famous—and most popular—production "race car" ever built by Ford, the Mustang, brought in its share of trophies as well.

But there is little sense discussing the Ford small block as an all-out competition engine these days. Ford factory racing is over. The last GT-40 and Shelby Cobra were assembled long ago. And how many of the readers of this book could consider owning or working on a Gurney Eagle or a Foyt Coyote?

Today the builder of a 289 or 302 Ford engine is looking for practical street performance. Millions of these small blocks are in circulation, and more are being built every day. The basic components, blocks, heads, cranks, manifolds and so on, as well as complete engines are plentiful and inexpensive, either from wrecking yards or over the counter. Parts selection is surprisingly straightforward because there have been relatively few changes or options in the small block family since its inception. If people are still trying to tell you that it costs too much to build, race, or just enjoy a Ford, here's the engine to prove them wrong.

The 90°V family was really the first modern Ford powerplant. The block is not only small (amazingly small, compared to other Ford engines), but it is also ultra light because of modern thinwall casting techniques. So are the heads. Plus, the block is very compact due to the radically oversquare dimensions—meaning that the bore is much larger than the stroke. This design also yields slower piston speed at a given rpm, resulting in less friction and wear; it allows a lighter reciprocating assembly because the connecting rods are relatively short; and, since the bore diameter is larger, it permits larger valves in the heads. This engine is so compact, in fact, that there isn't enough room around the crank throws for counterweights big enough for complete balancing, so these engines are "externally balanced," meaning that about 30% of the eccentric balance weight is carried in the flywheel and the front damper. A complete small block Ford weighs only about 450 pounds, is narrow enough to slip under the hood of a Model-T, and still puts out a very healthy amount of horsepower. Obviously, this short-stroker doesn't mind revving to the outer limits. There is hardly a point of comparison between this modern V-8 and its predecessor, the Y-block.

Our discussion will concentrate on the 289 and 302 cubic inch versions of the 90°V family. All information will of course apply to the earlier 221 and 260 as well (unless otherwise noted), but these latter versions are getting very scarce these days and are likely worn out. The 351 Windsor engine is also technically a small block and a member of this family, but, since there are so many differences involved, we will discuss it in a following section. Likewise, we will devote a chapter to the Boss 302, which is really a small block with Cleveland heads, though we will mention Boss 302 short-block components which will swap with the 289/302.

Unlike the other Ford engine groups, and partly because during the "Muscle" era there was a definite trend toward bigger-is-better thinking, there have been few special high performance small block packages. The most notable, of course, was the Boss 302—being both a radical departure and an all-out performance engine. The other specialty small block was the High Performance 289, offered as an option in '63-65 Comets and Fairlanes and '65-68 Mustangs. This Shelby-inspired 271-horsepower engine was much more than a cam/four-barrel/dual-exhaust advertising ploy; it was a strong and lively street performance small block designed for a relatively light chassis (i.e., the early Mustang) and built to live with an enthusiastic teenager pulling the four speed. Beginning with a stouter block, the engine package also included a high-rpm-balanced, high-nodular iron crankshaft, forged steel connecting rods with 3/8-inch bolts, cast flat-top pistons, a solid-lifter cam with a healthy profile, screw-in rocker studs in the heads, a 480-cfm four-barrel carb, streamlined exhaust manifolds, and a dual-point distributor. Given the typical application of Ford small blocks today, this package needs little

PRODUCTION SPECIFICATIONS (inches, except as shown)						
Displacement (Cu. In.)	221	260	289	289	302	351 Windsor
Carburetor Venturi	2V	2V	2V	4V and High Performance	2V & 4V	2V & 4V
Horsepower (Bhp/rpm) (72 specs SAE "net")	145/4400	164/4400	195/4400—63-64, 68 200/4400—65-66-67	210/4400—64 225/4800—65-66-67 271/6000—HP	210/4400, 2V—68-69 220/4600, 2V—70 230/4800, 4V—68 210/4600—71 140/4000—72	250/4600, 2V 290/4800, 4V 240/4600—71 153/3800—72
Torque (lb-ft/rpm) (72 specs SAE "net")	216/2200	258/2200	282/2400—63-67 288/2400—68	300/2400—64 305/3200—65-66-67 312/3400—HP	300/2600, 2V 310/2800, 4V—68 296/2600—71 239/2000—72	355/2600, 2V 385/3200, 4V 350/2600—71 266/2000—72
Compression Ratio	8.7:1	8.7:1	9.0:1—63-64 9.3:1—65-67 8.7:1—68	9.0:1—64 10.0:1—65-66-67 11.6:1—63 HP 10.5:1—64-67 HP	9.5:1, 2V 9.0:1, 2V—Early 68, 71 10.0:1, 4V 8.5:1—72	9.5:1, 2V 10.7:1, 4V 9.0:1, 2V—71 8.3:1—72
Head Volume (cc)	43.6-46.6	53.0-56.0	52.5-55.6 61.7-64.7—68	52.6-55.6 47.7-50.7—63 HP	61.7-64.7, 2V—Early 68 52.0-55.0, 4V—Late 68, 2V 56.7-59.7, 2V—69-72	58.9-61.9
Bore	3.50	3.80	4.00	4.00	4.00	4.00
Stroke	2.87	2.87	2.87	2.87	3.00	3.50
Bore Spacing	4.38	4.38	4.38	4.38	4.38	4.38
Crankshaft Mat'l Journal Dia.—Main —Rod	Nodular Iron 2.2486 2.1232	Nodular Iron 2.2486 2.1232	Nodular Iron 2.2486 2.1232	Nodular Iron 2.2486 2.1232	Nodular Iron 2.2486 2.1232	Nodular Iron 3.000 2.311
Cam Journal Dia.			#1—2.081 #2—2.066	#3—2.051 #4—2.036	#5—2.021	
Centerline of Crank to Top of Block (Block Deck Height)	8.206	8.206	8.206	8.206	8.206	9.503—71-72 9.480
Head Gasket Thickness					0.047—72	0.038—72
Head Gasket Volume (cc)					10.0—72	8.14—72
Total Clearance Vol. (cc)					77.54—72	91.0—72
Top of Piston to top of Block (Deck Height Clearance)	0.016	0.016	0.016	0.016	0.0235—72 0.016—68-71	0.035 0.0475—72
Compression Height	1.60	1.60	1.60	1.60	1.60	1.739
Con Rod Length (Ctr-to-Ctr)	5.155	5.155	5.155	5.155	5.090	5.956
Valve Head Dia.—Intake	1.582-1.597	1.582-1.597	1.662-1.667—63-64 1.773-1.783—65-68	1.662-1.667—63-64 1.773-1.783—65-68	1.773-1.783	1.834-1.852
—Exhaust	1.381-1.396	1.381-1.396	1.442-1.457	1.442-1.457	1.442-1.457	1.535-1.548
Valve Stem Dia.	.310	.310	.342	.342	.342	.342
Valve Spring Load—Closed (lbs/Installed Ht)	57-63/1.77	57-63/1.77	71-79/1.78—63-66 56-64/1.64—66½ 71-79/1.66—67-68	83.5-92.5/1.77	71-79/1.66—68 76-84/1.69—69-72	79-87/1.79 75/1.79—71-72
Valve Spring Load—Open	161-178/1.38	161-178/1.38	160-178/1.39—63-66 157-175/1.25—66½ 174-192/1.27—67 171-189/1.23—67½-68	234.5-259.5/1.32	174-192/1.27—67 171-189/1.23—67½-68 190-210/1.31—69-72	204-226/1.34 200/1.34—71-72
Valve Lifters Lash (Mech)	Hyd	Hyd	Hyd	Hyd—4V, Mech—HP 0.020 Hot	Hyd	Hyd
Rockerarm—Ratio —Type	1.60 Pressed Stud—Adj	1.60 Pressed Stud—Adj.	1.60 Pressed Stud—Adj.	1.60 Threaded Studs—HP (Only)	1.61 Pressed Stud—Adj. (68) Pressed Stud—Non-Adj. (69-72)	1.60 Pressed Stud—Non-Adj. Positive Stop
External Balance	Yes	Yes	Yes	Yes	Yes	Yes
Firing Order	1-5-4-2-6-3-7-8	1-5-4-2-6-3-7-8	1-5-4-2-6-3-7-8	1-5-4-2-6-3-7-8	1-5-4-2-6-3-7-8	1-3-7-2-6-5-4-8

The small block is *small*—light, compact, diminutive compared to any other Ford.

From the outside, you can detect a Boss 302 block by the screw-in core plugs. The big advantage is the extremely stout four-bolt mains at #2, 3, and 4.

improvement. Finding a good Hi Perf 289 might be a little difficult (only 17,000 were produced); but imitating it when building your present 289 or 302 is simple and rewarding.

A regular four-barrel 289 was offered from '65 through '67 (rated at 225hp), a 235-horse four-barrel 302 appeared in '68, and a four-barrel 351 Windsor with close to 11:1 compression was listed in '69 and '70. All the rest of the 90°V small blocks, including those of recent years, have been two-barrel models. But it doesn't take much to wake them up. Following is an uncomplicated rundown on the parts and pieces to do it.

BLOCKS

Other than the 351-W, which is bigger and taller, you have three basic cylinder block choices. The best, by all means, is the Boss 302 (D1ZZ-6010-B) offered in '69 and '70. The major benefit of this casting is the very hefty four-bolt main bearing caps on journals two, three and four; but it also is cast of a higher nodular iron with thicker cylinder walls than the standard 289 or 302 blocks. The easiest way to externally identify a Boss block is by the large screw-in freeze plugs, but you will be a long time looking before you find one. They are still available from Ford, though they are expensive (about $700). And one note about these and all other out-of-production Ford performance parts still listed on the books: supplies are obviously limited to what stock remains, and the last part might be sold tomorrow. Also, inventories left at this point sometimes consist of parts that were once rejected—don't assume that one of these blocks or a set of connecting rods is perfect just because it is new. Have them Magnafluxed, pressure check the water jacket, inspect all bolt holes, threads, and so on, before doing any work on the part. On the other hand, many customers currently feel that something like a Boss block is worth the price even if it isn't perfect, assuming that it can be repaired.

The next best cylinder block is the High Performance 289, which supposedly has a higher nodularity and comes with two-bolt main caps that are visibly sturdier than the standard caps. You could, of course, install these main caps on any block (if you can find some), but then you would have to have the block and caps align bored. The benefit might not be proportional to the hassle. A simpler way to add extra strength to the bottom end of a two-bolt small block is to install a set of Gapp and Roush main-cap supports (GR5T-63A33B), consisting of a machined bar which fits across the top of the cap and a pair of longer, grade-10 bolts. Slight machining is required on the top and sides of the main caps, but they don't have to be align bored afterwards.

There were a few design changes in the small block line which we should mention. In the middle of the 1965 production year Ford switched from a smaller five-bolt bellhousing to the

The High-Performance small block came with recognizably stronger main bearing caps than standard blocks. Tapped bolts at #2 journal allow attachment of windage tray.

By comparison to Boss or Hi-Perf main caps, stockers appear puny. But they'll hold up fine under most street conditions. For racing consider something stronger.

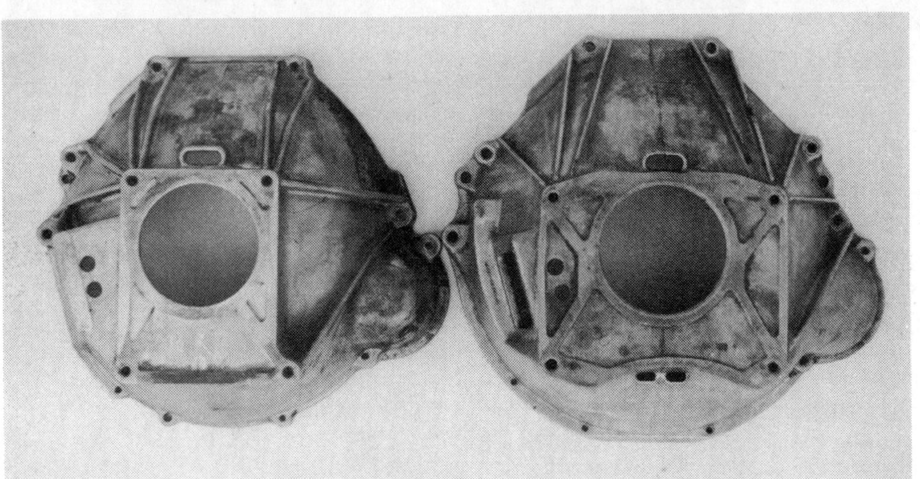

Pre-'65 small blocks require a five-bolt bellhousing (left). In the middle of '65, Ford switched to the now-standard six-bolt design (right) which accepts 11-inch clutches. Note different transmission bolt patterns, as well.

now-standard six-bolt design. All 221 and 260 engines are five-bolts, all 302's and 351-Windsors are six-bolts, but a 289 may be either. If you are shopping for a 289, you would probably prefer a six-bolt since these will accept 11-inch clutches and flywheels, the top-loader four-speed transmissions, and specialty scattershield bellhousings. In some instances the smaller bellhousing might help, however, such as an installation in an early Ford chassis (like a pre-'49) where you don't have much room in the firewall or floor area.

Second, 221 and 260 blocks are cast differently than the 289. They *cannot* be bored out to four inches. If you want a 289, get a 289 block—they're plenty cheap in junkyards. The 302 block is also slightly different from a 289; the cylinder bores extend a little further at the bottom to provide a bit more support for the pistons at the bottom of the stroke. However, there is only .130-inch difference in total piston travel between the two engines, and most builders feel the 302 crank can be swapped into the 289 block with no problem—though a 302 block would of course be preferable. What it all boils down to is, use the block you have if it is good (they are all thinwall castings, and a .040-inch overbore is maximum for performance use). If you are starting from scratch, shop around for the best block to meet your needs.

CYLINDER BLOCKS

Part Number	Engine	Description
C4AZ-6010-B	289	5-Bolt Bell Hsg.—Std. Engine
C4OZ-6010-C	289	5-Bolt Bell Hsg.—HP w/H.D. Main Caps
D1TZ-6010-B	289	6-Bolt Bell Hsg.—Std. Engine
C5OZ-6010-C	289	6-Bolt Bell Hsg.—HP w/H.D. Main Caps
D1TZ-6010-B	302	6-Bolt Bell Hsg.—Std. 302
D1ZZ-6010-B	302	6-Bolt Bell Hsg.—Boss 302 w/4-Bolt Main Caps
D1AZ-6010-B	351-W	6-Bolt Bell Hsg.

CRANKSHAFT

The '69 Boss 302 came with a cross-drilled steel crank, and it was the best unit made for a small block—but you'll probably never find a good one out of an engine. The '70 Boss motor had a similar steel crank (DOZZ-6303-A) but it wasn't cross-drilled (meaning it has two oil holes per throw like most standard cranks, instead of four). All "service" (replacement) Boss 302 cranks have been two-holers; these are supposedly still available new. If you are planning to wind your small block into the 8000-10,000 rpm range, this is the crank you should use. But you don't need it for street or weekend racing.

All other small block crankshafts are cast iron. The High Performance 289 unit (C3OZ-6303-B) is of higher nodularity than others, and it also came with a .150-inch thick add-on counterweight at the front to improve high-rpm balance. If you are using this crank, with the extra counterweight, be sure to use the proper timing chain crank sprocket; and if you want to install a multi-index crank sprocket, mill .150-inch from the back surface to retain proper alignment. As a note in passing, Ford small blocks used two different types of timing gears, a "thick" set and a "thin" set. Pre-'65 engines use the thick gears and timing chain, and the crank sprocket has a spacer that fits behind it. All '65 and newer engines use the thinner chain and gears, and the crank sprocket has a shoulder which spaces it properly from the crank. Entire sets can be interchanged from one engine to another, but do not mix components from a thick or thin set.

The 221 through 289 engines share the same 2.87-inch stroke length and the cranks are all identical except for the Hi Perf 289. The 302 has a stroke of three inches, and this crank can be substituted in the smaller engines. The 351-Windsor, with a 3.50-inch stroke, has the same bore spacing as the other small blocks, but the main journals are larger so you *can't* drop in the Windsor crank to get a ½-inch longer stroke. Even if you could, the counterweights would hit the piston

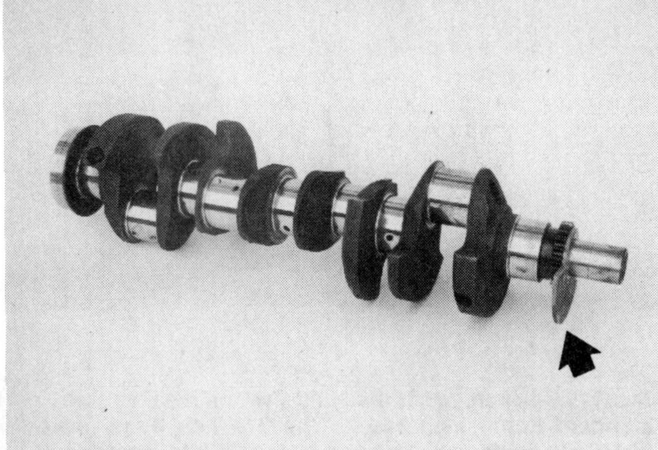

The high-performance 289 crankshaft is of higher nodularity than standard, and comes with add-on counterweight (arrow) for optimum high-rpm balance.

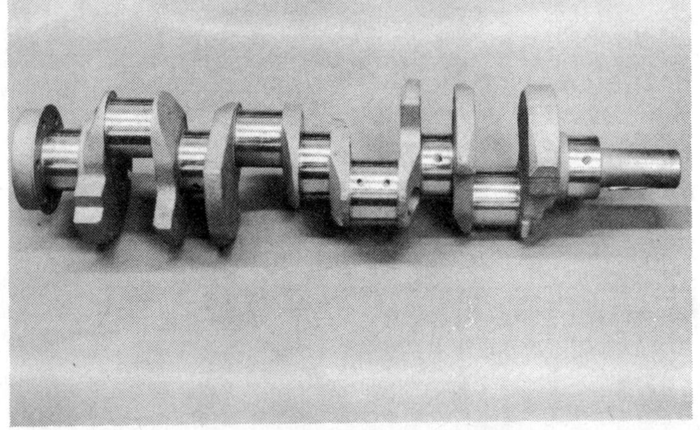

The standard small block crank is extremely rugged because of the short throws. For good street or weekend racing performance, have it Tufftrided and chamfer the oil holes as shown.

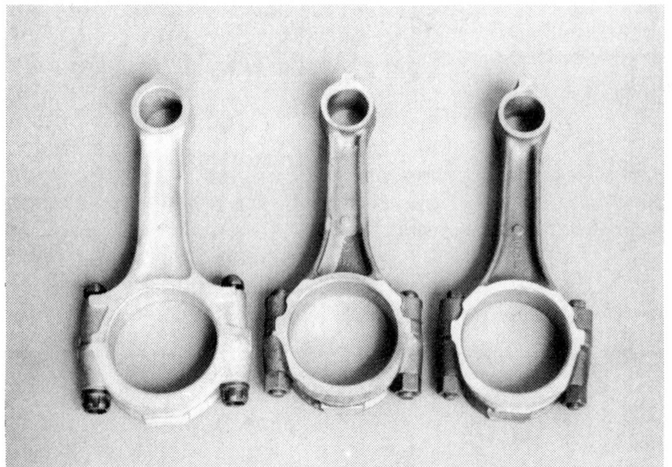

Beefy con rod on the left is a very rare part made for the Trans Am 302 racing engine. Boss 302 rod, center, is as strong as most racing engines need. Stock rod, right, is almost as well built, but has much weaker bolts.

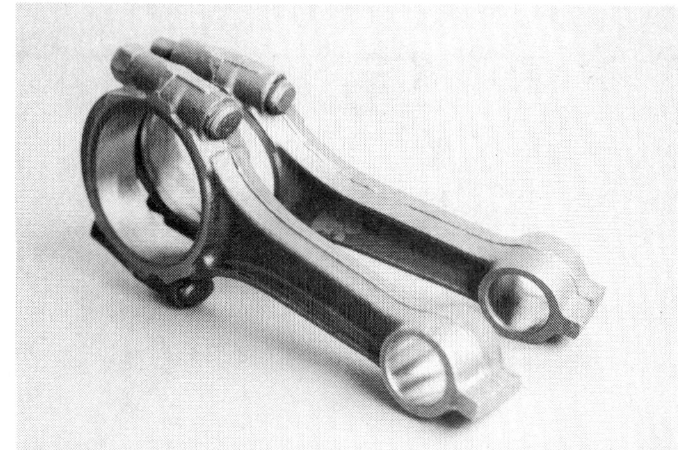

Boss 302 rods are still available from Ford, and are the same length as standard 289 rods. There have been some variations in production—note extra strengthening rib at shoulder of front rod.

CRANKSHAFT I.D. CHART AND APPLICATION

Part Number	Engine	Year	Journal Diameters		Stroke	Material
			Main	Rod		
C3AZ-6303-F	221/260/289	62/68	2.249	2.123	2.87	Iron
C3OZ-6303-B	289 HP	63/67	2.249	2.123	2.87	High Nod Iron
C8AZ-6303-A	302 2V, 4V	68/72	2.249	2.123	3.00	Iron
D0ZZ-6303-A	302 Boss	69/70	2.249	2.123	3.00	Steel
C9OZ-6303-A	351-W	69/72	3.000	2.311	3.50	Iron

skirts—that's why they had to make the 351-W block taller. So the story on crankshafts is like that for cylinder blocks. For most cases, what you have will work fine. For best performance and durability have it Tufftrided, chamfer the oil holes, and micro-polish the journals. Of course, the entire reciprocating assembly should be balanced, and since the small block cranks are externally balanced, the harmonic balancer, flywheel, and even the pressure plate should be balanced as a unit with the crankshaft. Be sure you have chosen the parts you want to use on the engine before it's time to have them balanced. If you swap any parts—pistons, rods, flywheel—you should have the assembly rebalanced.

RODS

The weakest point in a standard Ford small block is the puny 5/16-inch rod bolts in the regular 221, 260, 289 and 302 connecting rods. The rods in the three smaller engines are the same length (5.155 inches long), while the 302 rods are similar but slightly shorter (5.090 inches). Realizing the hazard of using these rods in performance engines, Ford offered three alternatives. The best is the Boss 302 rod (C9ZZ-6200-B), which is the same length as the 289 unit (the Boss piston uses a different pin height than the standard 302); it will swap into the 221, 260, and 289 engines. These rods have much stronger 3/8-inch diameter bolts with "football" heads, and the shoulders are circular spot-faced where the bolt head seats, thus leaving more metal and strength in this critical area than the standard broached, or square cut, shoulder. The production High Performance 289 rod was identical to the Boss except that the 3/8-inch bolts had rectangular heads and the shoulders were broached. The Boss rods, which superseded the Hi Perf 289 rods as a replacement part, are still available from Ford, but they cost about $50 each. Good sets of used Hi Perf 289 rods are more affordable, and aren't too difficult to find. For the standard 302 Ford offered a similar heavy duty rod (C9OZ-6200-B) in the 5.090-inch length which had football-head 3/8-inch bolts and spot-faced shoulders. If you are planning to turn 7000 rpm regularly, one of the above sets of connecting rods is highly recommended.

However, for a stout performer there is an easier and much less expensive alternative. Some manuals and articles have suggested drilling the stock rods to accept the 3/8-inch bolts—don't do it. The standard rods do not have enough metal in the bolt area for this operation, so you would actually be weakening the rod. None-

High-Performance 289 engines came with rods similar to the Boss 302 except that the bolts had square heads and the shoulders were square cut—a big difference in terms of strength.

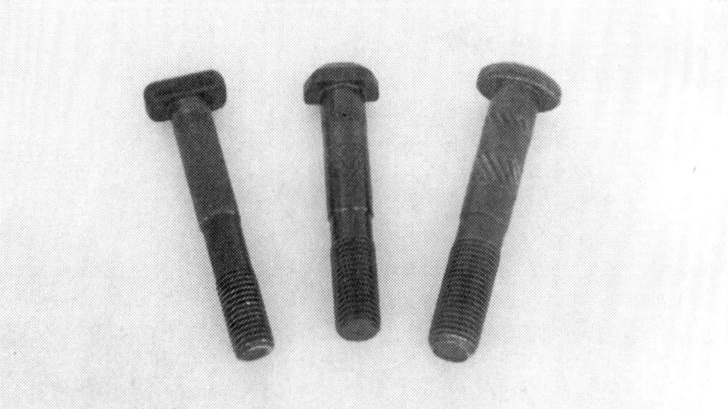

Stock 5/16-inch rod bolts (left) are the weakest part of a standard Ford small block. The 3/8-inch Boss rod bolts (right) are obviously superior, but too big to install in stock rods. You can, however, drill stock rods to 11/32-inch and install Chevy small block bolts (center) for an added margin of safety.

ÇON ROD I.D. AND APPLICATION

Part Number	Engine	Year	Weight (grams)	Ctr-to-Ctr Distance (inches)	Bolt Seat	Bolt Size	Remarks
C2OZ-6200-A	221-260	62/63	521-533	5.1535-5.1565	Broached	5/16	
C3AZ-6200-D	260 289	64/65 63/67	521-533 521-533	5.1535-5.1565 5.1535-5.1565	Broached Broached	5/16 5/16	
C9ZZ-6200-B	302 Boss 289 HP	69/70 64/67	581-593 581-593	5.1535-5.1565 5.1535-5.1565	Spot Faced Spot Faced	3/8 3/8	
D1OZ-6200-A	302	68/72	557-569	5.0885-5.0915	Broached	5/16	"Standard Duty"
C9OZ-6200-B	302	68/70	557-569	5.0885-5.0915	Spot Faced	3/8	"Heavy Duty"
C9OZ-6200-A	351-W	69/70	698-710	5.9545-5.9575	Spot Faced	3/8	
D0ZX-6200-A	302 T.Am.	OHO	751	5.3165-5.3135	Spot Faced	7/16	Use Special "Competition Only" Piston

theless, you can safely drill them (have a good machine shop do it) to 11/32-inch and install SPS-type high strength rod bolts, from a reputable supplier, which are actually made for small block Chevys. These bolts cost about $35 a set—but that's cheap life insurance for your engine.

Of course, the usual performance prepping—Magnafluxing, polishing along the beams, and shot-peening—is further insurance against failure on these or any connecting rods being installed in a performance engine.

PISTONS

Since all 260, two-barrel 289, and two-barrel 302 engines (meaning the vast majority of small blocks built) came with dished pistons averaging 8:1 or 9:1 compression, one of the expensive priorities of building a high performance small block will be a set of new pistons. Considering the current octane quality of gasoline, between 9:1 and 10:1 will be the practical compression range to aim for in a street-driven motor. If you have a late model 302 and it is still fresh, you could approach this compression with stock pistons by swapping on a set of early 289 small-chamber heads. But a set of special pistons will probably be the best bet because a dished piston is not a high performance design (a flat-top promotes optimum flame travel); stock cast pistons are not nearly as tough as forged performance pistons (though forged pistons are certainly not mandatory for street motors); and the majority of engines torn down for a full rebuild will require reboring and a new set of pistons anyway.

Early production 289 engines came with a flat-top piston with no valve reliefs. If by chance you have or find a set of these pistons in usable condition (which is unlikely), they must have reliefs cut in the top for use with a high-lift cam. All other four-barrel 289 and the '68 four-barrel 302 engines came with cast flat-tops with four valve-relief eyebrows. They yield 10½:1 compression with early regular production heads (53.5cc). TRW makes an excellent forged flat-top with eyebrows (L 2218-F) also rated at 10½:1, and it is the best street piston for these engines.

Since both 289 and 302 pistons are the same bore size and have the same pin height, you would probably surmise that this piston also fits the 302. Such is unfortunately not the case. The longer-stroke 302 crank counterweights hit the pin boss and skirt of this piston when the piston is at the lowest point of travel in the bore. What is worse, neither TRW nor any other manufacturer makes a flat-top specifically for the 302. One solution, practiced by several engine shops we contacted, is to mill approximately .200-inch from the bottoms of the pin bosses and around the radius of the skirt on the TRW 289 pistons. This operation should be done on a Bridgeport mill by a competent machinist—it is a lot of work to get a flat-top for a 302.

Since Ford has offered so many different sizes of cylinder heads (combustion chamber volume) for small blocks, there is a more practical method for arriving at a livable, yet peppy, compression ratio in one of these engines. TRW offers a forged pop-up piston (L 2249-NF) which fits both 289 and 302 engines with no clearance problems. Commonly referred to as a 12½:1 piston, it actually yields closer to 10:1 in a late 302 with big-chamber heads. Here's a breakdown: With a .047-inch head gasket (.030-inch compressed) and -.012-inch piston deck height (down the bore), the TRW L 2249-NF gives 12½:1 compression with a 52.34cc head; 12¼:1 with the more common 53.5cc head; 10½:1 with the 63.2cc '68-76 302 head; and between 9½ and 10:1 with the '77-later 302 head listed at 67.5-70.5cc. You can also mill some of the dome from this piston to lower the compression. The TRW pop-up is an excellent quality forged racing piston, but it costs about twice as much as the forged TRW flat-top for the 289. You can therefore decide, according to your budget and which set of cylinder heads you have, what piston you will need to come up with the compression ratio you want.

If you are rebuilding a 289 for the street, you will probably need a new set of pistons (since you will have to run a clean-up over-bore on most 10-year-old-plus motors), and you will probably have the 53.5cc heads on it. The TRW L 2218-F flat-top will give 10:1 compression with this combination, which is just what you want. Milling these heads .040-inch will bring the

The TRW L-2218 piston is a high quality forged flat-top that will boost compression to 10½:1 in a standard 289. But it will not fit the 302 without some machining.

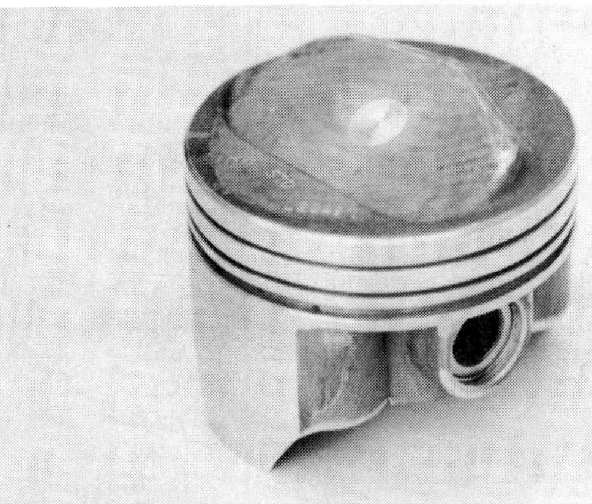

The TRW pop-up fits both 289 and 302 engines, and is a good solution for making about 10:1 compression with late big-chamber heads

Recommending camshaft profiles in print is like prescribing medicine by mail. Let a knowledgeable camshaft dealer tell you what you need, after you give him plenty of specific data about your car.

Valve spring specs are dictated by the camshaft. At left is a typical performance combination from Crane (#99836) in standard diameter. For two-barrel heads, a good choice would be Chevy Z/28 off road springs (right), which can be matched with stock two-barrel retainers.

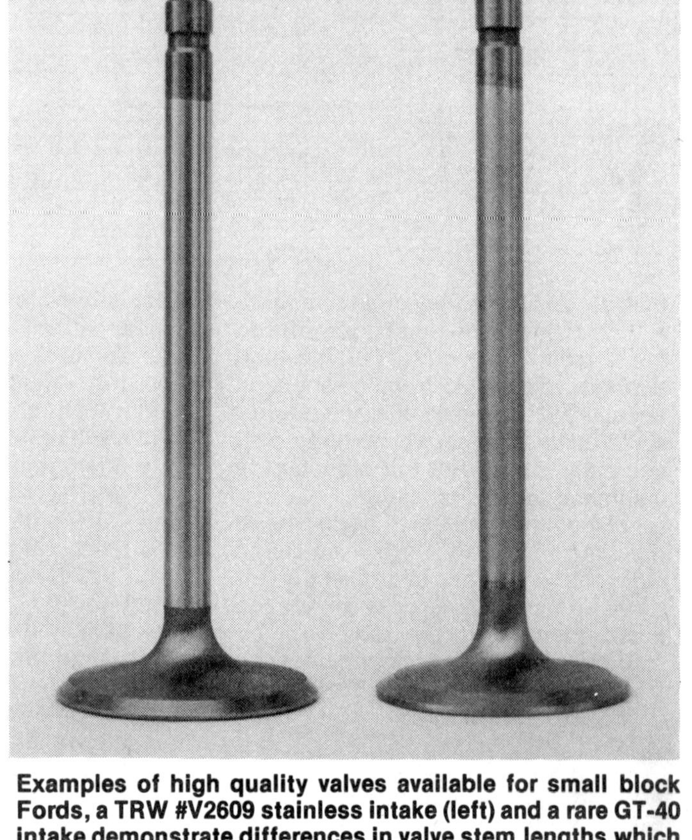

Examples of high quality valves available for small block Fords, a TRW #V2609 stainless intake (left) and a rare GT-40 intake demonstrate differences in valve stem lengths which occur in these engines.

combination up to about 11:1.

If you are building a 302 there are a few choices. If you have, or want to use, small-chamber cylinder heads you can either buy the TRW 289 flat-tops and mill the bottoms to fit in the 302; or you could buy the pop-ups (which are more expensive, remember) and mill off some or all of the dome. Either way you are talking about machine work on the pistons. Probably more practical, especially if you have a post-'68 302, is to retain the large-volume heads and install the pop-up TRW pistons without modification, giving 9½ to 10½:1 compression, depending on whether the heads are pre- or post-'77. Such an engine would also be a good candidate for the 351-Windsor head swap, since you would gain the larger valves and intake ports without sacrificing a major compression drop. Incidentally, Ford did offer a pop-up piston (C90Z-6109-B left, C90Z-6108-AA right) specifically for the Windsor head conversion on a 289. It had a 10cc dome volume and gave approximately 10½:1 compression with the C90Z-6049-F (59cc) 351-W heads on a 289. However, these were not forged pistons and they were part of the Muscle Parts program, so they would be hard to locate these days.

Finally, another recent alternative for builders of both 289 and 302 engines, especially those on a budget, are decent quality cast pop-up pistons now offered by at least three replacement parts manufacturers—Triplex, Badger, and Hy-Duty. The pistons are basically identical (Hy-Duty #197-XHCP) and give 11:1 compression in a 289 with the standard head. These pistons are not the best for extreme high performance or racing situations (since they are cast rather than forged), but they are inexpensive and they would be a practical way to boost compression 1½ to 2 points in a '73 or later 302 (rated 8-8½:1 stock), giving a decent ratio for a peppy street engine.

CAMSHAFTS AND VALVETRAIN

Ford made two high performance camshafts for the small block, the C30Z-6250-C mechanical which came in the 289 Hi Perf engine, and the C90Z-6250-C hydraulic. They are still available, and both have been acclaimed as excellent street performance cams, even today, by many name engine builders (including Jack Roush). The solid-lifter cam specs out at 310° duration and .450-inch lift on intake and exhaust, while the hydraulic is 290° and .470-inch lift (if you are comparing these figures to specifications for current specialty cams, remember that the Ford specs are not taken at .050-inch lift like many are these days). A couple of other mechanical cams were offered for the small block through the OHO program, but these are rare. One (C7FE-6250-A) was known as the Le Mans cam (318° Intake, 304° Exhaust; .510-inch lift) and the other by OHO part number DOZX-6250-B (324°, .589-inch lift). And, of course, there were a few different grinds offered for the Boss 302, which will slip right into any small block—but remember that the Boss engine uses 1.73:1 ratio rockerarms while all other small blocks use 1.60:1 rockers. Using a Boss cam with standard rockers, or Boss rockers with the standard cam, will alter actual valve lift. The High Performance 289 solid-lifter cam is very similar to the production Boss 302 cam, when each is set up with its respective rockers. But don't use a Boss cam in a standard-head small block.

Although the first two high performance Ford cams mentioned do work very well for street engines, they are outdated. Cam grinders have learned a lot in the last few years, and advanced technology both in lobe designs and spring combinations has allowed modern performance cam companies to offer very effective street camshafts featuring higher lift and shorter duration (thus maintaining a decent idle and good low-end response, yet flowing plenty of mixture through the wide open valve). Good cam companies abound, and each offers several selections for small block Fords—any small block cam will fit in a 221 through a 351-Windsor. (In this section, as well as in others in this book, we will refrain from recommending particular cam grinds for particular engines since the choices are far too numerous to cover adequately and fairly, and different applications require different cam grinds—that's why so many are offered.) Our recommendation is, let the cam company tell you what sort of cam you need; most of the better companies have accessible representatives who should know their products better than anybody else. Your job is to give the salesperson definite and accurate information: other equipment in the engine, weight of the car, gear ratio and tire height, type of transmission and converter or clutch, and—most important—how you are going to use the car and where you want the power. If you say you are going to drive the car on the street, most companies will recommend a milder cam with some bottom-end torque, a decent idle, and probably a power band in the 2500-4500 rpm range. That's a practical recommendation. However, if you really mean that you are going to drive the car on the street *sometimes* (not 30 miles to work every day), and you don't care if it idles at 1200 rpm and you have to slip the clutch or chirp the tires to get moving, and you definitely want the engine to wind to eight grand while still pulling in the lights, then tell the person selecting your camshaft exactly what you expect. You'd be sadly disappointed if he gave you an RV hydraulic street grind.

Then, when the salesperson suggests a long list of "extra" components to go with the camshaft, listen closely. A cam can't do the job by itself. Of primary importance is matching valve springs of proper tension and size to handle the cam profile. Stock springs are hardly ever adequate; use the ones recommended by the cam manufacturer or others of exactly the same specs. Second, never install used lifters on a new cam. If they are the least bit worn they will destroy the cam lobes in a matter of minutes. And a high performance hydraulic-lifter cam requires a good, modern anti-pumpup lifter to function properly. Third, other "kit" components listed by the manufacturer are usually necessary to withstand the increased loads of the new cam and the rev potential it creates, or they may be necessary to fit the new custom pieces or align them properly with adequate clearances.

If you buy a high performance camshaft with a coordinated installation kit (lifters, pushrods, valve springs, retainers and keepers) from a reputable manufacturer, you can assume that the parts will work together properly (e.g., the springs won't bind at full lift and the retainers won't hit the valve stem guide). But never take this for granted. Check everything in the valve train at least twice. It'll mean some extra work, like installing the heads more than once, but it is imperative. Most cam manufacturers explain clearance checking and cam degreeing operations in their catalogs (even if you have to pay for the catalog, this information is usually worth the price), so we will discuss them only briefly here. The main points to check when installing a higher-than-stock lift cam in any engine are piston-to-valve clearance, coil bind, rockerarm travel, and clearance between the valve guide and spring retainer.

Start with the springs. The manufacturer will give you a recommended installed spring height (distance between the bottomside of the retainer and the spring seat on the cylinder head), which should yield the recommended seat pressure with the valve closed. Most speed shops or engine shops will have a spring testing machine on which you can check these specs before installing the springs on the valves. Assemble the entire spring combination (inner and outer spring, spring and dampener, three springs, etc.), place it in the machine, and compress it to the correct installed height. The scale on the spring tester should read the proper pressure, in pounds, recommended by the cam manufacturer for the valve in the closed position. If you are using other than the manufacturer's springs, compress them until they read the proper pressure and measure their height. Now, further compress the springs exactly the amount listed for the net lift at the valve. At this point the scale should read the recommended open spring pressure (if it doesn't, you need a different spring combination to match the cam; too much pressure may wear the lobes, too little may allow the valves to float prematurely). Then, compress the springs as far as they will go past the "full lift" measurement and note the travel. In most cases this extra travel margin, before the coils bind, should be a minimum of .040-inch.

When installing the springs on the heads, again measure for the correct installed spring height, and use shims under the springs to make adjustments. Once the heads are assembled on the engine and valve lash is set, you can recheck for coil bind by passing a .040-inch feeler gauge between at least two coils of each spring with the valve at the full open position.

To check for proper clearance between the valve guide and retainer: after the valves and seats have been ground, slip a valve in place with an oil seal, install a retainer with keepers on the stem, and pull the valve into the closed position. Measuring with a machinist's rule at the lip of the retainer, open the valve the amount of the net valve lift. Beyond this point you should be able to open the valve at least another .040-inch before the retainer hits the guide. If not, you can try different retainers, or you can mill a slight amount of material from the tops of the guides, the bottoms of the retainers, or both.

Checking the clearance in the slot in the rockerarms is difficult. For any high performance cam installation, solid or hydraulic, you should use early 289 rockers rather than the "rail rockers," standard on all later engines. Ford recommended, as a matter of course, opening the fulcrum slot on these rockers .030-inch when installing a high-lift cam. Otherwise, the rocker could bind on the rocker stud at full lift, either causing wear on the cam or breaking the stud. One way to check the actual clearance is to install a rocker on the head (on the engine), with a pushrod, but without a valve. Adjust the rocker so the valve end is the same

CAMSHAFT I.D. AND APPLICATION

Part Number	Application		Lifter		Intake Events		Exhaust Events		Duration		Lift		Overlap	Identification	
	Engine	Year	Type	Lash	Open	Close	Open	Close	Intake	Exhaust	Lobe	Valve		Mark	Location
C3OZ-6250-B	221/260	62/65	Hyd		21°BTC 26°ATC	51°ABC BDC	57°BBC 10°BBC	15°ATC 36°BTC	252°	252°	.238	.380	36°	UA	Between last lobe and journal
C3AZ-6250-V	289 302	65/68 68/72	Hyd		16°BTC 40°ATC	70°ABC 8°ABC	44°BBC 1°BBC	20°ATC 27°BTC	266°	244°	.230—I .237—E	.360—I .380—E	36°	UA	Between last lobe and journal
C3OZ-6250-C	289 HP	63/68	Mech	.019	46°BTC 12°ATC	84°ABC 26°ABC	94°BBC 36°BBC	36°ATC 22°BTC	310°	310°	.298	.460	82°	∀ E	Between dist. gear and first journal
C7FE-6250-A	All Except 351-C	All	Mech	.020—I .025—E	52°BTC 6°BTC	86°ABC 30°ABC	82°BBC 40°BBC	42°ATC 4°BTC	318°	304°	.330	.510	94°	C7FE-A	Stamped on end of shaft
C9OZ-6250-C	All Except 351-C	All	Hyd		36°BTC 16°ATC	74°ABC 20°ABC	84°BBC 32°BBC	26°ATC 28°BTC	290°	290°	.290	.470	62°	C9OZ-C	Stamped on end of shaft
D0ZZ-6250-A	302 Boss	69/70	Mech	.025	34°BTC 15°ATC	76°ABC 25°ABC	86°BBC 47°BBC	24°ATC 27°BTC	290°	290°	.290	.477	58°	VED	Stamped on end of shaft
D0ZX-6250-B	302 Boss	OHO	Mech	.025	58°BTC 12°BTC	86°ABC 32°ABC	88°BBC 42°BBC	56°ATC 2°ATC	324°	324°	.355	.589	114°	D0ZX-A	Stamped on end of shaft
C9OZ-6250-A	351-W	69/71	Hyd		11°BTC 34°ATC	65°ABC 15°ABC	68°BBC 15°BBC	22°ATC 33°BTC	256°	270°	.260—I .278—E	.425—I .450—E	33°	8 F	Stamped on end of shaft
D0ZX-6250-C	302	OHO	Mech	.025	66°BTC 20°ATC	84°ABC 33°ABC	94°BBC 47°BBC	64°ABC 11°ATC	330°	338°	.355—I .368—E	.600—I .620—E	130°	D0ZX-C	Stamped on end of shaft

Valve lift is computed for "stock" rockerarm ratio.
(1.73 for 400, 351-C and 302 Boss; 1.60:1 for all others)

height as the installed valve tip; then depress the valve end of the rocker the amount of full cam lift. If the rocker binds, you may need shorter pushrods (more on this in a moment). If the slot comes close to hitting the stud at full lift, you can simply grind or file the slot a little larger (incidentally, TRW replacement rockers for the early 289 come with longer fulcrum slots).

There are two ways to check valve-to-piston clearance. The traditional method is to coat the top of the piston with modeling clay, install the head with valves, set the valve lash to "checking clearances," and then turn the crank by hand through at least one complete cycle (two revolutions). Remove the head, carefully slice the clay at the lowest depression made by each valve, and measure the thickness. Clearances should be specified by the cam manufacturer, but a rule of thumb is .080-inch on the intake and .100-inch for the exhaust. A newer method is to install light springs on the valves (available from Isky cams, or the hardware store), install the heads and set the lash, turn the crank until each valve is at full lift, then set a dial indicator on the retainer and push the valve by hand until it contacts the piston, noting the distance traveled on the indicator. Normally such checking need only be done on one cylinder; but if you haven't blueprinted the rest of the engine, remember that deck heights of pistons in stock engines can vary .010-inch or more. At least measure each piston deck height at TDC and take your piston-to-valve clearance reading on the cylinder with the least deck height. Better yet, match the "long" connecting rods with those pistons which have "short" pin heights to equalize the deck heights as much as possible.

Each of the above checking procedures applies to any engine in which a high performance cam is to be installed, and of course this includes the other Ford engines discussed in this book. Following each of these procedures will also eliminate some of the confusion and prevent mishaps when mixing and matching valve train components.

The major point of confusion concerns a difference in valve stem and pushrod lengths between the 289 and 302. Even official Ford information varies, but apparently a change to longer-stem valves (with an altered keeper groove, thus altering valve spring height) was made on 302 engines built after 10-21-68. Consequently, .060-inch longer pushrods were used in these engines to maintain the correct rockerarm angle. Some 302 engines built before this date used .060-inch thick valve stem caps on the exhaust valves. Supposedly, the longer valve stem length was required for clearance with rail-type rockerarms, though rail rockers were introduced over two years before this. The main point is that there is a difference in pushrod lengths between the two engines, and the problem arises when the long pushrods (302) are used with short valves (289) and stock rockerarms. In such a situation the rockers will bind on the studs at full lift, often breaking the studs. The solution in such a case is not simply to grind the slot in the rocker larger, but to install shorter pushrods to correct the rocker angle (otherwise you will be losing some of the rockerarm ratio).

A secondary problem arises when installing 289 springs on 302 valves. Ford offered a few different retainers to help correct the situation, and a chart is included here that shows the proper matchup for Ford components. If it looks confusing, just remember that any high performance valve spring is designed to be installed at a specific height, which must ultimately be measured when the spring is installed on the head. If the installed height isn't correct, adjust with spring shims if it's too long, or with a "taller" retainer if it's too short. Never assume that everything is fine just because you have installed the "correct" set of part numbers.

The difference in valve stem length on the 302 corresponds to a switch at that date by Ford to a two-piece valve spring retainer, supposedly designed to allow the valve to rotate on the seat. The benefit of valve rotation is debatable; but these retainers are too sloppy for high-rpm use. Earlier heads have one-piece retainers, those on the two-barrel engines being smaller than those on four-barrels. These stock retainers are plentiful and cheap and can be used for most street performance engines. Otherwise, several varieties of trick retainers are available from cam manufacturers—some designed specifically to match their springs—in hardened steel, aluminum, or titanium. Aluminum retainers, however, are not recommended for an engine that will be driven regularly on the street, especially with a flat-wound inner damper (it will chafe the aluminum).

SMALLBLOCK VALVE SPRING HEIGHT CHART

Year	Engine	Production Spring Ht.	Recommended Valve Spring Ht.	Retainer
63-66½	289	1.78	C9OZ-6513-C 1.66	C9OZ-6514-E .090 offset (plus .030 shim B3Q-6515-A)
66½-67	289	1.64	C9OZ-6513-C 1.66	C7AZ-6514-A
67-68	289	1.66	C9OZ-6513-C 1.66	C7AZ-6514-A
63-68	289 HP	1.77	C3OZ-6513-A 1.77	C3OZ-6514-A
68	302	1.66	C9OZ-6513-C 1.66	C7AZ-6514-A
69-72	302	1.69	C9OZ-6513-C 1.66	C9OZ-6514-E
69-72	351-W	1.79	C9OZ-6513-A 1.79	C9OZ-6514-D Hydraulic Cam
			C3AZ-6513-B 1.82	C9OZ-6514-E Mechanical Cam

Ford offered several varieties of valve springs for small blocks. The combination used on the High Performance 289, consisting of an outer spring and a damper (C90Z-6513-C), is a good unit for many applications and is still available. They should be installed at 1.66-inch, and to get this height Ford suggests retainer C90Z-6514-E plus a .030-inch shim on '63-65 vintage 289 and '69-72 vintage 302 heads, and retainer C7AZ-6514-A on '66-68 vintage 289 and '68 vintage 302 heads. Another good possibility from the Ford shelves is the 390 GT valve spring and damper (C3AZ-6513-B) which should be installed at 1.82 inches giving 85 pounds on the seat (and 268 pounds at 1.32 inches). Install them on small block heads with retainer C90Z-6514-D and hardened keepers C9ZZ-6518-A. And, here's a neat tip for those of you rebuilding a set of 289 two-barrel heads: if you want to save about $30 on a set of specialty retainers, you can use the small two-barrel Ford type with Z-28 Chevy offroad valve springs (you can buy them at most parts stores under McQuay-Norris part number VS541, or from Crane under number 99836). They give 110 pounds installed at 1.700 inches and will usually handle cams up to .520-inch lift without coil binding. But, once again we will stress, if you are uncertain about a hybrid combination, follow the camshaft manufacturer's recommendation for the setup that will make his bump stick work the best in your small block.

Another big point of difference in the small block valve train is rockerarms. All Ford small blocks (except the High Performance 289 and the Boss 302) made after February 1966 came with "rail rockers." This, of course, includes all 302's and all 351-Windsors. These rockers have a unique tip on the valve end with a pair of tabs which fit down over the valve stem to keep the rocker aligned on the valve. This system works well enough on low-rpm engines equipped with hydraulic cams running at zero lash. They are no good for a performance engine with a solid cam or a high-lift hydraulic. To begin with, they make valve adjustment with a feeler gauge virtually impossible. Furthermore, at high speeds they tend to chew away at the valve tip, sometimes destroying

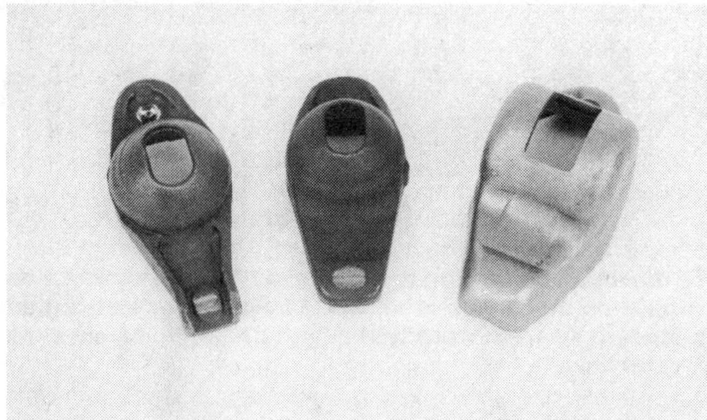

Variety of stock rockerarms used on factory small blocks includes (left to right): "rail" type rocker, standard-tip rocker, and stamped steel, sled-fulcrum Boss 302 rocker.

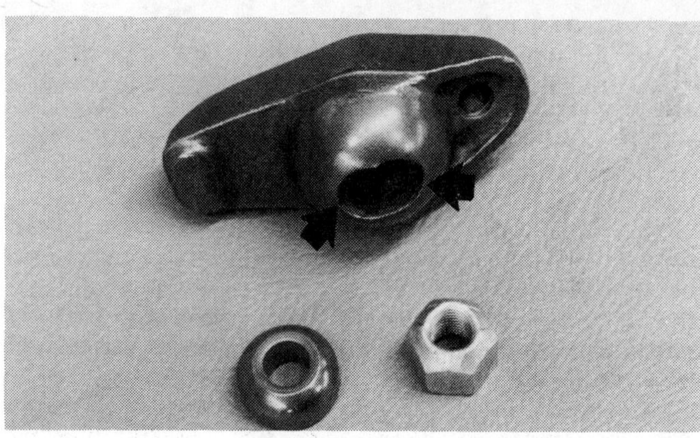

Conventional-tip cast-iron rockerarms came on all pre-'66 small blocks. If you use stock rockers with a high-lift cam, enlarge ends of pivot slot (arrows) at least .030-inch. TRW replacement rockers already have larger slot.

Heads converted from rail rockerarms require guide plates (Manley #42152 shown) to keep standard rockers aligned, plus screw-in studs (Chevy LT-1, #397446 shown) to attach guide plates.

Two-piece valve spring retainer (left) is not for performance engines. Four-barrel engines came with larger springs and retainers (center), while two-barrel heads used the smaller retainers shown at right.

it. And finally, with a higher-than-stock-lift cam the rockerarm "rails" can sometimes strike the spring retainer, pushing it down and thereby allowing the keepers to pop out—subsequently allowing the valve to drop into the cylinder. End of engine! The point is simple: use the standard early-289 cast rockers on any high performance small block. You can rob them off a junkyard motor if you don't have a set, you can buy them from Ford (C20Z-6564-A), or you can get them from your parts store under various brand names (TRW 44036K; McQuay-Norris 1RM30). If your heads came with rail rockers, you will have to install screw-in rocker studs, guide plates, and heat-treated pushrods to use these rockers (see the next section on cylinder heads for particulars). This may seem like a lot of work, but this should be considered as practically a mandatory changeover for any performance cam installation other than a mild RV-type hydraulic.

The final valve train consideration for small blocks concerns variation in rockerarm studs. All but the High Performance 289 have press-in studs. Those in regular 289 and '68 vintage 302 engines allow for adjustment of the rockers. But the studs in '69-later 302 and all 351-W engines are of the "positive stop" type, identifiable by a wider shoulder below the threads. These studs do not allow valve adjustment, so they obviously cannot be used with a mechanical cam. Furthermore, either of the press-in studs are prone to pulling out of the head when used with performance valve springs of over 100 pounds seat pressure. So, at the risk of repeating, remember that the best bet on a performance smallblock engine is to install screw-in studs and guide plates.

CYLINDER HEADS

Although Ford parts books list more than 14 different numbers for replacement small block heads, the situation is actually much less complicated than it appears (especially compared to other Ford engines, such as the FE big block). Three basic cylinder head types have been used on small blocks: the production 221, 260,289, 302 variety, the 351-Windsor, and the Boss 302. (The Boss head, completely different from the others in every detail except bolt pattern, is actually a Cleveland head with small block water outlets.) Within these three groups there have been several minor differences in port, valve, and chamber sizes, plus different types of smog control apparatus.

The 221 heads have the smallest chamber volume, at 43.5cc, (therefore giving the highest compression of any small block casting. The 260 heads were identical except that the chambers were larger, 53cc. Both came with 1.59-inch intake valves and 1.39-inch exhausts. The 289/302 heads can be immediately distinguished from 221/260 heads (off the engine) by their unique combustion chamber shape, which appears "pinched" around the spark plug. Ford engineers said this design promoted even burning in the cylinder and less carbon buildup. More perceptible improvements in the 289/302 heads include bigger intake ports (.180-inch taller) and larger

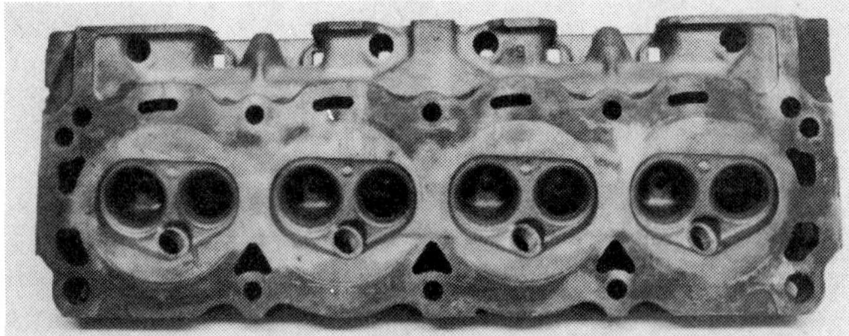

The 221 heads, rare these days, had the smallest combustion chambers and noticeably smaller valves than other small block heads.

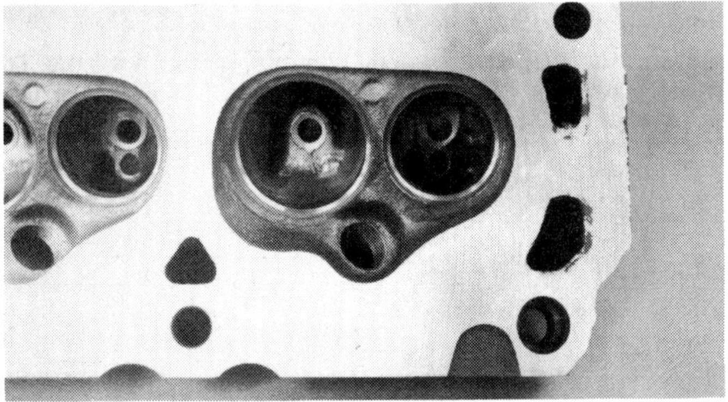

The 289 and 302 heads have a unique combustion chamber shape. Also note crescent shape of water passage above chamber. This was changed on newer engines.

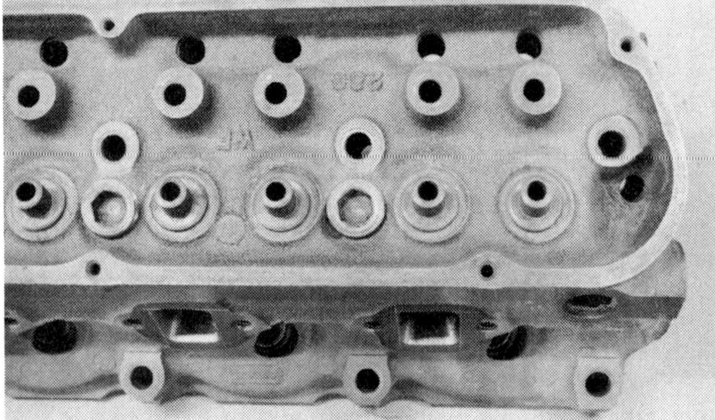

This is a typical post'66 small block head, which came with rail rockerarms and pressed-in rocker studs. Large round pushrod holes necessitate guide plates when converting to standard rockers.

High-Performance 289 heads came with screw-in rocker studs, standard rockerarms, slotted pushrod guide holes (as on all pre-'66 heads), plus cast-in valve spring seating bosses.

To eliminate rail rockerarms, any post-'66 small block head should be machined to accept screw-in studs and guide plates—a virtual necessity if a high performance cam is to be installed.

Most head shops agree—Ford small block heads need little porting for excellent street/strip breathing. Just match the opening to the gasket, blend the passage smoothly for the first 3/4-inch.

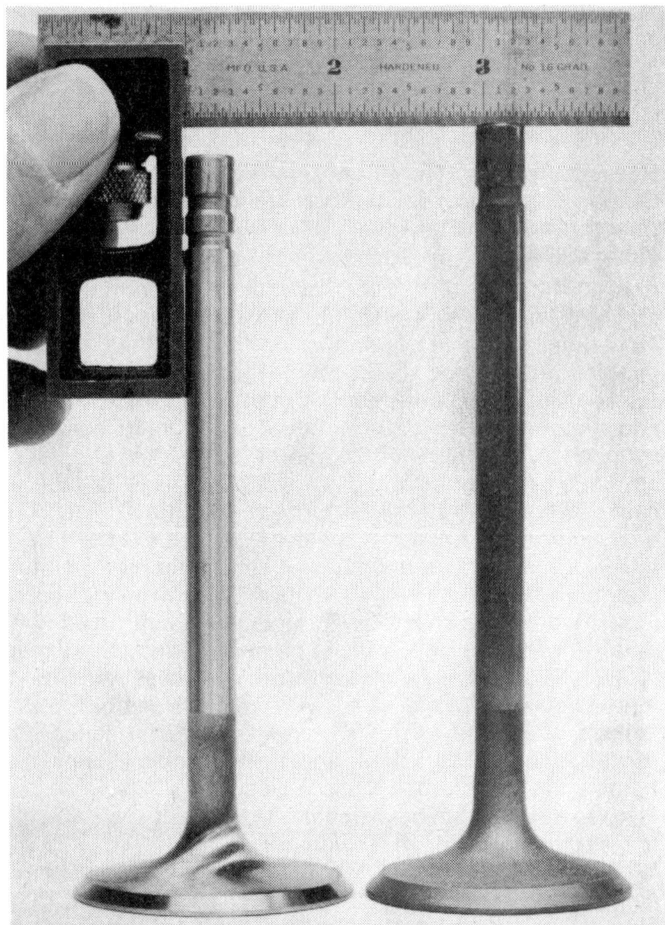

TRW makes high-performance stainless steel oversize valves for Ford small blocks. They are excellent, but expensive. You can save more than $30 by substituting TRW valves for a 327 Chevy (shown at left, next to a stock 302 Ford valve). Shorter tip is main difference.

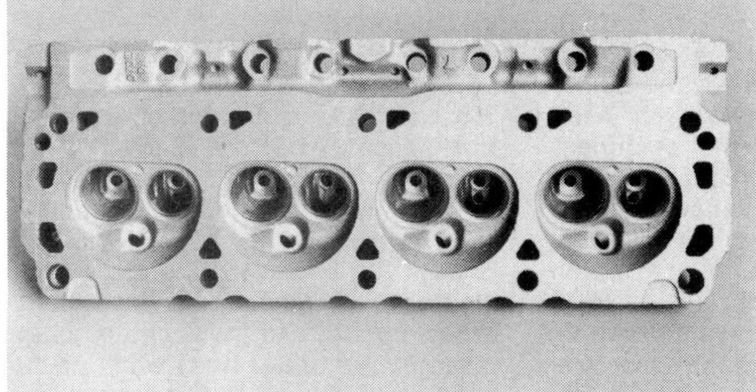

The '77 and later 351-Windsor and 302 heads all have the same small valves and giant combustion chambers—a low-compression, low-performance part.

The Boss 302 head is obviously a radical departure from previous and subsequent small block cylinder head designs—it's actually the same as a four-barrel Cleveland head except for water passages. You can bolt them on any small block, but much of the engine must be changed to match.

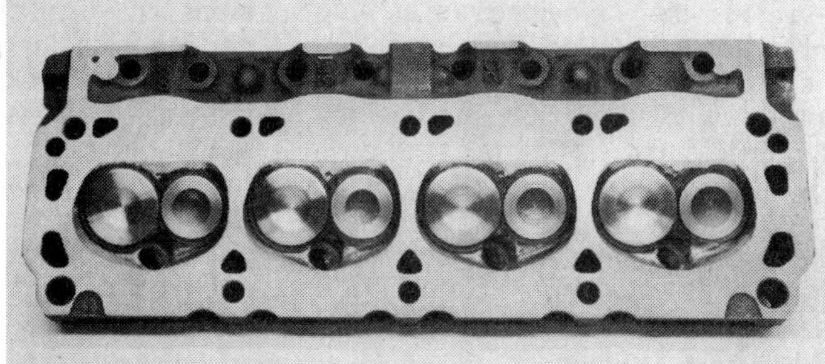

Swapping an early set of 351-Windsor heads onto a late "smog" small block is an easy way to raise compression, plus you'll get bigger valves and ports. Oval chambers decrease valve shrouding.

CYLINDER HEAD I.D. AND APPLICATION CHART

Part Number	Engine	Year	Chamber Volume (cc)		Valve Sizes (inches)		Port Sizes Intake	Port Sizes Exhaust	Rockerarm Type
			Min	Max	Exh	Int	W x H	W x H	
C3OZ-6049-AE	221	All	48.3	51.3	1.45	1.67	1.00 x 1.76	1.00 x 1.24	Conv.
C3OZ-6049-AF	260	All	52.0	55.0	1.45	1.78	1.00 x 1.76	1.00 x 1.24	Conv.
C3AZ-6049-AF	289	63/65	52.0	55.0	1.45	1.78	1.04 x 1.94	.96 x 1.24	Conv.
C5OZ-6049-B	289 HP	63/67	52.0	55.0	1.45	1.78	1.04 x 1.94	.96 x 1.24	Conv.
C6OZ-6049-AE	289	66	52.0	55.0	1.45	1.78	1.04 x 1.94	.96 x 1.24	Conv.
C7OZ-6049-E	289	67	52.0	55.0	1.45	1.78	1.04 x 1.94	1.00 x 1.24	Rail
C7ZZ-6049-B	289 HP	67	52.0	55.0	1.45	1.78	1.04 x 1.94	.96 x 1.24	Conv.
C8DZ-6049-D	289	68	61.7	64.7	1.45	1.78	1.04 x 1.94	1.00 x 1.24	Rail
C8AZ-6049-F	302, 2V	68	61.7	64.7	1.45	1.78	1.04 x 1.94	.96 x 1.24	Rail
D0OZ-6049-B	302, 2V	69/70	56.7	59.7	1.45	1.78	1.04 x 1.94	.96 x 1.24	Rail
C8OZ-6049-G	302, 2V	68	52.0	55.0	1.45	1.78	1.04 x 1.94	.96 x 1.24	Rail
C8OZ-6049-C	302, 4V	68	52.0	55.0	1.45	1.78	1.04 x 1.94	.96 x 1.24	Rail
C8ZZ-6049-A	302, 4V	68	52.0	55.0	1.45	1.78	1.04 x 1.94	.96 x 1.24	Rail
D0ZZ-6049-A	302 Boss	69/70	57.2	60.0	1.71	2.19	1.75 x 2.50	1.74 x 2.00	Guide Plate
D0OZ-6049-C	351-W	69/70	58.9	61.9	1.54	1.84	1.76 x 1.94	.96 x 1.24	Rail
C9OZ-6049-F	351-W	69/70	56.3	59.7	1.54	1.84	1.76 x 1.94	.96 x 1.24	Rail

valves. On '63½-64½ engines the intake valves measured 1.67 inches, on all other 289/302 models (except the Boss) the valve sizes are 1.78-inch intake and 1.45-inch exhaust. There have been several variations in chamber volumes in these heads (see specifications chart) ; the smallest was the '63 Hi Perf 289 version at 47.7-50.7cc, then came the early production 289 head at 52.3cc, but the majority of 289 heads are listed as "standard" at 53.5cc. There were some variations in early 302 chamber volumes, but the majority of post-'68 heads are considerably bigger (i.e., low compression) at 63.2cc.

In 1977 Ford began using the same cylinder head castings for both the 302 and the 351-W (we will discuss the peculiarities of the earlier 351-Windsor heads in a minute). The combustion chambers on these heads measure 67.5-70.5cc, which would drop compression approximately one more full point over the "big" '68-76 heads. Since factory engines from '77 on are rated at slightly higher compression ratios (8.4:1 as opposed to 8.0:1 for all '73 through '76 engines), we must surmise that compression adjustments have been achieved by altering the piston. All of these later small blocks came with dished pistons.

If you want to increase compression on a late model 302, you can gain more than two points by bolting on a pair of 289 heads. Furthermore, any of these heads can be milled up to a maximum of .050-inch (.040-inch is safer), and you can gain approximately one compression point for every 5½cc reduced from the chamber. Other suggestions for altering compression are discussed in the section on pistons.

Modifications to production small block heads are relatively uncomplicated. For excellent response on a street or bracket type motor, most builders have found that matching both intake and exhaust ports to the manifolds is critical. Simply blend the first ½ inch in from the port with a grinder, and do the same for the first ½ inch under the valve into the pocket. This minor amount of work with the grinder usually produces as much increase in flow as several more hours of porting and polishing will yield.

If you want to increase valve sizes on 289/302 heads, you have a couple of different choices. TRW makes chrome stem, swirl-polished 1.900-inch intakes (V2609) and 1.600-inch exhausts (S2608) to fit the Ford heads. To install them, you will have to have a machinist cut the seats and valve pockets larger—a relatively simple operation. An alternative that could save you about $2 apiece on a new set of valves, however, would be to use 327 Chevrolet high performance valves. They are also available from TRW, have chrome stems and swirl-polished heads. The intakes (V2351N) measure 1.940 inches and the exhausts (S2469) are 1.600 inches. They have the same stem diameter as the Fords. The only difference is that the stems on the Ford valves are longer to clear rail rocker tips; the keeper grooves are in almost the same position, however. If you do elect to use the Chevy valves, be sure to check correct valve spring height and rockerarm alignment as discussed in the section on cams and valve train. In most cases, using 289 pushrods with the Chevy valves gives proper alignment on either 289 or 302 engines.

Rather than installing larger valves in 289 or 302 heads, the factory performance literature and most early magazine articles suggested swapping on a set of 351-Windsor heads. With these heads (pre-'77) you get 1.84-inch intake valves, 1.54-inch exhausts, and 1/8-inch wider intake ports. However, combustion chambers are also larger on the Windsor heads—in the range of 60cc—almost 10cc bigger than early 289 heads. On the other hand, the larger, oval-shaped Windsor combustion chamber provides less valve shrouding and better breathing around the bigger valves; and if you are starting with a late 302, the chamber size difference is minimal, or even in your favor. Another variation is that the Windsor heads are drilled for ½-inch bolts (standard on the 351-W), whereas other small blocks use 7/16-inch head bolts. Also, pre-'77 351-W heads have L-shaped water passages on the intake manifold surfaces and an extra manifold bolt hole is located next to each water passage. Furthermore, Ford moved the location of a water passage on the intake side of the combustion chamber deck surface (late 302 heads match the Windsor heads in this respect).

Ford originally sold a kit for installing the Windsor heads on other small blocks. It consisted of the pop-up pistons previously mentioned, special head gaskets (C8OZ-6051-B), manifold gaskets (D1AZ-9433-C) and custom 7/16-inch head bolts with integral large-shoulder washers. Most of these parts are no longer available. To attach the Windsor heads to a 289 or 302 these days you could install cylinder head washers under the stock 7/16-inch bolts; you could drill and tap the block for ½-inch Windsor head bolts; or you could drill and tap the block for 1/2-inch studs. If you are going to make the swap, the best Windsor heads to get are the '69 models (C9OZ-6049-F) which have 59cc chambers. Install them with 351-W intake manifold gaskets and the C8OZ-6051-B head gaskets which have "butterfly" holes to connect the misaligned water passages (these are still available from Ford). Whether this conversion is really practical these days depends on how inexpensively you can locate a set of early Windsor heads (though it shouldn't be difficult), and how good the valves are. If you are going to have to replace worn or burned valves, you might as well use the heads you have and put the TRW valves in them. Do not use '77 or later 351-W heads, since they have the same size valves as the original 289 and 302 heads, and have the big, low-compression chambers.

Whether you are using 351-Windsor heads or standard 289 heads, a modification you will have to consider (unless you have a High Performance 289) is converting them to screw-in rocker studs and pushrod guide plates. Although early heads came with adjustable, conventional rockerarms, the press-in studs tend to pull out with high-lift cams and high-pressure valve springs. On post-'66 heads which came with rail-type rockers this conversion is mandatory for any high performance application—you need conventional rockers so you can adjust the valves. Consequently, you need guide plates to keep the pushrods, rockers and valve stems aligned on these heads (which don't have pushrod aligning slots), and as a result you need to install screw-in studs to attach the guide plates.

The job is simple and can be handled by any competent machine shop. After removing the stock studs, have the shop mill .300-inch from the rocker pedestals (.230-inch if guide plates aren't going to be used). Drill and tap the bosses to accept either Ford 289 Hi Perf screw-in studs (C3OZ-6A527-B) or the more readily available and almost identical Chevy small block screw-in studs (GM #3974416). Rail rocker heads have large round pushrod holes and therefore require guide plates (Ford part C9OZ-6A564-B or Manley #42152). Pre-'66 heads have slotted pushrod guide holes which do not require guide plates, but with a high performance cam either a flat tappet or a healthy hydraulic, screw-in studs are still a wise and inexpensive addition. If you want to install guide plates on early heads, drill the pushrod holes in the head to 1/2-inch. In all cases with guide plates be sure you are using hardened pushrods. Most 289 engines came with them (you can check by running the edge of a file over the pushrod; if it cuts easily, it isn't hardened). Hardened 302 pushrods were available under part number C9OZ-6565-F, and they are also sold by TRW and Manley, among others. Even with stiff springs and radical cam profiles, the stock 5/16-inch diameter pushrods seem to hold up fine in the 289 and 302 engines (other than the Boss) because of their relatively short length.

Finally, we come to the ultimate head swap for the small block—the Boss 302. Boss heads are still available from Ford (about $230 each, bare, at last count), and they can be bolted onto any 289 or 302 (they won't fit the smallbore 221 or 260 because the valves will hit the cylinders). These are a completely different design of head than those on other small blocks, with significantly different port shapes and and valve configuration. Consequently, nearly everything in the engine short of the block, crank, oil system and ignition will have to be changed to match the heads.

Boss 302-type pistons must be installed to match the Boss canted-valve chamber design (don't use stock Boss 302 pistons; use TRW replacements—see the Boss section). Boss pistons have a different pin height than the standard 302, and therefore require Boss connecting rods which are 5.155 inches long, as opposed to stock 302 rods which are 5.090 inches. Incidentally, the Boss rods are the same length as 221, 260, 289 standard rods, so they can be swapped into these engines using standard heads and matching pistons; but never use the weaker 221-289 rod, with the smaller 5/16-inch bolts, in a Boss 302 conversion. If you wanted to put the Boss heads on a 289, you would have to have a custom set of

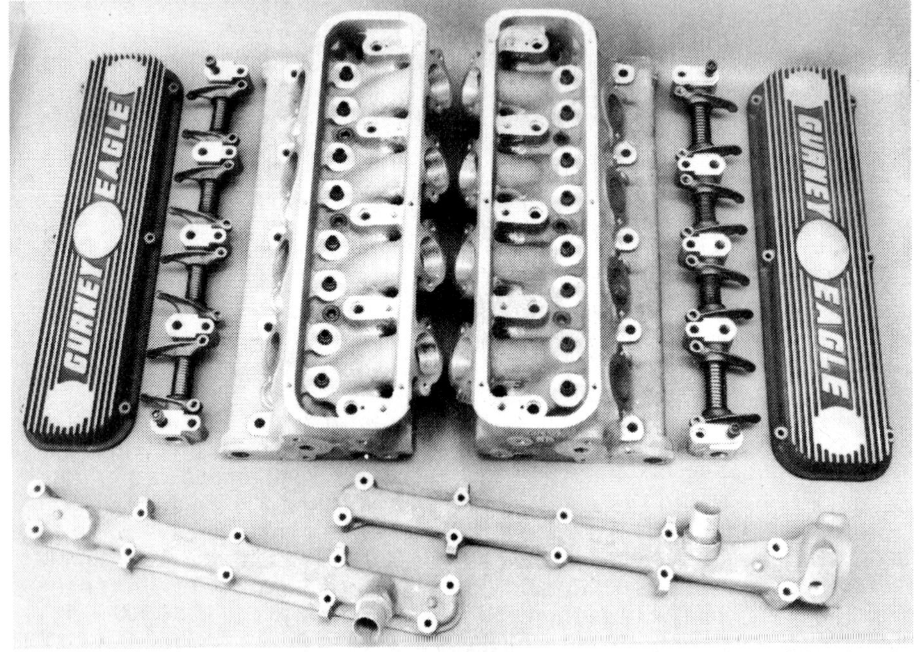

A famous, though esoteric, head swap kit for Ford small blocks is the Gurney-Weslake, now called the Gurney-Eagle. All American Racers reportedly still has several kits like this stashed in their warehouse.

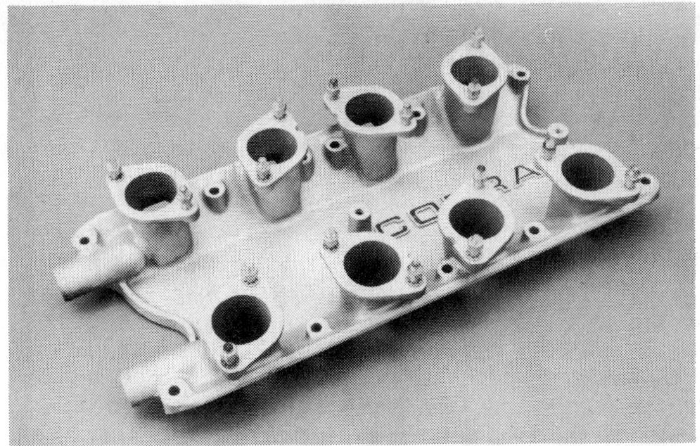

During the Sixties, you could buy just about any sort of induction system you could imagine right from your Ford dealer. This Shelby manifold accepts four downdraft Weber carburetors. Such parts are not uncommon at swap meets these days.

Offered by Ford Muscle Parts in the late Sixties, this triple Holley two-barrel setup is rare today, but is a very practical and potent street induction for a small block.

pistons or rods made to facilitate the shorter stroke length (obviously installing a 302 crank would be easier). You would also have to get a Boss 302 valve train, including a new cam to match the Boss rockerarm ratio, plus a Boss 302 intake system. When you were all finished you would have a 2-bolt main, cast crank, Boss 302 engine. Considering the scarcity and high price of individual Boss 302 components you would be wiser searching for a complete Boss engine to begin with, or buying a much cheaper and easier to find 351 Cleveland instead.

INDUCTION SYSTEM

Between the Ford Muscle Parts Program of the late 60's and all the goodies offered by Carroll Shelby for small block Fords, just about any sort of carburetion you'd care to bolt on top of a 289 or 302 was offered—from single four-barrels to four downdraft Webers. Shelby manifolds haven't been available for several years, but plenty of them were sold and you can often find them at swap meets or on the used parts shelves at speed shops. (The great thing about manifolds is that they don't wear out.)

For all-around street performance most Ford performance experts agree that you can't beat the factory special-order aluminum high-rise single four-barrel intake (C90Z-9424-D), which is a dual-plane design. This manifold is still readily available, either new or used, and with a carburetor in the 600cfm range is good for at least 30 bolt-on horsepower. Ford originally recommended the 600cfm center-pivot Holley C8AZ-9510-AD for use with this intake. Other Holleys that would work well are the 600cfm C90Z-9510-N used on the '68 GT 350 Mustang and on 390 GT Fairlanes, or the 650cfm Holley (Holley part R-4777-AAA). As a point of reference, '64-68 four-barrel 289 engines came with a cast iron manifold (C40Z-9424-H) and a 480cfm carb—this includes the High Performance engines.

Naturally, all of the currently popular specialty manifold designs are available to fit the small block Ford. Edelbrock, Holley, Offenhauser, and Weiand each make at least a couple of street, RV, or street/strip intakes for Fords—they are easy to buy, they're relatively inexpensive, and your preference in this market must be guided primarily by how much you believe the advertising or sales people. The modern single-plane, "spider" type manifolds all seem to make an excellent compromise between mid-range efficiency and top end power. And last, though a worthwhile consideration, we will skirt the issues of supercharging, turbocharging, nitrous oxide injection, and induction systems other than straight carburetion, since these subjects really apply to all engines in general and require lengthy discussions in themselves. (For an in-depth study of these subjects, see *Super Power: Turbocharging, Supercharging, Fuel Injection and Nitrous Oxide;*

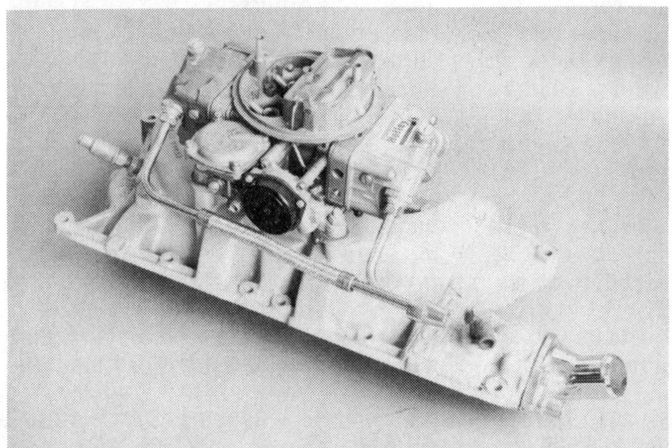

The most common intake for street performance on a small block today is a single four-barrel. The factory aluminum hi-rise, still available new, is the most recommended; use a carb in the 600cfm range for most applications.

Also excellent for all-around street and strip performance are modern single-plane, "X-type" manifolds. Edelbrock Torker is shown; similar products are made by Holley, Weiand, and Offenhauser.

Standard Ford high-performance ignition for years has been the factory centrifugal-advance dual-point (C5OZ-12127-E) distributor, which can still be found. Plenty of modern alternatives are for sale at the local speed shop, however.

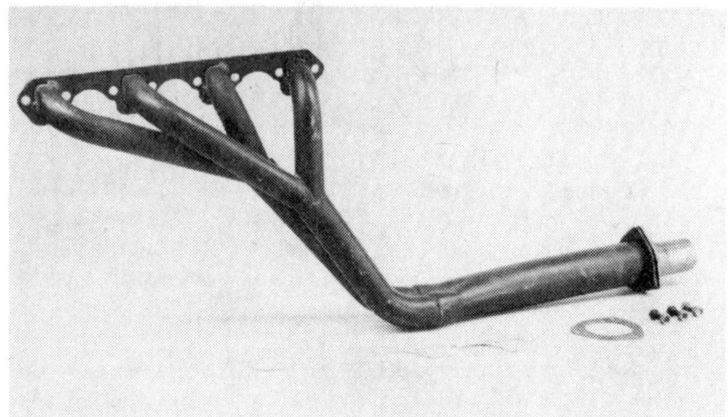

Probably the best header for street use and mid-range performance is the tri-Y design. These were installed on later Shelby Mustangs, and are currently available from Maier Racing in Hayward, Ca.

The Shelby deep-sump, finned aluminum oil pan not only improves oiling, but really dresses up a small block. They're available from most Ford specialty parts houses.

INTAKE MANIFOLD I.D. AND APPLICATION

Part Number	Engine	Year	Type	Material	Bore Diameter		Port Sizes	
					Primary	Secondary	Width	Height
C3AZ-9424-G	260	62/65	2V	Iron	1.44		.84	1.60
C4OZ-9424-E	260	64/65	2V	Iron	1.44		.84	1.60
C4AZ-9424-F	289	64	2V	Iron	1.60		.90	1.82
C3OZ-9424-C	289	63 & 65	4V	Iron	1.60	1.60	.90	1.82
C4OZ-9424-H	289 302	64/68 68	4V	Iron	1.60	1.60	.90	1.82
D1OZ-9424-A	289 302	64/68 68/72	2V	Iron	1.60	1.60	.90	1.82
C9OZ-9424-D	289/302	OHO	4V Hi Riser	Alum.	1.60	1.60	.90	1.82
D1ZZ-9424-E	302 Boss	69/70	4V	Alum.	1.74 x 1.76	1.74 x 1.76	1.68	2.38
D1AZ-9424-C	351-W	69/70	2V	Iron	1.64		1.02	1.82
C9OZ-9424-B	351-W	69	4V	Iron	1.64	1.52	1.02	1.82
D0ZX-9425-A	302 Boss	OHO	4V-8V	Alum.			1.68	2.38

"Cross-Boss" plenum (base only).
Use D0ZX-9C483-A cover for in-line carbs.
For other carburetors, fabricate cover.

available from S-A Design Publishing.)

Any intake manifold designed for a small block Ford will fit a 221, 260, 289, or 302 (except the Boss 302 manifolds, which fit only this one engine). When swapping 351-Windsor heads on a 289 or 302, use a 289-302 manifold and ignore the two extra bolt holes near the water passages on each head (on later Windsor heads these bolts have been eliminated). Manifolds cannot be swapped from a 351-W engine to other small blocks and the small block manifolds cannot be used on a 351-W, since the manifold flanges of the 351-W heads are spaced wider apart.

Finally, since intake port sizes vary—especially in the case of 351-Windsor heads used on smaller engines—it is important to match the manifold ports to the intake ports in the head. On a 221-260 use a 289-302 gasket as a template; on a 289-302 with 351-W heads, use the 351 gasket.

IGNITION

Ford has always been big on dual-point distributors. There are three varieties available from the factory for small blocks. The best is the centrifugal-advance (no vacuum advance), special-order distributor C5OZ-12127-E, which is still available if you shop for it. More popular in the early days because it gives basically the same setup for less money was the Ford dual-point conversion kit for stock distributors (D1AZ-12A132-A). Another dual-point distributor, this one having dual vacuum-advance diaphragms, came on the Boss 302 engines (C9ZZ-12127-E). The dual-diaphragm was intended to produce a suitably low idle speed (700 rpm) to allow an automatic transmission behind the Boss, despite the very healthy flat-tappet cam, but it also had a built-in rev limiter (see Boss section). It should be installed with a vacuum line connected from the intake manifold to the outer diaphragm cannister only, and timing should be set to 16° advance, idling at 700 rpm with the vacuum line plugged. However, these days it would be much smarter to install a higher stall speed converter with the automatic transmission, letting the engine idle at a faster speed without bogging or building up tranny heat, rather than trying to get the engine idle speed below 1000 rpm.

Although dual-point distributors are inexpensive and uncomplicated, they have been made obsolete in terms of both performance and maintenance by breakerless electronic ignitions. Several excellent electronic ignitions are available for Fords (add-on kits generally fit distributors for *all* modern Ford engines because the distributor heads are all the same). As with the popular specialty intake manifolds and cams, we are not going to argue the differences or benefits of one brand over another—the point is, breakerless electronic ignitions are well worth the money and when *properly installed* any of the reputable systems should provide consistent high-quality ignitions. Ford offers their own solid state breakerless kit for all '67-74 engines under Motorcraft part number DZ-5003. Accel makes a complete distributor assembly for the small block with a mechanical tach-drive (30201 T), and their BEI breakerless ignition is excellent. Hays makes a breakerless kit that installs in the stock distributor housing, and ignitions such as the Autotronic Controls MSD Multi-Spark or the Jacobs/Clifford capacitive discharge unit are highly respected systems that will work with suitable Ford distributors.

Whether you use a stock distributor housing or a specialty item, and whether or not you install an electronic ignition with it, it is always a good (and very inexpensive) idea to take the distributor to a *reputable* shop and have the advance curve dialed in on a machine. It may or may not have to be "recurved" for optimum performance for your type of driving, but you should know exactly how much the distributor advances, and at what rpm full advance is achieved, so you can set ignition timing properly.

As far as ignition timing is concerned, the experts are decisive if not exactly specific. Jack Roush says simply, "Set the advance curve to be as quick as possible before the engine begins to ping during acceleration." Bill Carroll is adamant that 10° initial advance is good, but total ignition lead over 38° "will be totally dangerous." For drag racing he recommends 26° advance in the distributor at 7200 rpm. Incidentally, Ford recommends Autolite BF-32 spark plugs for high performance; Carroll amends that to BF-32 for street, BF-22 (one step colder) for drags.

MISCELLANEOUS

We won't devote a separate section to exhaust systems for small block Fords, as we will for the other engines, because there isn't much to say. The 289 High Performance engine came with smooth-flowing cast iron manifolds (C5ZZ-9430-B, right; and C3OZ-9431-B, left), which will do a fine job in most situations and will bolt to all small blocks other than the Boss. An extra advantage of these manifolds is that they hug closely to the engine (which is narrow to begin with), so the whole package will fit easily into the engine compartment of most cars. More popular these days, and more efficient as well (though not as durable), are steel tube headers. Just about every header company makes "cheapie" sets for as little as $39.95 to fit small block Mustangs and other Fords of various years. For the price, you can't beat them, even if they aren't "tuned" for maximum performance. If you do want an engineered performance header, one of the best designs ever produced for excellent response at both mid-range and top end (meaning it's great for the street as well as the strip or race track) is the traditional tri-Y header. Such headers were installed by Shelby on the '65-66 GT-350 Mustangs, and if you'd like a set try contacting Maier Racing Sales, Hayward, CA, who have them listed in their current catalog (part number 259).

In the following sections on other Ford engines we will spend a great deal of time talking about modifying oil systems to make them live under performance/racing conditions. Happily, such is not the case with the small blocks, which have an excellent oil system design. If anything, install a Melling (M68HV—also sold through other suppliers such as TRW) high-volume, deep-rotor 302 oil pump, and possibly a deep-sump oil pan. The early Cobra finned aluminum pan is a good looking piece and it works very well; you can still find them here and there. Moroso also markets a deep-sump pan and pickup for the small block. With either a regular or a deep-sump pan, an excellent and inexpensive horsepower maker is the Boss 302 windage tray (C9ZZ-6687-B) which fits all small blocks, is readily available, and only costs about 10 bucks.

For those of you contemplating the installation of a small block Ford in an earlier chassis where the front oil pan sump will likely interfere with a front crossmember, you should know that the Bronco came with a rear-sump oil pan (C6TZ-6675-D), which must be installed with an extended oil pickup tube (C6TZ-6622-D) and a screen-support bolt that attaches to the main cap (C6TZ-6345-C). Another very helpful oil system goody that will help out in tight spots is the Econoline right-angle oil filter adapter (C5TZ-6881-A, plus bolt C5TZ-6894-A), which can be rotated to mount the filter forward or straight down rather than protruding to the left as it does normally. This adapter fits all other modern Ford engines (including sixes) except the FE big blocks.

Finally, once you have modified a small block to rev seven or eight grand, it is wise to add a heavier damper to the front of the externally-balanced crankshaft to reduce flexing and vibration at higher rpm. For a 289 use the Hi Perf 289 damper (C5OZ-6316-A) with the Hi Perf add-on counterweight (C3OZ-6A360-A) and the "thin" timing chain sprocket (C3OZ-6306-A) and matching components. For a 302 use the Boss 302 damper (C9ZZ-6316-A) with the 289 Hi Perf counterweight and the thin timing gear set.

As you readily see, making a high performance piece out of a Ford small block is a relatively easy and inexpensive operation. To begin with, the fact that close to ten million 289 and 302 engines have now been produced makes the propostion attractive. And, these well-designed and thoroughly modern little hustlers respond surprisingly well to the basic backyard bolt-on hop-up tricks: camshaft, induction, exhaust, ignition swaps and minor cylinder head rework. In essence, that's about all any Ford small block really needs.

THE 351 WINDSOR

It's hard to believe an engine the size of the 351-Windsor can be a small block, but it falls into this category primarily because it belongs to the

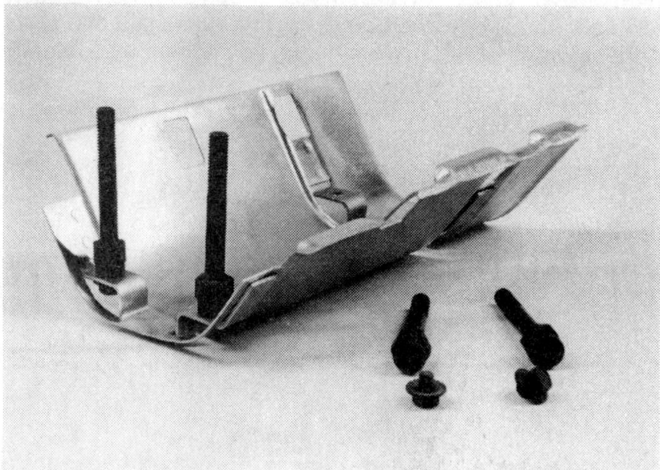

Dollar for dollar, you get more performance from a windage tray than from any other component. These came standard on the Boss 302, but fit any small block.

If you are swapping a Ford small block into some other chassis, the problem of a protruding oil filter can be solved with an Econoline right-angle adapter (C5TZ-6881-A), available from the dealer. It will fit all modern Ford engines except the FE.

Although the design is the same, the 351-W block is recognizably taller and wider than 289 or 302 small blocks.

Although two-bolt mains are fitted on all Windsors, the caps are obviously sturdy. Main journal size is larger than on other small blocks.

221, 260, 289, 302, 351-W
BLUEPRINT SPECIFICATIONS

	STOCK	PERFORMANCE
Main Bearing Clearance	.001-.00125	.002-.0025
Rod Bearing Clearance	.002-.003	.0025-.003
Rod Side Clearance	.014-.024	.0025
Piston-to-Bore Clearance	.0025-.003 (cast)	.004-.0045 (forged)
Piston Pin Clearance	.0003-.0005	.0008
Piston Ring Gap	.017 #1 & 2	.015 #1 .012 #2
Piston Ring-to-Groove	.002-.004	.001-.002
Piston-to-Valve Clearance	.070—I .100—E	.100—I .100—E
Piston-to-Deck Height	.015	.015
Crankshaft End Play	.004-.008	.004-.008
Valve Stem-to-Guide	.0008-.0018—I .0011-.0021—E	
Lifter-to-Bore	.0007-.0027	
BOLT TORQUE SPECIFICATIONS		
Cylinder Head	Step 1 50 Step 2 60 Step 3 65-72	55 65 95-100
Intake Manifold	23-25	23-25 28-32
Connecting Rod Bolts	19-24	40-45 (3/8-inch)
Main Bearing Caps	60-70 (221-302) 95-105 (351-W)	95-105 (289 HP & 351-W)
Rockerarm Stud		30-35

same family as the 90°V engine. When you list the parts that interchange between the 351-W and other members of the family—almost none—you still wonder what the relationship can be. Actually, the 351-W derives from the same basic design as the other 90°V small blocks, it has just been stretched an inch on each side to give the crank and pistons room for the extra ½ inch of stroke over the 302. Because of the taller block, neither intake manifolds nor distributor housings will interchange with the 289 or 302. Then, to give added strength to the longer-throw crankshaft, they increased the sizes of both the rod and the main journals. As a result, the connecting rods have bigger bottom ends, besides being almost an inch longer than those in other small blocks. Although both engines have the same bore size (4.00 inches), the piston pin is approximately .140-inch higher in the 351 piston than in the 302. About the only part that will interchange between the 351 and other small blocks is the camshaft. However, the firing order in the 351-W (1-3-7-2-6-5-4-8) is different from that in the other engines (1-5-4-2-6-3-7-8)—the change being made, according to Ford, "to revise main bearing loads." So, if you are going to use a 289-302 camshaft in a 351-Windsor (which is perfectly all right; most specialty cams are made to fit all small blocks, including the 351-W), you must simply rewire the distributor in the 289-302 firing order. Nothing else in the engine is affected.

We have already discussed the 351-W cylinder heads which, though not exactly identical to those on other small blocks, are another component that can be interchanged. Initial Windsor heads ('69-70) had 58.9-61.9cc combustion chambers, giving a healthy 10.7:1 compression with flat-top pistons in the four-barrel 351 engine, and even a very respectable 9.5:1 in the two-barrel with dished pistons. In '71 the compression dropped to 9.0:1 and by '73 it was 8.0:1. In 1977 Ford began using the same cylinder head castings for both the 302 and the 351-W, the only difference being that the 351 heads are drilled for the larger ½-inch head bolts. These heads have 67.5-70.5cc chambers and the smaller 302 size valves—1.78-inch intakes and 1.45-inch exhausts as opposed to 1.84-inch intakes and 1.54-inch exhausts in pre-'77 Windsor heads. Up to 1978 the 351-W came with rail-type rockerarms and all but a few '69-70 heads have non-adjustable positive-stop rocker studs. In '78 the Windsor were fitted with stamped steel rockers.

Given the existence of the 351 Cleveland Ford engine plus all the specialty parts available to make it go even faster than it does, the question of building a full-race 351 Windsor sounds almost silly. For the amount of money you'd spend on the Windsor, including having non-available parts custom made, you could buy at least a

The '69 four-barrel 351-W came with a cast flat-top piston (all others use dished pistons), which will give about 10:1 compression in pre-'77 Windsors. If they are used in conjunction with a high-lift cam, the valve-reliefs should be cut deeper, as shown on right piston.

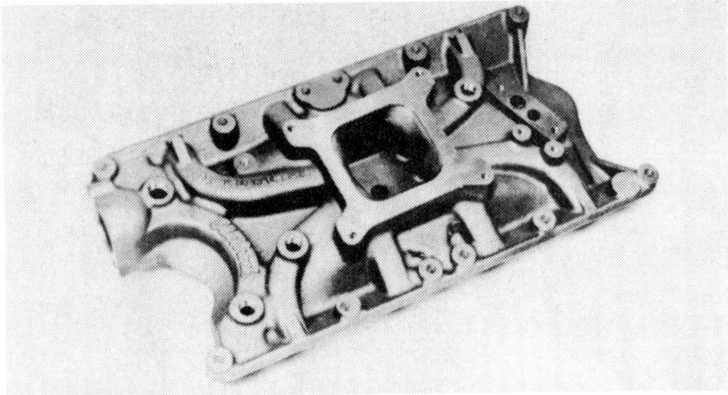

Nobody makes all-out performance intake manifolds for the 351-W, but manufacturers are finally introducing "RV" type four-barrel intakes for this engine. Edelbrock Streetmaster, shown, is designed for low-rpm torque and driveability.

couple of Clevelands that would run circles around it. Of course, it can be done, to prove a point or to specific class racing rules, as there are custom components available for the 351-W. But, in the vast majority of cases hopping up a 351-Windsor should be strictly a bolt-on or basic rebuild situation. We can't ignore the fact that a few million of these engines have been, and are still being, produced; and fortunately the performance parts manufacturers are waking up to this ready market. If you have a 351-W in your car, some quick and inexpensive cam, compression, and carburetion changes will make it come alive.

There are no "good" or "bad" 351-W blocks. All have two-bolt mains and come with the same cast crankshaft. However, these parts are relatively stout, the big-journal crank being designed to reduce flexing and the block having thicker cylinder walls and beefier main bearing webs and caps than the other small blocks. Connecting rods are the same on all 351-W engines. So start with the components you have, and if you are rebuilding the engine follow basic high-performance techniques: tolerance checking, Magnafluxing, deburring, Tufftriding and micro-polishing of the crank, shot-peening of the rods.

Only one four-barrel version of the 351-W was ever made, in 1969 (a few carrying over to '70). If you are lucky, you might be able to find the cast iron intake manifold from one of these engines in a junkyard, or you might locate one at a dealer (part C9OZ-9424-B). But considering the weight and scarcity, you might as well buy an aluminum four-barrel intake such as the Holley Street Dominator (#300-18). Ford also offered a Muscle Parts aluminum high-rise manifold for the Windsor (C9OZ-9424-E), as did Shelby, both of the dual-plane design, but these would be hard to find and might pose hood clearance problems on some cars.

Of greater concern, the 4V 351-W also came with the only flat-top pistons ever made for this engine. They are cast aluminum with dual eyebrows and are still available (C9OZ-6108-A). Similar pistons are also available from some rebuild suppliers such as Badger and Silver-lite. They give 10.7:1 compression with the early (59cc) heads, or about 10:1 with '70-76 heads (about 63-64cc). These pistons are inexpensive (especially the rebuild brands), and they are plenty good for a street-type engine. The only high performance forged racing pistons currently available for the 351-W are TRW pop-ups (L-2442-F) rated at 11:1 with '77-later cylinder heads (67.5-70.5cc). These pistons will fit *only* in the '77 and newer engines; with earlier heads they hit the combustion chambers. However, as of this writing, TRW is designing a new pop-up for the pre-'77 351-W, which should be available by the time you read this. Another alternative would be to machine the 5cc dome from the TRW pop-up, producing a suitable forged flat-top for a 351-W. Such a machining operation is fairly straightforward and inexpensive, and would produce a good, rugged performance piston for a Windsor that would live with street gasoline and with weekend passes at the bracket races. In stock form all 351-W engines, other than the '69 4V, have dished pistons.

We have already discussed cylinder head options and modifications for the 351-Windsor. Obviously, the same head, camshaft, and valve train selection advice applies to the 351 as given for the 289 and 302. The only real difference between the two is pushrod length—those in the Windsor being about 1.250-inch longer. Because of this difference, plus the fact that all Windsor heads have rail rockers and therefore nonguiding pushrod holes, it is very advisable to install screw-in rocker studs and pushrod guide plates (and, of course, conventional rockers) no matter if you use a hydraulic or a solid-lifter cam. If you choose a

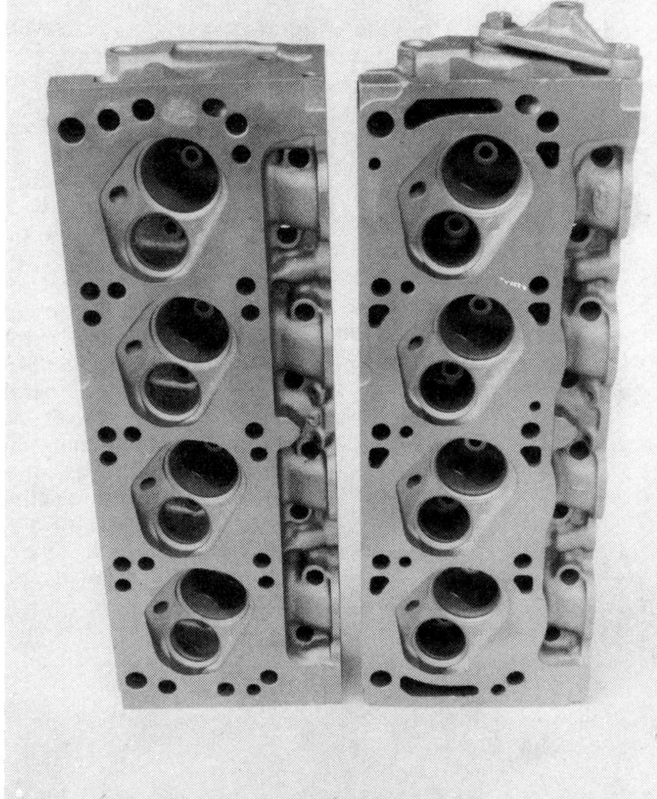

The '69 Boss 302 heads had the biggest valves (left), but '70 versions with 2.19-inch intakes work a little better (right). Note water passage differences.

The one "underdesigned" component of the Boss 302 is the factory piston (darker of the two), which has become notorious for cracking at the skirt. A good replacement is the forged TRW, which has a pair of reinforcing ribs (arrow) in the vulnerable area.

radical cam with hefty springs, you should switch to 3/8-inch hardened pushrods with corresponding guide plates, as available from Manley or from most cam makers. Since the 351-W used several different pushrod lengths (they vary slightly according to production requirement), and since valve tip and spring heights can vary depending on the parts you use, it would be wise to coordinate all valve train components according to the cam manufacturer's recommendations.

If you are working on a '77 or later 351-Windsor, one of the easiest ways to bring it to life would be to buy a set of earlier Windsor heads (the most preferable being the '69, C9OZ-6049-F) at the wrecking yard, give them a good valve job, and bolt them on. You'll not only bring the compression back up to 9½ or 10:1, but you will get the larger intake and exhaust valves as well. If you are planning a camshaft change, you might as well upgrade the valve train and match the ports at the same time. Other than this, your basic 351-W hop-up consists of the usual carb (650- to 700cfm) and manifold change, a set of headers, and a modern performance ignition system.

THE BOSS 302

There really isn't much to say about the Boss 302 engine. If you have one, you are likely a collector, you value what you have, and you know that it is worth most if left in (or restored to) original condition. If you don't have one, your chances of finding a Boss 302 these days are not impossible, but slim.

The Boss 302 small block, an outgrowth of the short-lived Tunnel-Port 302 and predecessor of the Cleveland engine design, was produced only in 1969 and '70 and came in limited production Boss Mustangs and a few Mercury Cougar Eliminators. It was designed for F.I.A. Trans Am competition, and it did very well. Naturally, racing versions of the Boss 302 underwent modificaton, using some Ford Muscle parts such as super strong T/A connecting rods (DOXZ-6200-A), needle-bearing rockerarm fulcrums (DOXZ-6A585-A), dual valve springs (DOXZ-6A511-A), titanium intake valves (DOXZ-6057-A), and special exhaust valves (DOXZ-6505-A). Several special induction systems were produced for the Boss 302 (Boss small block manifolds are unique, they won't fit any other Ford engines); and factory optional inductions are very rare—such as the Cross Boss (DOXZ-9425-A, base; DOXZ-9C483-A, top) with the four-throat inline Autolite "Weber" carb (DOXZ-9510-A), quad Weber setups, fuel injection, or dual four-barrel tunnel rams (still offered by Weiand, #1989). Other factory-touted racing modifications included camshaft selection, head modification, and oil system trickery.

But the majority of Boss 302 engines in existence today will be used on the street (since there are few instances where class racing will call for this specific engine displacement). And, the production Boss motor is just about as tough, strong, and sophisticated a street hot rod engine as you could want, even in stock form. It does have a couple of weak points, one of which should definitely be rectified, but first let's start with some differences in production engines.

The basic Boss 302 package included a rugged four-bolt main block, a forged steel crank, forged connecting rods, a windage tray, Cleveland-type heads with huge ports and canted valves, a 290° solid-lifter cam, 10.6:1 pistons, a 780cfm Holley four-barrel on a high-rise, aluminum, dual-plane manifold, and a dual-point distributor. If you were to pick and choose parts for the best Boss, you should select the '69 cross-drilled crankshaft and the '70 heads. The cross-drilled crank was available only in 1969 production engines; the only replacement crankshaft offered was the '70 type (DOZZ-6303-A) which is also forged steel and identical except that it has only two oiling holes per journal instead of four.

The slight change in heads between '69 and '70 will tell you a lot about the Boss 302. For the second year of production, the factory *reduced* valve size on this engine (from 2.23-inch intakes in '69 to 2.19-inch intakes in '70), and the latter heads are the ones that work better. To be honest, the ports and valves in Boss 302 heads are way too big for street use on an engine this small. And, with the

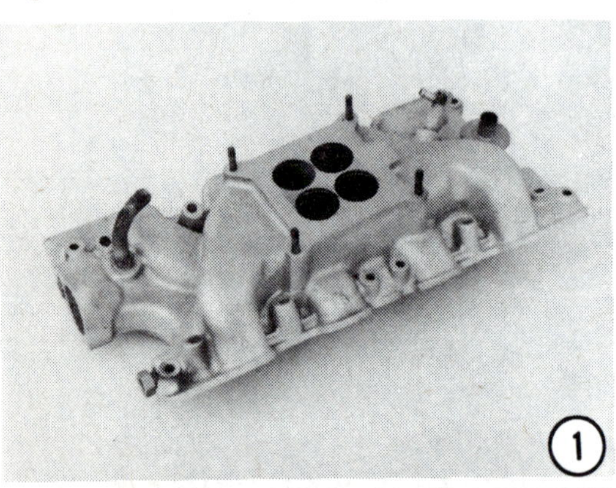

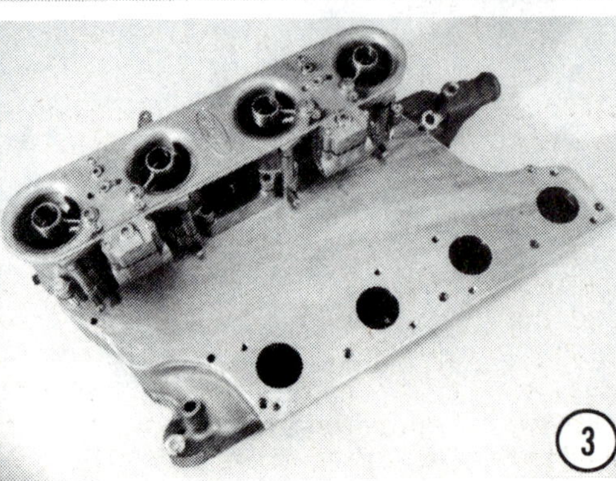

There are only a few inductions for the Boss 302, including: 1) the stock Boss 302 aluminum high-riser with 780cfm Holley (a more-than-plentiful setup); 2-3) the extremely rare (and valuable) Cross Boss manifold with the inline-four Autolite carbs, one of the most extraordinary pieces of exotica ever dreamed up by Ford engineers; 4) and a Boss 302 single-plane X-type manifold designed and built by Jack Roush (GR7X-9425-A, costing about $275). Not shown here but also available is a Weiand tunnel-ram intake to fit the Boss 302 heads.

stock 780cfm Holley, it's over-carbureted. Running a close-ratio four-speed and extremely low rear gears on a road course, a tight-winding small block can make use of the cavernous induction system. On the street in a dressed out '69-70 Mustang (which is pretty heavy), you are going to experience a boggy bottom end and gas consumption that we'd rather not think about these days. To make it more responsive between red lights, run as low a rear end ratio as you can live with on the street, and/or a high-stall converter (around 1500 rpm) if you have to have an automatic trans. Obviously, this solution will make fuel "economy" even worse. But we will assume that most Boss 302 Mustangs still on the street today are being used more for recreational driving.

Other than crankshaft oiling and intake valve size, components on all Boss 302 assemblies remained the same. If you are planning to rebuild one of these motors and most of the original parts are still in good condition (such as cam and valve train), there is little point in making modifications if it is still going to be run on the street. The major weak point of the Boss 302, however, is the stock piston design; they lacked reinforcing in the skirt area, and they are notorious for cracking or breaking. Some of the original 10.6:1 stock pistons (DOZZ-6108-A) are still on Ford parts shelves, but for a rebuild you should use the TRW 10½:1 Boss 302 replacement piston (L2324-F) instead. It is the same as the stock part, except ribbed in the skirt area for more strength. They are also available in oversizes up to .040-inch whereas Ford's only go to .003-inch over. For racers, TRW also makes a 12.1:1 Boss 302 piston (L2325-F).

You might also want to do some upgrading of valve train components on your Boss 302. All production engines came with a solid-tappet cam (290° duration, .484-inch lift), but there is little reason why you couldn't install an equally effective, quieter, and maintenance-free high performance hydraulic grind. Brand name preference is up to you; but any of the major cam grinders can supply you with a cam and related components that will perform best under your specific driving conditions. A couple of things to remember: The Boss 302 accepts any small block camshaft, but it uses Cleveland-type components for the rest of the valve train. Standard Boss 302 rocker-arms have a ratio of 1.73:1 whereas all other small blocks have 1.6:1 rockers. Consequently, a camshaft designed for a regular 289 or 302 will give the same "advertised" duration if installed in a Boss 302, but it will net 8.125% more lift at the valve. Considering the current trend to mild duration, super high-lift cam profiles, this could mean interference between valves and pistons on the Boss. Remember, this engine breathes *too well*, if anything. So there's little sense running close valve-to-piston clearances or pushing valve spring limits with ultra-fast valve acceleration rates. In other words, it wouldn't be smart to install a regular small block cam of over .500-inch net lift in a Boss 302. As always, follow the cam manufacturer's recommendations once you have supplied him with accurate information.

The same holds true for most of the valve train, especially concerning valve springs. The stock setup on Boss motors—with stamped steel rockers, screw-in studs, guide plates, heavy springs with dampers, hardened retainers, and spring cups to keep the springs from walking on the head—is better than you will find on just about any production engine anywhere. With a more radical cam you might need an inner coil spring, which would necessitate PC-type valve stem seals for clearance. As discussed in the Cleveland section, the sled rocker fulcrums will benefit from Tufftriding. And, if you are thinking of locating the optional needle-bearing rocker fulcrums (DOXZ-6A585-A), consider that competition aluminum roller rockers are generally cheaper and stronger. Big block Chevy-type (Isky #204-96) roller rockers, with a 1.7:1 ratio, fit the Boss heads. A set of these roller-tip rockers will cure the problem of rocker tip wear often associated with Boss or Cleveland stamped rockers. The one part of the valve train that definitely should be changed on the Boss 302, however, are the 5/16-inch pushrods. At high rpm under heavy spring loads, they can flex or bend—the problem being more severe in a Boss because of the taller heads and the pushrod inclination for the canted valves. Replace them with Manley 3/8-inch hardened pushrods (#25728—same as for small block Chevy) and matching guide plates. Incidentally, to achieve rocker-to-valve tip alignment, many engine builders cut the guide plates apart to position each pushrod independently as the rocker stud is cinched down.

The factory performance bulletins (there was one devoted entirely to modification of the Boss 302) suggest and show diagrams for porting and polishing the Boss heads. This may help a little for all-out, high rpm racing, but for the street...DON'T DO IT. The ports certainly don't need to be any bigger, and the as-cast roughness will help keep the fuel in suspension, rather than "wetting out" on the port walls.

About the only other area that needs particular attention on your Boss 302 is the ignition. Production engines came with a dual-diaphragm, vacuum-advance, dual-point distributor and standard coil ignition. This distributor has a built-in rev limiter designed to hold maximum engine speed to approximately 6000 rpm. If you want to retain this distributor, connect a vacuum line from the manifold to the outer cannister only. Otherwise, you could install the Ford centrifugal-advance, dual-point distributor kit (DOAZ-12A132-B) along with a standard 13° breaker cam (C5AZ-12210-A), and discard the vacuum-advance mechanism entirely. Or you could install the 289 Hi Perf dual-point distributor (C5OZ-12127-E), which is also a centrifugal-advance unit. In either case, Ford performance manuals recommend 16° initial advance, 38° total. Any distributors that will fit the 289-302 will fit the Boss, so your best bet these days would be to install a modern electronic ignition system in a standard single-point distributor (because they're plentiful and cheap), and bolt it in the Boss.

PRODUCTION 302 BOSS SPECIFICATIONS
Nominal (inches) except as shown

Displacement (Cu. In.)	302
Carburetor	4V, 780-cfm
Horsepower (Bhp/rpm)	290/5800
Torque (lb-ft/rpm)	290/4300
Compression Ratio	10.5:1
Bore	4.00
Stroke	3.00
Bore Spacing	4.38
Head Volume (cc)	61.3-64.3—69 57.0-60.0—70
Crankshaft—Material —Journal Dia—Main —Rod	Forged Steel 2.2486 2.1226
Con Rods—Material —Length (Ctr-Ctr)	Forged Steel 5.150
Pistons—Material —Compression Height —Deck Clearance	Forged Aluminum 1.529 0.013-0.033
Centerline of Crank to Top of Block	8.201-8.211
Camshaft—Timing—Open/Close —Duration/Overlap —Lift —Journal Dia.	Int-34°/76°—Exh-86°/24° 290°/58° 0.290 #1—2.081 #4—2.036 #2—2.066 #5—2.021 #3—2.051
Tappets	Mechanical
Rockerarm—Ratio —Type	1.73:1 Lightweight stamping with threaded stud—Adj.
Valves—Head Dia.—Intake —Exhaust	2.225-2.235—69 2.185-2.195—70 1.702 1.717
Valve Stem Diameter	0.342
Valve Spring Load—Closed (lbs/installed ht) —Open	88-96/1.82 299-331/1.32
Firing Order	1-5-4-2-6-3-7-8
Initial Advance (Vacuum Disconnected)	16°BTDC
Breaker Point—Gap —Dwell	0.020 30°-33°
Spark Plug Gap	0.032-0.036
Manifold Vacuum (Idle)	11 inches of mercury

HOW TO BUILD A 90°V SMALLBLOCK

Each of the four sections of this book will be followed by a photo essay detailing the assembly of a Ford engine of the family being discussed. This way you can see how the parts go together, and, since each engine was built by a performance expert, you will hopefully pick up some good engine assembly tips. Since the majority of Ford small blocks being modified today are driven on the street, we have chosen this engine to demonstrate a practical, though peppy, budget build-up. The job was done by Dave Smith of Precisioned Speed in Anaheim, California; he's a meticulous and studied engine builder with years of Ford experience. The engine is a '66 two-barrel 289; it will be driven exclusively on the street, so components were chosen to give the best performance per dollar spent. Including parts and shop labor, assembly of the short block and heads, as shown here, would cost about $500.

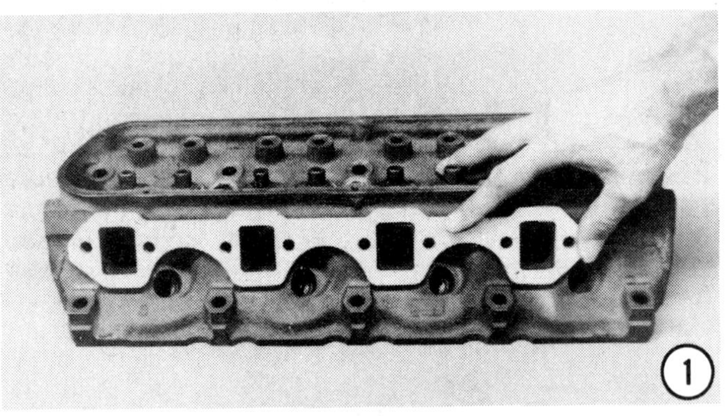

Beginning with the heads, which happen to be '66 two-barrel versions, Dave strongly recommends matching intake and exhaust ports to the gasket openings.

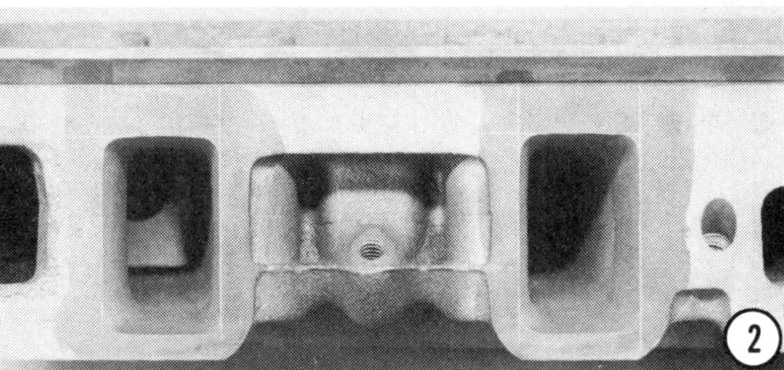

The ports are ground out to scribed outlines, then blended smoothly to the stock as-cast passage. Dave has proven on his flow bench that complete enlarging and polishing of small block ports yields little gain over this simple and inexpensive procedure.

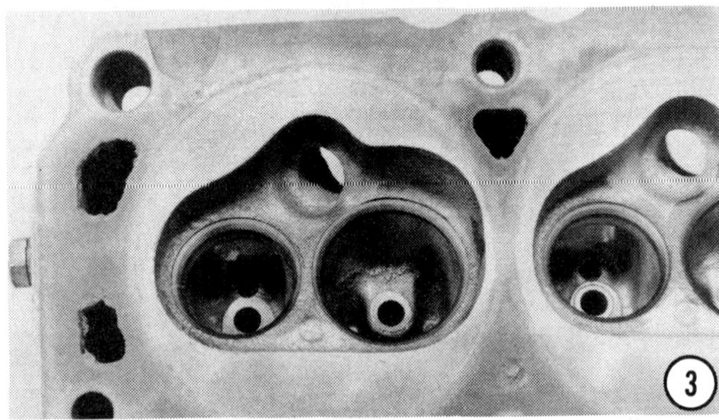

The first .500-inch under the valve seat should similarly be cleaned up with the hand grinder. Then Dave gives the seats and valves a 15°, 45°, 70° three-angle cut, keeping the valve seat width .060-inch for street. Stock valves will be used; however, the stem tips have been refaced, since they've been chewed up by the rail rockers.

Any '66 or later small block fitted with a performance cam should be converted to conventional rockerarms. First, extract the press-in rocker studs. The rocker pedestals must then be cut down .300-inch, and this is best done on a mill, as shown.

Tap each pedestal to accept screw-in studs. Since each hole must be 90° to the base, this should also be done on a mill.

These heads will be assembled with inner and outer valve springs, so Dave will install small diameter Perfect Circle teflon valve stem seals, which require the trimming of each guide. Use a special cutter (P.C. #VST-17) with a hand drill.

With valves and seals in place, heads are now ready for final assembly. Valve springs are Crane #99836, single outers with inner dampeners. Installed at 1.700 inches they give 110 pounds pressure with the valves seated. These Chevy Z/28 springs can be used with stock two-barrel retainers, which are fine for street duty.

Dave is using Manley guide plates (#42152) and Chevy LT-1 screw-in studs (#3974416). Use a sealer on threads because they penetrate the water jacket. Torque each stud to 40 ft-lbs.

The '66 and later heads have a thermactor hole on the exhaust port side. If the smog pump isn't used, plug the hole with a 7/8-inch cup plug.

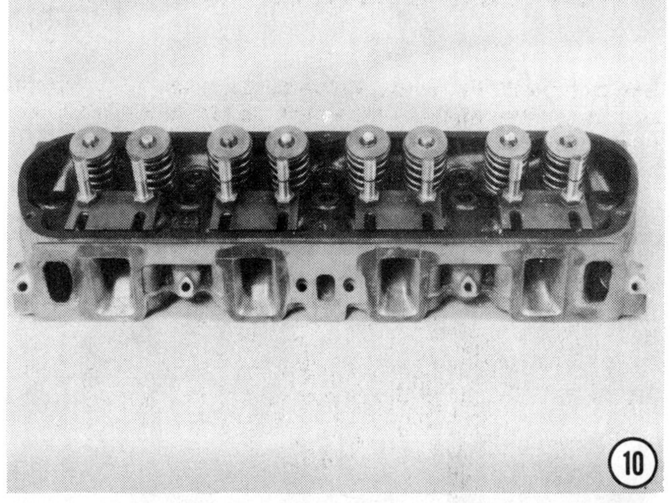

Completed heads for this economy street performance small block include matched ports, three-angle valve cut, Crane springs, stock valves, screw-in studs, and guide plates; They will be fitted with replacement early small block rockerarms (TRW #44036K; McQuay-Norris #1 RM 30). If you want to spend more money, you can also install larger valves.

For the low-buck hop-up the block was hot tanked and the cylinders were bored .040-inch oversize. Be sure to keep main caps in order (they're numbered).

The crank journals should be ground undersize if they are heavily scored. For the final finish the journals should be micro-polished and the oil holes chamfered, as shown. Tufftride heat-treating (optional) will increase journal surface toughness, inexpensive extra insurance on Ford cast crankshafts.

Keeping things clean is the most important part of engine assembly. Dave uses regular motor oil for lube; he coats bearing and journal surfaces only. Of course, the engine should be thoroughly primed before it's fired by driving the oil pump while rotating the crank assembly by hand (or with the starter).

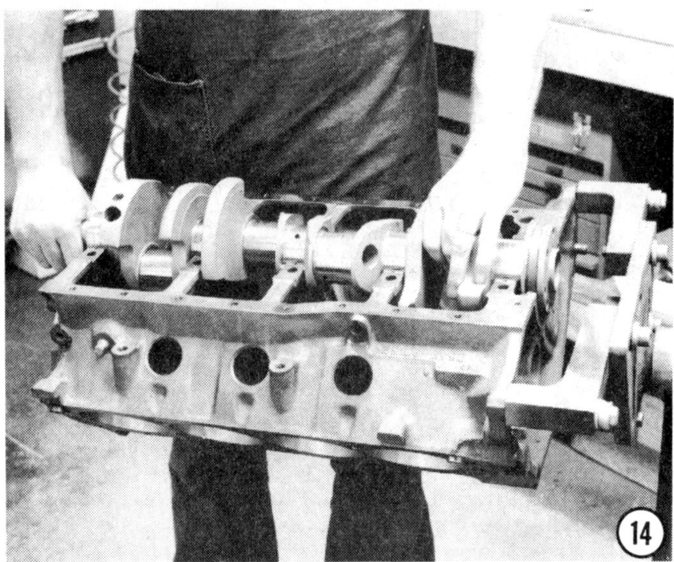

Drop in the crank, and torque main bearing bolts to 70 ft-lbs.

Spin crank by hand to make sure it turns freely.

These .040-inch oversize Triplex cast pop-up pistons will yield 10½:1 compression in this engine. The rods are completely stock; a very wise extra expense would be the addition of stronger rod bolts (see text).

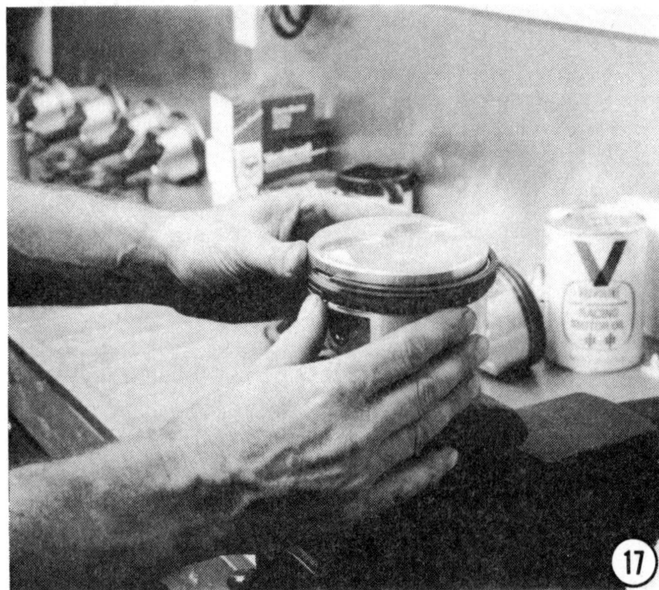

A standard ring set, such as McQuay-Norris #1508 "single moly" (molybdenum-faced top ring with a standard iron-faced second ring) is good for a street motor.

Installing pistons is one of the touchiest parts of engine assembly. Use a good ring compressor of the proper size and strike piston top with resilient object (Dave likes the handle of a Compothane hammer). Piston should slip right in; never force it or you will jam or break the rings. Don't forget to cover the threads on the rod bolts to prevent damage to the crank.

Double check bearing clearances (Plasti-gauge is fine for this), then lube bearings and journals, install rod caps and torque to no more than 25 ft-lbs (this is critical) with stock bolts.

Automotive Alliance of Santa Barbara, Calif., makes excellent low cost camshafts in grinds very similar to Ford Muscle Parts cams. This customer chose #612535, a hydraulic profile giving .506-inch lift and 288° net duration. Use good anti-pumpup lifters.

Always use a new timing chain; for street, the stock Ford type will work adequately, especially with a metal cam gear, as shown. Be sure to match the right parts on a small block: this is the "narrow" ('65-up) chain; the wide chain/gears require a spacer behind the crank gear.

Nothing real fancy about this short block, but it will be plenty lively on the street. Assembled in a professional rebuild shop (with pop-up pistons and performance cam already mentioned) it would cost about $350. This customer also wisely tacked on another $40 for balancing.

After the short block and heads have been machined and assembled by a good shop, even a novice mechanic can bolt the rest of the engine together. Take your time, use quality gaskets and sealants, and pay strict attention to bolt torque specs.

This street performance 289 is topped off with an Edelbrock Torker intake, and will get a 600cfm four-barrel, headers, and an electronic ignition kit. It's an inexpensive package—but it's just about all you need to build a healthy little Ford.

THE "FE" BIG BLOCK
332,352,360,361,390,391,406,410,427 and 428 ENGINES

THE "FE" BIG BLOCK SERIES

In some ways a big block can be the most complicated of Ford engines. In other ways it can be the most simple. The complicated part is sorting through all of the numerous parts changes and the special-order and racing-only goodies offered by Ford during the dual purpose (workhorse and race motor) career of the FE engine. The simple part is that building a high performance big block Ford, even of the most radical variety, entails little more than screwing together the right combination of original factory parts. As stated by Ford, the 427 side-oiler was an out-and-out racing engine reflecting the state of the art 15 years ago—and the art of building Ford wedge engines hasn't really progressed much since then. Unless you're going to mix octane booster with your gasoline at every fill-up, there is little sense in building even a "stock" 11½:1 compression 427, circa 1964. The point is, however, that Ford made just about any component you might want to put into a big block Ford engine, and even today the engines need very little modification of any sort to meet the most rigorous of street, strip, off-road, or drag boat demands.

Where and how do you get specialty parts for an engine that hasn't been produced for 10 years? Surprisingly, most of the high performance 427 components are still available from the factory. High-Riser and Tunnel-Port heads are no longer listed, nor are most of the specialty intake manifolds other than the single four-barrel types, but side-oiler blocks, Medium-Riser and Cobra-Jet heads, solid-lifter cams, steel cranks, factory pistons, and so on, are still available as of this writing. Obviously, supplies are limited on most components, and in the case of some parts (e.g., blocks) what is available is the last of the pickings; and once you have ordered it from the factory you can't return it. Prices for some components are fairly steep: about $620 for a 427 side-oiler block, $320 each for bare Medium-Riser heads, $45 each for factory high performance pistons, $15-$25 each for the trick valves; but it is possible to build a brand new Medium-Riser 427 today with all new factory parts. The "list price," when added up, would come to around $3500-$4000, excluding labor to assemble all the pieces. It should also be mentioned that these parts are now designated "Class C" items, which are ordered through the Ford National Parts Depot in Livonia, MI, and will therefore take about one month to arrive at your local dealer. On the other hand, a few Ford specialty

SPECIFICATION CHART

Displacement (Cu. In.)	352	390	390	390	406	410	427	428
Carburetor Venturi	2V & 4V	2V	4V	6V	4V & 6V	4V	4V & 6V	4V
Horsepower (Bhp/rpm) (bhp/rpm)	220/4400—2V—61-63 235/4400—2V—60 250/4400—4V—64-66 300/4000—4V—58-60 360/6000—4V—Hi-Perf 60	250/4400—63-65(L-M) 255/4400—71 266/4600—64-65(L-M) 265/4400—66, 68-70 270/4400—67 275/4400—66 AT 280/4400—67-70 PF	300/4600—61-65 315/4600—66-68 320/4800—67 GT, 69 325/4800—68 GT 330/5000—62-65 PI 335/4800—66 GT 375/6000—61-62 HP	340/5000—63 401/6000—61-62	385/5800—4V 405/5800—6V	330/4600	390/5600—68, 4V, Hyd 410/5600—4V 425/6000—8V	335/5200—CJ 345/4600 360/5400—PI
Intake (lb-ft/rpm)	336/2400—2V—61-63 350/2400—2V—60 352/2800—4V—64-66 380/2800—4V—54-60 380/3400—4V—Hi-Perf 60 395/2800—4V—58	378/2400—63-65 376/2600—71 390/2600—68-70 403/2600—67 67-70 PF 405/2600—66	427/2800—61-68 427/3200—PI, GT, 69 427/3400—61-62 HP	430/3500 430/3200—63	444/3400—4V 448/35006V	444/2800	460/3200—68,4V, Hyd 476/3400—4V 480/3700—8V	440/3400—CJ 459/3200—PI 462/2800
Compression Ratio	8.9:/—2V—61-63 9.3:1—4V—64-66 9.6:1—4V—59-60 10.2:1—4V—58 10.6:1—4V—Hi-Perf 60	9.4:1—64-65 9.5:1—66-70 10.5:1—PF 8.6:1—71	9.6:1—61-63 10.1:1—64-65 10.5:1—66-69 PI 10.6:1—61-62 HP		10.9:1 Nom 12.1:1 Max	10.5:1	11.6 Bumper Piston Max 10.9—68 13.1 Dome Pop-up Max 14.1 Service Pop-up Max	10.6:1—CJ 10.5:1
Head Volume (cc)	69-72—58 70.4-73.4—59 72.8-75.8—60 59.7-62.1—60 Hi-Perf 71.2-74.2—61-66	71.2-74.2—63-67 67.1-70.1—68 68.1-71.1—69-71	59.7-62.7—61-62 HP 62.6-64.6—61-62 HP 71.2-74.2—61-67 67.1-70.1—68 68.1-71.1—69	10.5:1—63 10.6:1—61-62	62.6-64.6—62 64.0-67.0—62-63 56.4-61.0—Opt, Alt	71.2-74.2	64.0-67.0—Early 63 72.8-75.8 66.0-69.0 Opt Alt	71.2-74.2—65-67 67.1-70.1—68 68.1-71.1—PI 72.8-75.8—CJ
Bore	4.00	4.05	4.05	4.05	4.13	4.05	4.23	4.13
Stroke	3.50	3.78	3.78	3.78	3.78	3.98	3.78	3.98
Bore Spacing	4.63	4.63	4.63	4.63	4.63	4.63	4.63	
Crankshaft Matl Journal dia—Main Rod	Nodular Iron 2.749 2.438	Nodular Iron 2.749 2.438	Nodular Iron 2.749 2.438	Nodular Iron 2.749 2.438	Nodular Iron 2.749 2.438	Nodular Iron 2.749 2.438	Iron—63-64, 68 Steel—65-67	Iron Steel—65-67
Cam Journal Dia	2.1238-2.1480	2.1238-2.1480	2.1238-2.1480	2.1238-2.1480	2.1238-2.1480	2.1238-2.1480	2.1238-2.1480	2.1238-2.1480
Centerline of Crank Top of Block (Block Deck Height)	10.17	10.17	10.17	10.17	10.17	10.17	10.17	10.17
Top of Piston to Top of Block (Back Height Clearance)	0.010-0.030—4V 0.036-0.056—60 Hi-Perf 0.046-0.066—2V	0.010	0.010-0.030	0.010-0.030	0.045-0.065	0.015	0.035	0.015
Compression Height	1.836-1.842	1.778-1.782	1.778-1.782	1.778-1.782	1.743-1.747	1.678-1.672	1.753-1.757	1.678-1.672
Con Rod Length (Ctr to Ctr)	6.538-6.542	6.486-6.490	6.486-6.490	6.486-6.490	6.486-6.490	6.486-6.490	6.486-6.490	6.486-6.490
Valve Head Dia—Intake —Exhaust	2.022-2.037 1.551-1.566	1.551-1.566	1.551-1.566	1.551-1.566	1.645-1.660	1.551-1.566	2.022-2.037—63, LR 2.080-2.097—64, LR, 68 2.185-2.195—65-67, MR, HR 1.660-1.645—63-64 LR, 68 1.723-1.733—65-67 MR, HR	2.022-2.037 2.080-2.097—CJ 1.551-1.566 1.652-1.660—CJ
Valve Stem Dia				0.371	0.371	0.371	0.371	0.371
Valve Spring Load—Closed (lbs/Installed Ht)	94-104/1.82	80-90/1.82—64-66 85-95/1.82—67-71	78-84/1.82—61-66 80-90/1.82—67 & GT, PI, HP 85-95/1.82—68-70	80-90/1.82	80-90/1.82	80-90/1.82	80-90/1.82	80-90/1.82 85-95/1.82—67-69 69-70 CJ
Valve Spring Load—Open	180-198/1.42	235-255/1.38—64-65 209-231/1.38—67-71	190-208/1.42—61-66 209-231/68-70 233-257/1.38—67 255-280/1.32—GT, PI	255-255/1.38	255-280/1.32	233-255/1.38	255-280/1.32	233-254/1.38 255-280/.38 255-280/1.32—68 CJ 66-68 PI 271-299/1.34—69-70 CJ 69 PI
Valve Lifters Lash(Mech)	Hyd Mech—Hi-Perf & Early 58 0.028 Cold/0.025 Hot	Hyd	Hyd Mech PI & HP	Mech 0.028 Cold 0.025 Hot	Mech 0.028 Cold 0.025 Hot	Hyd	Mech—68 Hyd 0.028 Cold 0.025 Hot	Hyd
Rockerarm—Ratio —Type	1.76 Shaft—Hyd-non-adj Mech-adj	1.73 Shaft—non-adj	1.76 Shaft—Hyd—non-adj Mech—adj		1.76 Shaft—adj	1.73 Shaft—non-adj	1.73—Hyd, 1.76 Mech Shaft—Hyd—non-adj Mech—adj	1.73 Shaft—non-adj
External Balance	No	No	No	No	No	No	No	Yes

parts houses have been established recently which stock many of the older high performance parts or can get them quickly. Notable is John Vermeersch's Total Performance, 40631 Irwin, Mt. Clemens, MI 48045, an independent business specializing in Ford high performance products of all types. Being in the local area, he can get one day shipment on Class C parts, plus he has a large inventory of on-the-shelf components. John says 90% of his business deals in FE parts or modification.

Second, and probably one of your better markets, is the vast array of used big block equipment still in circulation. If you have something specific in mind these parts can be a little difficult to track down (begin at your local race track, speed shop, or boat shop and ask Ford racers about spare parts), but often you can find good serviceable components at decent prices—especially parts like intake manifolds which never wear out. The independent Ford high performance parts dealers, such as Total Performance or Ford Power Parts (12200 E Washington Blvd., Unit C., Whittier, CA) are also excellent sources of good used big block parts. If they don't have the part in stock, they can often locate one for you. So let's take a look at the various components that go into a big block Ford wedge stormer, and give you a shopping guide to the myriad of 390-427-428 parts and pieces.

All FE Ford engines are based on a big and rugged cylinder block that underwent only minor changes throughout its long history. The block on the left is the standard version with two-bolt mains, small oil passages (note oil pump hole, upper right pan rail), and standard freeze plugs. Block on right is a side-oiler 427 with cross-bolted mains at #2, 3, & 4, larger oil passages, and screw-in freeze plugs.

BLOCKS

Although FE engines ranged in size from 332 cubic inches to 428 inches over the years, we will discuss primarily the 390-427-428 big blocks, since these are the most popular, the more recent, the most advanced, and they are still commonly available. Other than some problems of valve-head-to-cylinder-bore clearance, all parts and procedures discussed herein apply to any FE engine. All critical dimensions and bolt patterns remained the same throughout the line.

Although all FE blocks appear basically the same externally—big, brawny, and heavy with the characteristic Ford "Y-block" extended bottom skirt, and all have the same bore spacing, deck height, and bearing sizes—there are nevertheless three distinct versions of the big block.

The "standard" FE block, as used on smaller displacement non-High Performance 390 and all 428 engines, is characterized by two-bolt main bearing caps and a comparatively restricted oiling system. In this design the main oil gallery runs down the middle of the block, to the cam bearings, to the filters, to the rockers, and finally to the crank. Oil passages are fairly small with sharp bends at corners. Both the 352 and the 390 blocks can be bored to 428 size (4.13 inches); '68 and '69 428 blocks reputedly were made with more metal between the bores and slightly beefier main webbing. All replacement 428 blocks sold by Ford after '74 were bored-out 391 truck blocks, characterized by vertical ribs on the outside of the block plus a 3/8-inch pipe plug at the lower side of the block for the truck-engine external oil return line (see introduction for info on FE truck engines).

From '61 through '63 a high performance version of the 390 was offered, and this block differed from previous FE castings. It used two-bolt main caps, but beefier bottom end webbing, larger oil galleries, and a pressure relief valve and spring located at the end of the main (center) oil gallery to direct more oiling back to the crankshaft (especially on cold start-ups). Since only mechanical camshafts were used in these engines, they

The FE extended block skirt allows the use of cross-bolted main bearing caps which provide excellent bearing stability and strength in two planes.

A side-oiler block can be easily identified from the outside by three small screw-in plugs just above the main cap cross bolts on the left side. Also note generous size of oil filter passages (arrow).

427 CYLINDER BLOCK COLOR CODING

COLOR	OIL SUPPLY	BORES	GRADED	USED FOR	TYPE
Blue/Green	Side	Standard	1-6-A-B-C	Racing	SOHC
Blue/White	Top	Standard	1-2-3	Street	Wedge
Blue/Red	Top	Standard	1-2-3	Industrial	Wedge
Blue/Yellow	Top	Standard	1-2-3	Marine*	Wedge
Blue	Top	Standard	1-2-3	Street	Wedge
Blue	Side	Scalloped	1-6-A-B-C	Racing	Wedge
Blue/White	Top	Scalloped	1-B	Service**	Wedge

*Equipped with brass threaded plugs
**Replaces Blue/White "Street" engine in service applications.

Side-oiler cam bearings (left) must be used with a camshaft grooved at the second and fourth journals to provide oiling to the rockershafts. The standard FE has a grooved bearing (right, upper). Make sure the camshaft and bearings are compatible and that the bearings are properly aligned with oil passages in the block.

have no lifter gallery oil passages. The High Performance 390 block can be identified by an "HP" cast in the front right side of the block (behind the generator), in the back of the block behind the flywheel, and also inside the lifter gallery. This same block design was also used for the early 406 and the '63-64 427 engines. Late 406 and some early 427 assemblies (8V Low-Risers and most High-Risers used cross-bolted main caps in this block.

The most desirable FE block is the "side-oiler," introduced in 1965 for the 427 SOHC and used on all '65-67 427 engines. Like the previous Hi Perf 390/406/early 427 blocks they had no provision for oiling hydraulic lifters, they all came with the cross-bolted mains, plus they had a completely revised oiling system which put the main gallery on the lower left side of the block to feed the main bearings directly. In 1968 the same side-oiler 427 block was used, but extra oil passages were added to the lifter galleries because hydraulic cams were used in these engines. If a hydraulic-cam block is to be used with a solid-lifter camshaft, these passages should be plugged so that pressure isn't lost (kits are available from Gapp & Roush and Total Performance). It is also imperative that the proper cam bearings and camshafts be used in the side-oiler block, a necessity since the rocker shafts receive oil from the second and fourth cam bearing jour-

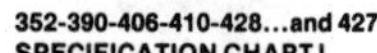

352-390-406-410-428...and 427
SPECIFICATION CHART I

	332	361 Edsel	360 Truck	361 Truck	390 Truck	391 Truck
Bore	4.00	4.05	4.05	4.05	4.05	4.05
Stroke	3.30	3.50	3.50	3.50	3.786	3.786
Bhp	225/4400 (2V-59) 240/4600 (2V-58) 265/4600 (4V-58)	303/4600	215/4400	210/4000	255/4400	235/4000
Torque	325/2200 (2V-59) 340/2400 (2V-58) 360/2800 (4V-58)	400/2800	327/2400	345/2000	376/2600	372/2000
Comp Ratio	8.9:1—59 9.5:1—58	9.6:1—59 10.5:1—58	8.4:1	7.4:1	8.6:1	7.4:1

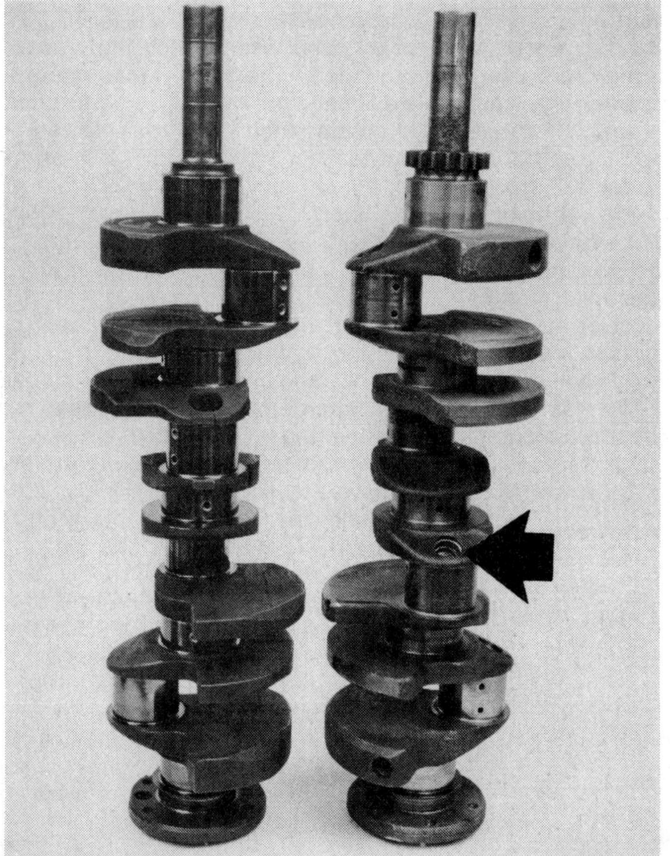

A comparison of a standard cast FE crank (left) and a fully cross-drilled forged steel crank (right) shows four oil holes on each throw of the steel crank plus removable plugs (arrow) for the oil passage drill access holes.

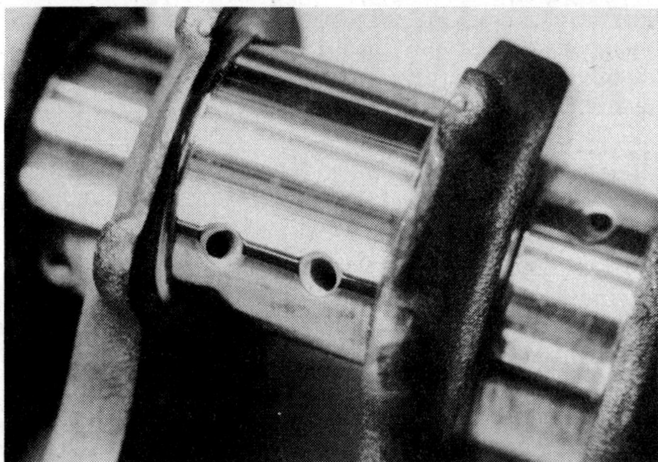

On this crank the rod journals were turned down to 2.374-inch, giving a .125-inch radius at the shoulder for added strength. The oil holes have also been chamfered and the surfaces micro-polished.

nals. These bearings must have two oil holes each (other FE blocks have only one), and the camshaft must be grooved at the second and fourth journals to carry oil from one passage to the other. Since the grooved cams can be used in any big block, most are now of this type—be sure to use only the grooved cam in a side-oiler.

As mentioned, late side-oiler blocks (with lifter oil passages) are still available from the factory, as are 428 blocks. If you are shopping for one of these, however, it is wise to thoroughly check it, if possible, before buying it since these are the last of the production runs. Greg Foreman, an experienced FE builder, recommends that you first check the block for unwanted porosity by installing a pair of torque plates (or heads), filling it with water, pressurizing it, and then looking for leaks. Secondly, check the cylinders for possible overboring, since some of these blocks have been "corrected" at the factory for cylinder flaws. Remember that the maximum overbore for one of these blocks is .030-inch, it would be unwise to buy one already at this limit. On the other hand, this is not a buyer's market. If you need a specific FE block, you may have to take what you can get, and then sleeve it, weld it, or do whatever is necessary to make it ready for use.

CRANKSHAFTS

Since all FE blocks have the same bore spacing and the same main bearing diameters, all crankshafts will interchange (there would be cylinder skirt clearance problems with certain crank and rod combinations in 352 or 332 blocks). A small assortment of cranks has been offered for the 390-427-428, most of which are cast iron. But the FE is not notorious for bottom end breakage even with cast cranks, two-bolt mains, and less than superior oiling.

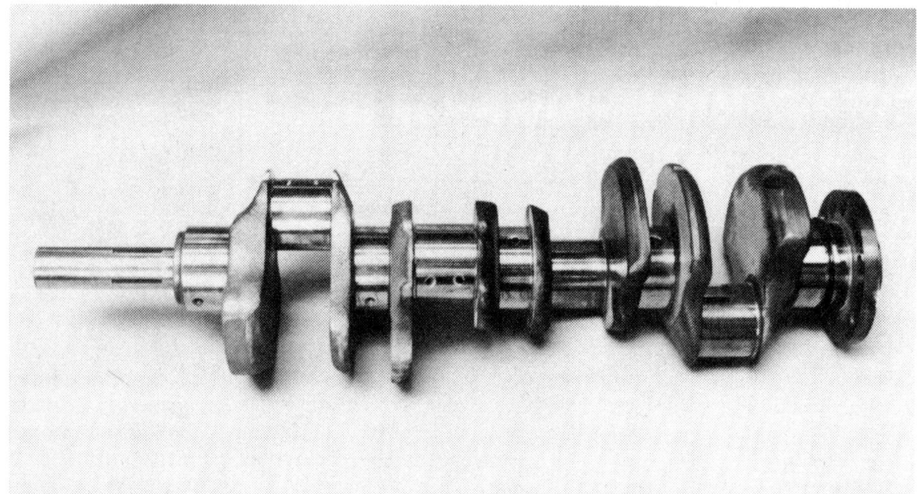

This 427 steel crank by Mondello was made from a 391 truck crank by turning down the front snout. It is not fully cross-drilled.

Until '65 all FE cranks were cast iron, including those for 390, 406, and early 427 versions. They took plenty of abuse in all kinds of racing ventures in the early 60's, including Nascar Grand National and Super Stock drag racing. Ford says they are good to 6000-7000 rpm in drag race engines of up to 600 horsepower (unblown). The only notable cranks in the early FE line were the High Performance 390/406 units (C3AZ-6303-C) which had grooved main bearing journals for increased lubrication, as well as a larger harmonic balancer for high rpm use.

All 428 engines came with cast cranks. They have the longest stroke of any FE (3.98 inches). Four different part numbers are listed for 428 cranks (C9ZZ-6303-B, E, A, or D), the only difference being a balance variation for slightly varying piston weights. The main difference between 428 cranks and other FE units—cast or steel—is that they are externally balanced and must be installed with the correct flywheel and damper. The 428 crank, flywheel and damper must be balanced as a unit.

The '65-67 vintage 427 assemblies came with a steel crankshaft (C5AZ-6303-C), known as the Le Mans crank. These are cross-drilled for better oiling, meaning that each rod journal has four oil outlets and each main journal has two. Press-in cup plugs with snap ring retainers seal the ends of the oil passages (some later cranks use screw-in pipe plugs—a wise modification); remove these plugs to thoroughly clean the crank. When balancing a cross-drilled crank, allowance should be made for 15 grams of oil contained in each throw during operation. The Le Mans crank is excellent for any high performance situation; they are still available new, but cost about $300 each. Also offered for the 427 as a special order item was the steel Nascar crankshaft (C9AZ-6303-D), recommended by Ford for continous 7000-9000 rpm use (just in case that is what you intended). This crank features 0.080-inch wider connecting rod journals than other FE cranks, and must therefore be used with appropriately wider Nascar rods and bearings (C7OE-6200-A).

Another alternative for an inexpensive steel crank to fit a 390 or a 427 would be the readily available 391 truck crank (C7TE-6303-B). It has the same bearing sizes as other FE cranks, but it is not cross-drilled and the front snout must be turned down (to 1.375 inches) to accept a smaller passenger car damper and pulley. It should also be rebalanced for high rpm use. Given the reliability of the cast FE cranks, such a swap is probably of questionable practicality, considering the work and cost involved.

RODS

Despite a multitude of different parts within the family, the blessing of the FE is that just about everything is

CRANKSHAFT I.D. AND APPLICATIONS

Part Number	Application Engine	Year	Journal Diameters Main	Rod	Stroke	Material	Remarks
C4AZ-6303-E	352	60/63	2.749	2.438	3.50	Iron	
C4AZ-6303-L	352	64/66	2.749	2.438	3.50	Iron	
C4TZ-6303-F	361—T	All	2.749	2.438	3.50	Steel	
C3AZ-6303-J	390/390—SPL 390—PI	61/63 61/63	2.749 2.749	2.438 2.438	3.78 3.78	Iron Iron	Before 11/1/62 Before 1/15/62
C4AZ-6303-G	390—SPL 390 390—PI	63 63/65 64/65	2.749 2.749 2.749	2.438 2.438 2.438	3.78 3.78 3.78	Iron Iron Iron	After 11/1/62—Use W/C3AZ-6200-B Rods (Grooved Main Brgs) After 11/1/62
C6AZ-6303-A	390	66/72	2.749	2.438	3.78	Iron	
C3AZ-6303-C	390—SPL 390—PI/406	61/62 62/63	2.749 2.749	 2.438	3.78 3.78	Iron Iron	Hi-Perf and Police orig equip—(Grooved Main Brgs) After 1/15/62
C4AZ-6303-H	427—4-6V	63/65	2.749	2.438	3.78	Iron	
C5AZ-6303-C	427—4-8V	66/67	2.749	2.438	3.78	Steel	
C8AZ-6303-B	427—4V Hyd	68	2.749	2.438	3.78	Iron	
C9AZ-6303-D	427—All	All	2.749	2.438	3.78	Steel	Wide Crank req Nascar C70E-6200-A Rods, brgs, & balance
C4TZ-6303-G	391—T	All	2.749	2.438	3.78	Steel	
C9ZZ-6303-B	410 428—Std/PI/CJ 428—PI 428—CJ	All 66/68 69/70 69	2.749 2.749 2.749 2.749	2.438 2.438 2.438 2.438	3.98 3.98 3.98 3.98	Iron Iron Iron Iron	 Before 12/26/68
C9ZZ-6303-E	428—CJ	69/70	2.749	2.438	3.98	Iron	After 12/26/68
C9ZZ-6303-A	428—SCJ	69	2.749	2.438	3.98	Iron	Before 12/26/68
C9ZZ-6303-D	428—SCJ	69/70	2.749	2.438	3.98	Iron	After 12/26/68

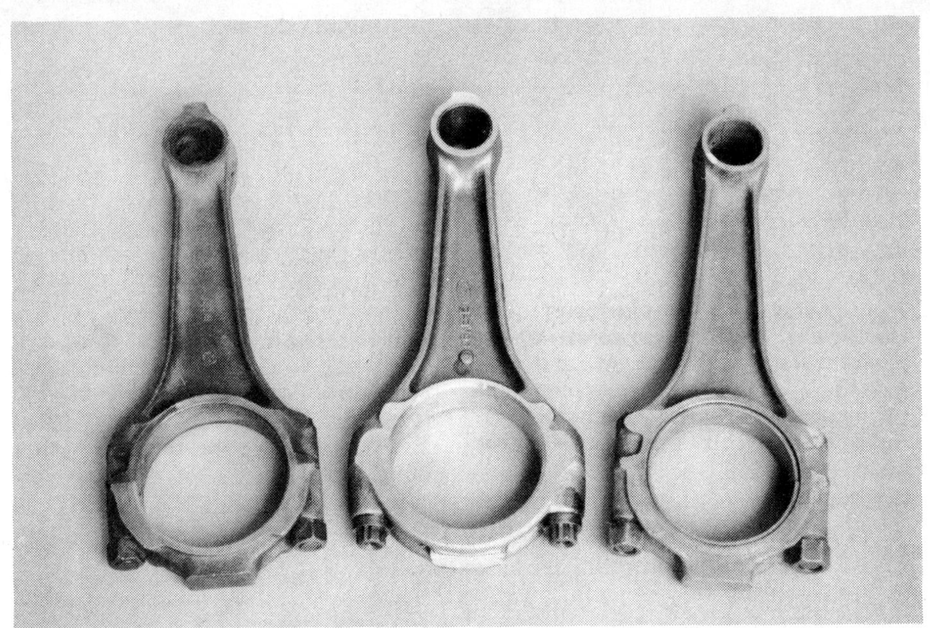

Common FE production connecting rods include, from the left, a standard 390 unit, the 427 Le Mans capscrew rod, and a 427 Low-Riser/428 Cobra Jet rod.

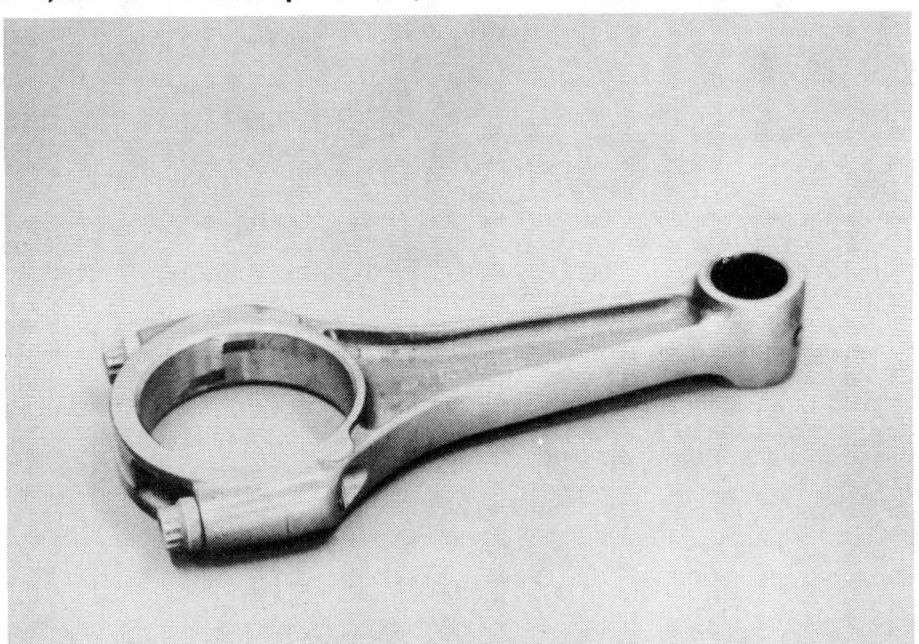

An excellent part and the one widely preferred by FE builders is the 427 Le Mans connecting rod. This one has been polished and shot-peened.

interchangeable. For instance the 390, 427, and 428 all use the same length connecting rod. The 390 High Performance, Police Interceptor, 406, and the '63-64 vintage 427 all used identical rods featuring a 3/8-inch thru bolt (C3AZ-6200-F). Next in line in terms of performance is the thru bolt con rod used in '68 hydraulic-cammed 427 engines and in '66-70 Police Interceptor and CJ 428 engines (C6AZ-6200-C). This rod has a slightly thicker beam and a 13/32-inch bolt. The favorite choice of most high performance big block engine builders, however, is the Le Mans capscrew rod (C5AZ-6200-D), which came in all the '65-67 Medium-Risers and in special order High-Risers, '65-68. This same rod was also intalled in '69-70 vintage 428 Super Cobra Jets, but it went under a different part number (C9ZZ-6200-A) because it used a short-head capscrew to provide block clearance with the longer stroke. The one problem with these rods, which are excellent otherwise, is the stock tri-lobe capscrew which has a necked-down shank. As you probably know, nearly all rod failures derive from bolt failure, and these bolts have been notorious for breaking. In fact, they are one of two weak links in an otherwise almost bulletproof factory engine. More than one well-known engine builder has been heard to say "use them once and throw them away" (that is, install new rod fasteners every time you tear the engine down). Fortunately, these days there are better alternatives. The large shank capscrew from the stock Ford Nascar rod can be substituted instead, or similar bolts from several current manufacturers are now also available (Ford Power Parts; SPS bolts from Gapp and Roush). Be sure to chase the threads in the rod with a regular tap before installing new bolts; the stock tri-lobe bolts are designed for an interference fit.

The toughest connecting rod

CON ROD I.D. AND APPLICATION

Part Number	Application		Weight (Grams)	CTR-to-CTR Distance	Bolt Seat Finish	Bolt Size	
	Engine	Year					
C1AZ-6200-C	352	60/66	727-740	6.540	Spot Faced	3/8	Use w/C4AZ-3 or L ungrooved crank
C1AE-6200-C	390/390—SPL 390—PI	61/63 61/62	716-728	6.488 6.488	Spot Faced Spot Faced	3/8 3/8	Before 11/1/62 uses C4AZ-6303-E or L ungrooved crank Before 1/15/62 uses C4AZ-6303-E or L ungrooved crank
C3AZ-6200-B	390/390—SPL 390	63/65 65	762-774	6.488 6.488	Spot Faced Spot Faced	3/8	From 11/1/62 use w/C4AZ-6303-G grooved crank (w/C3AZ-6303-D crank)w/C3AZ-6303-D crank)
C3AZ-6200-F	390—PI 390/390—SPL 406 427	63/65 61/62 62/63 63/65	762-774	6.488 6.488 6.488 6.488	Spot Faced Spot Faced Spot Faced Spot Faced		After 1/15/62 use w/C4AZ-6303-G grooved crank
C6AZ-6200-C	428—PI, CJ	66/70 68—Hyd	762-774	6.488 6.488	Spot Faced Spot Faced	13/32	
D1TZ-6200-A	390—All 410 428—2V/4V	66/70 66/67 66/68	761-775	6.488 6.488 6.488	Spot Faced Spot Faced Spot Faced	3/8	
C7OE-6200-A	427—All	65/68	936-1036	6.488	Spot Faced	7/16 Cap Screw	Use w/C9AZ-6303-D crank & SPL wide brgs
C9ZZ-6200-A	428—SCJ 427—MR/HR	69/70 65/68	833-845	6.488 6.488	Spot Faced Spot Faced	7/16 Cap Screw	"LeMans" type

made by Ford for the FE is the Nascar rod (C7OE-6200-A), which has the .080-inch thicker big end and, therefore, requires wider bearings and can only be used with the "wide-journal" 427 crank. These rods were designed explicitly for sustained high rpm use (such as Grand National stock car racing), and they are really much heavier than necessary (almost 1000 grams each) for any type of drag racing or street use. For high rev drag racing one of the several brands of aluminum rods would be better.

The Le Mans rods are still available from Ford or through the special dealers, and with premium capscrews they seem to be the favorite of the FE builders. To install them in a 390, you will have to grind the block slightly for clearance at the bottom end. And for extra insurance, they should be Magnafluxed and polished along the beam. Some builders recommend shot peening and some don't: but this step should always follow polishing if it is done.

PISTONS

It is difficult to be objective about piston choices these days. To begin with, there were at least a dozen different varieties offered by the factory, some of which were used in production engines and many others that were offered as special order items. The discussion is further complicated by the fact that factory pistons were offered only in standard bore and .003-inch oversize, and most used FE blocks will be worn beyond these limitations. Second, the majority of

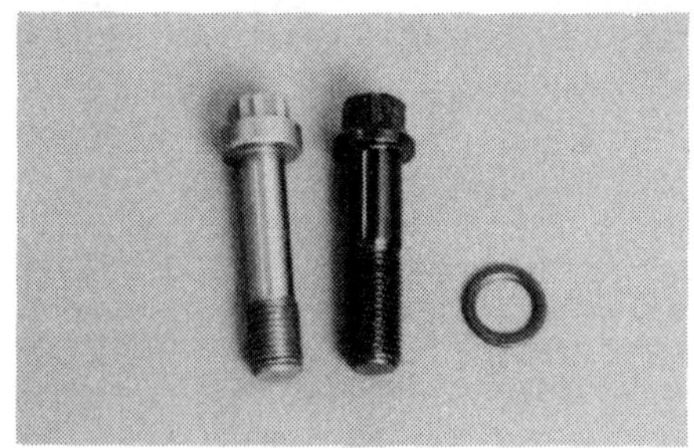

The one drawback to the Le Mans rod is the stock "tri-lobe" capscrew which has a turned down shank and has gained a reputation for breaking. Stronger replacement capscrew, at right, is available from Ford Power Parts.

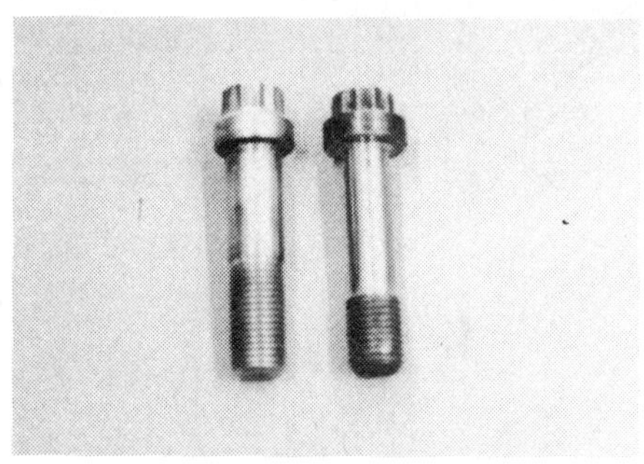

Another good alternative to the Le Mans bolt is the thickshank capscrew made by Ford for the Nascar 427 rod. Very tough SPS bolts for the Le Mans rods are also available from Gapp and Roush.

For non-stock drag racing or drag boat applications you might want to use a light aluminum connecting rod, such as this Ansen design now marketed by Bill Miller. This is actually a Chrysler hemi rod (6.850 inches long) which will fit the turned down Mondello crank shown previously. The forged aluminum pop-up piston was made by Arias (#HW-425-SS), and will obviously require considerable hand shaping of the dome before it's ready to run.

TRW also lists the special-order 427 pop-up (L-2299-f) which gives 12.5:1 compression with Medium-Riser heads, 14:1 with High-Risers, and 12.6:1 with Tunnel-Ports.

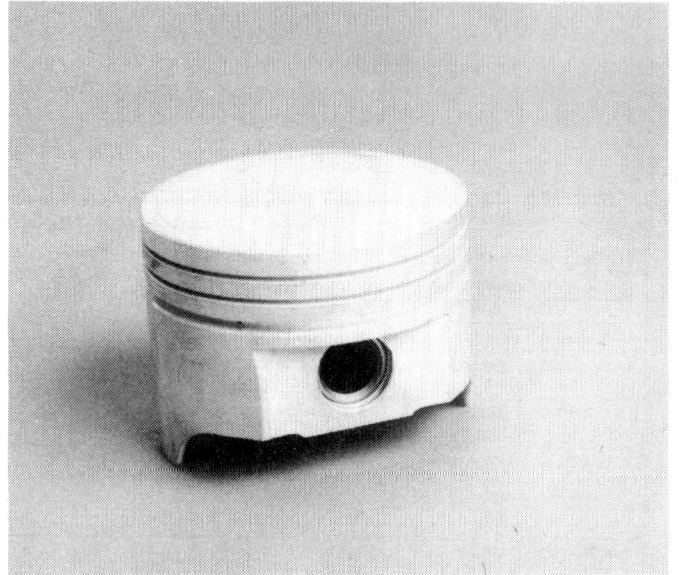

Ford offered all sorts of standard and special-order pistons for FE's, most of which were manufactured by TRW and many of which are still available under the TRW brand. This is the standard Medium-Riser piston (TRW part no. L-2244-F) which gives 12:1 compression.

The selection of pistons for the 390 and 428 engines is rather limited—the standard "dished with eyebrows" and the TRW 12:1 domed CJ 428 (shown on left) are the most common. Some domed pistons can be machined to 11:1 compression, but be certain the dome thickness permits this modification.

the FE specialty pistons produced compression ratios of 11:1 or more (even up to 14:1), and such ratios just are not feasible in any sort of recreational engine these days. And finally, there are several excellent specialty piston manufacturers today, and their expertise is such that they can machine pistons for just about any engine and any specific application. Considering that the 427 and 428 blocks are both very touchy on overboring (0.030-inch maximum), you might even want to have pistons made for an odd overbore size, like 0.015-inch, to increase cylinder wall strength. Your best bet for piston shopping is to visit your local speed shop or engine builder, look over the piston catalogs, and perhaps, contact a manufacturer directly for recommendations (given your specific head/crank/bore combination and the intended use of the engine). Incidentally, most of the factory performance Ford pistons were originally made by TRW (marked both "Ford" and "TRW" inside). TRW still has most of these piston designs available under their own brand, in popular oversizes.

HEADS

Here's where things start to get complicated, or at least confusing. But this is where much of the "building" of a big block takes place. During the late Sixties the Ford factory was into performance, and the majority of their energy (not to mention considerable tooling expense) went into various head designs. (Let's face it, most engines are pretty much alike until you bolt the heads on.) As a result, you can make several different engines out of the same FE short block by swapping cylinder heads.

Any of the FE series heads, including the SOHC, will physically bolt onto any block in the family. (The SOHC heads, just in case you happen to run across a set, require special provision for oil drainback if installed on a non-SOHC block.) The only problem that arises when swapping heads is interference between larger valves on 406, 427, and 428 CJ heads and smaller bores of the other FE blocks. Since all production 332, 352, 390, 410, and standard 428 heads used exactly the same valve sizes (2.04-inch intake, 1.57-inch exhaust), any of these heads will retrofit. But, to install Medium-Riser, High-Riser, or Tunnel-Port heads on 406 or 428 blocks, you will have to chamfer the tops of the cylinder bores for valve clearance. According to Ford information these heads should not be used on 390 blocks because too large a notch would have to be cut in the cylinder (a better choice would be the 428 Cobra Jet heads), and they definitely won't go on a 352 block. (If you are a 352 aficionado, special heads COAZ-6049-H offered in '60-62 had the same port size as Medium-Risers, with standard size valves but considerably smaller chamber volume and, therefore, higher compression; see chart.) All of the standard production FE heads (for 332, 352, 390, 410, 428) go by part number C8AZ-6049, with a varying final letter. These heads, besides the standard valves, have 68-71cc chamber volumes, 1.34-inch by 1.93-inch intake ports, and 1.28-inch by 1.84-inch exhaust ports. Incidentally, the exhaust ports on all the FE heads are the same, except that '66-68 vintage 390 and

CYLINDER HEAD I.D. AND APPLICATION CHART

Part Number	Application		Chamber Volume (cc)		Valve Sizes		Port Sizes				Emission Control	Notes
	Engine	Year			Exhaust	Intake	Intake Width	Intake Height	Exhaust Width	Exhaust Height		
C0AE-6049-H	352/390—SPL	60/62	59.7	62.7	1.57	2.04	1.34	2.34	1.28	1.84	PCV	
C8AZ-6049-M	352/390 390 410	60/65 69/70 All	68.1 68.1 68.1	71.1 71.1 71.1	1.57 1.57 1.57	2.04 2.04 2.04	1.34 1.34 1.34	1.93 1.93 1.93	1.28 1.28 1.28	1.84 1.84 1.84		
C8AZ-6049-A	352 390/428	66 66/68	68.1 68.1	71.1 71.1	1.57 1.57	2.04 2.04	1.34 1.34	1.93 1.93	1.28 1.28	1.84 1.84	T	
C8OZ-6049-B	390	66/68	68.1	71.1	1.57	2.04	1.34	1.93	1.28	1.84	Except T	*Slanted bolt pattern on exhaust studs
C8WX-6049-A	427—4V/Hyd	68	72.8	75.8	1.66	2.09	1.34	1.93	1.28	1.84	T	*Slanted bolt pattern on exhaust studs
C8AZ-6049-K	427—LR 406	63/68 62/63	72.8 72.8	75.8 75.8	1.66 1.66	2.09 2.09	1.34 1.34	1.93 1.93	1.28 1.28	1.84 1.84	 T	
C5AZ-6049-C	427—MR	66/67	88.0	91.0	1.733	2.195	1.34	2.34	1.28	1.84		
C4AE-6049-F	427—HR	All	73.20	76.25	1.733	2.195	1.34	2.72	1.28	1.84	PCV	
C8AX-6049-A	427—TP	All	88.0	91.0	1.733	2.250	2.17	2.34	1.28	1.84	PCV	
C7AZ-6049-A	428—PI	66/67	68.1	71.1	1.57	2.04	1.34	1.93	1.28	1.84	Except T	
C8AZ-6049-N	428—PI 410	67/69 All	68.1 68.1	71.1 71.1	1.57 1.57	2.04 2.04	1.34 1.34	1.93 1.93	1.28 1.28	1.84 1.84	T	
C8OZ-6049-K	428—CJ/SCJ	68/70	72.8	75.8	1.65	2.09	1.34	2.34	1.28	1.84	T	

(T) Thermactor
*Staggered exhaust manifold bolt pattern. All others vertical.

some '68 vintage 427 castings used a staggered exhaust manifold bolt pattern. All the rest are identical, meaning that, with the exceptions noted, headers are interchangeable throughout the FE line.

Other than the special 352 heads just mentioned (which were also used on the '61-62 High Performance 390), the only other early variation in head design (other than slight combustion chamber differences for compression ratio adjustments) was the 406 head, which measured the same as the special 352/390 unit, except that it had larger exhaust valves (1.66-inch). This same head (C8AZ-6049-K) became the 427 Low-Riser, as used from '63 through '68, and later the 428 CJ from '68-70.

HIGH-RISER

With the introduction of the 427 in '63 came rapid changes in head design for the FE. The first special order head, the High-Riser (C4AE-6049-F) is so named because the intake ports, though the same width as other designs, were almost 4/5-inch taller than standard FE ports. The head casting itself is almost one inch taller above the ports; consequently it requires a shorter rockershaft pedestal (C3AZ-6531-A) so that standard length pushrods, rockers, shafts and valves can be used. These pedestals, like the bare head castings, are no longer available from Ford, so if you find a set of used heads be sure the rocker stands are with them. Valve sizes for the High-Riser were increased to 2.195-inch intake and 1.733-inch exhaust, special new lightweight valves were used (see following section), and the combustion chambers were fully machined to 86cc minimum volume. Only Ford High-Riser intake manifolds will fit these heads, and these manifolds raise carburetor height 2-3 inches higher than other FE designs. Interestingly, the intent behind the High-Riser head/manifold combination was not only to increase port area, but also to raise the intake runners for a more direct shot into the cylinder—the same theory that is proving so successful in current port reworking, especially for Pro Stock drag racing. Compared to other FE head designs, however, the High-Risers deliver noticeable gains only in the 5000-7000 rpm range, and most builders question their desirability (especially given the scarcity of heads and necessary complementary pieces) for modern high performance applications. There would be little point in running them on the street.

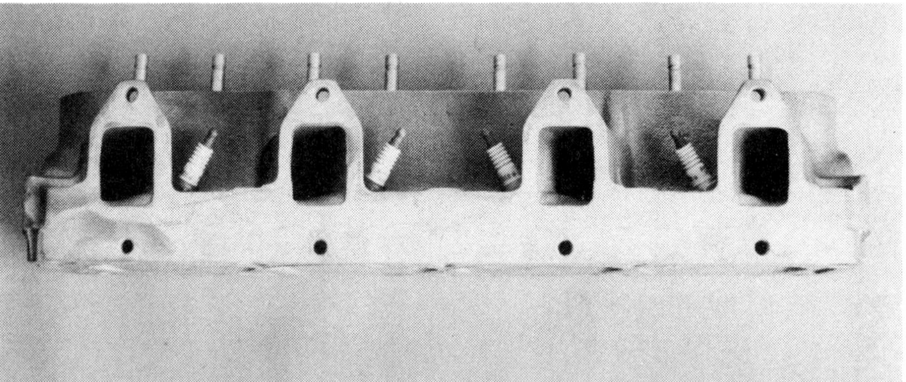

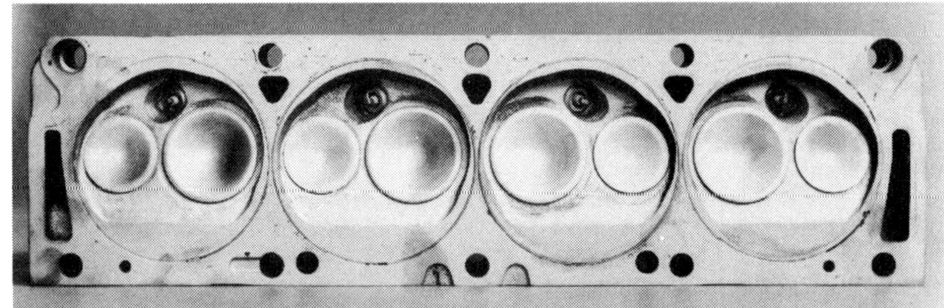

The first special-order head for the 427 engine was called the High-Riser and is characterized by its tall, vertical intake ports. The theory behind these heads and the accompanying high-rise intake manifolds was to raise the port runners for a better angle into the chamber—a sound theory. But the combination did not allow clearance for a stock hood, so the High-Risers were sold only as an over-the-counter option. Valve sizes were 2.195-inch intake and 1.733-inch exhaust, and the exhaust ports remained the same size as all FE heads.

Because of the increased height of the intake port, High-Riser heads require a special short rocker stand (C3AE-6531-A); these are no longer available new. And since High-Risers, Medium-Risers and Tunnel-Port heads had bigger valves spaced slightly further apart than standard heads, they must use .120-inch wider rocker stands. The Medium-Riser/Tunnel-Port part, shown in the center, is C5AZ-6531-A; the Low-riser, 428, and 390 used the thinner stand, C5AE-6531-B.

MEDIUM-RISER

The 427 Medium-Riser head (C5AZ-6049-C) is basically the same as the High-Riser except that the intake port height was reduced back to 2.34 inches. Valve sizes are the same as on the High-Riser and, to accommodate the bigger valves, they are accordingly spaced farther apart than the valves on regular heads. This requires special, wider rockershaft stands (C5AE-6531-A), to space the rockerarms farther apart. Be sure to use the proper stands on these heads (as well as on Tunnel-Ports) to assure proper alignment of rockers and valve stems—mixing them up is a common mistake. The Medium-Riser heads also feature fully machined combustion chambers, but they are quite large (88-91cc), a point to consider if these heads are to be used on another engine, especially one of smaller displacement. Installation on a 390 is not recommended by Ford, since bore chamfering necessary for valve clearance can break through the cylinder walls. Medium-Riser head castings are supposedly still available in limited supplies (plus many were installed on production 427 engines). One of their major advantages is that all FE intake manifolds other than High-Riser or Tunnel-Port inductions can be used with them.

TUNNEL-PORT

Considered by most Ford enthusiasts to be the ultimate wedge head, the Tunnel-Port (C8AX-6049-A) features the same machined combustion chambers as the Medium-Riser; even larger intake valves (2.25 inches); and huge, round intake ports that dump directly into the valve pockets rather than bending around the pushrods as on other FE heads. Tunnel-Ports were special order items to begin with, and are strictly collectors' items today (though some are still being used on specialized race engines). Special Ford Tunnel-Port intake manifolds *must* be used with these heads. They are readily identifiable by the large, round ports with small pushrod tubes through the centers. Like the Medium-Risers, these heads also require special wider rockershaft pedestals (the same part number).

COBRA JET/LOW-RISER

The exact same head used on the 406 and the Low-Riser 427 was reintroduced by Ford as the "new" Cobra Jet head for the 428 in 1968 (also Super Cobra Jet 428); the part number for all three is C8OZ-6049-K. Readily available and comparatively low priced, these heads are an excellent choice for improved street, boat, or bracket racing performance. They are quite similar to Medium-Risers except that the combustion chambers are

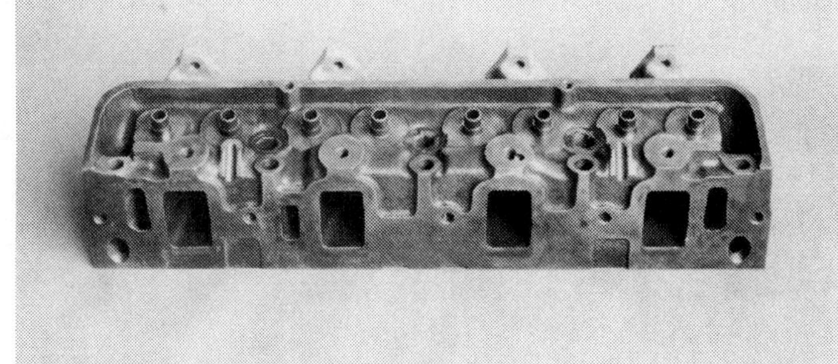

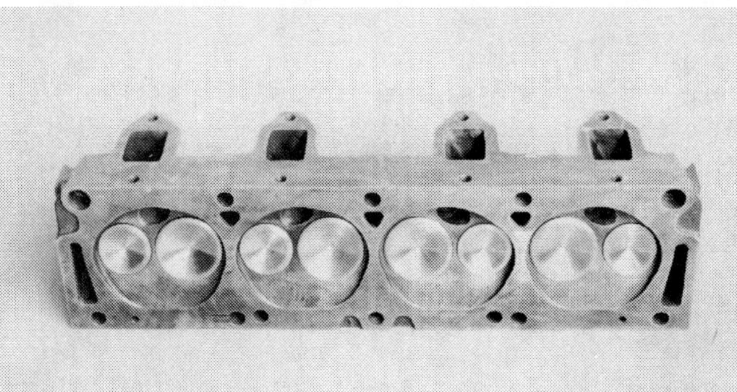

For the production side-oiler 427 Ford made the Medium-Riser head, which was very similar to the High-Riser except that the intake ports were almost an inch shorter. It came with fully-machined combustion chambers and the same lightweight valves as the High-Riser.

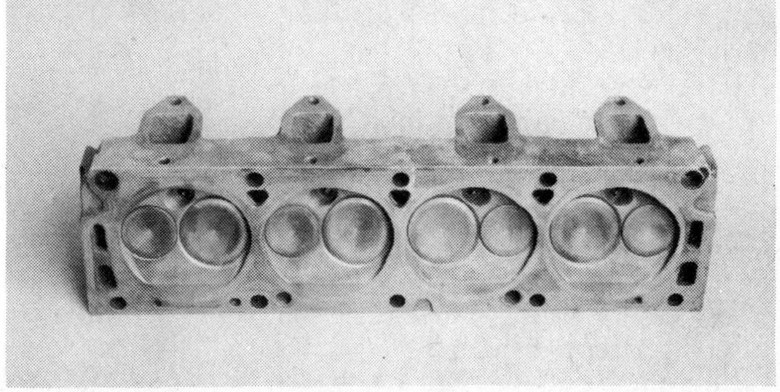

The most radical pushrod FE head was the Tunnel-Port, also only available over-the-counter. There's no mistaking the wide-gaping intake ports which dump right into the extra-large 2.25-inch intake valves. Exhaust ports remain standard size.

rough cast rather than machined (a quick way to tell them apart), and the valves are slightly smaller (2.09-inch intake, 1.66-inch exhaust) and closer together. Consequently, these heads will bolt right on to all FE engines—even the 352, if you notch the cylinders. Adding Cobra Jet heads to a production 390 is a popular and helpful swap, but since the combustion chambers are slightly larger (72-75cc) they will drop compression on a 10.5:1 ratio 390 to 9.6:1. To compensate, you can mill .030-inch from the heads and use steel shim head gaskets (C3AZ-6051-B) which are .020-inch thinner than the sandwich type. This will bring compression up to 10.7:1. Then, to make the intake manifold fit properly, mill .030-inch from each manifold port face and .042-inch from the bottom (block mating) surfaces. If you are running a hydraulic cam with non-adjustable rockerarms, also install .060-inch shorter pushrods (C4TZ-6565-D).

ROCKERARMS

Not much need be said here. All FE engines used one of two types of rockerarms, the adjustable, 1.76:1 ratio unit (B8A-6564-B) for all solid-lifter applications, or the non-adjustable, 1.73:1 ratio arm. Each is cast iron and shaft mounted. They are your only two choices. Obviously the adjustable rockers are preferable in all instances for their slight increase in ratio. They are available either from Ford or from Manley (#43128), or you should easily be able to find some decent used ones on an old junked 352 (all early ones had mechanical cams). The non-adjustable rockers use a double ball-end pushrod. while the adjustables need a pushrod with a cup on the rocker end. Fortunately, pushrod lengths for all the standard FE head combinations remain the same.

If you use the adjustable rockers with hydraulic lifters, here's the "official" method for setting the valves: bring number one piston to TDC on the compression stroke. Bleed the intake and exhaust lifters to the fully compressed position. Then adjust the rockers on number one cylinder for a clearance of 0.110- to 0.210-inch with the valve stem end. Repeat this procedure for each cylinder in succes- of firing order (1-5-4-2-6-3-7-8-), rotating the crank a quarter turn at a time in the direction of normal operation.

VALVES

This is the second touchy area of big block Ford engine building.

Currently a very popular high performance head for the FE because it is still available new, is plentiful used, and will fit all engines without valve clearance problems is the 428 CJ part. The same head was also used on High Performance 390, 406, and Low-Riser 427 engines. Note dual bolt patterns for exhaust manifolds.

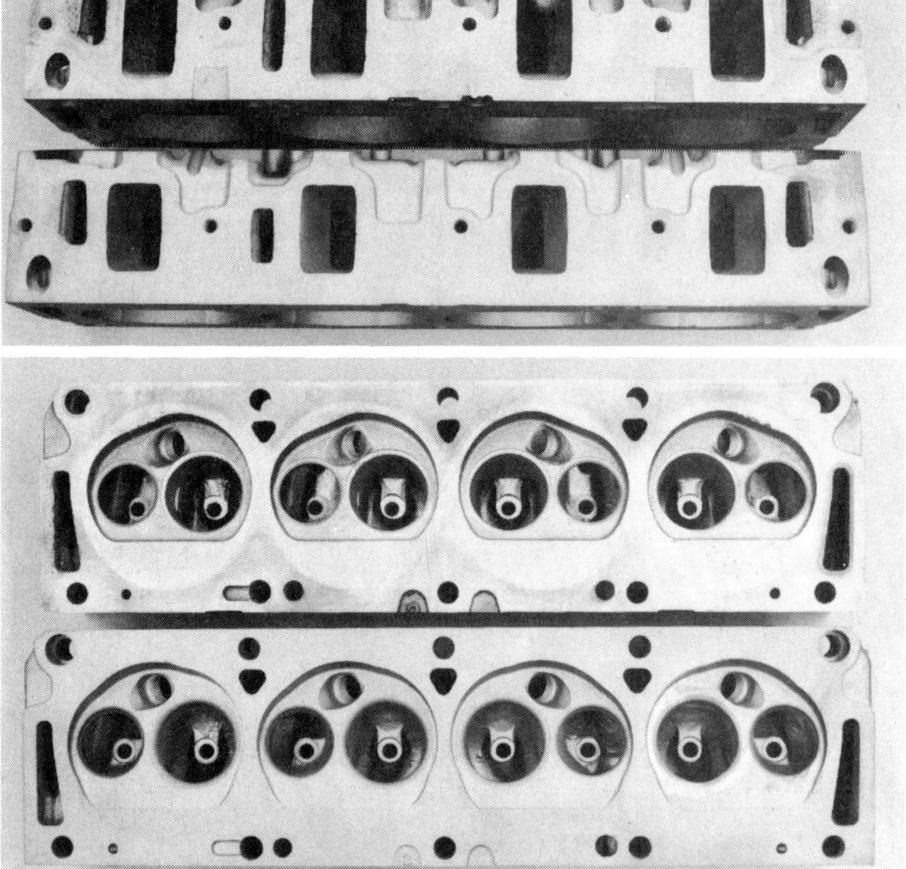

The 428 CJ head and the 427 Medium-Riser appear quite similar until they are placed side by side. The Medium-Riser, shown at the bottom in both photos, has machined combustion chambers (the CJ chambers are rough cast and smaller), larger valves (spaced wider apart), and actually has slightly smaller intake ports than the CJ (but note that they are "filled" on the bottom of the runner—they flow just as well).

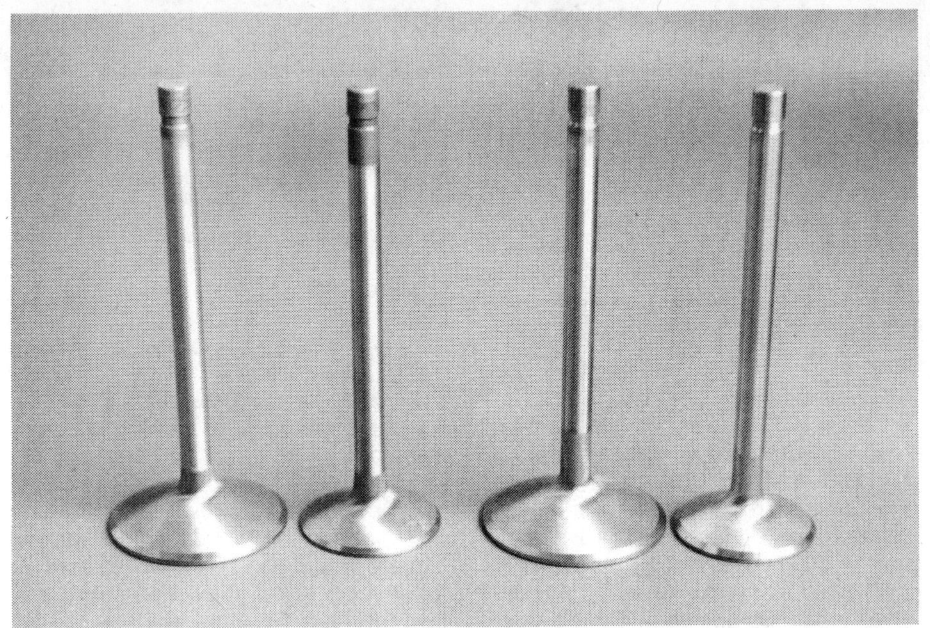

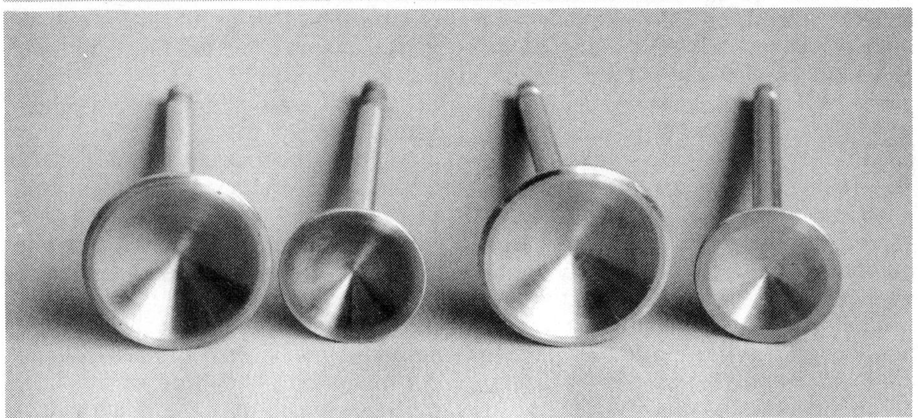

427 High-Risers, Medium-Risers, and Tunnel-Ports came with super-light hollow-stem intake valves and sodium-filled exhausts, but the exhausts have gained a bad reputation for losing their heads under conditions of stress. A set for a Tunnel-Port, shown on left, includes a big 2.25-inch intake and 1.73-inch exhaust. Not nearly as light, but much more rugged, are new Manley stainless steel FE valves for TP, HR, or MR (right).

Racers disagree somewhat, but the general consensus appears to be that the Ford highly-touted and much recommended (by the factory) special lightweight, sodium-filled, hollow-stem exhaust valves have a tendency to lose their heads. Many drag race builders use them anyway—valuing their significant weight savings—but paying very close attention to the cam grinders' specified open and closed valve spring tensions (which will vary according to cam and springs being used), constantly checking valve lash settings, and also religiously tearing the engine down for Magnafluxing or Zyglowing of all critical parts (especially the valves). Even in such cases, most of these builders would admit to one or two engine failures due to broken valves; but they figure the risk is worth a fraction of a second on the drag strip.

For street use or low-maintenance recreational performance stock valves are plenty big in all FE heads, the *smallest* intakes being 2.04 inches in diameter. If you are after a good rugged valve, the best bet are Manley's new one-piece stainless steel intakes (#11804) and exhausts (#11825). They come in Tunnel-Port size (2.25-inch intakes) but can be cut down to fit the other heads. They are somewhat heavy—heavier than stock valves,—and they are slightly expensive at about $100 a set.

The super light Ford valves are very expensive today, in the neighborhood of $15-$25 each. For the record, the sodium-filled exhausts (these are the ones that are known for breaking) came in two sizes: C8AX-6505-A with 1.65-inch head diameter for use in the

INTAKE AND EXHAUST VALVES

			Exhaust Valve					Intake Valve				
Engine	Cylinder Head	Valve Description	Length	Head Dia	Stem Size	Stem Dia	Part Number	Length	Head Dia	Stem Size	Stem Dia	Part Number
390-406	C8OZ-6049-K	Std Weight	5.42	1.65	Std	.3705	C9OZ-6505-N	5.44	2.09	Std	.3715	C9OZ-6507-U
410-428	(428 CJ/SCJ	Solid Stem			.003		C9OZ-6505-R			.003		C9OZ-6507-V
	or											
427 LR	C8WY-6049-A				.015		C9OZ-6505-S			.015		C9OZ-6507-Y
427 Hyd	(428 Hyd)				.030		C9OZ-6505-T			.030		C9OZ-6507-Z
	or											
	C8AZ-6049-K											
	(406-427 LR)											
		Light Weight Chrome Stems Exh Valve-Sodium Filled Int Valve-Hollow	5.42	1.65	Std	.3705	C8AX-6505-A	5.44	2.09	Std	.3715	C8AX-6507-A
427	C5AZ-6049-C	Light Weight	5.45	1.72	Std	.3705	C5AZ-6505-N	5.45	2.19	Std	.3715	C5AZ-6507-N
406-428*	(427 MR)	Chrome Stems			.003		C5AZ-6505-P			.003		C5AZ-6507-P
	or	Exh Valve-Sodium Filled			.015		C5AZ-6505-R			.015		C5AZ-6507-L
	C4AZ-6049-F	Int Valve-Hollow			.030		C5AZ-6505-S			.030		C5AZ-6507-M
	(427 HR)											
427	C8AX-6049-A	Light Weight	5.45	1.72	Std	.3705	C5AZ-6505-N	5.45	2.25	Std	.3715	C8AX-6507-B
	(427 TP)	Chrome Stems			.003		C5AZ-6505-P					
		Exh Valve-Sodium Filled			.015		C5AZ-6505-R					
		Int Valve-Hollow			.030		C5AZ-6505-S					

*427 Medium Riser or High Riser heads can only be installed on 406-428 blocks if the cylinder walls are notched for valve clearance.
NOTE 427 Tunnel-Port heads can not be installed on 406-428 blocks, because excessive notching required for the intake valve may cause a cylinder wall fracture.

406, 427 Low-Riser, and 428 CJ heads; and C5AZ-6505-N with 1.72-inch head diameter for use in the 427 Tunnel-Port, High-Riser, and Medium-Riser. Exceptionally light and not-so-fragile hollow-stem intakes came in three versions: C8AX-6507-A with 2.09-inch diameter head for the 406, 427 Low-Riser, and 428 CJ engines; C5AZ-6507-N with 2.19-inch diameter head for the 427 Medium-Riser and High-Riser; and C8AX-6507-B with 2.25-inch diameter head for the 427 Tunnel-Port. These valves are designed to be installed with a 30° seat for the intakes and 45° for the exhausts, though contemporary three-angle cuts are generally preferred today. Furthermore, keep in mind that street or recreational engine use demands wider valve seats than does drag strip competition. For street use, keep seat width to 0.070-inch for intakes and 0.080-inch for exhausts; for the strip use 0.035-inch for intakes and 0.050-inch for exhausts.

VALVE HEAD DIAMETER-STOCK CYLINDER HEADS FE ENGINES

Engine	Intake	Exhaust
390-410-428-428 Police	2.04	1.57
406-427 LR-427 Hyd-428 CJ/SCJ	2.09	1.65
427 MR-427 HR	2.195	1.72
427 Tunnel	2.25	1.72

CAMSHAFTS

For years literature on big block Fords has recommended factory high performance camshafts. For the record, there were five factory performance cams offered for the FE, three solid grinds and two hydraulics. At least two of them (the C3AZ and C4AE solid grinds) are still available and sell for around $50 each. Here are the factory numbers:

C6OZ-6250-B 428 CJ hydraulic; 270° in., 290°ex., .500 lift, 46°overlap.

C8AX-6250-C 427/428 Special hydraulic; 282°in., 296°ex., .500 lift, 58°overlap.

C3AZ-6250-AA Stock Medium-Riser 427 mech.; 306°duration, .500 lift.

C4AE-6250-B Special-order mechanical; 324°duration, .500 lift.

C8AX-6250-D Special-order mechanical; 330°duration, .600 lift.

Each of these cams was advertised as "definitely streetable" except the C8AX-6250-D solid-lifter design. This cam also requires non-stock Ford springs (any of the stockers will coil bind with .600-inch lift) and either non-stock retainers that will clear the valve guide tops or else .100-inch must be machined from the tops of the guides. When installing any high performance camshaft in any engine, always be sure to carefully check for spring bind and retainer-to-guide clearance.

Technology in cam design has improved dramatically in the last ten years, however, and given the large number of excellent specialty camshaft grinders doing business today, it seems slightly archaic to rely on hard-to-get factory parts. As is the case with current replacement pistons, recommending a specific camshaft grind or type in a book of this sort would be foolish. Dozens of camshaft profiles exist simply because each job requires a specific camshaft design. Iskenderian, Crane, Clay Smith, Cam Dynamics, General Kinetics, Sig Erson, Lunati and several others make good cams for the big block Ford, and there are legions of racers and engine builders devoted to each. (If there is any consensus among FE builders, it appears to lie with Crane. Two of their solid-lifter profiles seem quite popular: the CC 280, a dual-profile cam reading 280°/.579-inch lift intake and 290°/.605-inch lift exhaust; and the CC 290 at a straight 290° and .591-inch lift. Carl Holbrook, on the other hand, one of the leading authorities and racers of 428 Cobra Jets, prefers Lunati cams and has worked with them on several grinds specifically for FE combinations.

Drag racers, unless restricted by class, almost all run flat tappet cams (Holbrook has been known to use a roller), not only for the rev potential but also for the extra oiling available to the bottom end when the lifters do not have to be pressure oiled (see block building section).

If you are building an older 406, 390, or 352, there is one minor modification necessary before a later cam can be installed. Engines built before mid-1963 use a spring and thrust button at the front of the cam to hold it in place. Later engines use a thrust plate which bolts to the front of the block. To install a post-'63 cam in an early engine remove the two small cup plugs on either side of the front cam bearing, thread the holes with a 7/16-NC tap, and use the later thrust plate (C3AZ-6269-A), spacer (C8AZ-6265-A), crank sprocket gear (C4AZ-6306-A), narrower cam sprocket gear (C3AZ-6265-A), timing chain (B8A-

CAMSHAFT I.D. AND APPLICATION

Part Number	Application		Lifter	Lash	Intake Events		Exhaust Events		Duration		Lift		Overlap	Identification	
	Engine	Year			Open	Close	Open	Close	Intake	Exhaust	Lobe	Valve		Mark	Location
C0AZ-6250-A	352/390	60/62	Hyd		26°BTC 31°ATC	64°ABC 5°ABC	67°BBC 10°BBC	23°ATC 36°BTC	270°	270°	.232	.401	49°	AA	Between Dist Gear and First Journal
C2SZ-6250-A	390—6V	61/62	Hyd		28°30 BTC 29°30 ATC	77°30 ABC 14°30 ABC	76°30 BBC 18°30 BBC	29°30 ATC 33°30 BTC	286°	286°	.258	.446	58°	Pink Stripe	Between Dist Gear and First Journal
C3AZ-6250-D	390/406—4V, 6V, 8V 428—PC	63 66	Mech	.025	40°30 BTC 14°30 ATC	85°30 ABC 29°30 ABC	88°30 BBC 33°30 BBC	37°30 ATC 18°30 BTC	306°	306°	.298	.500	78°	∀B	Between Last Lobe and Last Journal
C3AZ-6250-T	390/PC	63/65	Mech	.025	28°30 BTC 28°30 ATC	73°30 ABC 16°30 ABC	76°30 BBC 19°30 BBC	25°30 ATC 31°30 BTC	282°	282°	.264	.440	54°	∀ AA	Between Last Lobe and Last Journal
C3AZ-6250-U	352/390—2V	65/62	Hyd		22°BTC 35°ATC	68°ABC 9°ABC	68°BBC 11°BBC	22°ATC 37°BTC	270°	270°	.232	.401	44°	YA	Between Last Lobe and Last Journal
*C3AZ-6250-AA	427—4V/SPL, 8V/SPL	63/67	Mech	.025	40°30 BTC 14°30 ATC	85°30 ABC 29°30 ABC	88°30 BBC 33°30 BBC	37°30 ATC 18°30 BTC	306°	306°	.298	.500	78°	∀ BA	Between Last Lobe and Last Journal
C3SZ-6250-A	390—6V/SPL	63	Hyd		22°BTC 36°ATC	68°ABC 9°ABC	68°BBC 10°BBC	22°ATC 37°BTC	270°	270°	.232	.401	44°	∀ A	Between Dist Gear and First Journal
*C4A5-6250-B	427	63/67	Mech	.025	56°BTC TDC	88°ABC 28°ABC	88°BBC 31°BBC	56°ATC 3°ATC	324°	324°	.248	.500	112°	∀ M	Between Dist Gear and First Journal
C6AZ-6250-A	390/428 390—GT	67 69	Hyd		16°BTC 32°ATC	68°ABC 8°ABC	55°BBC 7°BBC	21°ATC 31°BTC	256°	256°	.253	.438	37°	∀ U	Between Dist Gear and First Journal
C6OZ-6250-B	390—GT 428—CJ	66/68 68/70	Hyd		18°BTC 30°ATC	72°ABC 22°ABC	82°BBC 28°BBC	28°ATC 24°BTC	270°	290°	.278 .283	.481—I .490—E	46°	Light Blue	Both Sides of No. 3 Journal
C7AZ-6250-A	390—2V	67	Hyd		13°BTC 35°ATC	63°ABC 22°ABC	63°BBC 14°BBC	23°ATC 28°BTC	256°	266°	.247 .249	.427—I .431—E	36°	∀ X	Between Last Lobe and Last Rear Journal
*C8AZ-6250-A	427—Auto	68	Hyd		18°BTC 29°ATC	72°ABC 23°ABC	82°BBC 29°BBC	28°ATC 19°BTC	270°	290°	.278 .283	.481—I .490—E	46°	ABAB	Between Last Lobe and Last Rear Journal
*C8AX-6250-D	427	63/67	Mech	.025	60°BTC 13°BTC	90°ABC 39°ABC	94°BBC 47°BBC	56°ATC 5°ATC	330°	330°	.355	.600	116°	C8AX-D	On End of Last Journal
C8AX-6250-C	427	63/67	Hyd		24°BTC 22°ATC	78°ABC 30°ABC	82°BBC 34°BBC	34°ATC 18°BTC	282°	296°	.289	.500	58°	C8AX-C	On End of Last Journal

*Has grooves in 2nd & 4th journals.
Requires 0.100-inch milled off valve guide bosses and special non-Ford lightweight valve springs, retainers and pushrods because of 0.600-inch valve lift.

Valve lift shown is for stock rockerarm ratios for noted engine and cam type (1.73:1 for HYD or 1.76:1 for MECH)
Two sets of lift figures denotes different lifts for (1) intake and (2) exhaust lobes.

6268-A), and timing gear key (7357-S).

Finally, once again, remember that you must use a camshaft grooved at the second and fourth bearing journals in the side-oiler 427 block.

INTAKE MANIFOLDS

The story on intake manifolds is like the story on cylinder heads—for big block Ford wedges you can rely on Ford factory high performance products (because most of them are generally available and they are good), but you must match the particular type of head with the manifold that fits.

For the Tunnel-Port heads, you have the choice of a dual-plane, dual four-barrel (C7OE-9424-B) designed for street and strip use; a single-plane, dual four barrel (C7OE-9424-A); or a single-plane, single four-barrel (C8AX-9424-B) manifold. The latter two manifolds are strictly swap-meet items these days and are usually expensive.

For the High-Riser, Ford offered an all-purpose, dual-plane, single four-barrel manifold (C4AE-9425-G) designed for use with a 780-cfm Holley carb and a dual-plane, dual four-barrel intake (C4AE-9425-F). These are the only two manifolds made with ports that match the tall High-Riser heads. They are also second-hand shop items.

Fortunately, the rest of the FE intakes will interchange between Low-Riser, Medium-Riser, and CJ heads, and there is a very good supply. The first factory high performance intake for the Ford big block was the three two-barrel setup for the 390 and 406. Quite a few of these were sold, and they are readily found at swap meets—usually quite inexpensively. With progressive linkage and three good Holley two-barrels, this would make a practical, cheap, and impressive-looking recreational performance induction system. The best all-around high performance intake for the FE, however, is the single four-barrel

Tunnel-Port heads weren't exactly designed for street use. The only dual-plane manifold made for them is this 8V model.

The only single four-barrel intake made for the Tunnel-Port was this 360° manifold designed strictly for Nascar competition.

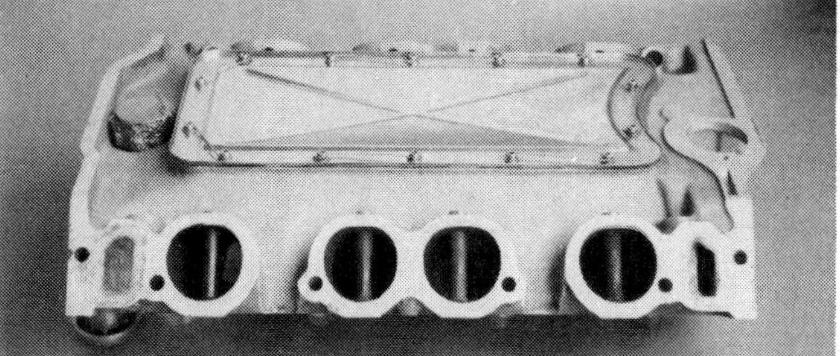

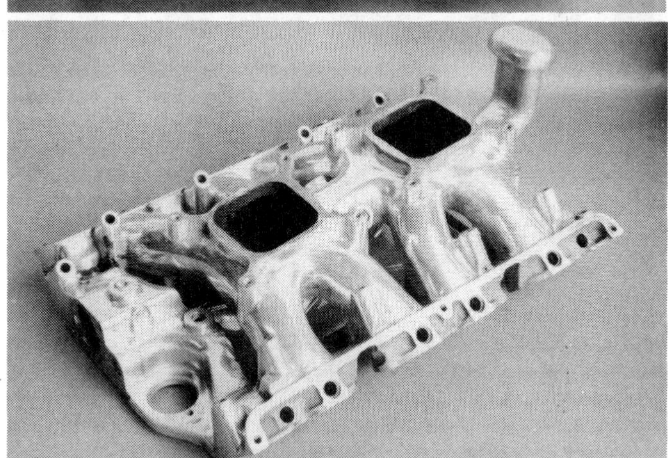

Drag racers' delight, and probably the closest thing to a tunnel ram intake ever made by Detroit, was the single-plane, dual four-barrel, Tunnel-Port casting. Underside clearly shows the small pushrod tubes which "tunnel" through the ports, plus the bolt-on oil baffle plate.

High-Riser nomenclature derived as much from manifold design as from the port shape, as shown by this definitely "hi-rise" single four-barrel intake. It is also easy to see, from the location of the pushrod guide holes at the lower edge of the manifold, the restrictions on intake port shape and size (until they devised the Tunnel-Port).

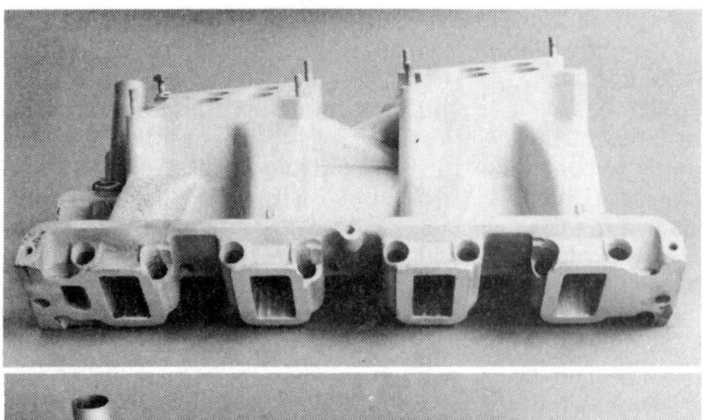

The other intake offered by Ford for the High-Riser was this dual-plane, hi-rise, dual four-barrel. These are the only two manifolds that will fit HR heads.

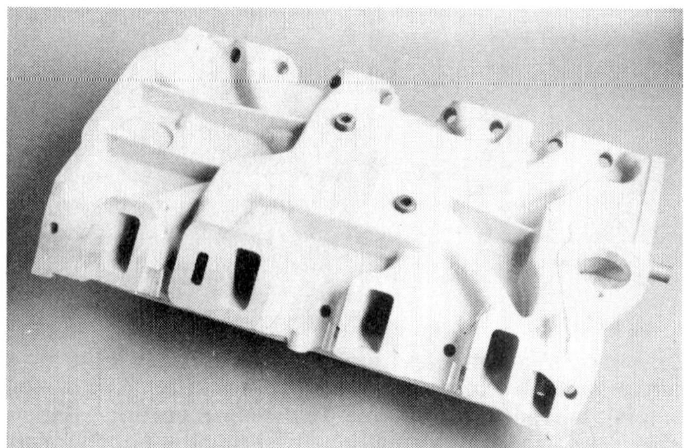

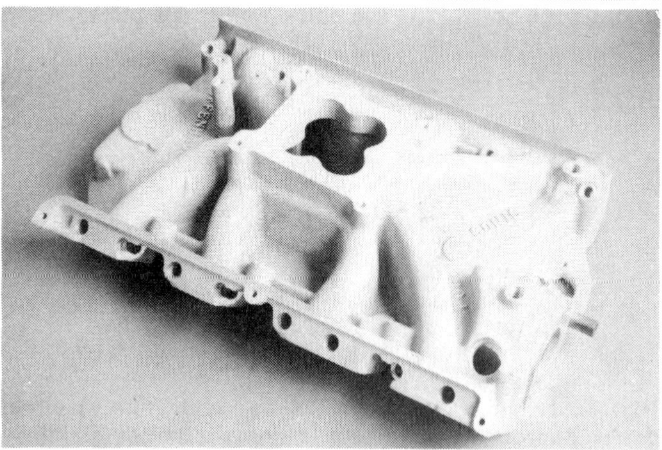

The most highly recommended specialty/performance FE intake for racing purposes is the Offy Port-O-Sonic single-plane.

Three two-barrel induction systems are considered outmoded by most racers these days, but don't overlook the early 390/406 triple Holley intake as a good, practical, and impressive-looking street system. Though they are hunted by collectors and restorers, you can still find them readily at swap meets or second-hand parts stores.

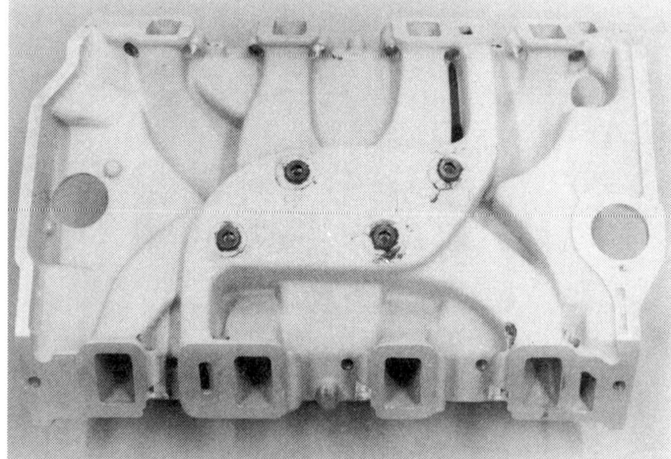

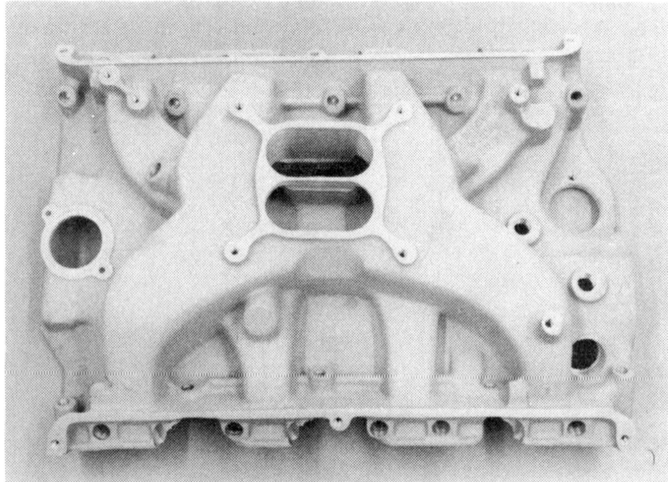

An even more practical and readily available intake, and one very popular with the many Stock or Super Stock drag racers running FE Fords is the "sidewinder" single four-barrel originally offered with a 780 Holley for the Medium-Riser 427. It also works very well with 428 CJ heads.

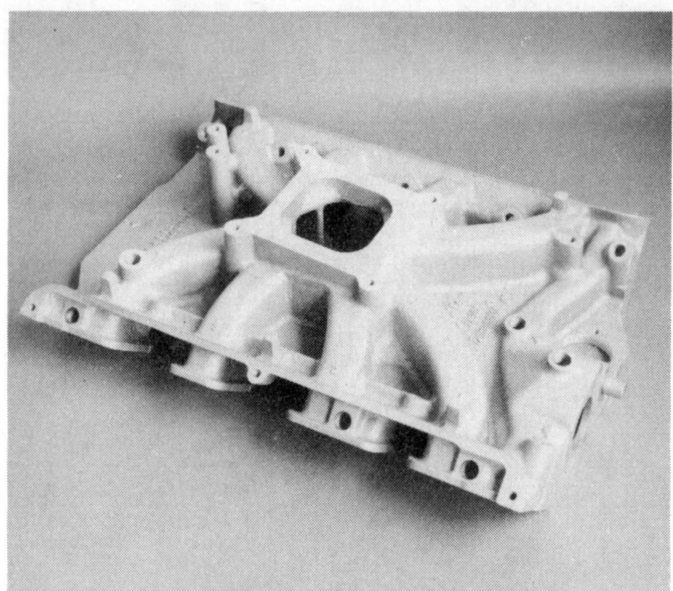

Both Holley and Edelbrock are making street "X-type" intakes for the FE. These are your basic recreational intakes—perfect for street use, low-rpm power, and mileage improvement.

Remember we mentioned that the big valves on Medium-Risers are spaced farther apart, requiring wider rocker stands? This means that the pushrods are also farther apart, allowing a slightly "fatter" intake port between them. Ford engineers took advantage of this situation to adapt the highly successful Tunnel-Port dual-four manifold design to Medium-Riser rectangular ports. The result is known as the "tunnel type" intake for Medium-Risers.

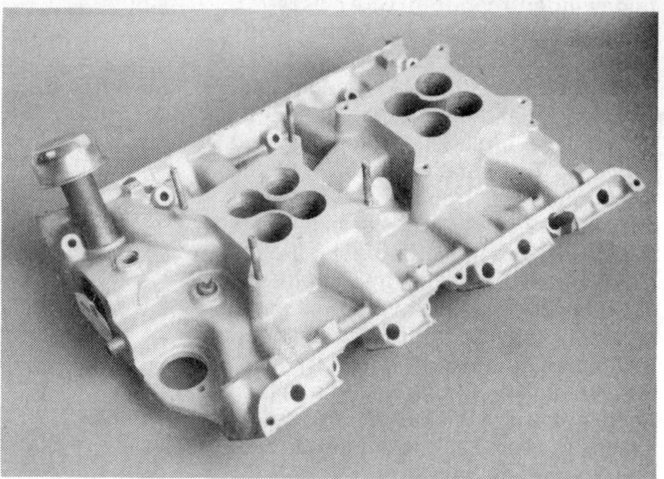

For the '63-64 Low-Riser 427, Ford made this dual-plane, dual four-barrel intake with 1.62-inch carburetor bores (C5AZ-9424-C).

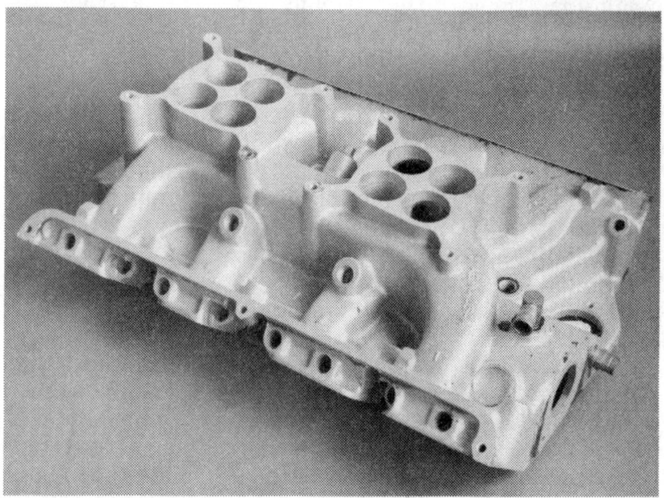

The Medium-Riser got a slightly bigger (1.72-inch bores) dual-plane, dual four-barrel.

Although a direct comparison of the two intake manifolds above shows that Low-Riser ports (left) are higher than Medium-Risers, don't be confused. The names refer to the profiles of the topsides of the manifolds, as can be clearly seen in the prior photos.

"sidewinder" manifold (C6AZ-9424-M), designed for use with a 780-cfm Holley on the Medium-Riser 427. It is immediately recognizable because the carburetor flange is offset to one side to provide equal runners to each cylinder. This intake is still available for about $150 from Ford. The next best factory single four-barrel setup is the special-order 428 Cobra Jet (Police Interceptor) aluminum manifold (C6AZ-9424-H) which is also the same as the 427 standard four-barrel model. Incidentally, the cast iron 428 manifold, which you should be able to pick up for about five bucks at a junkyard, is exactly the same as the aluminum one, just 55 pounds heavier.

While we are on the subject of single four-barrel intakes, both Holley and Edelbrock offer street four-barrel manifolds. These are low-to-mid range, stump-pulling, RV type intakes...the sort of thing you should be using in a street driver, a pleasure boat, a four-wheel drive, or a 360-powered pickup truck. For high-rpm performance, the only specialty intake generally recommended by big block builders is the Offenhauser Port-O-Sonic (#6147). While the other two manifolds are generally good up to 5500 rpm, the Offy builds horsepower above 6000.

For multiple carburetion it is strictly Ford's market. You get your choice of a dual-plane, dual four-barrel (C5AZ-9424-G) or a single-plane, individual-runner, "tunnel-type," dual four-barrel (C8AX-9424-A) manifold. Both of these manifolds were offered as options for the 427 Medium-Riser, the latter being the all-out competition model patterned after the Tunnel-Port intake with large, round, raised, individual runners which neck down to the standard rectangular ports. Both of these manifolds are supposedly still available from Ford or from the Ford specialty parts dealers.

As originally set up, either of the 427 dual four-barrel manifolds used a pair of Holley 625-cfm carburetors (C8OF-9510-AC front, C8OF-9510-AD rear) and the hot tip for both drag racing and circle trackers in the early days was to turn both carbs around so that the primaries were to the front. This would keep the front two cylinders from leaning out. For tuning, Ford recommended starting with number 77 main metering (primary) jets, and number 71 jets in the secondaries. For the single four-barrel manifolds some racers prefer a 735-cfm Holley carb (C9AZ-9510-U; standard on Cobra Jets) over the 780; tuning should start with number 67 main metering jets and number 79 secondaries.

INTAKE MANIFOLD I.D. AND APPLICATION BLUEPRINT SPECIFICATIONS

Part Number	Engine	Year	Type	Material	Bore Diameters		Port Sizes		
					Primary	Secondary	Width	Height	
C1AE-9424-A	352	60/61	2V Dual	Iron	1.60		1.16	2.14	
C3AZ-9424-F	352	62/63	2V Dual	Iron	1.60		1.16	2.14	1/4 inch Temp Sending Unit
C4AZ-9424-A	352/390	63/64	2V Dual	Iron	1.60		1.16	2.14	1/8 inch Temp Sending Unit
C4AZ-9424-B	352/390	63/64	4V Dual	Iron	1.60	1.60	1.16	2.14	1/8 inch Temp Sending (Police)
C6AZ-9424-D	390	65/67	2V Dual	Iron	1.60		1.16	2.75	
C9AZ-9424-E	390	68/70	2V Equal	Iron	1.60		1.16	1.82	
C1AE-9424-B	352/390	60/61	4V Dual	Iron	1.60	1.60	1.16	2.14	
C3AZ-9424-E	390	62/63	4V Dual	Iron	1.60	1.60	1.16	2.14	
C9ZZ-9424-A	352/390	65/69	4V Equal	Iron	1.70	1.60	1.16	1.82	
C3AZ-9424-C	352/390/406	60/63	4V Dual	Alum	1.62	1.72	1.16	2.14	
C3AZ-9424-D	390/406	61/63	6V Single	Alum	1.56 All		1.16	2.14	
C3SZ-9424-A	390 SPL	62/63	6V Dual	Alum	1.56 All		1.16	2.14	
C8AZ-9424-C	390/410/428 Std	67/68	4V Dual	Iron	1.60	1.60	1.16	1.75	
C3AZ-9424-J	427 LR	63/64	4V Dual	Alum	1.72	1.72	1.14	2.20	
C4AE-9425-G	427 HR	All	4V Dual	Alum	1.72	1.72	1.24	2.60	
C6AZ-9424-M	427 MR	68	4V Equal	Alum	(2) 1.78 x 2.50 Oval		1.24	1.94	(Before 11/1/66)
C8AX-9424-B	427 TP	All	4V Single	Alum					Rounded Tunnel-Ports
C5AZ-9424-C	427 LR	63/65	8V Dual	Alum	1.62 All		1.14	2.20	
C8AX-9424-A	427 MR	All	8V Single	Alum	1.72 All		1.24	1.94	
C5AZ-9424-G	427 MR	67	8V Equal	Alum	1.72 All		1.24	1.94	
C4AE-9425-F	427 HR	All	8V Dual	Alum	1.62 All		1.24	2.60	
C70E-9424-A	427 TP	All	8V Single	Alum	(2) 3.75 x 3.75 Square		2.20	2.05	Rounded Tunnel-Ports
C70E-9424-B	427 TP	All	8V Dual	Alum	1.72 All		2.20	2.05	Rounded Tunnel-Ports
C6AZ-9424-H	428 PI	66/69	4V Dual	Alum	(2) 1.78 x 2.50 Oval		1.24	1.94	
C8OZ-9424-B	428 PI 428 CJ/SCJ	66/70 68/69	4V Dual	Iron	1.60	1.70	1.24	1.94	

EXHAUST

Beginning with the early 390, Ford offered all sorts of fancy cast iron exhaust "headers" for the high performance FE. There aren't many of these around today, and most racers, performance builders, and even RV drivers tend to prefer steel tube headers. You won't find a whole lot of listings for big block Fords in current header catalogs (other than for late pickups with a 360 or 391), but fortunately all FE heads will accept the same headers, with the exception of the '66-68 390 and '68 hydraulic cam, four-barrel 427, which have a different bolt pattern. If the engine is installed in a late Mustang, Fairlane, or Torino, you shouldn't have any problem finding a set to fit. For 390-428 engines the header size recommendation is one with 2-inch i.d. primary tubes, 36 inches in length, having a 3½-inch i.d. collector, 12 inches long for manual transmission cars and 16 inches long for automatics. For serious drag racing, Hooker adjustable headers for Mustangs and Fairlanes (#6375) are better for the bigger engines. They use the same diameter primaries and collectors, but can be adjusted down to 30-32 inches primary length. The rule of thumb on header "tuning" is longer length and smaller diameter for low-rpm horsepower and torque gains, shorter length and larger diameter for high-rpm peak power.

IGNITION

Before breakerless, there was one standard high performance ignition setup for big block Fords—the dual-point, centrifugal-advance 427 distributor (COAZ-12127-L). It is still readily available and for an all-purpose, relatively low cost (about $50) unit it is hard to beat. As with valve timing, exact settings depend entirely on particular engine components and intended use (compression ratio, grade of fuel, type of transmission, etc.), but general recommendation calls for a total of 38° lead, with an initial of 12° and a curve that looks something like this:

Distributor rpm	250	500	1000	1500	2000
Distributor Degrees	0°	3°	10½°	12½°	14½°

For street or recreational use, you would probably want the extra mileage benefits of a vacuum-advance distributor. A good choice would be the 428 CJ dual-point, dual-advance unit which has a very fast curve:

Distributor rpm	250	750	1000	2000	3000
Distributor Degrees					
Auto Trans	0°	2½°	4°	8°	13°
Man Trans	0°	1½°	2½°	6°	10°

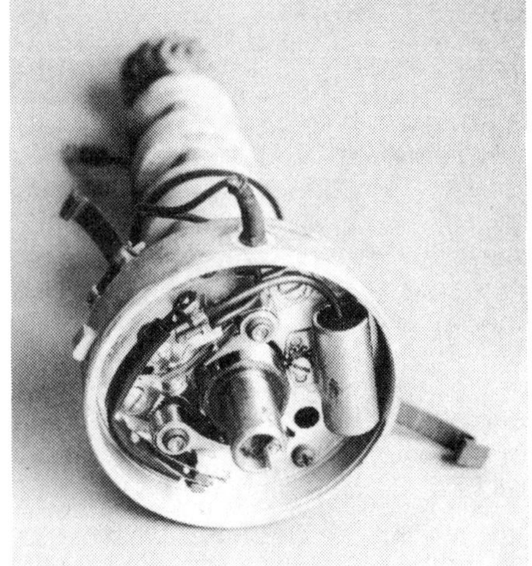

A very good general purpose performance ignition is the still-available and inexpensive 427 dual-point, centrifugal-advance distributor.

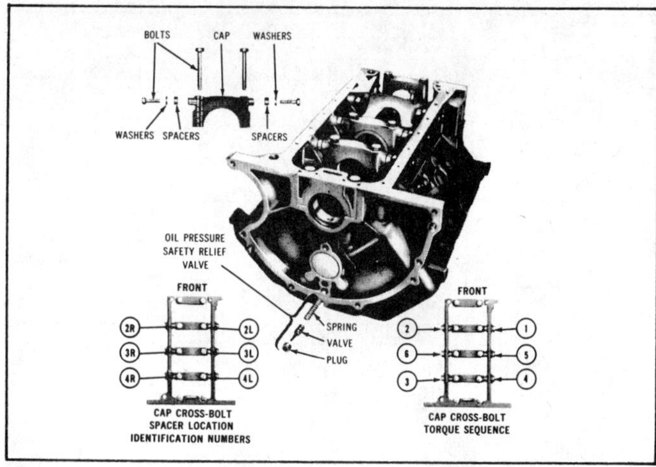

All FE Family engines are of the "Y" block design with the block lower skirt extending below the crank centerline. The '63 vintage 406 cid, '63-64 vintage 427 cid four-barrel, and the '65-67 four-barrel and dual four-barrel engines were fitted with "cross-bolted" main caps to increase bottom end strength. Some 406 blocks were cast with provisions for the cross-bolt caps but the bosses were not drilled.

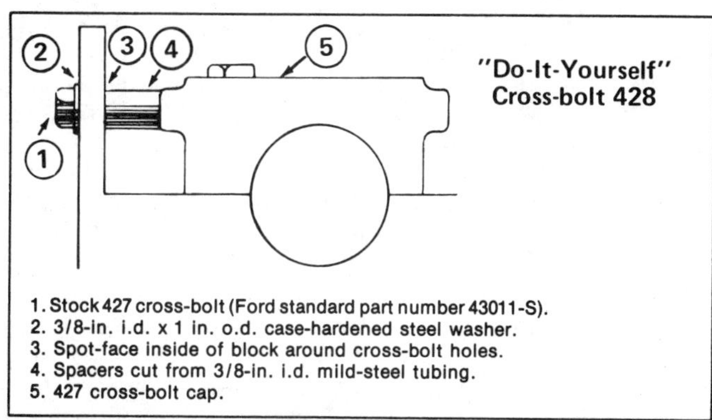

1. Stock 427 cross-bolt (Ford standard part number 43011-S).
2. 3/8-in. i.d. x 1 in. o.d. case-hardened steel washer.
3. Spot-face inside of block around cross-bolt holes.
4. Spacers cut from 3/8-in. i.d. mild-steel tubing.
5. 427 cross-bolt cap.

The FE blocks can all be fitted with cross-bolted main caps on the #2,3 and 4 main journals if "used" or specially-made caps are obtainable. Drill three holes in each block skirt to line up with the three caps. Blocks other than the 427 vintage are wider and require spacers between the cap and the inside of the skirt to absorb torque stresses. Spotface the inside of the skirt to assure the spacers seat squarely. Align-bore the journals to assure correct alignment.

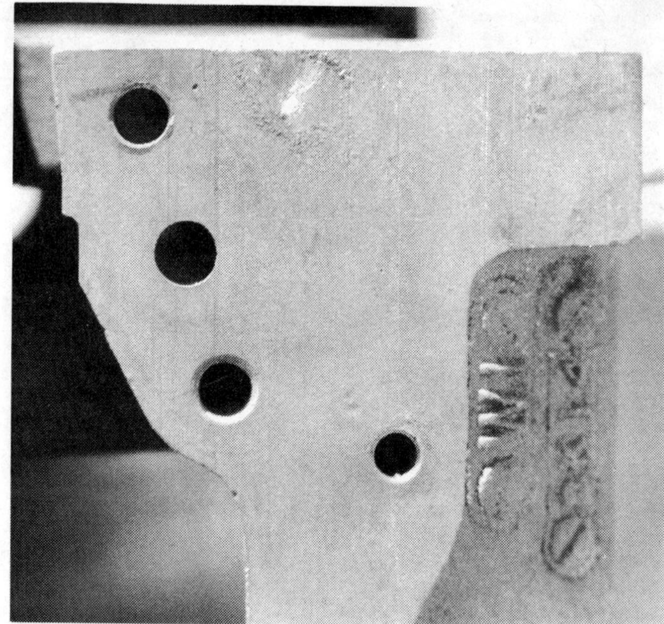

If you are building an FE other than a HP 390 or a 427, that little 3/8-inch oil pump passage is far too small to feed the big block. Drill it out to 1/2-inch and chamfer the opening with a grinder.

The only fault anyone seems to have found with stock Ford distributors is that they have a slight tendency to wear out upper bushings. Check them for runout—a wobbly shaft can wreak havoc with timing. If worn, you may have to select a standard bushing that will fit the case and ream it to fit the shaft. Otherwise, if good points are used and breaker-point spring tension is properly maintained, these distributors should be good to 7000 rpm.

Of course, electronic breakerless ignitions are the hot setup these days, and most manufacturers have complete distributors or kits that will fit the FE. By far the most popular with racers seems to be the Hays "Stinger" which installs in the stock distributor. Runners-up would be the Accel BEI or the Autotronic Controls MSD multi-spark ignition.

BIG BLOCK BUILDING TIPS

As with most Ford engines, the real story behind building the FE correctly lies in getting oil to the right places so the engine can run hard. This is undoubtedly a tough engine, but any big block other than the 427 side-oiler requires some small, but critical, modifications to the oil system. On any nonside-oiler, regardless of intended use, the first thing you must do is enlarge the oil passages from the oil pump to the filter and to the main oil gallery. The passage from the pump to the filter, located in the lower front left corner of the block, is dismally small on all standard 390 and 428 blocks. Drill this passage to ½-inch diameter. Next use a small die grinder to flare the openings at each end of this passage and also at the opening of the passage from the filter to the main gallery. If your engine is equipped with an early oil filter adapter, swap it for the larger side-oiler type adapter with flared openings, which is now the standard replacement part (COAZ-6881-A). A good high-volume, high-pressure oil pump is also mandatory, such as the stock 427 unit (C9ZZ-6600-A) which flows 22 gallons per minute at 70-80 psi, or the readily

The passages leading to the oil filter adapter/mount should also be chamfered to reduce oil turbulence. This passage normally will not have to be enlarged but every effort should be made to gain smooth oil flow throughout the system.

And, if your engine still has the early, small-entry oil filter adapter, rush down to your parts store for the bigger, 427-size adapter (right) which is now the service part.

available TRW (Melling) high-volume pump for the big block. Use a grinder to flare the outlet on the high flow pump to match the larger opening you've made in the block. The higher volume pump will also help reduce spark scatter problems at the distributor by evening the load on the intermediate shaft (which connects the pump to the distributor shaft). You might also consider a beefler 7/16-inch diameter intermediate shaft available from Ford Power Parts.

To ensure that the bigger pump and passages have plenty of oil to feed them, install a larger diameter (5/8-inch) oil pickup tube (COAZ-6622-E) which is available from Ford. Better yet would be the Ford special-order seven-quart, deep-sump oil pan (C8AX-6675-A) which has a baffle and a scraper and was designed to be installed with a deep-sump oil pickup (C5AE-6622-B). These parts are no longer available from Ford, but can be often found in Ford specialty shops. Similar deep-sump pans and pickups are currently offered by some performance companies as well, such as Moroso (#2061). Whether or not you use the extra capacity pan, an excellent low cost addition for free horsepower would be the 428 CJ windage tray (C9ZZ-6687-A), which simply sandwiches between the pan and the block. At less than ten bucks, it's the cheapest horsepower you can buy.

If you are not using a High Performance 390, 406, or pre-'68 vintage 427 block, and you are running a solid-lifter cam, you should plug the oil passages to the lifter galleries and enlarge the passage to the rear main. On blocks equipped for hydraulic-lifter oiling, you will find a pair of plugs in two protrusions in the main oil gallery "hump" in the center of the lifter chamber and toward the back of the block. Remove these two plugs and tap the two offshoot bores below the main gallery to receive small screw-in pipe plugs, then replace the outer plugs or convert them to screw-in type. This way you can remove the

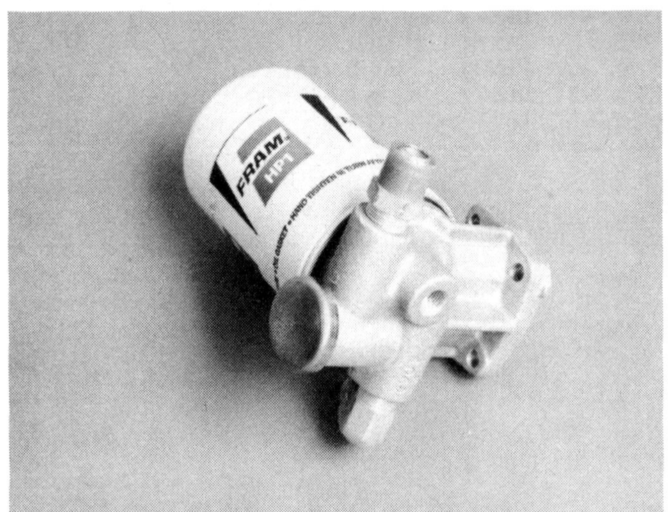

429 Super Cobra Jets came with an external oil cooler system, and the special dual take-off oil filter adapter will fit all Ford engines except the FE. Few builders know this gem exists—but there is a similar inlet-outlet oil filter adapter for FE engines (CNOZ-6881-B) to which you could connect an oil cooler, extra filters, whatever you want.

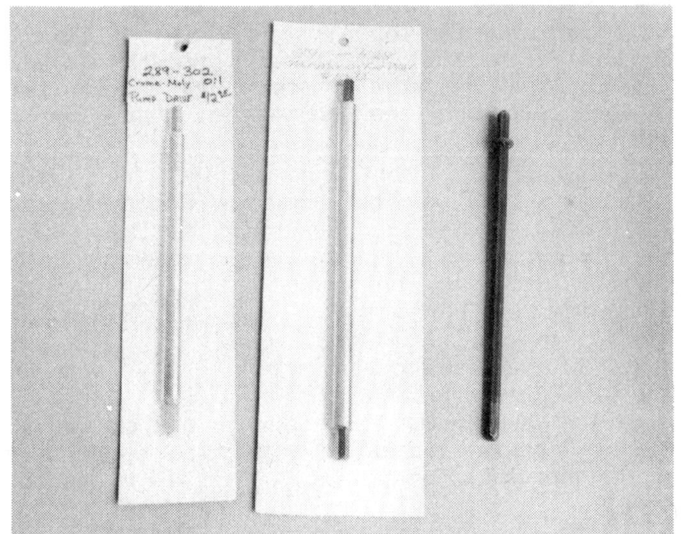

The FE doesn't generally break oil pump driveshafts, but if the thin hexagonal shaft flexes against the load of the oil pump, it can cause spark scatter in the distributor (at the other end). Ford Power Parts offers the plenty strong 7/16-inch chrome-moly steel shaft (center).

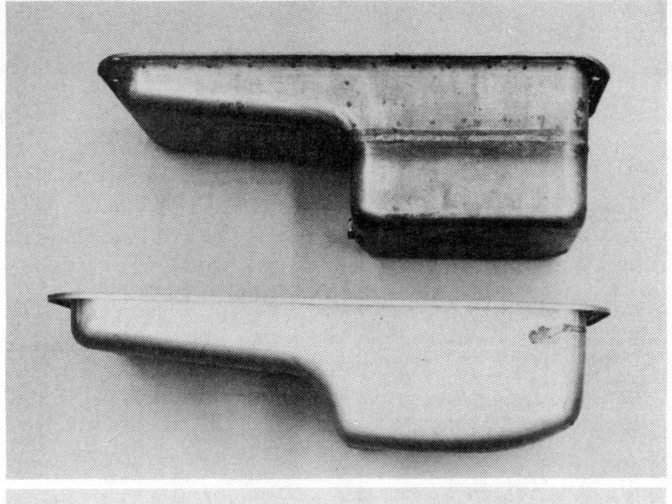

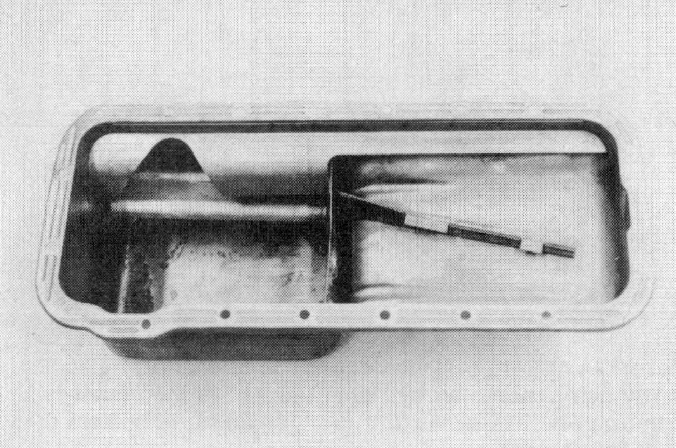

Ford no longer stocks the deep-sump oil pan made for the 427, which comes with a baffle and scraper inside, but they sold plenty originally and you can usually find one if you shop around.

In nonside-oiler FE blocks the main oil gallery is the "hump" down the middle of the block between the lifters. The two off-shoots near the rear of this passage feed the lifter galleries, which can be seen as smaller humps between the lifter bores.

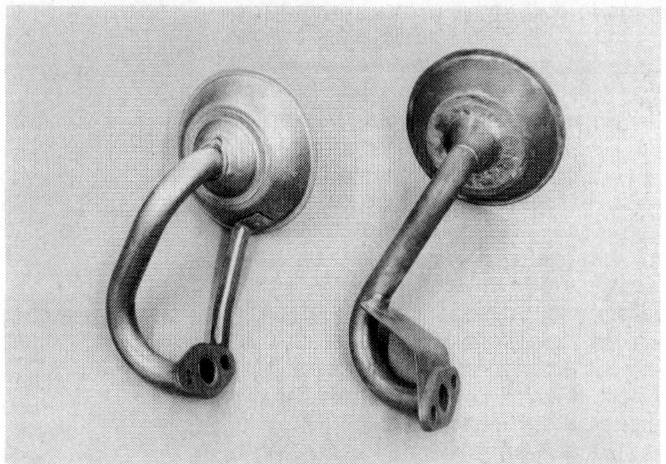

To go with the deep pan you need an extended (modified) oil pump pickup. Notice that the "bell" has been brazed in place—good insurance since they often crack. If you retain the stock pan, get the larger 5/8-inch oil pickup tube which is still available.

A windage tray is the racer's cheapest horsepower. Though not sophisticated in design, the FE tray is very inexpensive (about $7.95) and a snap to install.

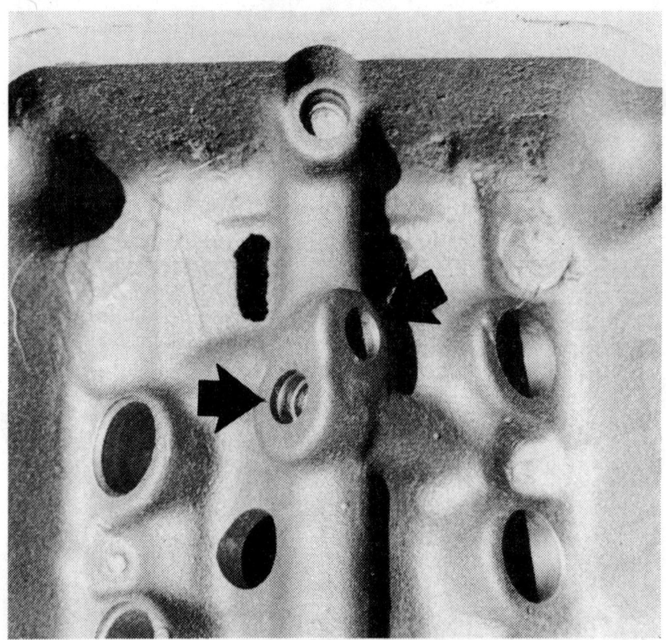

If you are going to use a solid-lifter cam you don't need to waste oil pressure on the lifters. Remove the two press-in plugs indicated, tap each passage below the level of the main gallery, insert screw-in pipe plugs to block the lifter galleries, and reinstall the outer plugs (or convert to screw-in type). If you wish to switch to a juice cam later, just remove the inner plugs.

plugs later if you wish to switch to a hydraulic cam at a later date. Since these blocks also have an obstruction cast into the main gallery just behind these offshoot passages but just before the rear main bearing passage (to route more oil to the lifters), remove the plug at the rear center of the block above the cam boss, drill out the obstruction, and replace the plug. Of course, this modification must be carried out before the block is cleaned or hot-tanked. Never do any drilling, grinding or filing to oil passages (or any other internal components) in an already assembled engine.

Finally, another good oil rerouting tip for any Ford FE is to restrict the amount of lubricant directed to the rockerarms. This end of the engine does not need a large supply of oil anyway, and these engines have been known (like Y-blocks) to suck extra oil down the valve stems. The modification is simple: cut a small piece of steel or aluminum rod stock to about ¾-inch long and approximately of equal diameter to the oil passage in the head. Drill a .090-inch hole up the middle and slip it into the oil passage (a slip fit is all it needs) and bolt the head in place. Your "restrictor" will stay in place and do the job until the heads are removed; then it will slip back out so the passage can be cleaned.

Dress-up parts are the favorites of Ford parts collectors. A new Cobra valve cover for the FE (top) is currently being marketed by Ford; the one in the center is the actual valve cover that came on Shelby Cobras (a collector's item); at bottom is the plain aluminum 428 CJ cover.

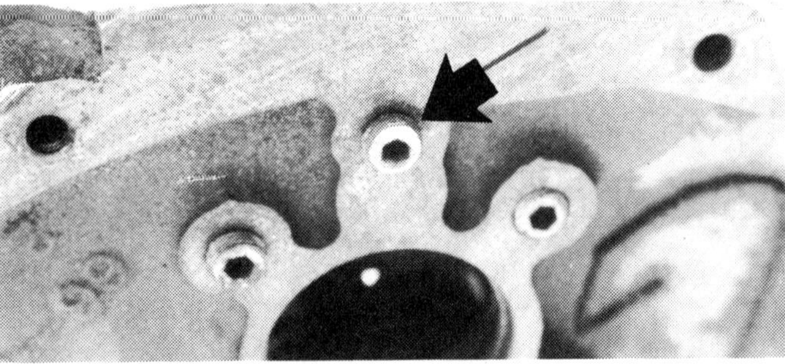

To help force oil to the lifters, non-HP 390 and 428 blocks have a restriction cast into the main oil gallery between the off-shoots and the rear main passage. To keep the rear main well supplied with oil, remove the pipe plug indicated at the back of the block and drill out the restriction.

Another source of oil pressure bleed-off in the FE is the rockershafts. A small passage under one rockerstand on each head carries oil to the shaft; you can insert a short length of solid rod in this opening, with a .090-inch hole drilled through it, to restrict oil flow.

FE BIG BLOCK

BLUEPRINT SPECIFICATIONS	STOCK	DRAG
Main Bearing Clearance	.0025-.0030	.0030-.0035
Rod Bearing Clearance	.0025-.0030	.0030-.0035
Rod Side Clearance	.014-.025	.025-.030
Piston-to-Bore Clearance	.007 (cast .0023-.0031 (forged)	.007-.009 (forged)
Piston Ring End Gap	.012-.015	.012-.015
Piston Pin Clearance	.0007-.0009	.0007-.0009
Crankshaft End Play	.004-.008	.004-.008
Piston-to Deck Height	.015-.025	.008-.012
Piston-to-Valve Clearance	.070—I (auto) .100—E .100—I (stick) .100—E	.120—I .120—E
Valve Seat Width	.070—I .080—E	.035—I .050—E
BOLT TORQUE SPECIFICATIONS		
	352/390 410/428	406/427
Cylinder Head	Step 1 70 Step 2 80 Step 3 80-90	90 100 100-110
Intake Manifold	32-35	25-28 (406) 32-35 (427)
Main Bearing Caps	95-105	95-105
Cross Bolts, Mains		42
Connecting Rod Caps	40-45 53-58 (428)	53-58
Rockerarm Shafts	40-45	40-45
Distributor Holddown	5-8	5-8
Exhaust Manifold	12-18	12-18

From the bottom the cammer looks just like any side-oiler 427, including the fully cross-drilled steel crank and cross-bolted mains.

The only difference between an SOHC block and a wedge side-oiler is an extra hole (arrow) in each bank to carry oil from the head back to the pan.

THE SINGLE OVERHEAD CAM 427

The ultimate FE was the Single Overhead Cam (SOHC) 427 introduced to the public market by Ford in the '66 model year. It was described by the factory as, "a high-rpm competition engine developed by the Ford Motor Company for retail sale through Ford automobile dealers. This engine is a direct result of experimental work done on the regular production 427 OHV engine that is available in Ford passenger cars. The addition of overhead camshafts and hemispherical combustion chambers to this basic engine provides a powerful competition engine capable of producing over 600 horsepower on gasoline." It is difficult to estimate how many com-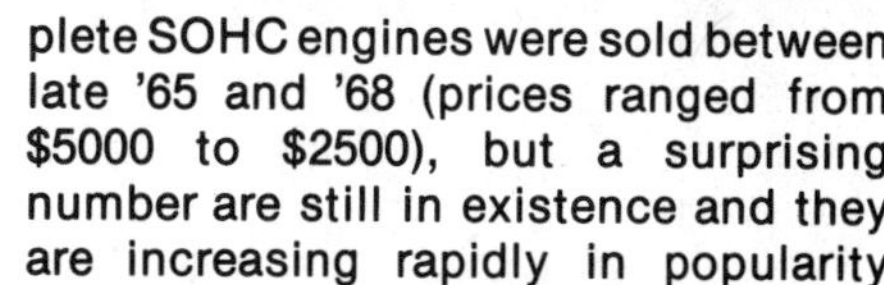plete SOHC engines were sold between late '65 and '68 (prices ranged from $5000 to $2500), but a surprising number are still in existence and they are increasing rapidly in popularity among collectors of Muscle-era Ford products.

The SOHC is based upon a short block assembly almost identical to the wedge side-oiler 427. The major difference is a pair of bosses cast into the rear of each cylinder bank and drilled to allow oil to run back to the pan from each head. A short stub shaft is inserted in the front of the block to drive a distributor in the standard location. Regular side-oiler cam bearings are installed in number one and two journals and the other three cam journals are plugged with steel rings to prevent oil loss, the number four ring being grooved on the backside to transmit oil to the right cylinder head. A wedge FE block (preferably a side-oiler 427) can be converted to accept SOHC heads if an external oil return line is fabricated to carry lubricant from each head back to the oil pan, and if the numbers three, four and five cam journals are sealed. If original SOHC cam journal rings are not available (they would be hard to locate), you can use regular cam bearings if you install them so that the oil holes do not line up with orifices in the journals. You must also cut a groove in the backside (the outside circumference) of the number four bearing. This groove must intersect both oil passages at that journal.

The SOHC used the same forged steel, cross-drilled crank (C5AE-6303-D) as the high performance 427, along with the Le Mans capscrew rods. As noted in the prior section, the stock tri-lobe LeMans capscrew should be changed for a tougher SPS-type capscrew. The stock SOHC pistons were forged aluminum of a fully hemispherical design rated at 11½:1 compression. A special Ford/TRW piston (C6AE-6110-AE) was also offered, rated at 12½:1. However, either of these pistons will be difficult to locate these days. If you must replace pistons in a cammer, you will probably have to have them made by one of the reputable specialty piston manufacturers such as Arias, Venolia, Forgedtrue, etc.

Naturally the SOHC used cross-bolted main bearing caps, plus a high output oil pump (C4AE-6600-E) rated at 20½gpm at 70psi, and the 7½ quart, deep-sump FE oil pan and pickup. According to Bud Gilbert, the SOHC expert at Louie Unser's engine shop

The Single Overhead Cam heads completely changed the character of the FE engine.

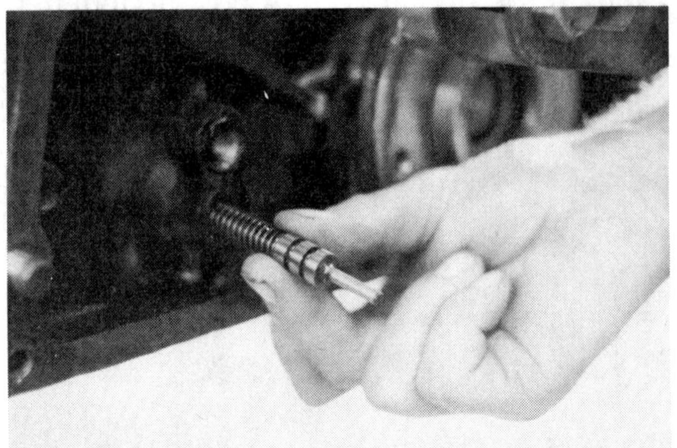

A good recommendation for cammers, as well as for all side-oilers, is to shim the stock oil-pressure relief spring (located at the left rear of the block) about 3/16-inch for more oil pressure.

Since stock pistons are very hard to locate, you will probably have to have a set made to specification by one of the specialty performance piston manufacturers. These were made by Venolia. The rod is by Carrillo, in standard 427 size and length.

(Santa Ana, CA), the cammer's weak point is the bottom end. "These engines like lots of oil pressure," says Bud, and he recommends at least 80psi hot with 50 weight oil in the engine. To keep the pressure up, he installs a 3/16-inch shim behind the oil pressure-relief spring located at the rear of the main oil gallery (at the back of the block). For the SOHC in particular, Bud strongly recommends a red line of 6500 rpm. For FE engines in general he warns, "Once the oil pressure gets below 60 pounds shut it off or the bearings will be gone." When these engines were being built for blown fuel drag racing by the likes of Ed Pink and Mickey Thompson, considerable reworking of the oil system (drilling the main passages larger and restricting secondary passages to the top end) was a standard practice. But, considering that these engines fall into the "collectible" category today and are used primarily for recreational rather than hard core racing purposes, we would suggest discretionary driving rather than major reworking of the block.

Although the short block is the familiar FE, the heads transform the SOHC into the completely unique engine that it is. Cast of aluminum from a single mold and then machined for right or left side fit, they each carry a single camshaft in the center flanked by identical roller-tipped rockers riding on hollow ground shafts. The combustion chambers are fully machined and are of a true hemispherical design. The huge intake and exhaust valves are similar to the wedge 427, except even larger in diameter; both are hollow stem, with the exhausts sodium-filled. Intake ports are circular, while the exhausts are D-shaped. The camshafts ride on small split-shell bearings secured by caps which also

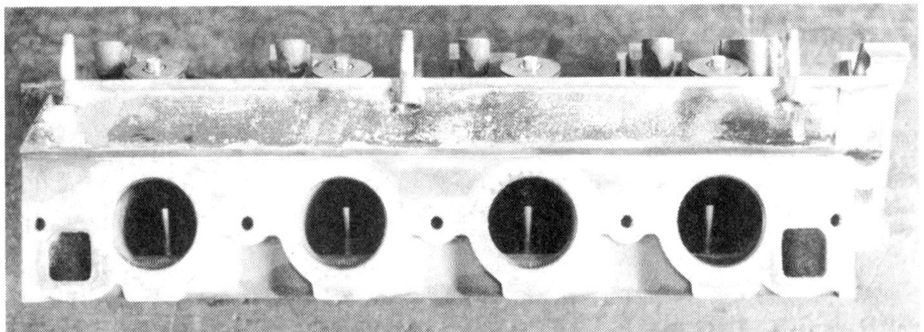

Although the Boss 429 is often referred to as the "Hemi," the SOHC 427 is the only production engine made by Ford that had a true hemispherical combustion chamber. Hollow-stem intake valves and sodium-filled exhausts are similar to the Tunnel-Port. Round intake and "D"-shaped exhaust ports are unique to this head—manifolds from other engines will not fit.

hold the rockershafts in place. Save the cam bearings if you can and keep them in sequence. Finding a replacement set will be very difficult. The retaining caps are numbered and must be replaced in the proper position. Early SOHC engines used non-adjustable rockerarms and valve adjustment was set with select-fit lash caps on the tops of the valve stems. Later engines used an adjustable "foot" on the valve end of the rockerarm. Since these adjustment feet would sometimes break off under competition situations, the simpler lash-cap arrangement was preferred for high performance or racing. If the engine is to be used primarily for recreation, the adjustable rockers will make maintenance easier. Actually, you probably won't have much choice in the matter—spare SOHC parts are almost nonexistent. If you find a complete engine, be sure that all the parts you get are good or be prepared for a long search for replacement parts.

Among the distinctions of the SOHC is one that is somewhat dubious. It has, at close to six feet, the world's longest timing chain. As a matter of fact, it has two timing chains. The first, called the main drive, is similar to a standard roller timing chain driving what would be the normal cam sprocket at one-half the speed of the crank sprocket. This "cam" sprocket is attached to the short shaft which drives the distributor and it is timed to the crank gear by aligning a pair of dots (as on most engines). The main drive also has a second sprocket which drives the long chain to operate the two camshafts. To install the secondary drive chain, with the camshafts in the heads and the idler pulleys in place, match the red painted link to the dot on the secondary drive pulley, the white link to the timing dot on the left-hand cam gear, and the blue link to the dot on the right cam gear.

That's the easy part. The difficult trick is getting the cams dialed in just right so that the engine will run the way it should even when the chain is stretching and throwing everything out of wack. Let's begin with the factory method. First, you must construct a special dial indicator extension or other means of checking piston top dead center (TDC) with the head on the engine. Bud Gilbert made his own TDC indicator by removing the porcelain from a spark plug, welding a tube to the spark plug bottom, and inserting a necked-down rod inside the tube so that the lip would protrude about ½-inch from the spark plug base. Then he attached a dial indicator to the top of the tube so the rod contacted the TDC indicator foot. This device can then be screwed into the spark plug hole in the head to measure the highest point of piston travel. Then, per Ford instructions, install the indicator in number two cylinder (second cylinder from the front on the right side), bring this cylinder to top dead center, install a degree wheel on the crank and set it to zero at this point. Turn the crankshaft clockwise as viewed from the front until the pointer reads 22° BTDC (always turn the crank clockwise for the rest of the timing operation so that chain slack will not produce false readings). At this reading the right cam should just begin to open the intake valve on the number two

The chain-driven camshaft rides in the center of each head; roller rockers mount on shafts on either side. For some reason the left cam has five bearing journals while the right cam has six. Dual valve springs are held in place by machined hardened-steel seats and retainers.

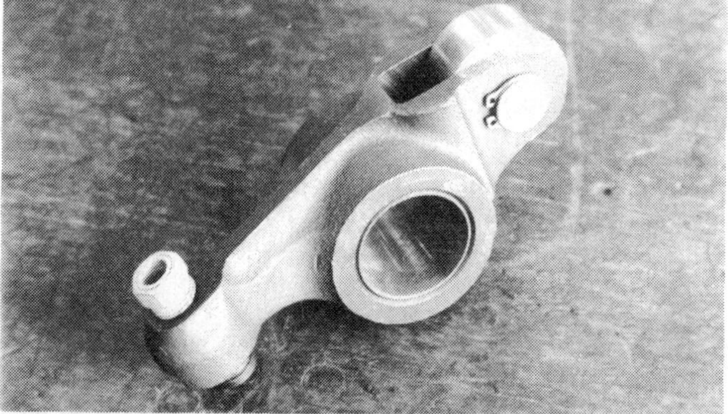

The rockerarms are common to all positions. This is a late adjustable type which uses a ball and socket at the end of the adjusting screw; they have been known to break under extreme conditions. Earlier rockers used valve stem lash caps for adjustment.

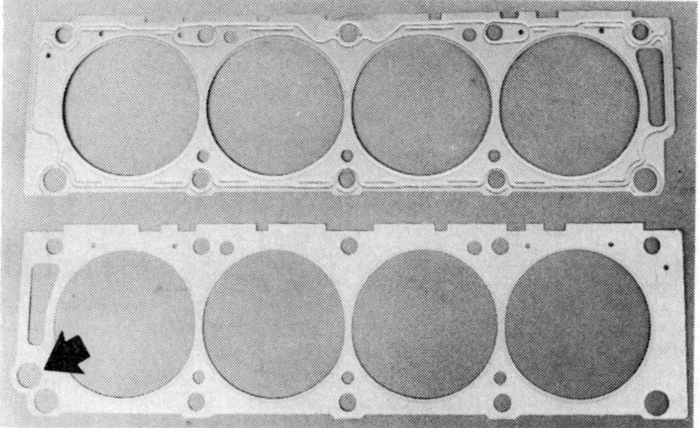

Since SOHC head gaskets are no longer available, you will probably have to modify wedge 427 gaskets to fit by cutting an extra hole for the oil drain back passage. If the gasket does not fit completely around the oil hole, use silicone sealer or cut a small piece of gasket to fit.

Installing cammer heads takes some muscle and dexterity. Tilt the block as shown and install bolts immediately to prevent this irreplaceable part from slipping off.

There are only ten bolts to hold the giant head in place, so bring the torque up very evenly (in at least four increments) to the specified 110 ft-lbs. The rockershafts cannot be installed until after the head is torqued down.

cylinder. If not, remove the bolts and roll pin attaching the sprocket to the cam, manually turn the cam until it is in the correct position, and then reinstall the roll pin in the hole that most closely lines up. Continue to rotate the crank until the degree wheel reads 50° BBDC; at this point the exhaust valve on number two cylinder should just begin opening. If not, split the difference between the two. Repeat the procedure on the other side of the engine.

Naturally, the above procedure assumes your engine has stock camshafts and that they haven't been reground at some time in the past. Incidentally, one of the few companies to offer alternative cam grinds for the SOHC was Crane, who supposedly can still supply cams for these engines, along with necessary specs for dialing them in properly.

The above procedure also assumes that you will want the cams to run "straight up," but this is not the habit of most builders familiar with the SOHC. Theories vary, but the general thinking is to advance the right camshaft, in relation to the left cam, to compensate for chain stretch between

You will probably have to make new gaskets to seal the front cover on a cammer, since these are also obsolete. Use a piece of gasket stock and "trace" a perfect outline of the mating surface by tapping around the edges with a ball peen hammer. Then cut out the gasket with scissors and punch out the bolt holes.

In place of the regular camshaft the SOHC uses this accessory drive sprocket shaft which rides in the first two cam journals and drives the distributor. Note that the second bearing journal is grooved to feed oil to the left head. The other cam journals are sealed in the SOHC by steel bushings, the one at #4 being grooved on the backside to transfer oil to the right head.

The trick to making a cammer run is in the way the camshafts are degreed. See text for varying theories. Note extended dial indicator screwed into #1 cylinder to determine piston TDC with heads in place. While adjusting cams, always turn the engine the same direction (clockwise) to keep constant tension on the chains.

This particular cammer, built in Louie Unser's shop, is used in a boat. Other than a marine oil pan, a magneto, and a pair of odd-looking Kendig carburetors it is externally stock. It looks impressive and performs in like fashion.

the two at high speed. For a racing SOHC, Ed Pink used to recommend advancing the right cam 8° and running the left cam straight up. For typical applications where the engine won't be run over 6500 rpm, Bud Gilbert prefers to advance the right cam 4° with the left cam straight up. For peak power in the 7000-7500 rpm range, he recommends advancing the right cam 4° and retarding the left cam 4°, which gives about 4° retard on both cams at this speed. With other builders the figures vary, but at least you know in what direction to experiment.

Also of significant effect on ultimate cam timing in cammers is the tension maintained on the chain. It is held in track by two idler pulleys, one of which is a tensioner, plus two nylon rubbing pads. You obviously want to keep the long chain from oscillating since this would effect valve timing. Tighten the nylon rubbing bars to take up as much slack as possible in the chain. Then, once the front cover is in place, tighten the tensioner sprocket adjusting bolt to a maximum of 25 ft-lbs. Over-tightening the chain will place undue stress on the front cam bearings causing them to wear out, so this is a touchy business. The Ford manual says to tighten the chain tensioner until a bolt placed in the center of the cam sprocket is deflected .005-inch (measured with a dial gauge), but they don't say at what distance from the face of the sprocket this measurement should be taken, which would make quite a difference.

When it comes to timing the ignition on a cammer, Bud Gilbert has found that, "They don't like a lot of timing—not over 30° total on gas or alcohol." For carbureted engines he recommends 18° advance in the distributor, for injected engines (such as in drag boats) he puts in 24°. The SOHC originally came with a dual-point distributor fired by a transistorized module. Any distributor that will fit an FE will work in the SOHC, provided it will fit behind the recess in the front cover plate. Spark plugs for the cammer fit inside metal tubes which seal the plugs from the rocker chambers. Do not use a gasket (sealing ring) on the spark plug itself. Insert the plug in the tube, fit a rubber O-ring around the lip at the bottom of the tube, slip the tube through the hole in the valve cover until the plug seats in the hole in the head, then torque the plug down to specification.

About the only other peculiarity in the assembly and operation of one of these engines is to make sure the large front cover seals properly so there will be no leaks of either oil or water. A couple of places that require special attention are the bolt just to the left of the accessory drive sprocket, which enters the water jacket (apply a little sealer under the head), and the point at which the head, the steel front plate, and the cast front cover meet along the valve cover sealing surface. Be sure that these three parts align properly, then spread an extra dab of silicone over this joint to prevent an oil leak.

If you have one of these engines, consider yourself lucky. Build it properly and run it judiciously for it is truly one of the marvels of American automotive engineering, the likes of which we will never see again.

BLUEPRINT SPECIFICATIONS	
Main Bearing Clearance	.002-.003
Accessory Driveshaft and Camshaft Bearing Clearance	.001-.003
Crankshaft End Play	.004-.008
Piston-to-Bore Clearance	.006-.007
Top-of-Block-to-Top (dome) of-Stock-Piston	+.6785-.7015
Rod Bearing Clearance	.002-.003
Rod Side Clearance	.014-.024
Camshaft End Play	.001-.007
Valve Lash Setting	.015-.018—I .022-.025—E
BOLT TORQUE SPECIFICATIONS	
Main Bearing Cap	95-105
Cross Bolt (main bearing)	38-42
Cylinder Head	100-110
Connecting Rod	58-62
Cam and Rocker Shaft Cap	35—(3/8-16) 20—(5/16-18)
Cam Sprocket-to-Cam	40-45—(7/16-14) 10-12—(5/16-18)
Intake Manifold	32-35
Spark Plug	15-25
Flywheel-to-Crank	75-85
Crank Damper-to-Crank	70-90

HOW TO BUILD AN "FE" BIG BLOCK

Not only are the engine building photo sections in each chapter of this book designed to illustrate the construction of the particular family of Ford engine being discussed, but also to demonstrate the different approaches to building any performance engine. Some are for street, some for racing; some are economical, others can be exceedingly expensive. Since the FE Ford engines are still very popular in NHRA stock class drag racing, here we show a big block being assembled by successful class racer Greg Foreman, recent holder of both NHRA A/S and B/S class records with his '66 427 Fairlane. The building procedure demonstrates most of the meticulous steps necessary to make a stock FE perform. However, the particular engine shown will be installed in a street-driven car, and therefore has also been given the benefit of a very popular and simple FE swap. Using a side-oiler 427 block, plus the longer-stroke 428 crankshaft, it yields a potent 454 cubic inches. Greg's shop is called Specialty Automotive Engineering, in Anaheim, CA.

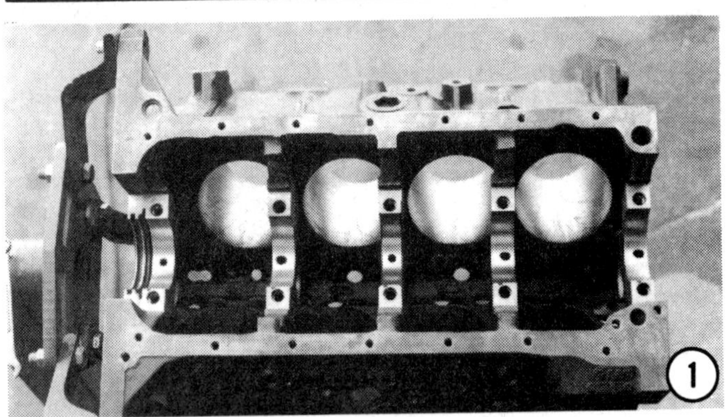

The block is a side-oiler 427, bored and honed to .030-inch over. It is thoroughly washed with strong soap and water just prior to assembly, then it is blown dry with compressed air.

The cast 428 crankshaft might not be quite as strong as the steel 427, but for a street motor it will do fine—plus the easy extra cubic inches are worth the swap. Originally externally balanced (unlike other FE cranks), it has been internally balanced by Engine Dynamics of Garden Grove, CA, then given usual performance prepping: Tufftriding, micro-polishing, chamfering of oil holes.

A professional double checks everything before bolting the assembly together. Torque main caps in place without bearings and mike diameter of opening; then measure thickness of each bearing shell, and subtract from opening size. Mike main journal on crank. The difference should be .003-inch clearance on a street performance engine such as this. Follow same procedure on rod throws and rod bearings, but measure big end opening of rods with bearings in place. Greg found clearances to be too tight (under .002-inch), and had to have crank journals resized. Often it is possible (and cheaper) to select a different set of bearings in order to obtain the desired running clearance.

When initially tightening main caps, preset thrust bearing by pushing crank forward and center main cap slightly backwards as you tighten bolts on center main cap (thrust bearing is on #3 main). Since the pressure plate pushes the crank forward when the engine is operating, this presetting procedure minimizes crank end-play. Torque main cap bolts to 105 ft-lbs.

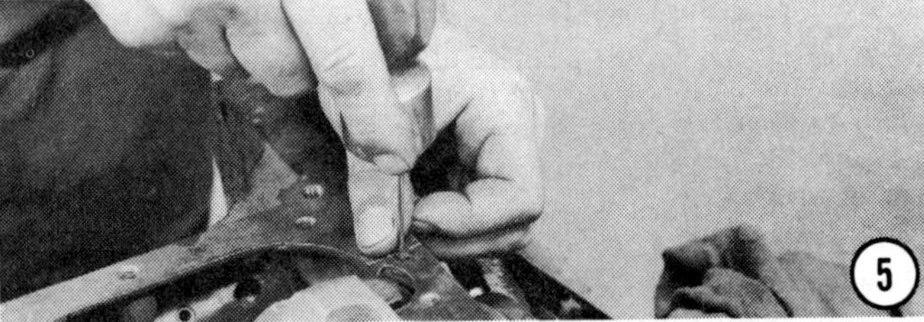

Greg prefers neoprene rear main seal instead of the original rope-type seal. After rear main cap is torqued in place, insert two neoprene strip gaskets into grooves on either side, then gently press metal rods behind them to push them tightly against the side of the block.

After all mains are torqued, check crankshaft end play with a dial indicator. Press crank forward and back with screwdriver between cap and throw, as shown. It should move .003-inch, according to Greg.

Next, tap steel spacers into place between main caps and block with a drift punch. Spacers are numbered (2R, 2L, 3R, etc.) and machined precisely to fit the indicated position. Be sure to replace them in the correct order. When aligned, install cross bolts and torque to 42 ft-lbs following sequence: 2L, 2R, 4R, 4L, 3L, 3R.

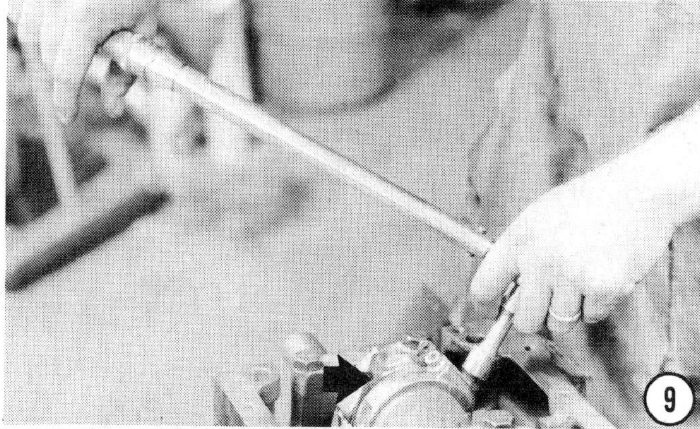

Greg uses TRW Clevite 77 bearings for mains and rods. With rod bearings and caps in place, torque cap screws to 55 ft-lbs. Note feeler gauge between rods (arrow) to take up side clearance (.025-inch); this keeps rod from twisting,and crushing edges of bearings, while bolt is being tightened.

After the cam is lubed and installed in the block (slide the cam in carefully to prevent damage to the cam bearings), Greg adds a double-roller chain and sprocket assembly. He highly recommends that Loctite or some similar thread-locking fluid be used on the single bolt used to hold the cam-drive sprocket in place (it also holds the fuel pump eccentric in place). Torque the bolt to 45 ft-lbs.

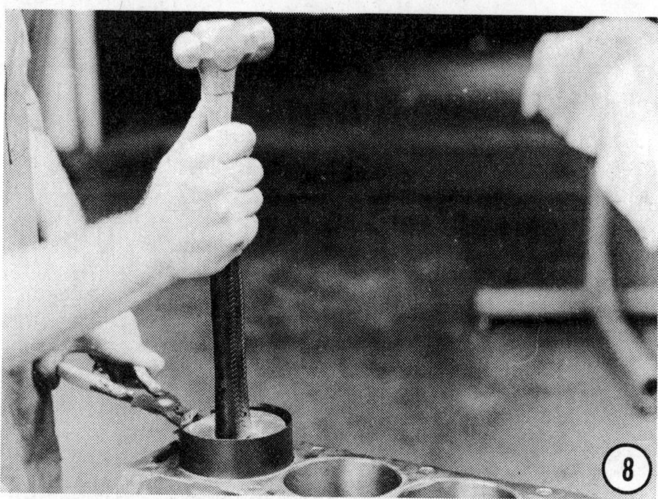

After double checking cylinder bore and piston skirt diameter to verify desired clearance of .004- to .006-inch, install rings, lube piston skirts, and slip the pistons into place.

Completed short block is now ready for camshaft installation. Notice that oil plugs (arrow), removed for block cleaning, are still missing. Be sure to install new ones before adding intake manifold.

To degree cam, randomly attach degree wheel to crank and fashion a simple wire pointer to attach on the block. Index the degree wheel with Top Dead Center (TDC) on #1 piston: attach bar across #1 cylinder; turn crank until piston dome stops against bar, and note reading on degree wheel; turn crank in opposite direction until piston stops against bar again, and take reading. Split difference in degrees between these two readings—this is "indicated" TDC. Turn crank until "indicated" TDC reading on wheel is across from the pointer. Loosen degree wheel and rotate the wheel until the 0° mark, the TDC index, is across from the pointer. To double-check indexing turn crank to left and right, the pointer should read an equal number of degrees "before" and "after" TDC on wheel (when piston contacts stop).

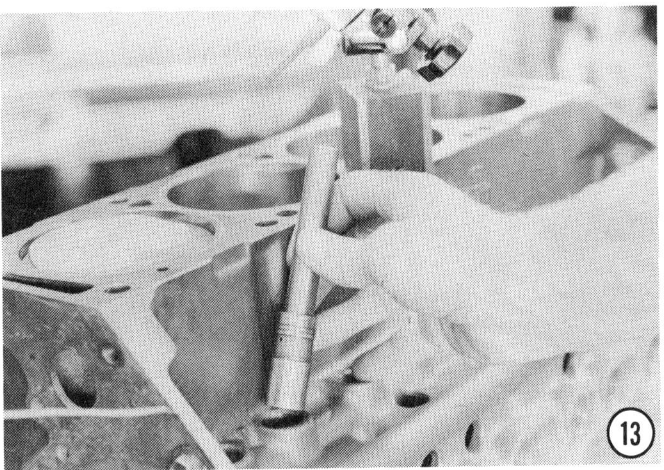

To check actual cam lift and duration with a dial indicator, Greg made a special "extended lifter" by brazing a length of bar stock to the top of a valve lifter. Cam specs tell when (in crank degrees) #1 intake and exhaust valves should open and close. Movement of dial indicator shows when valve action actually occurs as crank is hand-turned through cycle. It will also read actual cam lift. Everything checked out O.K.; adjustments could be made with offset cam gear bushing or key.

Slip oil pump driveshaft in place; then bolt on pump, using gasket.

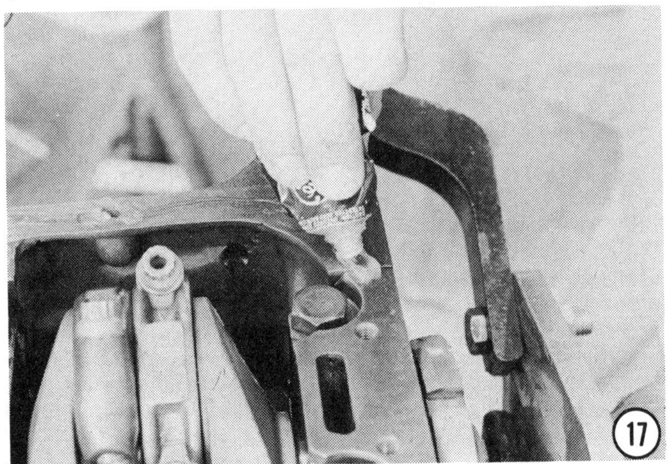

Another source of leaks on big blocks is gap between rear main and block. Add extra silicone here, as shown.

Before installing oil pump (TRW/Melling #50059), Greg replaces stock bypass spring with a 427 Ford "pink" high-pressure spring which gives approximately 100 pounds oil pressure. Also use this spring for relief valve at back of block, or shim stock spring 1/4- to 3/8-inch.

When bolting on cast aluminum timing cover, it is wise to use aligning tool (T61P-6019-B) available from your Ford dealer. Install gaskets, bolt cover loosely to block, slide aligning tool over crank snout and into cover, then tighten bolts. This assures proper seal around damper—a common source of leaks.

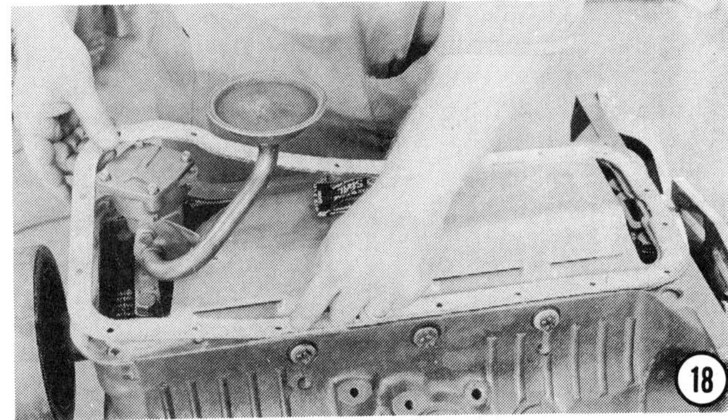

Greg uses silicone sealant, sparingly, for windage tray and pan gaskets. One gasket goes between block and windage tray. Another goes between windage tray and pan. Note that oil pump pickup (deep sump, high-volume type) is attached after windage tray is in place.

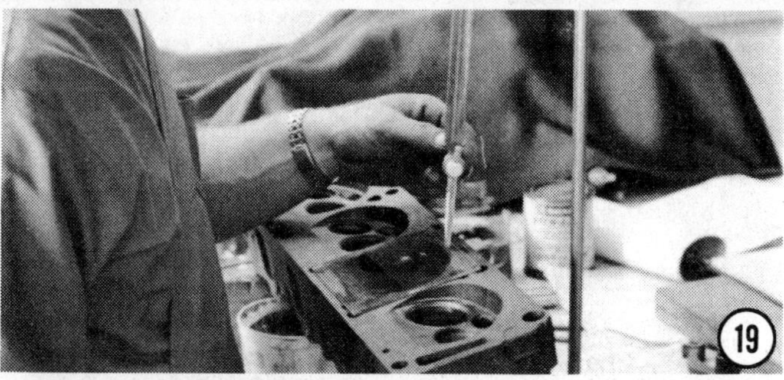

For stock class racing, head "cc-ing" (to check chamber volumes) is critical (to maintain as much compression as allowable), but Medium-Riser heads, with machined combustion chambers, allow little alteration. Greg believes equalizing chambers is important even on this street engine. To check, install valves and spark plug in cylinder. Spread white grease around edge of chamber; press clear plastic square over chamber, with small hole at top edge; then fill chamber with fluid (solvent works well) from graduated burette, noting volume of fluid (in cc's) required to fill chamber.

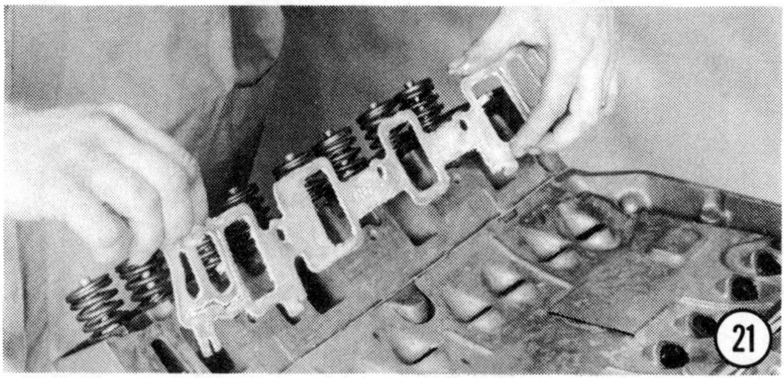

Oil splash baffle fits between heads, under lip of head gaskets. Intake gaskets also have tabs interlocking with notches on protruding head gasket edge. Greg uses white grease on intake manifold gaskets to make removal of manifold simple (should it be necessary in the future). You don't want to pry on a rare Ford aluminum manifold!

Pushrods and rockerarms cannot be installed until intake manifold is bolted in place. Barely visible is oil splash guard between rocker shaft pedestals and valve springs.

Carburetion is an original pair of 4150 Holleys (715cfm each) sold under Ford part numbers C5AF-9510-BC and C5AF-9510-BD, with vacuum-operated secondaries and stock 427 linkage. These are scarce, as are the tall pent-roof valve covers.

Porting and polishing isn't allowed for stock class, and isn't needed on these heads anyway. With valves and springs (Clay Smith dual springs, 140-lbs seat pressure) assembled, install heads. Torque evenly in 10 ft-lb increments to 110 ft-lbs (using clean, lubricated stock head bolts).

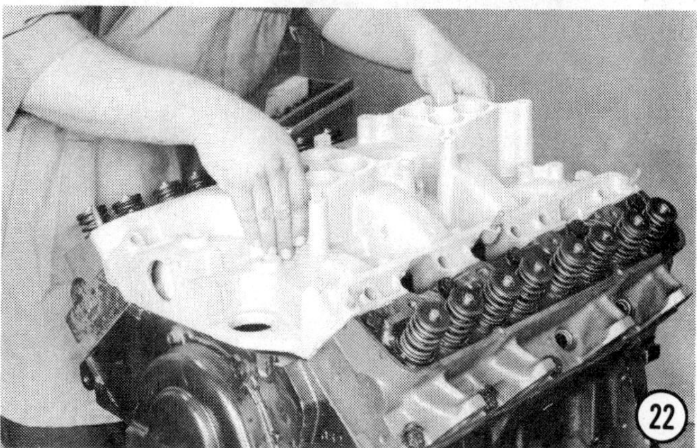

The rare intake in this case is a cherry 427 Ford Medium-Riser dual four-barrel manifold. Be sure to use grade 8 or better intake manifold bolts; torque to 35 ft-lbs.

The finished product is essentially a factory-type 427 with 30 extra cubes. It will put out a strong 425-450 horsepower, and is certainly street driveable.

THE CLEVELAND FAMILY
351 CLEVELAND, 351-BOSS, 351-M, and 400 ENGINES

PRODUCTION SPECIFICATIONS

	351C-4V, CJ, Boss, HO	400-2V
Horsepower (Bhp—rpm) Note: '72 figures are SAE "net" Bhp	300/5400—4V 70 285/5400—4V 71 280/5800—CJ 71 330/5400—Boss 71 266/5400—4V/CJ 72 275/6000—72 HO	260/4400—71 172/4000—72
Torque (lb-ft—rpm) Torque (ft-lb—rpm) Note: '72 figures are SAE "net"	380/3400—4V 70 370/3400—4V 71 345/3800—CJ 71 370/4000—Boss 71 301/3600—4V/CJ 72 286/3800—72 HO	400/2200—71 298/2200—72
Compression Ratio	11.0:1—4V 70 10.7:1—4V 71 9.0:1—CJ 71 11.7:1—Boss 71 9.0:1—4V/CJ 72 9.2:1—72 HO	9.0:1—71 8.4:1—72
Bore	4.00	4.00
Stroke	3.50	4.00
Bore Spacing	4.38	4.38
Head Volume (cc) (Includes valves & plugs)	61.3-64.3—4V 70 64.6-67.6—4V & Boss 71 73.9-76.9—CJ 71, 4V/CJ 72 & 72 HO	76.9-79.9
Head Gasket Thickness	0.047	0.038
Head Gasket Volume (cc)	10.29—4V 9.80—HO	8.31
Total Clearance Volume (cc)	90.36—4V 72.10—HO	103.9
Crankshaft-Material Journal Diameter Main Rod	Nodular Iron (Boss selected for hardness) 2.749 2.311	Nodular Iron 2.9998 2.3107
Con Rods-Material	Forged Steel (Boss Magnafluxed & shot peened) with 180,000 psi nut & bolt	Forged Steel
Length (Ctr-to-Ctr)	5.78	6.58
Pistons-Material	Cast Aluminum—4V and CJ Forged Alum—Boss	Cast Aluminum
Compression Height Deck Clearance	1.657—72 HO 1.631—71 Boss 0.035—4V & CJ 0.045—71 Boss 0.019—72 HO	1.65 0.0565—72
Centerline of crank to top of block		10.302-10.292
Cam-Timing Open/Close	Int. 14/72 Exh. 70/20—70-71 4V 18/72 82/28—71 CJ 14/76 78/32—72 4V/CJ 34/76 86/24—71 Boss 17½/77½ 77½/17½—72 HO	Int. 17/59 Exh. 71/21
Duration/Overlap	226/270/34—70-71 4V 270/290/46—71-72 CJ 290/390/58—71 Boss 275/275/35—72 HO	256/272/38
Valve Lift	0.427—I&E 0.480/0.488 0.477—I&E 0.491—I&E	0.422 Int. 0.427 Exh.
Cam Journal Diameter	No. 1—2.124, No. 2—2.066, No. 3—2.051 No. 4—2.036, No. 5—2.021	No. 1—2.124, No.2—2.066, No. 3—2.051 No. 4—2.036, No. 5—2.021
Tappets	Hydraulic 4V & CJ Mechanical Boss	Hydraulic
Rockerarm-Ratio Type	1.73:1 Lightweight stamping on pedestal 4V & CJ—non-adj., Boss—adj.	1.73:1 Lightweight stamping on pedestal —non-adj.
Valves	2.183-2.198 1.705-1.715	2.050-2.032 1.6595-1.6495
Valve Stem Diameter	0.342	0.342
Valve Spring Load CLOSED—Int. & Exh (Lbs—installed ht.) OPEN—INT & Exh	90/1.82 4V & CJ 92/1.82 Boss 285/1.32 4V & CJ 315/1.32 Boss	76-84/1.82 215-237/1.39
Firing Order	1-3-7-2-6-5-4-8	1-3-7-2-6-5-4-8

THE "CLEVELAND" FAMILY

It's a shame that the 351 Cleveland didn't arrive before the energy/emissions crunch. What Ford eventually intended for this brand new engine was fairly obvious. It was going to be a production-packaged killer.

The 351-C is the culmination of the reversal of Ford's performance image of building engines that wouldn't breathe (flathead, Y-block) to engines that would actually breathe too well. After all their experimentation with exotic, inventive, and oversized cylinder head designs, the Dearborn engineers finally settled on the one that gave the best results in a spectrum of situations—the Boss 302 big port, canted-valve arrangement—and designed a new, modern, lightweight, mid-sized engine to extract the full benefits of this head. The 351-C was designed bo be a *power*plant, no doubt about it. Too bad it died so young (it was produced in '71, '72, and '73 only); the performance engineers had even bigger plans for it.

The surprising fact is that more interest hasn't been shown in the 351-C in racing or high performance circles. As of January, 1973, over one million of these engines had been produced, with another full year of production yet to come. These engines are currently plentiful in the wrecking yards, and some selective shopping should easily dispel the myth that building a high performance Ford costs large amounts of dollars. It is true that specialty/performance products for the Cleveland are not plentiful, and that the more exotic components can be expensive because of the low volume of production. But, the 351-C is an engine that needs very little in the way of "specialized" parts to make it an excellent street, strip, off-road, or ski boat performer. The parts that you will want to play around with—camshafts, manifolds, carburetors, ignitions—are plentiful and competitively priced. One of the most expensive areas of engine building today is headwork. With a 350 Chevy or a 360 Mopar you will have to spend a few hundred dollars at the head shop to get the good valves and the right port contours, or else you will shell out several hundred bucks for a set of trick racing heads. On a Cleveland Ford this expense is totally unnecessary. For anything short of Pro Stock competition, you can't improve on the performance of the four-barrel heads (porting or polishing is actually discouraged), and even the "little" two-barrel versions come with 2.05-inch intake valves and 1.65-inch exhausts and very healthy-sized ports. The "small" Ford heads have bigger valves than even the "big" (2.02-inch) Chevy small block heads! The early two-barrel heads, with a ratio of 9.0:1, will give plenty of compression (with current gasoline) after an inexpensive milling (rather than having to buy new pistons). The four-barrel heads, at 10.7:1, might even be tighter than you'd want for a street engine. About the most involved building process for the Cleveland

1971-1973 COMPONENT COMPARISON 351 C...4V-CJ-BOSS-HO

	4V and CJ 1971	BOSS 1971	4V/CJ 1972-73	HO 1972-73
Cylinder Block	4V—2 bolt main caps CJ—4 bolt main caps	4 bolt main caps selected for hardness	Same as 71 CJ	Same as 71 Boss
Cylinder Head	4V—Quench chamber 64.6-67.6cc Non-adjustable rockerarm pedestal CJ—Open chamber73.9-76.9cc Induction hardened exhaust valve seats Otherwise same as 4V	Quench chamber 64.6-67.6cc Otherwise same as 71 4V, except rockerarm pedestal machined for mechanical camshaft	Same as 71 CJ	Open chamber 73.9-76.9cc Otherwise same as 71 Boss
Cylinder Head Gasket	4V—Production composition CJ—Reintz Repa comp. for 100 ft-lb torque	Reintz special comp. for 120 ft-lb. torque	Same as 71 CJ	Similar to 71 Boss
Intake Valve	2.19" dia head 11/32" dia solid stem Multi-groove key Sil-Chrome No. 1	2.19 dia head 11/32" dia solid stem Single groove key Sil-Chrome No. 1	Same as 71 CJ	Same as 71 Boss
Exhaust Valve	1.71" dia head 11/32" dia solid stem Multi-groove key 21-4N Steel	1.71" dia head 11/32" dia solid stem Single groove key 21-4N Steel	Same as 71 CJ	Same as 71 Boss
Rockerarm Stud	5/16" bolt	7/16" threaded stud	Same as 71 CJ	Same as 71 Boss
Rockerarm Fulcrum	"T" shaped—non-adj.	Cylindrical—adjustable	Same as 71 CJ	Same as 71 Boss
Rockerarm	4V—Production CJ—Stamped high-strength	Stamped high strength	Same as 71 CJ	Same as 71 Boss
Connecting Rod	1041-H Forged Steel 3/8" nut and bolt	1041-H Forged Steel Shot-peened Magnafluxed Improved durability 180,000 psi 3/8" Nut and bolt	Same as 71 CJ	Same as 71 Boss
Piston	Cast Aluminum—flat-top CJ—9.0:1 CR 4V—10.7:1 CR	Forged Aluminum pop-up 11.1:1—CR	Same as 71 CJ except CR is 9.0:1	Forged Aluminum—flat-top 9.2:1 CR
Piston Pin	0.912" dia I.D. non-tapered	0.912" dia I.D. tapered	Same as 71 CJ	Same as 71 Boss
Con Rod Bearings	Over-plated copper/lead w/increased eccentricity	Same as CJ	Same as 71 CJ	Same as 71 Boss
Oil Pan Assembly	Production w/welded windage baffle	Same as CJ	Same as 71 CJ	Same as 71 Boss
Oil Lever Indicator	Calibrated for 5 qts.	Calibrated for 6 qts.	Same as 71 CJ	Same as 71 Boss
Intake Manifold	Cast Iron—over/under	Cast Aluminum	Same as 71 CJ	Same as 71 Boss
Carburetor	4V—Autolite Model 4300-A w/std. bolt pattern CJ—Autolite Model 4300-D w/spread bore pattern	4V Autolite Model 4300-D	Same as 71 CJ	Same as 71 Boss, except with different calibration.
Distributor	4V—Single point dual diaphragm CJ—Dual point dual diaphragm	Same as CJ, except for calibration	Same as 71 4V	Same as 71 Boss
Rockerarm Covers	Stamped Steel	Cast Aluminum	Same as 71 CJ	Same as 71 Boss
Air Cleaner	Ram air—optional	Ram air	Ram air not available	Ram air not available
Oil Fill	5 qt. SAE 10W-30	6 qts. SAE 40 (summer) 6 qts. SAE 20 (winter)	Same as 71 CJ	Same as 71 Boss
Rear Oil Seal	Rope type	Split lip	Same as 71 CJ	Same as 71 Boss
Valve Spring	285 lbs/1.32 open	315 lb—1.32 open	Same as 71 CJ	Same as 71 Boss
Valve Spring Key	Multi-groove	Single groove-hardened	Same as 71 CJ	Same as 71 Boss
Valve Stem Seal	Production 351 C	Production 429 with shorter skirt for improved lubrication	Same as 71 CJ	Same as 71 Boss
Valve Spring Seat	None required	Stamped steel	None required	Same as 71 Boss
Push Rod	Production	Hardened and ground	Same as 71 CJ	Same as 71 Boss
Push Rod Guide Plate	None required	Same as 302 Boss	None required	Same as 71 Boss
Camshaft	Hydraulic 4V-duration 266°—I, 270°—E overlap 34°, lift 0.427 CJ-duration 270°—I, 290°—E overlap 46°, lift 0.480"/0.488	Mechanical duration 290°—I and E overlap 58, lift 0.477	Same as '71 CJ except valve events retarded 4°	Mechanical duration 275°—I and E overlap 35°, lift 0.491"
Tappets	Hydraulic	Mechanical Internal metering	Same as 71 CJ	Same as 71 Boss
Crankshaft	Cast Iron	Cast iron selected for hardness (902 nodularity)	Same as 71 CJ	Same as 71 Boss
Damper	0.10 inertia cast iron hub cast iron inertia ring non-bonded elastic member 28.2 oz. in unbalance	0.14 inertia nodular iron hub wider cast iron inertia ring bonded elastic member 27.3 oz. in unbalance	Same as 71 CJ	Same as 71 Boss

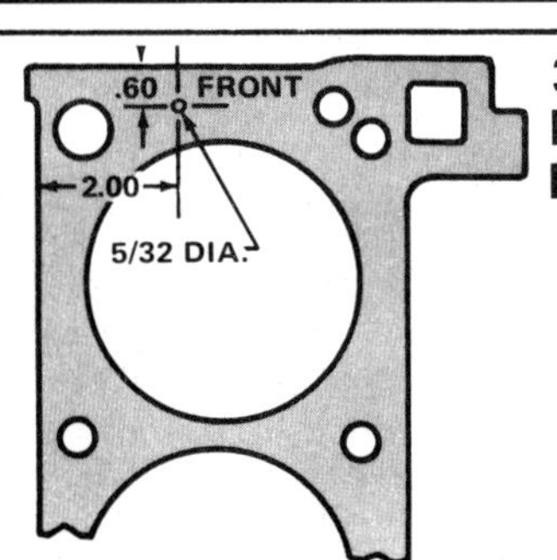

351C Head Gasket Modification

For extended high-rpm usage such as required in road racing or circle track competition cylinder head gasket durability can be improved by drilling a 5/32-inch hole in the location illustrated. This modification is not required for drag racing.

PRODUCTION 351 C SPECIFICATIONS

Displacement (Cu. In.)	351
Carburetor Venturi	2V & 4V
Horsepower (Bhp/rpm)	250/4600—2V 300/5400—4V
Torque (lb-ft/rpm)	355/2600—2V 380/3400—4V
Compression Ratio	9.5:1—2V 11.0:1—4V
Bore	4.00
Stroke	3.50
Bore Spacing	4.38
Head Volume (cc)	74.7-77.7—2V 61.3-64.3—4V
Crankshaft—Material —Journal Dia—Main —Rod	Nodular Iron 2.749 2.311
Con Rods—Material —Length (Ctr-Ctr)	Forged Steel 5.778
Pistons—Material —Compression Height —Deck Clearance	Cast Aluminum 1.65 0.035
Centerline of Crank to top of Block	9.213
Cam Timing—Open/Close —Duration/Overlap —Lift —Journal Diameter	2V—Int: 12°/66°, Exh: 66°/20° 4V—Int: 18°/70°, Exh: 81°/19° 2V—258°—I, 266°—E/32° 4V—268°—I, 280°—E/37° 2V—0.235, 4V—0.247—I/0.262—E No. 1—2.124, No. 2—2.066, No. 3—2.051 No. 4—2.036, No. 5—2.021
Tappets	Hydraulic
Rockerarm—Ratio —Type	1.73:1 Lightweight stamping on pedestal with positive stop threaded stud
Valves—Head Dia—Intake —Exhaust	2.036-2.046—2V 2.183-2.198—4V 1.650-1.660—2V 1.705-1.715—4V
Valve Stem Diameter	0.342
Valve Spring Load—Closed (Lbs/Installed Ht) —Open	76-84/1.82—2V 85-95/1.82—4V 199-221/1.42—2V 251-279/1.37—4V
Valve Lifters Lash(Mech)	Hydraulic
External Balance	Yes
Firing Order	1-3-7-2-6-5-4-8
Initial Advance (Vacuum Disconnected)	6° BTDC
Breaker Point—Gap —Dwell	0.021 24°-29°
Spark Plug Gap	0.032-0.036
Manifold Vacuum (Idle)	14 inches of Mercury

GENERAL SPECS (351 BOSS)

Bore Stroke Firing Order	4.00 3.50 1-3-7-2-6-5-4-8
Block ℄ of crank to head face Bore spacing Main bearing bore dia. Tappet bore dia.	 9.201-9.211 4.38 2.9425-2.9417 0.8752-0.8767
Cylinder Head Combustion chamber vol.(cc) Valve guide bore dia. (I & E) Valve seat width (I & E)	 64.6-67.6 0.3433-0.3443 0.060-0.080
Valves—Exhaust O.D. Stem dia. Length	 1.7145-1.7045 0.3418-0.3411 4.94
Valves—Intake O.D. Stem dia. Length	 2.195-2.185 0.3423-0.3416 5.136
Rockerarm Ratio Contact pad area with valve	 1.73 60% minimum
Valve Springs—Installed Ht. Stock spring (For reference) 3-piece spring D0ZX-6A511-A	 1.82/92 lbs. 1.69/130 lbs.
Piston Compression Height—stock —TRW (Reference Information) Deck clearance Stock specs for stock piston Blueprint specs for stock piston Stock specs using TRW piston Blueprint specs for TRW piston Piston to valve clearance	 1.638-1.624 1.652-1.638 0.0345-0.0555 0.010 nominal 0.0085-0.0295 0.010 nominal 0.070 min.—I & E/zero lash
Piston Pin Diameter Length	 0.9122-0.9125 3.02-3.03
Crankshaft Main bearing journal dia. Con rod journal dia.	 2.7484-2.7492 2.3103-2.3111
Connecting Rod Length—center to center Crank bore dia. Piston pin bore dia.	 5.7785-5.7815 2.3451-2.3469 0.9104-0.9112

would be converting hydraulic-cam heads to adjustable rockers, but this job is really no more difficult than putting screw-in rocker studs in any head; and, besides, the vast majority of recreational performance enthusiasts would prefer a good hydraulic grind anyway.

As in other sections we will categorize the various 351 Cleveland engine models and point out the "preferable" components for building the good combination. But, though there are some "better" Clevelands, you will quickly discover that none are deficient for good street-type performance. There are no dogs in the 351 Cleveland line. If any of the "335" family can be considered pokey or undernourished, it would be the over-smogged 400 or the half-breed 351-M, both current production engines. Yet even the very plentiful 400 is built just like the 351-C, and with a little Cleveland parts swapping and a new four-barrel performance intake, it can be livened up in no time. The 351-M is, unfortunately, an hermaphrodite—a compromise at best. So we won't discuss it here as a performance engine. However, all information that applies to the 400, and most to the 351-C, applies to the 351-M as well.

Other than extra holes drilled and tapped in the saddles, four-bolt and two-bolt 351-C blocks are the same. Cast housing for timing gears and fuel pump readily distinguish the Cleveland from the Windsor.

CYLINDER BLOCKS

You have two choices. Supposedly all four-barrel 351-C engines came with four-bolt main bearing caps, while all two-barrel engines used main caps of the same width and basically the same size but lacking the extra two bolts. Technically, the '71 vintage four-barrel engines had two-bolt mains while the CJ got the stronger bottom end—but inspection of engines shows that the assignment of blocks was sometimes random (for instance Panteras, all fitted with four-barrel 351-C engines, sometimes have two-bolt blocks, sometimes four-bolt). Actually it is a moot point, as stated by Jack Roush: "Virtually any 351-C block can be used, since there are no differences in materials or strength. In fact, the two-bolt main cap block is just as good as the four-bolt block. Even the caps seem to be equivalent in strength. So, unless you already have a four-bolt block, don't spend the extra bucks for this feature."[1] Roush recommends removing casting flash from the block (deburring), and he suggests radiusing the number two and number four main bearing saddles and webs, noting that these will eventually crack in most Cleveland blocks after *sustained* high speed operation. If you are shopping for a used block, be sure to Magnaflux it carefully before starting any machine work.

Other builders, such as Doug Cook, feel that the four-bolt mains do help control "walking" of the main bearings, and are therefore preferable ...though not necessary. All 351-C blocks will accept the four-bolt caps by simply drilling and tapping the web to accept the outer 3/8-16 bolts. Unfortunately the caps have never been available separately from the block, which means you'd have to scavenge them from another motor, which in turn would necessitate Magnafluxing the caps and align boring once the swap was made. So, unless you can find a four-bolt block complete, don't worry too much about it. By no means attempt to modify the two-bolt caps to accept four bolts; although they have the wide shoulder, drilling them would

1. Jack Roush, "Profecting the 351-C." *Car Craft*, Aug. 76, pg 50.

Extra strength afforded by four-bolt 351-C main caps is minimal. However, the extra bolts do help prevent twisting of the cap.

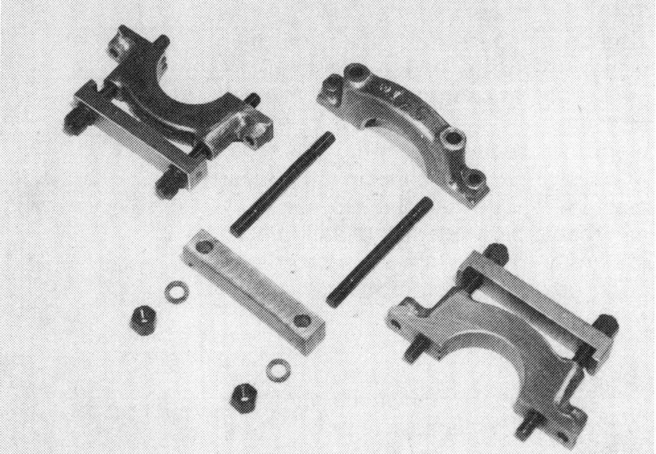

To add bottom end strength to either two- or four-bolt main caps you can install Gapp and Roush main support caps.

only weaken them.

A minor difference exists between four-bolt blocks. The '71-73 CJ 351 (block D1ZZ-6010-A) used a rope-type rear main seal, and consequently has a small pin in the rear main cap to hold the seal in place. The '71 Boss and '72 HO blocks (D1ZZ-6010-D) used a split rubber lip-type seal, and therefore do not have the pin in the cap. Racers would prefer the split seal for less friction (Mr. Gasket #1966 neoprene, or Ford CNOZ-6701-A), and these can be installed in the other block by pulling out the pin and sealing the hole with a spot of silicone sealant. (Personally, I have found that the rope-type rear main seal gives the best service for day-in and day-out driving, especially if the crank has seen some miles.)

A couple of other considerations for junkyard block shoppers: The Cleveland block is a thinwall casting with cylinder wall thickness measuring .190-inch—.130-inch, depending on core shift. Ford sells replacement pistons only in .003-inch oversize, and some builders do not recommend boring a Cleveland block any more than this amount. Specialty pistons are available in larger sizes, or course, but the maximum overbore on a 351-C is .030-inch, at best. Any used Cleveland will have plenty of miles on it by now, so be sure to (1) check that the block hasn't already been overbored to .030-inch (overbore size should be stamped on the top of replacement pistons), and (2) mike the cylinder bores for excessive wear or taper.

Second, Jack Roush points out that Ford machines the cam bearings to size once they are in the block. Consequently replacement cam bearings may not be concentric when installed in a Cleveland (or a 90°V small block), and would have to be "align bored" in the block—a difficult process since each bearing is a different size (i.d.). He recommends saving the original cam bearings if at all possible, which means not hot tanking the block since caustic solutions attack bearing material. We haven't heard this problem mentioned by other sources, however, and a check with local machine shops revealed no cases of noticeable cam bearing misalignment in Fords. Not hot tanking a dirty block might lead to worse problems.

CRANKSHAFT

Again, there isn't much choosing to do. All Clevelands came with cast nodular iron cranks, the only differences being that the Boss 351 piece (D1ZZ-6303-A) is selected for higher nodularity. But don't let the lack of an

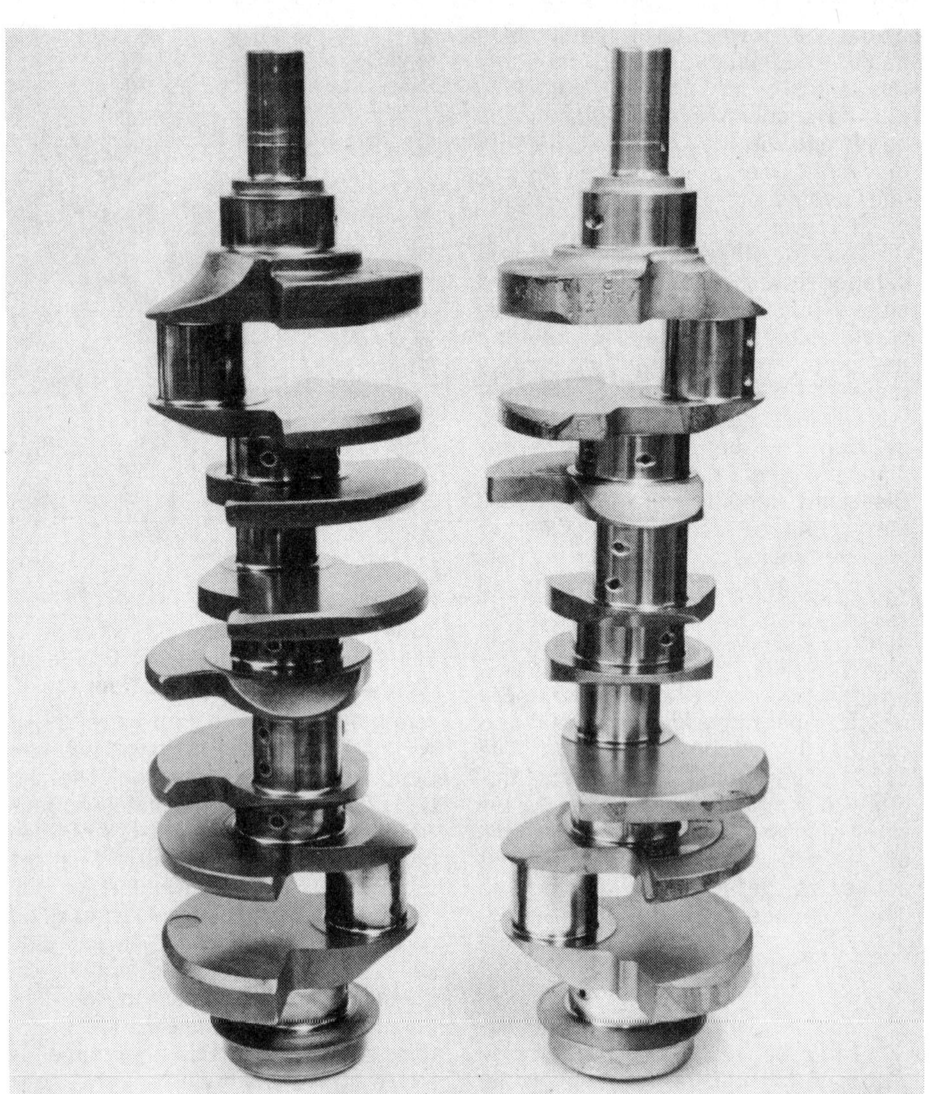

All production Cleveland crankshafts (right) are cast nodular iron and externally balanced. The example shown here has been micro-polished and had the oil holes chamfered. At left is a special chrome-moly steel billet crank made by Hank the Crank. Note the extra two large counterweights in the center of the crank to minimize flexing.

On any 351-C crank intended for high performance, chamfering of the oil holes and micro-polishing of the bearing surfaces is recommended.

The stock 351-C con rod (right), is a healthy part. This one has been polished along the beam and shot-peened. On the left is a considerably more expensive Crower custom steel rod.

Standard 351-C rod with flat-top piston shows rounded edges of full-bodied piston skirt.

available steel crank worry you; the Pro Stockers use the cast crank, even with undersized rod journals, and spin them to ten grand without problems. It would be a very good idea to have the crank micro-polished, chamfer the oil holes, and then have it Tufftrided for better durability. Since Tufftriding is a heat process, the crank should subsequently be restraightened and the journals lightly micro-polished once again. Roush recommends resizing the main journals to 2.7480 inches and the rod journals to 2.3088 inches, standard sizes being 2.749 inches and 2.311 inches, respectively. See accompanying charts for general blueprint specifications.

CRANKSHAFT I.D. AND APPLICATION

Part Number	Engine	Year	Journal Diameter		Stroke	Material
			Main	Rod		
D0AZ-6303-A	351C	70/72	2.749	2.311	3.50	Nod Iron
D1ZZ-6303-A	351C Boss	71/72	2.749	2.311	3.50	High Nod Iron
D1AZ-6303-A	400	71/72	3.000	2.311	4.00	Iron

Since the Cleveland crankshaft is externally balanced, rebalancing must be done with the flywheel and front damper to be used for the final assembly. Choose the components you wish to use before you visit the balancing shop, and take these pieces with you.

RODS AND PISTONS

Factory 351 Clevelands came with two types of connecting rods, both very similar in external appearance. The "good" rod came in the Boss engine (D1ZZ-6200-A), identified by casting number D1ZX-AA on the beam. It is forged of 1041 steel, shot-peened, and Magnafluxed, and comes with 180,000 psi, 3/8-inch bolts and nuts. These are excellent rods, considered good to 8,000 rpm. They could be improved slightly by polishing, but have them shot-peened once again because polishing destroys the surface stress created by the original peening.

The standard con rods used in all other 351-C engines, marked DOAE-A on the beam, are excellent for most general purpose applications. It would be very wise to install the stronger Boss bolts (D1ZZ-6214-A) and nuts (D1ZZ-6212-A) since they are the same size, and then resize the big end of the rod to make sure it is round. The best

CON ROD I.D. AND APPLICATION

Part Number	Engine	Year	Weight (grams)	CTR-to-CTR Distance	Bolt Size	Remarks
D0AZ-6200-A	351C	70/72	688-700	5.778	3/8	
D1ZZ-6200-A	351C Boss	71/72	688-700	5.778	3/8	Shot-Peened & Magnafluxed w/180,000 PSI Bolts
D1AZ-6200-A	400	71/72	846-858	6.58	3/8	

The most popular and practical replacement piston for street performance Clevelands is the flat-top TRW rated at 10½:1 compression with quench heads.

The current TRW pop-up for the 351 is similar to the '71 Boss piston. Rated at 12:1 with quench heads, it's a bit stout for street driving.

The specialty piston makers can cut just about anything you want on a 351-C blank. This line-up includes (from left) a supershort drag piston, two wide-skirt silicon alloy circle-track versions (notice different pin heights), and the TRW pop-up.

way to do this is to remove approximately .002-inch from the caps, and then rebore the rods with caps and new bolts in place to .0004-.0005-inch under spec (2.4360 inches). Magnaflux the rods before installing them in the engine.

Other than the several wild and varied Pro Stock designs, when it comes to pistons for your 351 Cleveland you have two basic choices these days. The standard piston used by most rebuilders and performance shops for street or recreation build-ups is the TRW flat-top, L-2379, which is similar to the '72 HO forged aluminum flat-top (D2ZZ-6108-C). Jack Roush prefers the Ford replacement piston because it has rounded edges on the skirt, unlike the sharp "corners" on the TRW (a strange difference since TRW also makes the Ford pistons). The problem is that the Ford piston comes only in .003-inch oversize, and they are not as readily available as the TRW pistons. Either of these pistons will give approximately 10.5:1 compression with the quench-type heads (zero deck height, .045-inch gaskets) or 9.2:1 compression with the open chamber heads (-.019-inch deck, .038-inch gasket). The TRW pistons can be ordered in .010-inch, .020-inch, and .030-inch oversize with .030-over being the limit for a street engine and .020 being the maximum for any competition use.

The other standard piston choice is the TRW pop-up, L-2348. Similar to the '71 Boss piston, except for the addition of a fire slot in the dome, this slug will boost the compression of your Cleveland to 12.0:1 with the quench heads (66.1cc chambers, .010-inch deck clearance, and a .038-inch gasket). For a little more practical street version, you can mill .100-inch off the dome for about 11.5:1 compression. The original Boss pop-up was rated at 11.1:1.

Just in case you are wondering about stock piston combinations used in Clevelands, here's the line-up: a cast aluminum flat-top gave 10.7:1 compression in the '71 vintage 4V engine with quench heads and 9.0:1 in the '72-73 CJ with open-chamber heads. A similar, but forged, aluminum flat-top was rated at 9.2:1 in the '72 HO with open-chamber heads. The forged pop-up came in the '71 Boss giving 11.1:1 compression with the quench heads.

Standard and TRW Cleveland pistons are designed for press-in wrist pins. A special tapered pin (C9ZZ-6135-E) was made by Ford for the Trans Am 302 and subsequently used in the Boss 351. Use it if you can find it. Hone the piston pin bore for .0008-inch clearance (.0006-.0012-inch interference) between pin and bore. Use Sunnen B-200 anti-seize lubricant while pressing the pins to prevent galling. Once in place, it should take a minimum of 1800 pounds force to move the pin. Ford discourages modifying pistons for full-floating pin operation.

Piston rings are available from all of the major manufacturers, of course, and your choice is primarily a matter of personal preference. For high performance, Ford recommends a Moly-faced top ring, and a cast iron second ring. The common choice of almost all engine builders surveyed was Sealed Power/Speed Pro set #R-9343 with a Moly-filled 5/64-inch top ring, a 5/64-inch cast iron second ring, and a 3/16-inch oil control third ring. Before installing these rings on the pistons you *must* check the end gap clearance of each ring in the respective bore. They are made specifically longer than necessary so that you can file them to proper specs (.015-inch top ring, .012-inch second). If you don't follow this procedure, as shown in the photo section, the ends of the rings will butt and consequently either break or score the cylinder walls.

CYLINDER HEADS

As we have stated in other sections, and as Ford had certainly learned well by the time they designed the Cleveland, the cylinder heads make the engine. Short of an all-out hemi head, the Clevelands are just about the ultimate in factory production configurations. Some critics will point out that Chevrolet pioneered the canted valve design, which may be true, but it is a well-known fact that the big Chevy suffers from the uneven lengths of the staggered intake runners. The Cleveland head is the ultimate refinement of

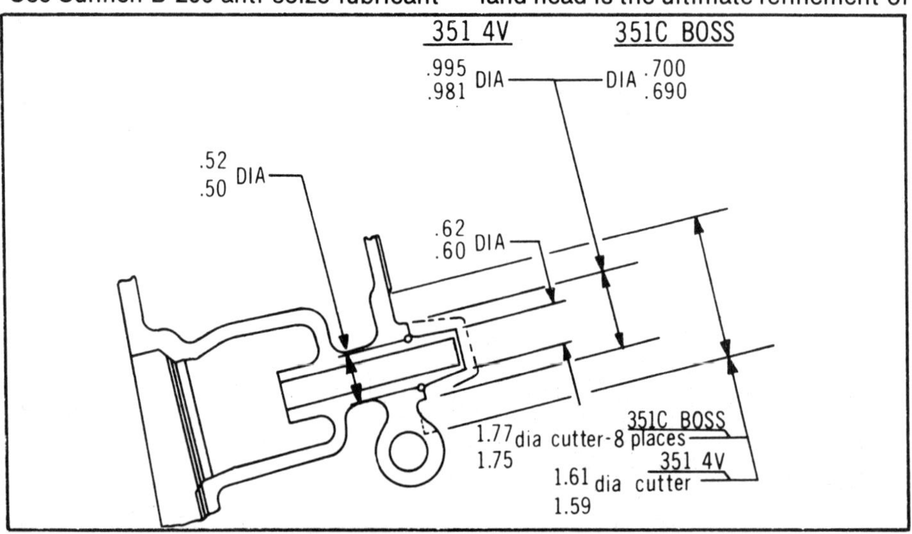

If special springs are to be fitted onto the standard four-barrel heads the spring seats may have to be machined for added spring clearance. This should be done by an experienced machinist. The specifications shown here are for machining a standard four-barrel head to duplicate the Boss 351 head (which was fitted with larger springs that also have a smaller inside diameter).

Even the "little" two-barrel head looks like it has a very healthy appetite with large oval intake and exhaust ports and 2.05-inch intake valves. All two-barrels have "open" combustion chambers and the same heads are used on 400 and 351-M engines. A look into the exhaust ports clearly shows that the passage is not as large as the opening—the bottom half of the port is virtually wasted.

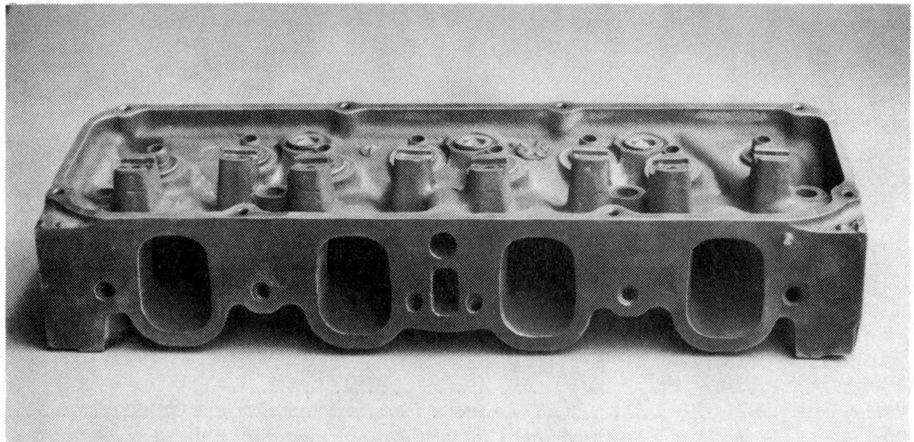

The two-barrel ports pale in comparison to the four-barrel Clevelands. Essentially the same as the race-proven Boss 302 heads, these ports are as big as any street motor could want.

the "poly-angle" chamber design as well as the ultimate in "bigger is better" thinking for port size and shape. Therefore, you don't have to do too much shopping for Cleveland heads—they are all good, and there were only a few variations.

CLEVELAND CYLINDER HEAD COMPARISON

Two Barrel (2V)
- Open chamber (76.9-79.9cc)
- Valve head diameter: Intake 2.050 inches, Exhaust 1.659 inches
- Small ports
- Valve train: Hydraulic cam, non-adjustable slotted rockerarm pedestal, multi-groove valve stem locks
- Usage: 1970-78—351-C-2V; 1970-78—400; 1975-78—351-M

Four Barrel (4V)
- Quench chamber (61.3-64.3cc)
- Valve head diameter: Intake 2.198 inches , Exhaust 1.715 inches
- Large ports
- Valve train: Hydraulic cam, non-adjustable slotted rockerarm pedestals, multi-groove valve stem locks.
- Usage: 1970-71—351-C 4V

Boss 351
- Quench chamber (64.6-67.6cc)
- Valve head diameter: Intake 2.198 inches, Exhaust 1.715 inches
- Large ports
- Valve train: Mechanical cam, screw-in studs, adjustable rockerarms, push rod guide plates, valve spring retaining cups, single groove valve stem locks.
- Usage: 1971 Boss 351

Cobra Jet
- Open chamber (73.9-76.9cc)
- Valve head diameter: Intake 2.198 inches, Exhaust 1.715 inches
- Large ports
- Valve train: Hydraulic cam, non-adjustable slotted rockerarm pedestals, multi-groove valve stem locks.
- Usage: 1971—Cobra Jet 351; 1972-74—351-C 4V

High Output (HO)
- Open chamber (73.9-76.9cc)
- Valve head diameter: Intake 2.198 inches, Exhaust 1.715 inches
- Large ports
- Valve train: Hydraulic cam, non-adjustable slotted rockerarm pedestals, multi-groove valve stem locks.
- Valve train: Mechanical cam, screw-in studs, adjustable rockerarms, push rod guide plates, valve spring retaining cups, single groove valve stem locks.
- Usage: 1972-74—High Performance 351-C 4V

There have been five distinct types of Cleveland heads offered. By far the most common are the "small" 2V type which came on all two-barrel 351-C engines beginning in 1970, and which have been used on all 400 cid engines and the 351-M. These heads have smaller intake and exhaust ports than any of the 4V types, large (approxmately 76cc) round open combustion chambers, 2.05-inch diameter intake valves, and 1.65-inch exhausts. All of these heads come with stamped steel rockerarms mounted with sled-type fulcrums on notched pedestals. The fulcrum holds the rocker in place so guide plates or guide slots in the head are not necessary to keep it aligned with the valve tip; however, this design does not permit lash adjustment of the rockers.

Four-barrel Cleveland heads are the ones with the gigantic intake and exhaust ports, plus they all have larger 2.19-inch intake valves and 1.71-inch exhausts. However, these heads came in four variations based on two combustion chamber shapes and two valve train options. The premium Cleveland heads are the '70-71 vintage 4V and the '71 Boss 351. Off the engine, either of these types is immediately recognizable by the smaller "quench" combustion chamber (61-67cc), which will, of course, yield higher compression on any Cleveland engine. The quench chamber is so named because it tends to actually extinguish the flame front as it travels to the corners of the chamber because the quench area remains relatively cool. This helps reduce detonation or "pinging" in the cylinder. It unfortunately increases hydrocarbon emissions since some fuel is left unburned—a situation which consequently led to the demise of the quench head. The major advantage of the quench design, other than providing an increase in compression, is to create turbulence in the chamber, which improves mixing of air and fuel (especially at lower rpm). This, in turn, yields more complete combustion and greater low- and mid-range torque. The quench heads came in two versions, the more common being the '70-71 vintage 4V type which was fitted with a valve train similar to the 2V heads and is, therefore, suitable only for use with hydraulic lifter camshafts (unless converted to adjustable rockers).

The '71 Boss 351 heads—which are obviously rare—were the best combination, being almost identical to Boss 302 heads. The major advantage is that they come with adjustable rockerarms to accommodate the solid-lifter cam fitted to this engine; but

The ports and valves (2.19-inch intakes) are the same on all four-barrel heads, but the '70-71 versions came with the smaller quench combustion chambers which are good for almost 1½ points more compression than the larger open-chamber heads shown at top.

The other distinction between Cleveland heads lies in the valvetrain. All hydraulic-cam engines (both two- and four-barrel) have slotted pedestals for nonadjustable rockers plus a spring-centering ridge around the valve guide boss (top). The '71 Boss (closed chamber) and '72 HO (open-chamber) heads have machined pedestals for screw-in rocker studs and machined spring seats for multicoil valve springs (bottom).

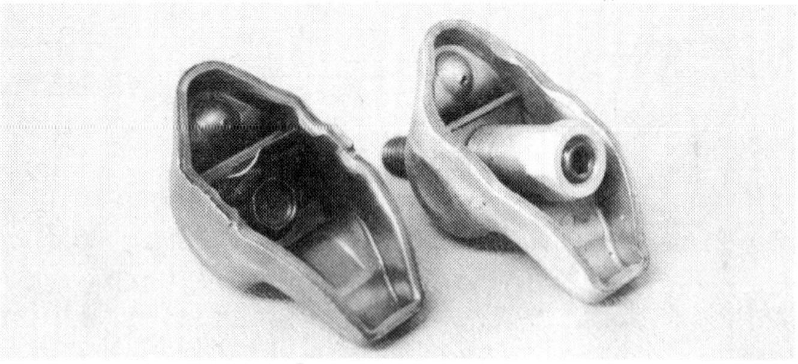

The rockers (though Boss and HO are specially hardened) look the same. The difference is in the attachment; the hydraulic-cam version, by far the most common, cannot be adjusted (left).

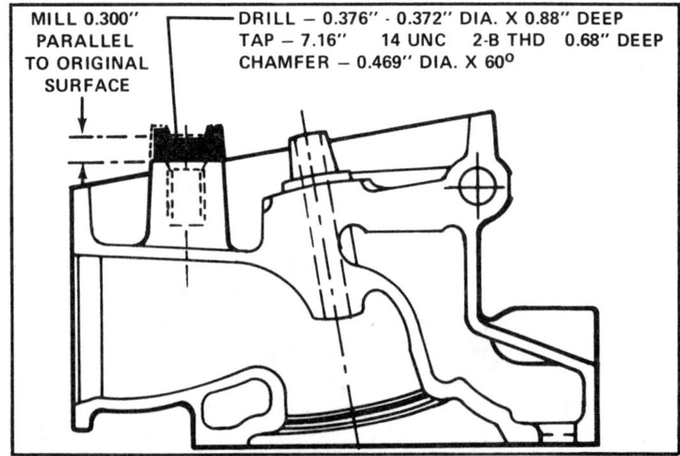

Standard four-barrel heads can be machined as shown to accept screw-in studs. The boss must be machined *parallel to the bottom of the original slot*, not parallel to the deck surface.

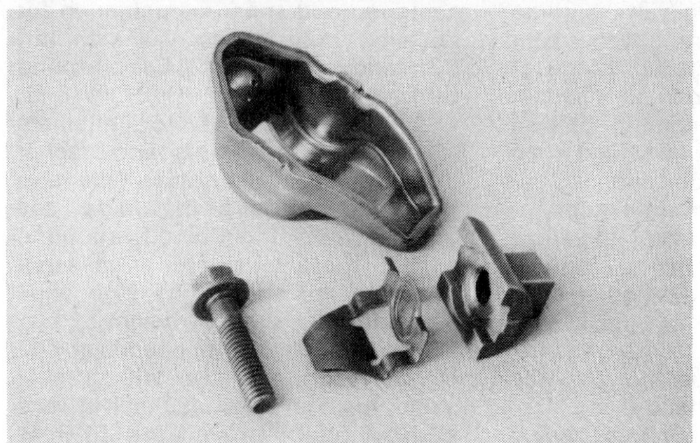

The standard hydraulic-cam rocker is aligned by the flat-sided "sled" fulcrum which bolts solidly into the slotted pedestal on the head. Two-barrel engines had aluminum fulcrums; change them to the sintered-iron four-barrel type for performance.

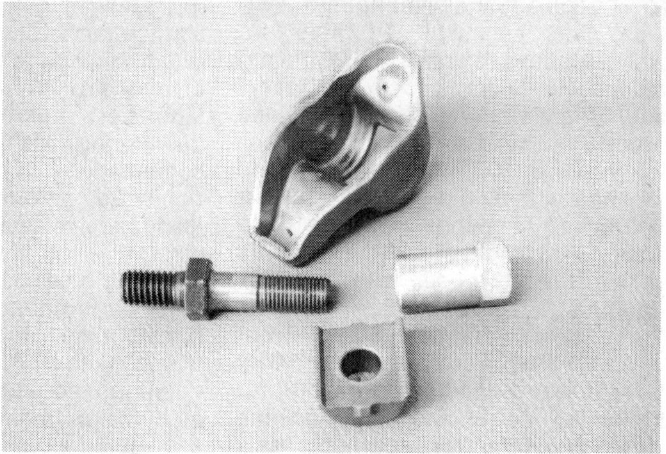

The Boss and HO engines retain the large stamped rocker and sled fulcrum for sake of parts conformity, but they also require pushrod guide plates for alignment. The screw-in stud is similar to Chevy types.

there are actually several subtle differences between these and other Cleveland heads. To begin with, the rocker pedestals are machined flat to accept 7/16-inch screw-in studs and guide plates to align the special hardened pushrods. The rockerarms are specially hardened also, and ride on sintered iron adjustable fulcrums with locking adjustment nuts. Also available were special-order needle-bearing rockers which are currently available from Maier Racing, Inc., in Hayward, CA. These were originally offered by Ford as a fulcrum kit (DOAX-6A585-A) that fits in the stock rocker. If you have a set of these rockers and they need new bearings, the needle bearing is still available separately from Torrington (#B-105). The Boss heads were also machined around the valve guide bosses to accept special spring seats which keep the bottom of the valve springs from shifting on the pad. The Boss motors, of course, came with heavier valve springs, as well as tougher retainers. And, finally, the valves in the Boss heads, although otherwise identical to other 4V 351 engines, are cut for single-groove keepers instead of the multi-groove locks used on all others. The multi-groove arrangement allows the two halves of the keepers to butt, holding the valve stem with a little clearance inside the locks. This supposedly allows the valve to rotate as it opens and closes, thus promoting better seat wear. It all sounds pretty theoretical, but the vast majority of Cleveland valves are of this type and the benefit of changing to the positive-grip Boss valves and locks would be questionable unless you were going to purchase new valves anyway. For high rpm runs, you would definitely want the single-groove valves. To give you a better idea of the exact differences in the Boss 351-C heads, here is a rundown of the specific parts:

Intake Valves	DOZZ-6507-A
Exhaust Valves	DOZZ-6505-A
Keepers	C9ZZ-6518-A
Valve Springs	DOZZ-6513-A
Valve Spring Seats	DOOZ-6A536-A
Retainers	C9ZZ-6514-A
Sintered-Iron Fulcrums	C9ZZ-6A528-A
Rockerarm Studs	C9ZZ-6A527-A
Rockerarm Stud Nuts	C8ZZ-6A529-B
Guide Plates	C9ZZ-6A564-A
Hardened Pushrods	DOOZ-6565-F
Rockerarms	C9ZZ-6564-A

Other than the different placement of water outlet passages and a slight increase in combustion chamber area (58.5-62.8cc), these heads are exactly the same as those used on the Boss 302.

The '72 Boss engine was given a new designation, the HO, the major change was a lowering of the compression ratio. The '72 HO heads have all of the special hardware to accommodate adjustable rockerarms, plus the large valves and ports common to all 4V engines, but they use the large open-type combustion chambers introduced on the 2V heads. The '71-73 CJ 351 and the '72 4V engines use the open-chambers along with the non-adjustable rockerarms for use only with hydraulic camshafts. Ford switched to the open-chamber heads not only to lower compression ratios to match the lower octane gasolines being mandated, but also because the open-chamber promotes more complete burning of fuel in the cylinder and thus discharges fewer pollutants. One performance benefit of the open-chamber design is that it completely unshrouds both valves. Unfortunately, however, nobody makes a domed performance piston to specifically match this chamber shape. Even with moderate compression ratios, however, the open chamber heads tend to "ping" and for any sort of performance, polishing the chambers would be a good suggestion. The best way to increase compression with the open-chamber heads would be to mill them; however, like the block, they are thinwall castings and .060-inch is the limit for cutting. The chart below shows the amounts to remove from intake manifold mating surfaces when 351-C heads are milled:

351C HEAD MILLING		
Amount removed from heads	Amount to remove from intake manifold	
	Sides	Bottom
.010	.010	.014
.020	.020	.028
.030	.030	.042
.040	.040	.057

Another method for controlling chamber volume, as well as for adjusting for piston deck height, is to alter head gasket thickness. The stock Ford gaskets for the 4V variety are .047-inch thick, as are the Felpro replacements. The stock Ford 2V gaskets are .038-inch thick, as are McCords (#6850M). The accompanying diagram shows how you can drill an extra 5/32-inch hole in each gasket to relieve pressure (steam), which might lead to early gasket failure, from the cooling system. This procedure is primarily recommended for circle track or other sustained high rpm use, but Jack Roush suggests using it on street motors as well.

VALVETRAIN

Besides the regular 2V intake and exhaust valves, the larger 4V intake and exhaust valves, and the Boss 351 single-groove keeper valves, Ford also offered "race only" titanium intakes

(DOZX-6507-A) and semi-hollow stainless steel exhausts (DOZX-6505-A) which weighed 85 grams and 95 grams, respectively, compared to 147 grams and 123 grams for stockers. Ford also offered a special-order three-piece valve spring (DOZX-6A511-A) designed for cams with .600- to .620-inch lift. It produced 130 pounds at the seat with an installed height of 1.69 inches. This spring was to be used with Boss 351 retainers, keepers, and spring seats. Since these components are not available from Ford any longer, they have been mentioned primarily for historical interest and as a guideline when shopping for specialty valve springs. Special valves for the 351-C are currently offered by several manufacturers. Manley lists both hollow-stem super-light intakes and exhausts (11711, 11710) as well as rugged one-piece stainless steel valves (11805, 11802). Maier Racing also lists one-piece stainless valves that cut weight 11% over stock (1624, 1625). Gapp and Roush list the original Boss 302/351 titanium intakes and hollow stainless exhausts (mentioned above) in their present catalog, plus a titanium exhaust made from cut-down intakes ...however they list for $43.40, $24.00, and $53.40 each, respectively. That's *per valve*, not per set.

When it comes to valve springs and related hardware, every cam grinder's catalog has a full range of components from which to choose. Most offer triple-coil springs, or else dual-springs with a damper, and such combinations will require the installation of Perfect Circle or similar spring-loaded valve stem seals to allow clearance for the inner spring. To install such seals, the valve guide boss must be trimmed with a special tool (i.e., Crane 99017) to a smaller diameter—a simple operation that can be performed with a hand drill. Most manufacturers also recommend using a Boss-type spring seat with high pressure springs. If you are not using Boss or HO heads to begin with, you will have to cut the spring seat area of the head to accept them. Your choice of valve springs should depend entirely upon the manufacturer's recommendation for the particular camshaft you decide to install. Always be sure to check each spring for recommended seat tension at the specified installed height, and use shims if necessary to attain the proper specs. Likewise, always check each spring combination for coil bind or for interference between the bottom of the retainer and the top of the valve guide at full lift.

If you wish to use Ford components, a good spring combination for relatively mild (up to .500-inch lift) hydraulic cams is the 428 CJ coil spring with inner damper (C9OZ-6513-E). These can be used with stock retainers (4V or service retainers are tougher than original 2V ones), stock-type valve stem seals, and can be installed on any of the heads without modification (no spring seat cups are necessary). These springs should give 90 pounds pressure at an installed height of 1.82 inches (closed) and 285 pounds at 1.32 inches (open). For use with a mild solid-lifter cam (up to .480-inch lift) or a slightly hotter hydraulic, the 351 Boss springs (DOZZ-6513-A), retainers (C9ZZ-6514-A) and spring seats (C9ZZ-6A536-A) are good. (These are single springs with inner dampers and can be used with standard valve seals. At an installed height of 1.82 inches they give 93 pounds at the seat and 315 pounds at 1.32 inches (open).

Of course, most specialty/performance cam grinders can supply you with springs comparable or identical to the Ford numbers. For more demanding cam profiles one good spring choice for street/strip activity would be Isky's inner-outer-damper combination (8005-A) which gives 140 pounds at an installed height of 1.825 inches and which coil binds at 1.060 inches. For

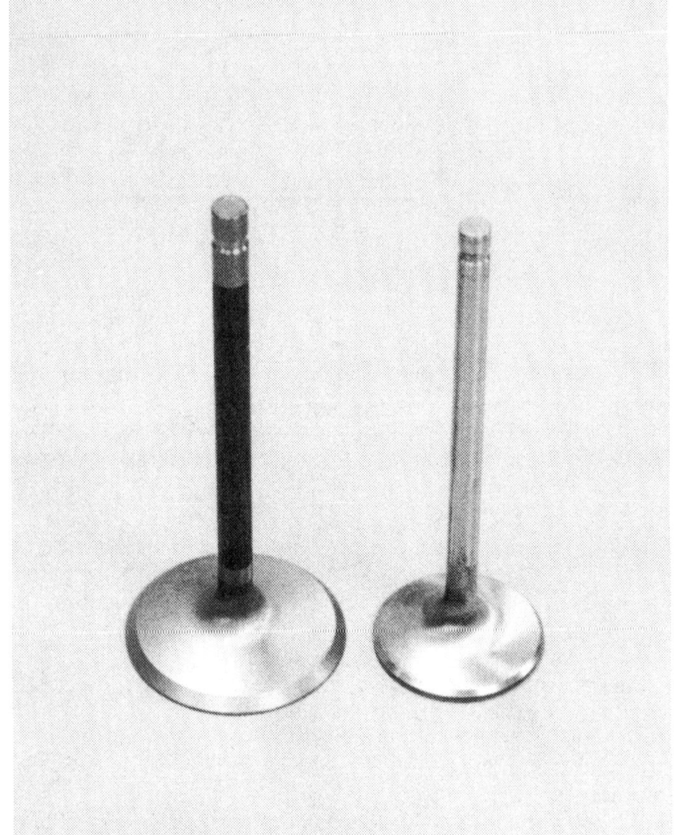

Ford offered "Pro Stock" titanium intake and semi-hollow exhaust valves for the 351-C as an over-the-counter option. They are hard to find these days, though.

Typical of current specialty performance valve spring combinations is Isky's inner and outer spring with flat-wound damper. Such a combination requires smaller-than-stock stem seals. An aluminum retainer should not be used with such a damper on the street.

Crane offers a triple spring combination for the Cleveland which gives exceptional travel before coil binding.

Stock guide plates for 5/16-inch pushrods and screw-in rocker studs are available from Ford.

Manley offers guide plates for larger than stock 3/8-inch pushrods.

any type of street or other low-maintenance/durability running, do not use an aluminum retainer with a spring using a flat-wound damper. They will chafe the underside of the retainer, not only weakening it but also sending fragments of aluminum into the oil. Better would be something like Isky's chrome-moly retainers, part number 507 ST.

All 351-C rockerarms appear identical, being of stamped steel with a 1.73:1 ratio. Incidentally, these are the same type used on the Boss 302 and on 429-460 engines. Supposedly, the Boss rockers are given a better heat treatment than the others (C9ZZ-6564-A), and of course they are used with adjustable type fulcrums. Two-barrel engines used aluminum nonadjustable sled fulcrums, and for any performance hydraulic-cam valve train these should be changed to the sintered metallic 4V type (DOOZ-6A528-A) which are identical except for material. Since both the rockers and the fulcrums are subjected to severe loads and large wear areas, a good and inexpensive tip for performance building is to have these pieces Tufftrided to increase surface strength. This will also reduce the chances of a pushrod tip poking through a rocker. In case you have any trouble locating the adjustable rocker/fulcrum combinations, these are available from Manely (43128) and well as from standard replacement parts houses such as TRW or McQuay-Norris. For another interesting solution to possible rocker-fulcrum failure in Clevelands, see the building tips section following.

The building tips section will also discuss the peculiarities of the Cleveland engine oiling system which initially routes all oil down the right lifter gallery. For this reason it is helpful to restrict oil being carried through the lifters and pushrods to the rockerarms. One way to do this is to install oil restrictor pushrods, such as sold by Gapp and Roush (GR5S-6565-C, -D, -G, or -H). These pushrods are also 3/8-inch in diameter, which is preferable over the stock 5/16-inch diameter rods for high rpm or high valve spring tension applications. Manley offers a 3/8-inch slot guide plate for use with such pushrods. Stock Ford 351-C pushrods are all identical except for Boss/HO units (DOOZ-6565-F) which are hardened so that they won't wear against the guide plates. When guide plates are used, it is imperative to install hardened pushrods. If in doubt, try cutting the surface of the pushrod with the edge of a triangular file; if it's hardened, the file should not cut it.

If nonadjustable rockerarms are used, pushrod length might need to be adjusted slightly to compensate for head milling or for valve tip facing. Ford pushrods are available in standard length (8.250 inches), .060-inch over, and .060-inch under. The G&R pushrods come in 8.250-inch and 8.300-inch lengths. Other things being equal, most builders recommend using the longer pushrods with anti-pumpup hydraulic lifters to reduce some of the "slop" from the valve train for better high rpm response. And, finally, a third consideration for pushrods in a Cleve-

For street or endurance racing engines something other than aluminum valve spring retainers are recommended. With single springs and mild-lift cams the stock retainers are fine. For more radical cams or multiple springs, Isky chrome-moly retainers are a good choice.

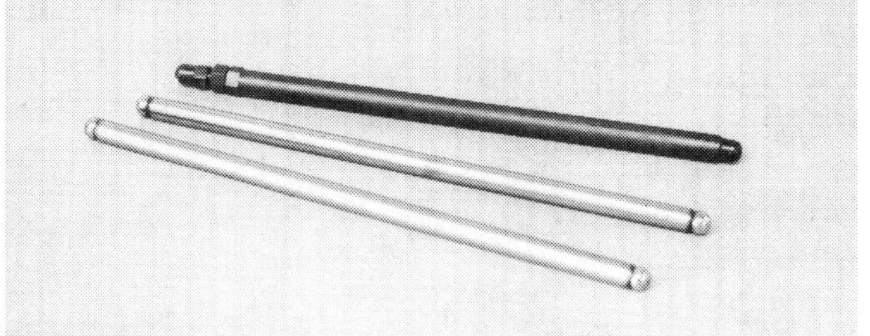

Standard Ford pushrods can be ordered in .060-inch longer or shorter-than-standard lengths to compensate for head milling, wear, etc. with nonadjustable rockers. Another alternative is the Isky adjustable pushrod (top) for the Cleveland.

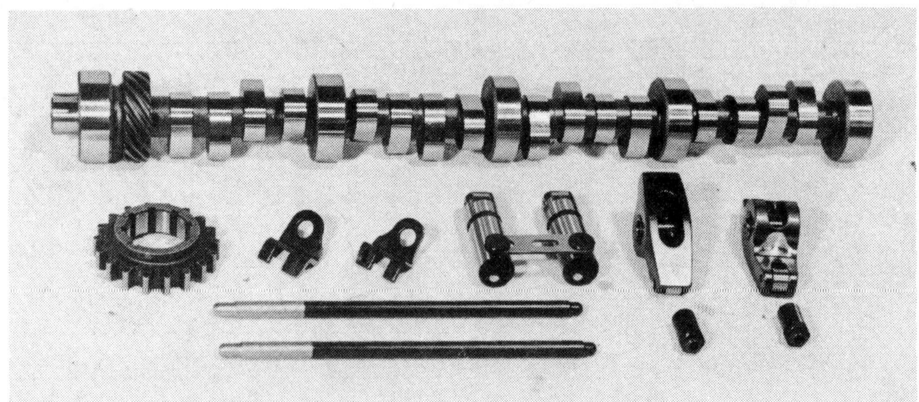

Since the Cleveland is a good and popular racing engine the performance parts manufacturers offer the racers all the exotic components they could want, plus research and development continue daily. This roller cam and related hardware are an example of high-technology components; notice the individual guide plates for precise pushrod alignment.

land would be an adjustable type, such as Isky chrome-moly tubular pieces (393 DA). If you want to run a solid cam in your 351 and you don't want to go to the trouble to convert the rockers to an adjustable type, this is your easy way out. Obviously it is a compromise (that is, it's not exactly the *right* way to do it) but it is quick and relatively simple. These adjustables can also be used in extreme cases where standard length pushrods will not match up properly with hydraulic lifters. However, they are relatively heavy, they are not as fool-proof as conventional pushrods, and they are generally considered to have a rev limit of 6000 rpm.

If you are using a solid cam, another way to control oiling to the rockers is to install "metering" type lifters. Known as "flapper-valve" lifters (because you can hear the metering plate "flap" inside if you shake it), they incorporate a small inertia valve inside to limit the amount of oil transferred to the pushrods. Ford made a lifter of this type for use with their "Pro Stock" solid camshaft (cam & kit D1ZX-6250-FA; lifter only D1ZX-6500-CA); however, this lifter and cam employed a unique lifter face radius different from all other Ford cams, and neither can be used with any other type. In all cases, be sure that the lifters you choose are compatible with the specific camshaft they will ride on. To be safe, buy cam and lifters from the same manufacturer as a matched set. Never use worn lifters on a new cam.

Most likely the majority of you will be using a hydraulic lifter setup anyway. There is little variation in hydraulic lifter types these days, and the anti-pumpup (high bleed rate) variety are excellent. Hydraulics such as Isky #202 HY "Superlifters" are good to 7000 rpm with proper valve springing. If you'd like a Ford part, try D1AZ-6500-B for their anti-pumpup.

CAMSHAFTS

Again, in a book like this, there is simply no way we could recommend a specific cam grind or type for each particular engine/usage. Everybody makes cams for Clevelands—and the same shafts will fit 351-C, 400, and 351-M engines—but these blocks only. Although smallblock and 351-Windsor cams may look similar, the Cleveland uses a larger (big block size) journal at the front of the stick.

As far as stock camshafts go, you have only a couple of decent choices. You will probably notice that duration figures on Cleveland profiles are relatively small; don't forget that there are giant ports and valves to dump air-fuel in and get exhaust out. What this engine needs, if anything, is some velocity in the intake manifold. Hence, the shorter duration, higher lift cams are preferable, especially for any application that requires some low- to mid-range response. The early ('70-71) 4V engines came with a surprisingly "small" hydraulic cam that measured 226° duration intake, 270° exhaust with .427-inch lift. The preferable Ford hydraulic grind is the '71-72 CJ cam, which has the same profile as the 428 CJ: 270°/290° duration and .481-inch/.490-inch lift (D1ZZ-6250-A). The '71 and '72 CJ cams have exactly the same profiles, but the '72 cam is indexed four degrees retarded. If you have a '72 CJ engine or camshaft, get the Ford (or

For all but the most radical performance applications, the most practical way to build a Cleveland is with a hydraulic cam. Modern anti-pumpup hydraulic lifters, such as these Isky "Superlifters," provide excellent street, boat, or bracket power with a minimum of noise and maintenance. They are good for a 7000 rpm rev limit.

One of the first things Ford did to meet smog restrictions, beginning in '72, was to retard the timing on existing camshafts. You can easily set cam timing back to a peppier position with this multi-index crank sprocket available either from Ford or most cam grinders.

one of the specialty) multi-index crank sprocket (D1ZX-6306-BA) and advance the cam four degrees. Ford offered two production solid-lifter cams, the '71 Boss and the '72 HO. The Boss grind is preferable (D1ZZ-6250-B) with specs of 290° duration and .477-inch lift. The HO cam reads 275° duration and .491-inch lift.

The '72 CJ cam is supposedly still available from Ford; but you'd have a hard time finding the Boss 351 stick. However, both the '71 CJ (also referred to as the 351 "GT" cam) and the Boss 351 mechanical camshafts and related kits are currently available from Maier Racing under part numbers 1040 and 1050, respectively. And of course, as mentioned, all current specialty cam companies offer several grinds for Clevelands, from economy or RV hydraulics to Pro Stock rollers. Talk (or write) to a customer rep and get an expert suggestion on a grind and type to fit your particular application. Just remember, when it comes to port and head design—and therefore camshaft profiles—the Cleveland Ford is a completely different animal from almost any other engine. Be sure you're talking to someone who knows the difference.

CAMSHAFT I.D. AND APPLICATION

Part Number	Application		Lifter		Intake Events		Exhaust Events		Duration		Lift		Overlap	Identification	
	Engine	Year	Type	Lash	Open	Close	Open	Close	Intake	Exhaust	Lobe	Valve		Mark	Location
D0AZ-6250-B	351 (C) 2V	70/72	HYD		12°BTC 38°ATC	66°ABC 11°ABC	66°BBC 11°BBC	20°ATC 37°BTC	258°	266°	.235	.400	32°	8 R	Between last lobe and journal
D0AZ-6250-C	351 (C) 4V	70/71	HYD		18°BTC 35°ATC	70°ABC 14°ABC	81°BBC 26°BBC	19°ATC 36°BTC	268°	280°	.247—I .262—E	.420—I .450—E	37°	8 R	Same as above and Grooved Dist. Gear
D1ZZ-6250-A	351 (C) CJ	71	HYD		18°BTC 30°ATC	72°ABC 22°ABC	82°BBC 28°BBC	28°ATC 24°BTC	270°	290°	.278 .283	.481—I .490—E	46°		Between last lobe and journal
D2ZZ-6250-B	351 (C) CJ	72	HYD		14°BTC 26°ATC	76°ABC 26°ABC	78°BBC 24°BBC	32°ATC 28°BTC	270°	290°	.278 .283	.481—I .490—E	46°		Between last lobe and journal
D1ZZ-6250-B	351 (C) Boss	71	Mech.	.025	34°BTC 15°ATC	76°ABC 25°ABC	86°BBC 47°BBC	24°ATC 27°BTC	290°	290°	.290	.477	58°	BY	Between last lobe and journal
D2ZZ-6250-A	351C HO	72	Mech.	.025	17½BTC 23°ATC	77½ABC 40°ABC	17½BBC 37°BBC	77½ATC 20°BTC	275°	275°	.298	.490	35°	OF	Between last lobe and journal
D1ZX-6250-FA	351 C	OHO	Mech.	.025	62°BTC 18°ATC	84°ABC 35°ABC	90°BBC 45°BBC	64°ATC 13°BTC	326°	334°	.355—I .368—E	.589—I .612—E	126°	D1ZX-CA	Stamped on end of shaft
D1AZ-6250-A	400	71/72	HYD		17°BTC 30°ATC	59°ABC 8°ABC	71°BBC 37°BBC	21°ATC 37°BTC	256°	272°		.422—I .427—E	38°	B U	Between last lobe and journal

INTAKE MANIFOLD I.D. AND APPLICATION

Part Number	Engine	Year	Type	Material	Bore Diameter		Port Sizes		Notes
					Primary	Secondary	Width	Height	
D1AZ-9424-D	351 C	70/72	2V	Iron	1.71		1.28	1.90	"Rounded" Ports
D0AZ-9424-C	351 C	70/71	4V	Iron	1.64	1.52	1.63	2.38	"Rounded" Ports
D1AZ-9424-A	400	71	2V	Iron	1.71		1.28	1.90	
D2SZ-9424-A	400	72	2V	Iron	1.71		1.28	1.90	
D1ZZ-9424-G	351 C	OHO	4V	Alum	1.64	1.52	1.63	2.38	Dual Plane
D1ZZ-9424-B	351C CJ 351C Boss	71 72	4V	Alum	1.40	2.27	1.63	2.38	Uses Motorcraft "Spreadbore" Model 4300-D Carb.
D2ZZ-9424-A	351 C	72	4V	Iron	1.40	2.27	1.63	2.38	Same as above
D1ZZ-9424-F	351C Boss	71	4V	Alum	1.40	2.27	1.63	2.38	Same as above
D1ZX-9424-FA	351 C	OHO	4V	Alum	2.0	2.0	1.63	2.38	Single Plane

INDUCTION SYSTEMS

There seems to be a little confusion over just exactly what types of four-barrel intake manifolds came on stock 351 Clevelands. Essentially, all four-barrel Cleveland manifolds are the same, but they came in either cast iron or aluminum and with either spreadbore (small primaries, large secondaries) or standard carburetor flanges. Everyone recommends the Boss 351 aluminum "high-rise" intake with standard carb flange (D1ZZ-9424-G)—which is an excellent all-purpose intake. But the truth is that all four-barrel 351-C manifolds *work* the same. The aluminum part will save you 31 pounds; it came in a spreadbore style on the '72 HO as well as with a standard flange on the '71 Boss. Early 4V engines ('70-71) came with a standard flange cast intake, while the '71 CJ, the '72 4V, and the '73 CJ used the cast manifold with a spreadbore. Spreadbore intakes came with an Autolite 4300-D carburetor of approximately 600-cfm capacity; it has never been popular as a performance piece—probably more because of its strange looks than anything else (although it has been known to suffer fuel starvation upon hard cornering). By far the most popular today are standard flange four-barrels—predominantly Holleys which are available in assorted sizes, though the Carter AFB series are also excellent.

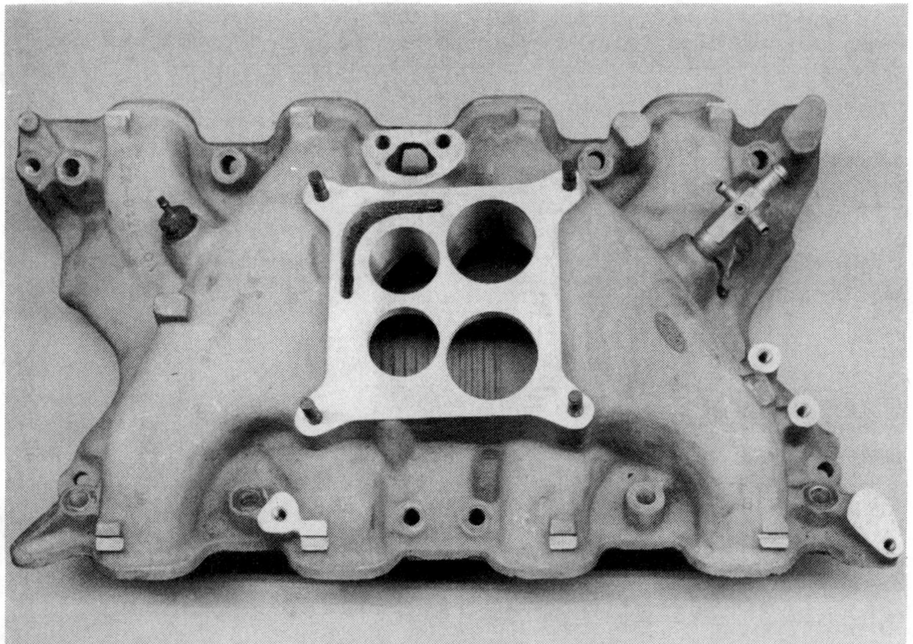

All Cleveland four-barrel intake manifolds were of the same design but some were aluminum, some were cast iron, some had conventional carb flanges, and some were for spreadbores. This is the '72 HO intake which was aluminum with a spreadbore carb flange.

If you have a two-barrel 351-C with the stock heads still on it, you can pick up a quick and cheap 35 horsepower just by bolting on a stock four-barrel manifold—regardless of port mismatch—plus a 780 Holley carb. You should be able to pick up both of these pieces at the "used parts" yard for about 25 bucks. When installing the four-barrel intake on 2V heads, it is recommended that you use paper-type manifold gaskets and rubber end seals (sold by Mr. Gasket, Rocket, etc.) rather than the stock stamped-steel gasket/valley baffle. Obviously your power increase will be substantially more if you install 4V heads to match the intake. But it would probably also help to enlarge the outlets of the 2V intake ports to match the head ports if you go this route. But the quick and dirty "bolt-on" 35 horses obtainable from this swap is hard to beat!

If you already have a 4V engine, you can pick up 11 horsepower by switching from the Autolite-Motorcraft carb to the 780 Holley (considering you have the early intake with the conventional 4300-A carb). If you want to order the 780 Holley from Ford, get D3ZZ-9510-E for stick-shift cars or DOOF-9510-R for

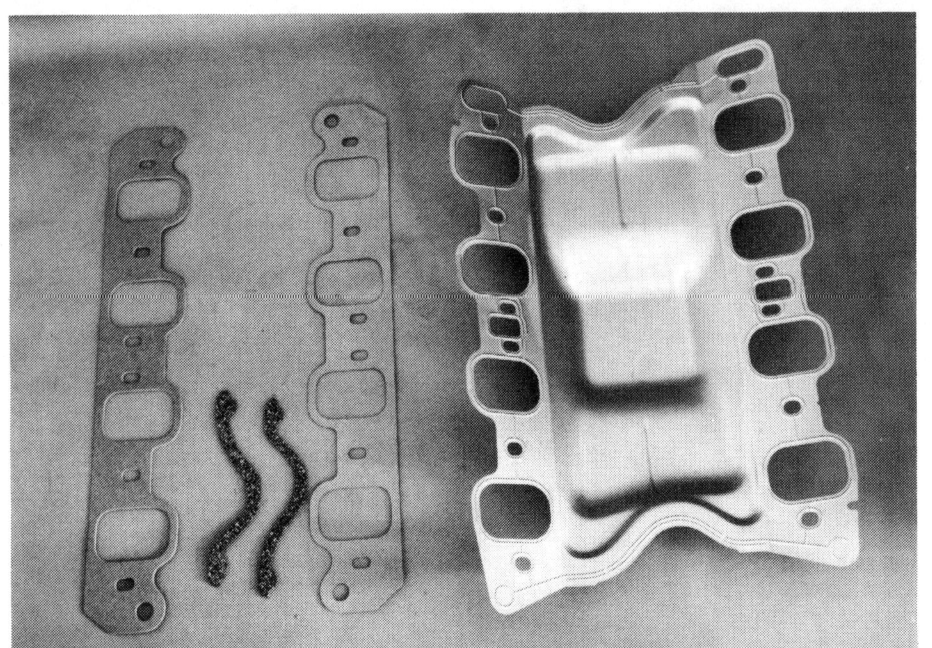

The stock Ford intake manifold gasket is stamped steel and incorporates a baffle pan to keep hot oil away from the underside of the manifold. Mr. Gasket, Rocket, and others offer thicker composition gaskets (left) which can provide better sealing especially if there is a port mismatch between manifold and heads (e.g., when putting a four-barrel intake on two-barrel heads). You can also trim the stock baffle and install it with the specialty gaskets.

automatics. The 780 with the Ford dual-plane intake is a good recommendation for all-around street performance with something like the CJ hydraulic cam.

If you plan to get into it a little deeper with a stouter hydraulic grind (and acceptable valve train) or else a solid-lifter cam, you'll want a little better manifold and definitely more carb. Early Ford factory testing showed that simply adding an 850-cfm Holley to the stock intake produced an increase of 18 horsepower over the 780, or 29 horses over the stock four-barrel. The 850 Holleys come in two common types, the earlier R-4223 "center-squirter" and the later R-4781 "double-pumper". The center-squirt model has a single accelerator pump to feed four nozzles located in the center of the carb; the double-pumper, as the name implies, has a separate accelerator pump for each circuit (primary and secondary). The double-pumper is, of course, the one to get for the most demanding performance use. On the other hand, the Cleveland is an easy engine to over-carburete. If you aren't going to run it at wide open throttle very often, probably a better suggestion for a high performance street/strip carb would be the 800-cfm double-pumper, R-4780.

When it comes to specialty/performance intake manifolds for the Cleveland, you have plenty of choice. Ford even offered one—though it is quite rare—which would be excellent for longer circle track racing. It was a single-plane aluminum manifold for a single Holley Dominator (model 4500) carburetor, and it was listed as "competition only" (D1ZX-9425-FA). Much more readily available are the current offerings from Edelbrock, Holley, Weiand, and Offenhauser. If you would like a good street or ski boat performance intake, the Edelbrock #F-351-4V is very similar to the Boss 351 dual-plane intake, except that it has runners that are actually smaller than the stock Ford. Edelbrock claims that this intake not only can flow more volume than the intake ports, but that it even increases the flow through the ports by increasing velocity in the runners. This is the intake for any Cleveland suffering from "flat" low- or mid-range throttle response due to overly large ports for the given application (such as a heavy vehicle, high differential gearing, load-pulling, etc.). If you use this intake, *do not* open the manifold runners to match the intake ports; it is designed to work the way it is.

If you are looking for output in the upper rpm range, but still plan to drive the streets, an Edelbrock "Torker" or similar X-type intake is a good choice. Holley offers their "Strip Dominator" for serious single four-barrel competition (this is not a street manifold); and tunnel rams are available in both single and dual four-barrel configurations. Light, early model street rods with Cleveland engines seem to have very good success with a single four-barrel type tunnel ram intake, even in stop and go traffic or on cross-country runs.

IGNITION

The '71 Boss and '72 HO Clevelands came with a dual-point, dual-diaphragm, centrifugal-advance distributor (D1ZZ-12127-D) which works fairly well, especially in applications combining an automatic transmission with a healthy cam. With an automatic trans, hook up the outer diaphragm

An excellent street performance package for a 351-C is the Edelbrock F351-4V intake with a Holley #6619 (600cfm) carburetor. Doug Cook uses this combination on the majority of his Pantera installations.

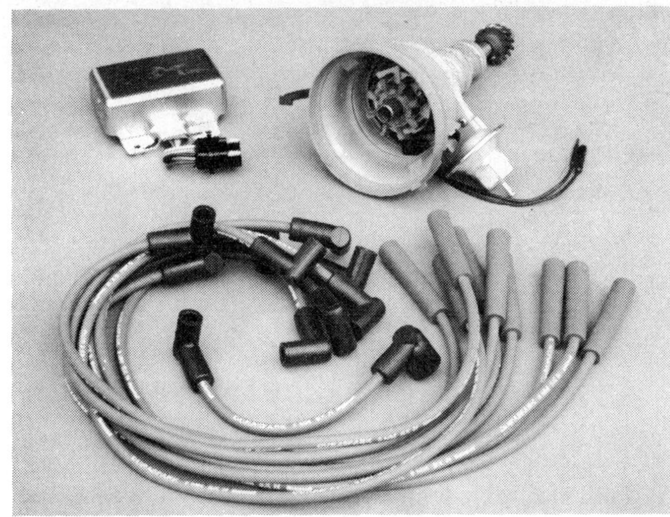

All new Fords come with electronic breakerless ignition systems and excellent 8mm high tension secondary wires. Control modules and hook-up wiring has varied from year to year, however, on stock units which are designed primarily for smog control. The Motorcraft solid-state electronic ignition conversion kit (DZ-5003), sold at all Ford dealers, will install in any '67-74 Ford single-point distributor.

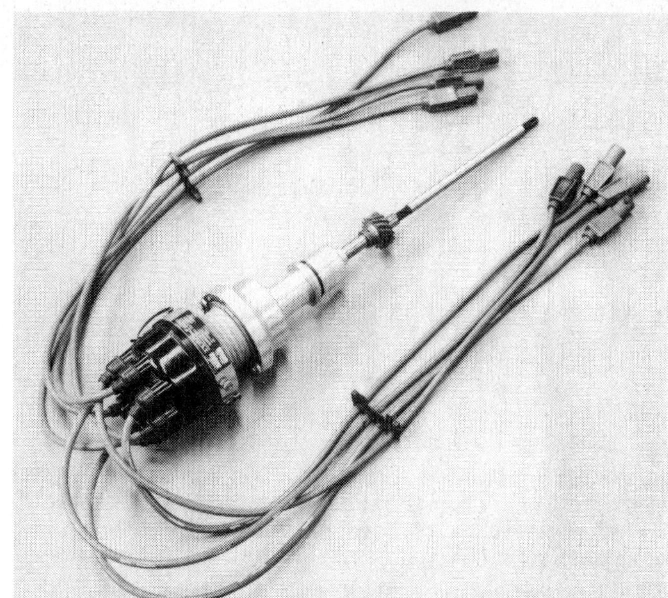

You'd be surprised what you can find in the way of specialty ignitions for Clevelands if you shop around. This is a Roto-Faze dual-point distributor (#SRS 8P) shown with a Milodon oil pump driveshaft and with 8mm spark plug wires.

cannister only, and connect it to manifold vacuum rather than venturi vacuum. If you have a single-point, dual-diaphragm distributor in your engine you can convert it to a dual-point operation with Ford conversion kit D1AZ-12A132-A. The stock single-point distributor admittedly has a performance limit of about 5000 rpm, at which point the advance plate begins to wobble (the condition will obviously be worse in worn units). When installing the dual-point kit, Ford states that the advance curve should not be modified other than with springs designated, which give the following curve:

DISTRIBUTOR RPM	DISTRIBUTOR DEGREES
400	0°
500	½°
750	3½°
1000	6°
1200	8½°
1300	9½°
1400	10°

This is with the kit installed in a "10 degree" distributor (early 351 distributors had 10°, 13°, or 15° advance-limit plates in them; there is a small inspection hole in the breaker plate, next to the coil wire outlet, through which you should read 10L). Once the converted distributor is installed, set initial advance to 16° at idle (800 rpm). This will yield a total of 36° advance by 2800 rpm—16° initial, 20° (crank) in the distributor. Maximum recommended advance is 38-40 degrees. (However, if the engine "pings" under heavy-load acceleration, you may have to use less total and less initial advance.) With the dual-points, set the breaker gap at .018- to ,020-inch for each point, or block off one set of points at a time with a piece of cardboard and set the other to 25° with a dwell meter. This will give a total of 32-34°dwell for the pair. To replace the contact points, use two sets of 289 hi-po points (C3AZ-12171-A). These are lightweight points that resist bounce, and they have a relatively high spring tension (27-30 ounces), so lube the cam with white grease and check regularly for rubbing block wear.

Ford did not make a high performance distributor, as such, to fit the 351-Cleveland, and they readily admit that ignition reliability above 8000 rpm requires a good specialty igniter, such as an Accel or Mallory. Nascar racers sometimes go to great lengths to camouflage one of these distributors to look just like a stock Ford (Nascar rules require a "stock-type" ignition). For non-restricted high performance use, one of these dual-point distributors would be a wise (and relatively cheap) investment. Maier Racing offers a special "Shelby" Mallory dual-point for the 351-C under part number

In recent years the Autotronic Controls MSD-7 transistorized ignition has gained wide spread notoriety. It provides several "sparks" during each firing cycle and will work either with breaker points or with most conventional "breakerless" triggers. It is also compatible with most electronic tachometers.

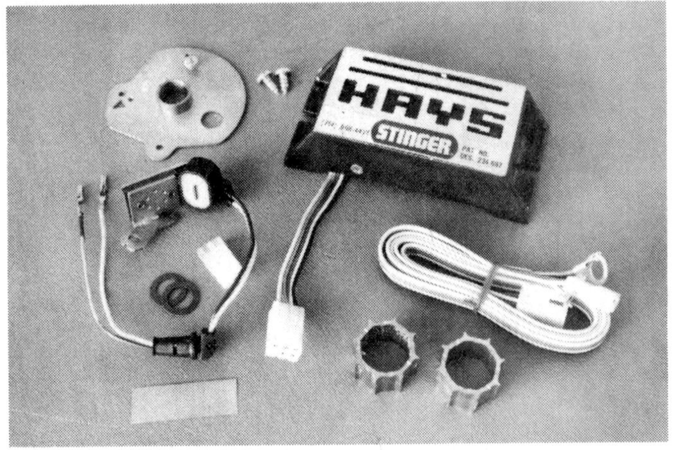

These days an electronic breakerless ignition system is the most practical performance choice, and the Hays Stinger is one of the favorite choices of drag racers. The Hays conversion kit for Fords installs in the stock distributor.

The Ford electronic ignition develops plenty of spark, but Doug Cook likes to combine it with an Accel Super Coil as well.

4502. If you would rather stick to stock Ford parts, here's a hot tip: 429/460 distributors also fit the Cleveland, and Ford Industrial/Marine dealers (located across the country—ask at your Ford dealer, or look in the Yellow Pages) offer an excellent Prestolite "Marine" distributor for the 460 under Ford part number D3JL-12100-G. It is a single-point unit, but is far superior to even the Boss 351 dual-point, showing no signs of breaking down until after 8000 rpm. It can easily be recurved to give 38-40° total advance in the engine, and to advance 15° by 1250 rpm in the distributor.

Electronic "pointless" ignitions are probably the wisest choice for any application these days, however, since they deliver both better performance and lower maintenance. Ford's Motorcraft division has recently introduced their own solid-state electronic ignition conversion kit for single-point distributors used in any Ford V-8 from '67-74. The kit, part number DZ-5003, contains a small electronic module, a simple plug-in wiring harness, and a trigger wheel that slips over the cam in the stock distributor. This kit can be used with the original cap, rotor, and plug wires, but it would probably be wise to also install the new Ford high-voltage distributor cap, spacer, and rotor (D7VY-12A217-A, cap; DR-323, rotor), and new Ford 8mm high-tension "Duraspark" plug cable set (D7PZ-12259-C). Or you may prefer to select one of the several specialty electronic ignition systems available for the Cleveland.

Cleveland engines use 14mm spark plugs. Don't think there is any speed secret involved—the smaller diameter was necessary to allow room for the big exhaust port boss and still get a socket wrench on the plug. A chart below shows heat ranges for AC 14mm plugs, which are readily available. One caution: do not use "Power Tip" or any other extended tip plug in the Cleveland if you are running the pop-up pistons. At high rpm the rods may "stretch" just enough to let the pistons nick the plugs, closing the gap.

AC 14mm SPARK PLUGS

	Standard Gap	Power Tip	Racing Gap
↑		AF 52	
		AF 42	
	AF 3	AF 32	
HOT	AF 2	AF 22	
COLD	AF 1	AF 12	
	AF 901		
	AF 701		AF503
	AF 501		AF 303
↓			AF 103

HEADERS

As usual, header recommendations depend upon several factors, including: the rpm range in which the engine will be expected to deliver max power, the weight of the car, the type of transmission and rear end ratio being used. What it usually boils down to, however, is who makes a set of prefabricated headers to fit the particular body style in which your Cleveland happens to reside. If it's a Mustang or a Torino/Ranchero, you should find a few choices; after that the pickings get slim. If you do get a choice of tube

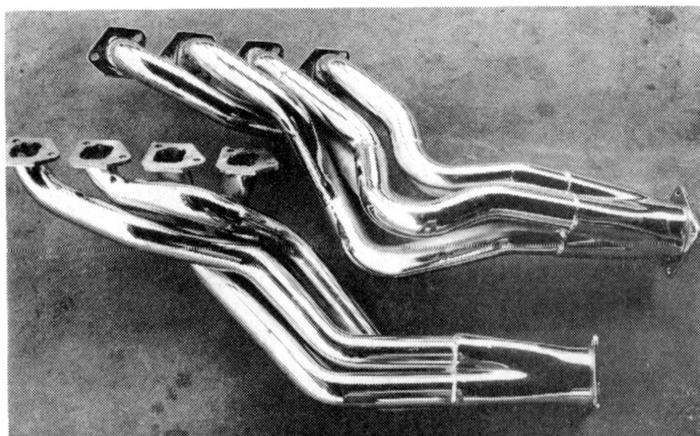

Several types of readymade headers are available for Cleveland engines in Ford bodies. These are by Appliance, designed for Mustangs but slightly modified to fit a 351-C in a '56 Ford pickup.

They won't fit in anything but a Pantera or a back-motor digger, but the wildest in headers are the 360° variety. These are made by Hall Pantera, Bellflower, CA.

High-volume oil pumps are readily available for Clevelands from TRW, Pioneer Products, or several of the specialty/performance suppliers.

Although gear drives are made for Clevelands, most racers use the inexpensive and rugged Cloyes "True Roller" timing chain and gear set (right). It comes with a three-position multi-index crank sprocket. If you retain the stock chain, use the steel replacement cam sprocket (left), rather than the plastic part.

sizes and lengths, here are some guidelines: 2¼-inch o.d. (or 2-inch i.d.) primaries, 34 inches long, with 3½- to 4½-inch diameter collectors for drag or circle track competition; 1.75- to 2-inch o.d. primaries, 40 inches long for street use.

MISCELLANEOUS

One of the major improvements for a 351-C that we haven't mentioned yet is a high-volume oil pump. These are available from several sources (such as Maier Racing), but you can probably get one at your local parts house. Pioneer Products makes one that produces 25% more volume (50086) and TRW sells a high-volume pump (M-84AHV). Jack Roush recommends installing a Moroso #2285 100psi relief spring in the stock oil pump, fitting the rotors for .002- to .003-inch clearance, and then deburring the pump case around the mounting flange and along the "neck" to prevent cracking under extreme conditions. Ford offered a similar oil pump spring (D2ZX-6670-A). Unfortunately, no one offers a windage tray for the Cleveland. There are all sorts of special oil pans on the market, many of which are made for specific uses such as oval racing. For drag racing, a rear-sump oil pan such as offered by Moroso would be smart if your chassis allows it. Roush suggests increasing the depth of the entire oil pan one inch (rather than just deepening the sump) by cutting and welding in a strip of metal just below the flange. The stock Ford Boss 351 oil pan came with a baffle inside (D1ZZ-6675-C) . . . if you can find one. You will probably find it interesting to note that HO and Boss 351 engines came with an oil dip stick calibrated for six quarts instead of the regular five, although the pan was the same.

Besides the standard part, you have two "performance" front crank dampers to choose from. The best (but expensive and elusive) damper is the large Boss/HO part with the counterweight in the center (left). The CJ came with a medium-sized damper with the counterweight on the circumference.

Finally, you should consider a replacement for the stock plastic timing gear—an excellent choice being the Cloyes "True Roller" chain system for the Clevelands. These are matched sets with Tufftrided crank and cam sprockets, and the crank sprocket allows for four degrees advanced or retarded timing installation, besides straight up. After you have the timing gear cover in place, you have your choice of three crankshaft dampers. 2V and 4V engines came with the regular small damper; CJ engines used a slightly heavier one (D1AZ-6316-A); and Boss and HO motors came with a large, degreed damper that may be expensive or difficult to find (D2ZZ-6316-A). We might also mention in passing that an aluminum water pump was at one time offered, but they are hard to find (even though they were touted in the final edition of the Ford OHO parts Newsletter). The Ford Pro Stock Pinto book states that the stock 351-C water pump, filled with straight impeller vanes, begins to cavitate at 5000 rpm and actually begins to drain horsepower from the engine at 6000 rpm. They suggest pressing a Boss 302 curved-blade impeller onto the 351-C shaft, and they further suggest turning the outer diameter of the impeller down .500-inch. This is obviously a complicated and expensive procedure, and possibly results in minimal return for the effort—at least according to extensive dyno tests recently conducted on this modification at Hank The Crank's. Using the cut down Boss 302 impeller with every other vane removed, they did not find any horsepower increase in the 6000-7500 rpm range, but they did experience some engine overheating. They found the best results with a Weiand aluminum water pump (8209).

This late model 400 Ford didn't need rebuilding, but felt extremely lazy at factory-rated 160 horsepower. Bolt-on modifications include a set of 351-C four-barrel exhaust manifolds, Holley four-barrel carb, and an RV-type hydraulic cam—and the performance increase is substantial.

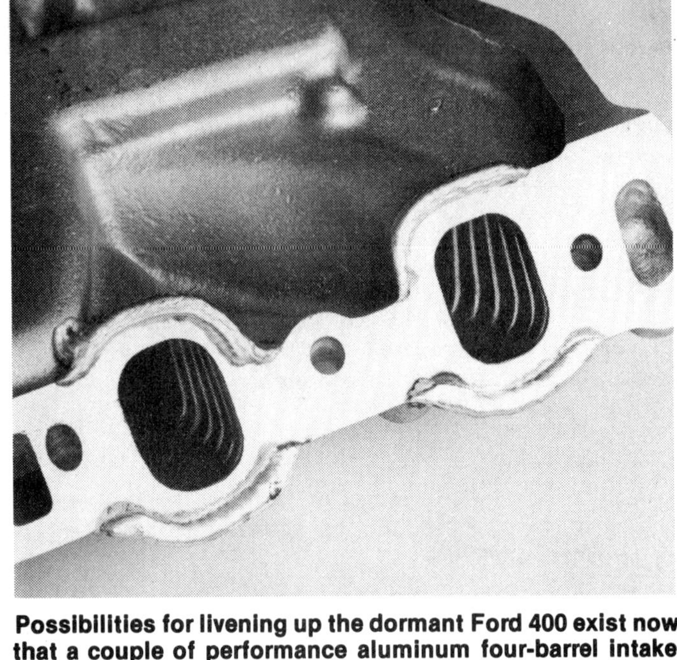

Possibilities for livening up the dormant Ford 400 exist now that a couple of performance aluminum four-barrel intake manifolds are available. You can also bolt high-compression, big-port 351-C quench heads onto the 400, but you must use the wider 400 intake manifold—with much smaller two-barrel ports (this includes the specialty four-barrel 400 manifolds). To seal the giant head port openings, extra material must be welded around manifold ports, as shown; then the manifold flanges must be milled flat. Install with composition 351-C four-barrel gaskets. It's certainly not a perfect parts match. Alternative is to use stock heads and install modified flat-top TRW 351-C pistons.

BUILDING TIPS

One indirect factory information source says of the Cleveland oiling system: "The left-hand gallery is connected to the right-hand gallery at a unique three-way junction at the number five bearing journal. No modification to this lubrication system is required, or recommended, other than using a deep-sump oil pan and installing the heavy duty OHO oil pump spring." Yet, modification of the oiling system seems to be one of the major concerns of Cleveland motor builders, especially for Pro Comp or Superspeedway racing. For good, hard street or boat use, the former evaluation is probably most applicable. But one simple oil system modification might help a little. In the Cleveland, oil is routed from the filter, across to number one main and cam bearings, and then over to a large gallery on the right side of the engine. This gallery intersects each of the lifter bores on that side. Offshoots from this gallery run down to the main bearings, and then oil is carried from the main bearings to the cam through adjacent passages which intersect the main bearing journals. At the rear main a groove in the journal receives oil from the lifter gallery, feeds it to the main bearing, and redirects it up a center passage to the rear cam bearing and up the left passage to the left lifter gallery. Moroso (2205) and others make a kit consisting of small screw-in restrictor plugs for the cam bearing oil passages and the left lifter gallery. To install the kit, simply tap each hole, apply a little Loctite to each plug, and screw the plug in (be very sure it seats far enough into the passage that it doesn't protrude above the saddle, causing the bearing to seat improperly). The thinking behind this modification is that some of the oil pressure intended for the main bearings gets diverted to the cam, and the restrictors allow just a minimum of lubrication to the cam bearings. Probably most helpful are the two restrictors at the rear main, especially the one in the big passage leading to the left lifter gallery.

The problem is that the right lifter gallery is the first source of oil loss in a Cleveland, and it is a problem that is rather difficult to remedy. We will show a couple of current Pro Stock solutions in a following section. But the most logical solution in a street motor is the use of either restrictor-type lifters or pushrods to limit oil flow to the top end, and if you are rebuilding a well-used Cleveland block, it might be wise to check the lifter bores for excessive wear which would allow too much oil to escape around the lifters.

Other than the oil system, there just aren't too many tricks to building a hard running Cleveland. Although not a "tip" as such, the other most common modification procedure is converting hydraulic-cam heads to accept screw-in rocker studs for adjustable rockerarms. As previously mentioned, only the Boss and HO heads came with adjustable rockers. All the rest have rocker pedestals machined with a slot in the top to hold the "positive stop" fulcrum in place and keep the rocker aligned with the valve. The conversion process is very similar to that shown for small block heads, except that the compound angles of the pedestals complicate setting up the job on a mill. Each pedestal should be cut down .300-inch, measured from the bottom of the slot. If you are doing the job on a mill, the angles for the cuts are 3° for the exhaust and 9°30'; 4°15' for the intake. By no means cut the pedestals parallel to the head on a Cleveland. For doing the job at home, you can use a Crane "Stud Boss Cutter" (#99023) with a half-inch drill, and it will align properly in the hole in the pedestal. Once the surfaces have been cut down, drill the holes .088-inch deeper with a .372- to .376-inch bit and then tap them to 7/16-14 UNC threads to accept Ford screw-in rocker studs (C9ZZ-6A527-A). Accompanying diagrams show dimensions for cutting the rocker bosses, as well as for cutting the spring seat and valve guide areas of other Cleveland heads to match those on the Boss (so that hardened spring seat cups and combination springs can be installed).

Clevelands have been known to have a bit of trouble with rockerarms. To begin with, though all Cleveland rockers are basically the same (they all have the same part number), Ford had some made by different suppliers. Ones that have a couple of bumps or "lugs" on the top rails at either side of the fulcrum will cause an interference problem with pushrods if used with a cam of .550-inch or greater lift. The head of the pushrod hits the back or heel of this rocker at full lift. Other Cleveland rockers do not appear to have this problem (though it is always wise to check not only pushrod clearance at full lift, but also to make sure the slot in the rocker is long enough so that it doesn't hit the stud at either extreme of travel).

Another problem experienced by some Cleveland owners is the cracking or breaking of rocker fulcrums under heavy duty running. Do not use aluminum 2V fulcrums, as we mentioned earlier. Tufftriding both the rockers and the fulcrums should also help alleviate the situation. But if you are willing to try a Chevy part in your Ford, here's a possible improvement for solid-lifter Clevelands. The "sled type" fulcrum is designed to hold the big stamped steel Ford rocker in place without the use of guide plates or other alignment hardware. But with a solid-lifter cam, guide plates are necessary anyway, and it would be possible to use a rocker that is not self aligning. So why not use a rocker and ball assembly from a big block Chevy instead? It is lighter, the ball fulcrum is stronger and affords much less friction than the sled type, and they hold up very well. The Chevy rockers do have a slightly smaller ratio than the Fords (1.70:1 as opposed to 1.73:1), but the difference would be minimal for most applications, and could be compensated for by the cam grinder in other situations. It's much cheaper than a set of aluminum roller rockers but remember, they must be used with pushrod guide plates.

THE 400 CID

Everything we have discussed so far in this section applies specifically to the 351 Cleveland, but most also applies indirectly to the 400cid Ford as well. The main differences between the 400 and the 351-C are the crankshaft, which has a .500-inch longer stroke plus larger main bearing journals in the 400 (so the 400 crank will not swap into the 351-C); the block, which is approximately one inch taller on the 400; and consequently the intake manifold, which is wider on the 400. However, there are several parts which will interchange between the two engines—such as heads, cams, and pistons—and therein lies hope for the 400.

Very little attention has been paid to the 400 up until now; it has served well as a big, lumbering powerplant for a variety of uses. But Ford has offered it only in low compression versions, and only with a two-barrel induction system (a four-barrel model was listed for the first year of production, but we have never seen one). But now that a couple of performance four-barrel intake manifolds are finally available for the 400—an Edelbrock "Streetmaster" (3190) and a Holley "Street Dominator" (301-14)—we would expect some interest in good basic bolt-on modifications from many of the hundreds of thousands of 400-powered pickups, Rancheros, and full-sized Fords.

A typical bolt-on hop-up for a 400 should probably begin with a set of tube headers and low restriction exhausts, a good specialty or Motorcraft electronic ignition system (if the engine didn't come with one from the factory) along with Ford good blue wires and cap, then a four-barrel manifold with a carburetor in the 600-700cfm range, and finally a relatively mild or RV grind hydraulic camshaft. Dozens of cam grinds are available for the 400, since the same cams also fit the 351-C. These modifications should considerably boost the output from the pitiful 160-170 horsepower beginning point. However, you still haven't done anything to perk up the compression ratio, which stands at 8.0:1 in all engines from '73 to date.

There are two ways to increase compression in the 400, other than milling the stock heads which will yield about half a point at best. The first is also a bolt-on: locate a pair of early 351-C "quench" 4V heads and screw them onto the 400. This will not only give you a good street compression ratio of about 9-9½:1, but you will get the added benefit of the big ports and larger valves as well—undoubtedly even more beneficial on the 400 than on the 351. But these heads are getting scarce and somewhat expensive. If the engine is due for a rebuild anyway, a better solution might be to install a set of flat-top TRW 351-C pistons (L-2379F). Since both the 351 and the 400 have the same bore and the same piston compression height (meaning the pin is located in the same place for both), the switch is relatively simple. The only problem is that the piston pin diameter is .975-inch in the 400, compared to .912-inch in the 351-C. Consequently, the pinhole in the 400 rod (which must be used, since it is longer) is too big for the 351-C piston pin. The .063-inch difference is too much material to hone out of the pin bosses in the pistons, so the simplest solution appears to be bushing the 400 rods and floating the pins. Any good machine shop can do this for you, including shortening the pin approximately .100-inch and cutting a pair of grooves in the piston pin bores so that a pair of Spirolocs can be installed to secure the pin. The TRW piston is cast with "outboard" pin bosses to allow this operation. This combination, with the stock 400 heads, yields about 10:1 compression, which should be plenty for most applications. If you want to really pump up a 400, you could use the quench heads and the TRW pistons—or even the pop-up 351 slugs—but you aren't going to find filling station gasoline that will run such an engine these days.

351 CLEVELAND/400 CID BLUEPRINT SPECIFICATIONS		STOCK	PERFORMANCE
Main Bearing Clearance		.001-.0025	.002-.0025
Rod Bearing Clearance		.002-.003	.0025-.003
Rod Side Clearance		.014-.024	.0025
Piston to Bore Clearance		.004	.0065-.0075
Piston Pin Clearance		.0003-.0005	.0008
Piston Ring Gap		.017—#1 & 2	.015—#1 .012—#2
Piston Ring to Groove		.002-.004	.001-.002
Piston to Valve Clearance		.070—I .100—E	.100—I .100—E
Piston to Deck Height		.015	.019
Crankshaft End Play		.004-.008	.004-.008
Valve Stem to Guide		.0008-.0018—I .0011-.0021—E	
Lifter to Bore		.0007-.0027	
BOLT TORQUE SPECIFICATIONS			
Cylinder Head	Step 1 Step 2 Step 3 Step 4	55 65 95-100 	60-70 75-85 95-105 120
Intake Manifold		23-25 (5/16) 28-32 (3/8)	
Connecting Rod Bolts		40-45	55
Main Bearing Caps		60-70	95-105
4-Bolt Main Outers		35-40	
Rockerarm Stud		65-75	
Rockerarm Bolt		17-23	
Oil Pan		7-9 (1/4) 11-13 (5/16)	
Cam Thrust Plate		9-12	
Cam Sprocket		40-45	
Flywheel to Crank		75-85	
Clutch to Flywheel		12-20	
Crank Damper Bolt		130-150	
Spark Plug (14mm)		10-15	
Front Cover		12-15	
Water Pump Bolts		12-15	
Exhaust Manifold		15-20	
Valve Cover		3-5	
Distributor Hold Down		12-15	

Comparatively speaking, Fords are popular in the Pro Stock ranks of drag racing. But that doesn't mean that there are more than a few dozen Pro Stock Fords in the country. We do not expect many of the readers of this book to become involved in an actual Pro Stock 351 Cleveland engine building project, but we do believe that the majority of you will be interested in the "state of the art" as well as in the several pointers you may be able to pick up from Pro Stock engine builders and subsequently apply to your own Cleveland Ford—whatever its ultimate use may be.

Pro Stock engines are sort of like Indianapolis engines in that horsepower extracted per cubic inch is much more important than total power output. Weight breaks for all drag racing classes continue to vary (if you ask a Ford racer, he will contend that they are never in his favor), but a typical Pro Stock Mustang II with a Cleveland will probably displace about 340 cubic inches. Unlike the Indy racer, the Pro Stocker is designed to build brutal amounts of power for very short periods of time. It'll be lucky to run a few miles before it gets torn down, inspected, and reassembled. Consequently, several of the Pro Stock techniques are not practical for engines that must be driven regularly, or even raced regularly, without continual teardowns. The average Pro Stock drag racer keeps a "quiver" of engines at hand: one in the car, another in the trailer for between-rounds swaps, and at least one or two back at the garage for back-up or for experimentation. That should give you an idea of what Pro Stock racing is like.

Though only a handful are being campaigned, the likes of Don Nicholson, Gapp and Roush, and Lee Hunter are keeping the Ford name in the limelight of professional drag racing. Keeping a Pro Stock Ford in the winner's circle means constantly redeveloping, running on the ragged edge, and carrying plenty of back-up motors.

We have mentioned that the heads make an engine. This maxim pertains directly to Pro Stock engine building—to the point that most competitive racers guard their latest port and chamber designs behind a cloak of secrecy. The basic approach to Cleveland heads for Pro Stock use has been fairly well known for several seasons, however. It is a unique set of circumstances: in the past a port grinder's main job was to get more mixture *into* the cylinder; but in the Cleveland the factory has taken care of most of that job. The deficiency lies on the exhaust side of the head, creating an "imbalance" between intake flow and exhaust port capabilities. The problem on the Cleveland is not so much the size of the exhaust port, but rather the angle of departure from the valve. True, the valve is slightly angled in the right direction to begin with (though not nearly as much as the intake is), but then the exhaust passage makes a hard dogleg turn before it exits the head. The bottom of the runner actually turns about 120°. The universal remedy is major surgery on the exhaust side of the head, by means of a mill, and the installation of a "high-port" plate

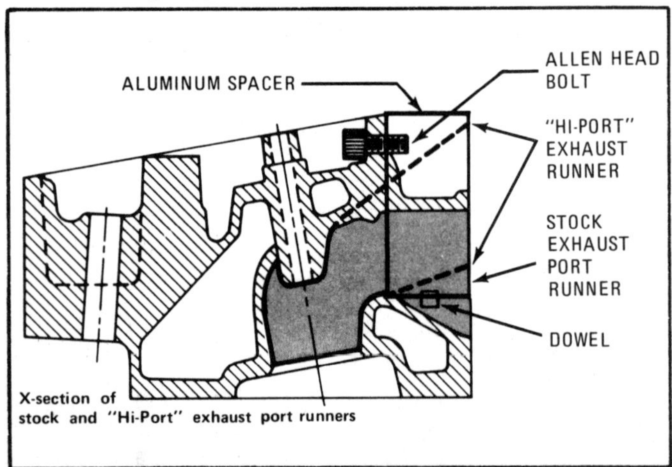

Though the Cleveland ports have gained a great reputation for flowing large quantities of intake mixture, the stock exhaust port configuration is very restrictive. The exhaust port was "bent" sharply to tuck the exhaust manifolds close to the block, allowing clearance for stock engine compartments. It is possible to improve exhaust flow by extensively modifying the head.

The most obvious design characteristic of a Pro Stock Cleveland is the raised exhaust port plate, a standard among frontrunners. A large slice is cut out of the head, even with the valve cover rail and just above the spark plugs. The effective exhaust port opening becomes obvious here.

The new port plate is cut from a billet of aluminum. Angled slots are milled for spark plug access.

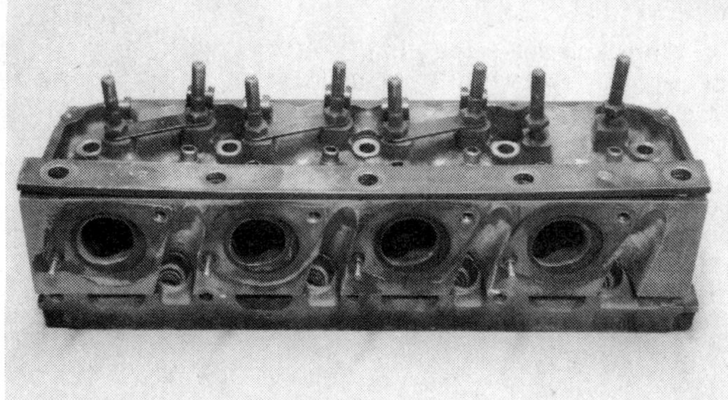

The installed port plate accepts stock head bolts (steel strap evens torque load and keeps bolts from chafing the aluminum), and raises the port outlets about one inch for much smoother flow. You can see "wasted" bottoms of original ports below the plate.

approximately one inch thick and three inches tall. This plate, with new exhaust ports cut in it, effectively raises the exhaust outlets about an inch and decreases the turn of the centerline of the passage from more than 90° to about 60°. In some cases the total area of the exhaust port is actually reduced, but flow is greatly increased. (The reason for the sharp angle of the stock exhaust ports was to allow the stock manifolds to tuck closely to the block and thereby afford more clearance in an already tight engine compartment.) Raised ports would, of course, be greatly compromised by any headers that turned sharply enough to fit in the stock chassis. Pro Stockers must use free-flowing "fender well" type headers to extract the full benefit of the reworked heads. And since every Pro Stock chassis is a little different, these headers must be custom-made to fit the car.

On the intake side, designs vary with individual builders, but generally these ports are also raised slightly by slabbing (welding or brazing) the bottom of the runner to improve the intercept angle with the valve centerline. The finished intake port usually ends up slightly smaller than stock, but relocated. All Pro Stockers currently use tunnel ram intakes, such as the Edelbrock UR-19 or the Weiand 2994, and these usually get as much building up and reworking as the heads (specific manifold modifications are, again, top secret). Standard selection on top of the intake is a pair of Holley Dominator carbs, usually as highly modified as the rest of the induction system.

Just as important as intake and exhaust tailoring is combustion chamber design. Several variables coexist in the combustion chamber, but basically this is a marriage of a chosen piston dome configuration and a complementary chamber shape that will maintain sufficient compression and allow free flow of gasses. The standard 4V Boss valve size is plenty big for most Pro Stockers, the particular choice for intakes usually being the TRW 2.190-inch titanium pieces and Manley 1.710-inch stainless steel exhausts.

Some racers choose specific bore and stroke combinations (for a given displacement) primarily to arrive at preferable rod-length-to-crank-stroke ratios, but Lee Hunter stresses that he prefers at least an .080-inch overbore in the 351 block to reduce cylinder wall shrouding of the valves, mainly for better intake flow. Obviously the Cleveland block poses overboring limitations—but more on this in a minute. Like most professional racers, Hunter has pistons custom made to his specifications (his are made by Venolia), but he will readily admit that even he has trouble distinguishing his

When it comes to winning with a Pro Stock Ford the real differences start right here: late night hours hand-shaping combustion chambers, piston domes, intake and exhaust ports, and intake manifold runners and then testing them on the flow bench and at the track. Each racer has his own tricks and his own secrets and none would dare divulge his latest design. By next week it would probably be obsolete, anyway.

The raised ports would be totally ineffective if headers that bend sharply downwards to clear a stock frame were used. Note how each pipe on these headers (custom built by Hooker) clears the head by several inches before turning downward.

What appears to be an assortment of off-the-shelf induction components is really another bag of racer's secrets. This setup, run by Lee Hunter, consists of a highly modified Edelbrock UR-19 tunnel ram manifold with a pair of Holley Dominator carbs modified by Braswell.

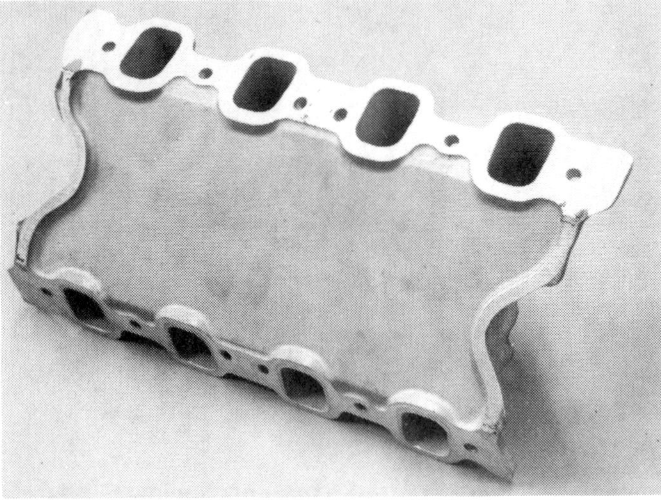

Keeping the intake mixture cool will increase the density of the charge and increase power. Most modern competition manifolds have an isolated plate across the manifold to prevent hot oil splash from reaching the intake runners. The example shown here is a Weiand tunnel ram. Lee Hunter's highly-modified manifold did not originally have an isolated valley cover but he removed the webbing between the runners and welded a separate plate across the valley opening.

"Hunter dome" from a "Nicholson dome" or a "Glidden dome." The fact is that the top Ford Pro Stock racers, given their various methods of approach, have arrived at many of the same conclusions on how to make the most power from a Cleveland. Hunter gets his pistons with a machined dome and predrilled gas ports—small holes drilled around the circumference of the piston top, intersecting holes drilled into the back of the top ring land (to increase sealing of the compression ring), and then hand contours the dome for maximum compression squeeze with his current combustion chamber shape. Given the smaller displacement of the 340 engine, plus the large diameter of the valves and correspondingly large valve reliefs in the pistons, getting a compression ratio of even 12½:1 is difficult. In the piston he installs an .088-inch wall full-floating B&B pin, retained with double Spirolocs (four per piston). With the gas-ported piston, he keeps the ring-to-land clearance on the top ring as close to zero as possible to eliminate flutter. The piston pin compression height is 1.660 inches. And to keep reciprocating weight as light as possible with maximum strength for short bursts of speed, he uses Childs and Alberts aluminum connecting rods. In the 340 motor with a 3.250-inch stroke the rod length is 5.850 inches, giving a 1.8:1 rod-to-throw ratio. Hunter claims that 1.73:1 would be optimum, but would require too heavy a piston for this combination.

It is interesting to note that all Ford Pro Stockers (that we know of) use the cast Cleveland crankshaft, and none report crank failure as a major problem. Of course, the crank is highly reworked. Since a good Pro Stock engine will rev into the 10,000 rpm area, the crank must be internally balanced. This is accomplished by adding "Mallory metal" slugs, a very dense and therefore heavy form of steel, to the counterbalance weights. To arrive at the 340 cubic inch size, Lee Hunter has the rod journals offset ground down to smallblock Chevy diameter (2.00 inches). This process removes more metal from one side of

Other bottom end components include stock four-bolt main caps and Childs and Alberts aluminum connecting rods. Hunter, like most Pro Stockers running Clevelands, has never broken a crank.

Most Pro Stockers use the stock cast Cleveland crankshaft, but have it internally balanced with slugs of Mallory metal in the counterweights.

Lee Hunter's pistons look something like this when they arrive from Venolia. A fire slot is machined in the crown and gas ports are pre-drilled. A piston like this is considered semi-finished, allowing the engine builder to carefully hand-form the dome to fit the combustion chamber for maximum compression and minimum detonation.

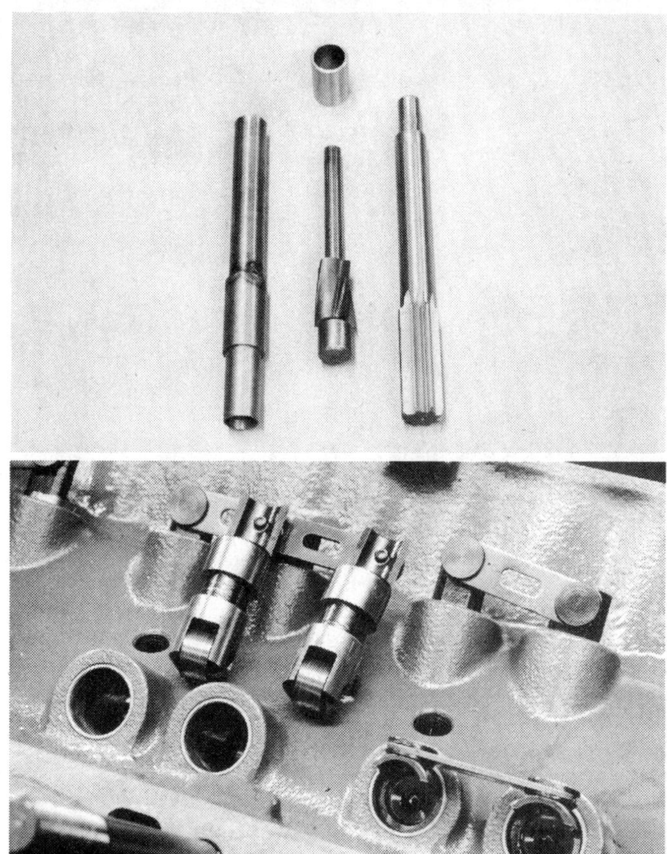

To insure that the Cleveland crank will live through 10,000 rpm races, however, requires major reworking of the oil system. Nicholson and Hunter, among others, install bronze sleeves in each of the right-side lifter bores to reduce oil loss to the lifters and to direct more to the main bearings. Each bore is enlarged with a specially-made self piloting ream, then reamed again to accept a standard bushing (pressed in place). Each bushing is drilled with a small hole to meter oil to the lifters.

the throw than the other, in this case destroking the crank to 3.250 inches without having to build up the throw with welding rod as in other stroking/destroking operations. The smaller throw not only allows the use of readily available Chevy rod bearings, but also reduces crank surface velocity across the face of the bearing, both increasing its life and reducing friction. Hunter's engine specs out to 4.080-inch bore by 3.250-inch stroke for a total of 339 inches.

Besides reworking the heads, the second major area of concentration by most Pro Stockers on the 351-C is the oil circuitry in the block. Jack Roush states that he simply uses the Moroso oil limiter kit (outlined earlier) in his Pro Stock engines, along with the bigger, high pressure oil pump and a rear-sump oil pan (Gapp and Roush part number GR5X-6675-A). Most other builders go to more elaborate oil control systems. Don Nicholson devised a relatively straightforward method for limiting oil flow to the lifters on the right side of the block, and this system is currently used by Bob Glidden and Lee Hunter, among others. They "sleeve" the eight lifter bores on the right side of the engine wtih bronze bushings (Kingwell #116 or Bunting #D-311) which are 1.5 inches long with an inner diameter of 7/8-inch and an o.d. of 1 1/16-inch. The major part of the operation is boring out the lifter holes to the larger size to accept the press-in sleeves, for which a special boring tool must be made. In each bronze bushing a .060-inch hole is drilled to meter oil to the lifter and thence to the pushrod and rocker. A notch is also ground on the outside of the bushing, in the area of the small hole and with a radius of about .50-inch, to allow as much oil as possible to flow down the right-side gallery. To control oiling to the left-side lifter gallery, a restrictor plug is inserted in the passage at the rear main journal as in the Moroso kit.

An alternative method for oiling the center mains in a Cleveland has been developed by Hank the Crank (North Hollywood, CA). Rather than altering the lifter galleries, it goes right to the target by drilling the number two, three and four main bearing oil passages all the way through the block (into the valley chamber) from the bottom, enlarging the upper ends of these new holes, and inserting tubes in them. The tops of the tubes are joined into a "manifold" with threaded elbows and short lengths of tubing, which in turn connect to a fitting inserted through the back of the block just above the bellhousing. This fitting is connected by a longer tube directly to main oil pressure at the oil filter by using an Econoline right angle oil filter adapter and brazing an oil take-off elbow into the head of the hollow bolt that connects the filter adapter to the block. Thus the center mains receive oil directly from the pump. A restrictor plug in the front of the right lifter gallery directs more oil to the front main, and a second oil line is inserted in the oil pressure gauge outlet to direct lubricant to the rear main. This system is available

Another approach to keeping the crank alive in a Cleveland is being marketed by Hank the Crank. Holes are drilled through the block directly to the #2, 3, & 4 main bearings and oil pressure is fed directly to them through this "manifold."

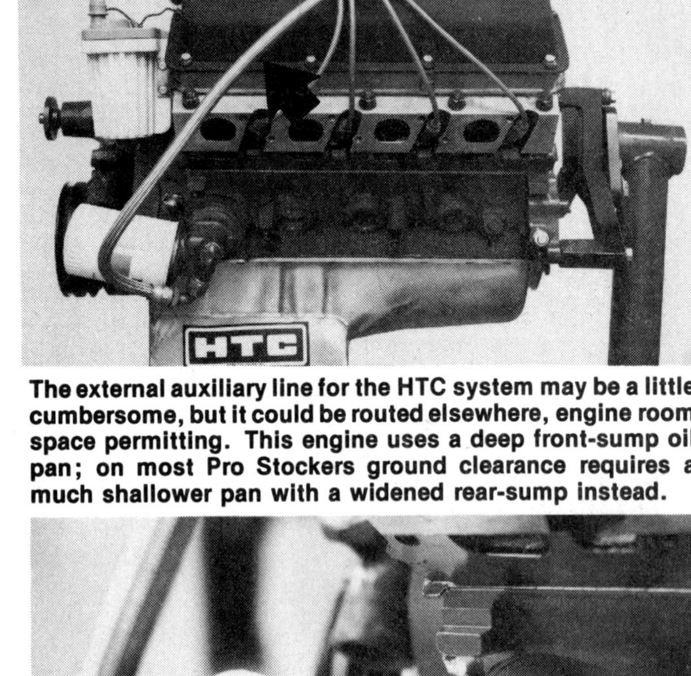

The external auxiliary line for the HTC system may be a little cumbersome, but it could be routed elsewhere, engine room space permitting. This engine uses a deep front-sump oil pan; on most Pro Stockers ground clearance requires a much shallower pan with a widened rear-sump instead.

The rear main receives oil through an external auxiliary line connected to the former oil pressure gauge take-off orifice. The #1 main is fed in the normal manner. Restrictor plugs are inserted in both lifter galleries.

To feed the HTC system a fitting is brazed to the head of a hollow oil filter adapter bolt, thereby tapping full pressure directly from the pump.

as a kit from Hank the Crank.

To contain the oil and circulate it through either of these highly modified systems, most Pro Stockers use relatively common pumps and pans. The major concern is a rear-sump pan and pickup so that oil feed is assured during acceleration. Ground clearance is usually a problem in a Pro Stocker, so most builders make their own pans. Lee Hunter's is about eight inches deep, with a sump only at the rear (rather than the full length of the pan), and it holds about seven quarts. He likes to use as little oil as possible, to keep it away from the crank in the shallow pan, and still maintain pressure. Hunter also uses a bone stock factory pump—says it does the job fine. Bob Glidden uses a dry-sump system in his Ford, and feels that it helps slightly. Most other Ford Pro Stockers (unlike Chevy drivers, who have found power advantages with a well-designed dry-sump) have not found the cost and hassle of a dry-sump warranted in a Cleveland.

Of course, another major concern of Pro Stock racers is the Cleveland block itself. You have probably noted that we previously cautioned against boring a Cleveland more than .040-inch for street use or .030-inch for competition. Boring one of these blocks .080-inch is certainly risky; and such an attempt will require checking several candidates for correct bore alignment, or minimal core shift, before the operation can even be considered. Lee Hunter has found that one of the big problems with running paper-thin cylinders in a Cleveland, besides the inevitable occasional ventilation that may occur, is that the cylinders will tend to flex out of shape at extreme rpm. To help subdue this problem on a couple of his blocks he has resorted to "pinning" the cylinders in place by installing a large "set screw" on either side of each cylinder. He can't vouch for the practical effect of this modification—it's primarily theoretical—but it is relatively easy to do and the engines have held up. The bolts are positioned on the right and left side of each cylinder, about half way down, one being inserted in a hole drilled and tapped in the valley wall and the other in a hole drilled and tapped in the outside of the block.

For a more bulletproof block, some Pro Stockers are now having special thick-wall cylinder sleeves

A big problem with Clevelands, especially if they are to be overbored, is the flexibility and weakness of the thinwall block. The new Australian block (see Circle Track Cleveland section) is one solution. Another approach used by a few Pro Stockers are these chrome-moly cylinder sleeves, which are over .250-inch thick. They can be furnace-brazed into the Cleveland block—a process which requires complete remachining of all surfaces but which yields a bulletproof large-bore block.

The topside of a typical Cleveland Pro Stock head reveals roller rockerarms held firmly in alignment by a stud girdle (this one by Jomar). If extra tall valve covers aren't used, a spacer must be installed to clear all the machinery. This head is attached with studs instead of bolts.

furnace-brazed into the bores. The sleeves, such as those available from Ramsco, are made from a centrifugally cast chrome-moly alloy and have walls slightly over .250-inch thick. The furnace brazing process actually siameses the cylinders together, so the problem of cylinder flexing is virtually eliminated. Unfortunately, the furnace-brazing process is rather complicated—only a few places will undertake the job and then delivery is usually slow—and when the builder gets the block back not only must the tops of the cylinders be machined back to deck height (they stick up above the block), but virtually every surface and bore must be remachined for alignment (the brazing process warps the entire block out of shape).

There are a couple of other alternatives, but they are equally obscure. Dyno Don Nicholson has acquired a few aluminum Cleveland blocks originally intended for Trans Am factory racing before Ford dropped the program. But Dyno has cornered the market on this rare commodity, and he is using them, along with a .250-inch steel stroker and aluminum T/A heads, only for match racing. Of slightly better availability—but not much better—is the "Australian" Cleveland cylinder block, so named because they are made in Australia for use in Australian Ford trucks. These blocks are made with a lot more metal all around, using pre-thinwall casting methods. Such a block has more meat in the cylinders (for possible overboring) as well as much more beef in the main bearing web area where Clevelands are known for cracking. They are denoted by an "XE" casting number on the outside of the block (XE 192540). These blocks have been imported in unmachined form and have been made available so far only to a chosen

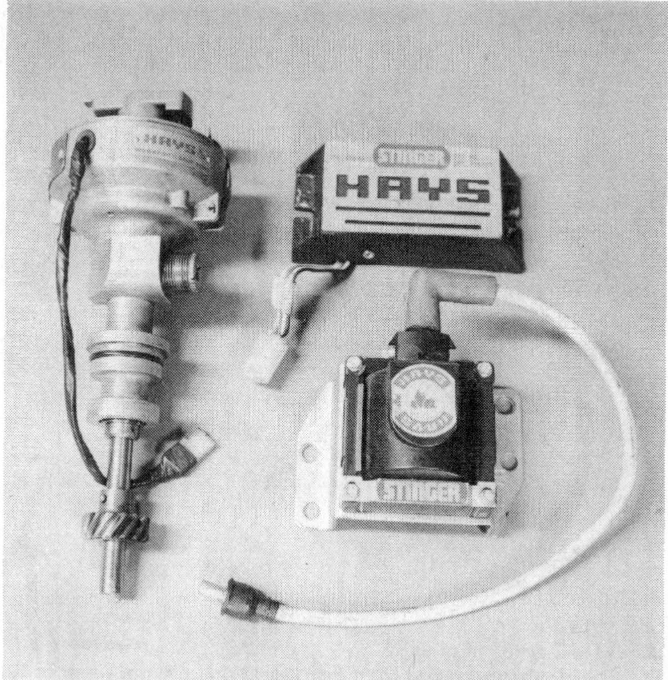

One of the most popular ignitions for Fords for drag racing is a Hays Stinger breakerless system mounted in an Accel tach-drive distributor housing.

No need to waste horsepower on a water pump and fan when a small electric motor can do the job just as well (actually better since the pump can be turned on only when the engine has come up to temperature, and then water will be circulated at a constant rate). A fan? You bet. It is not at all uncommon to see Pro Stockers driving back the return road and around the pits under their own power.

few. Those that have gone on the market have been exceedingly expensive. If you're in the market try Gapp and Roush or Holman-Moody.

Other hardware in a typical Pro Stock Cleveland would naturally include a roller cam and roller rockerarms with a stout stud girdle. Many Pro Stockers today prefer timing chains (such as the Cloyes double roller, mentioned previously) to gear drives, claiming that gear drives steal horsepower. The majority of the big-name Ford Pro Stock builders feel that a standard distributor ignition is adequate for the Cleveland (as opposed to a crank-triggered ignition) since the distributor mounts at the front of the engine (thus eliminating cam-twist problems experienced by Chevys). The Accel dual-point body with a tach-drive take-off is probably the most popular, fitted with an electronic triggering head such as the Accel BEI or a Hays Stinger. Just about every racer we interviewed touted the Hays setup very highly, the usual comment being, "It never breaks."

351 CLEVELAND PRO STOCK
BLUEPRINT SPECIFICATIONS

Main Bearings	.0030-.0035
Rod Bearings	.0030-.0035
Crankshaft End Play	.004-.010
Rod Side Clearance	.020-.025 (steel rods) .030-.035 (Aluminum Rods)
Valve Stem-to-Guid Clearance	.0011-.0022—E .0007-.0018—I
Piston-to-Valve	.100 Minimum
Piston-to-Bore	.0055-.0065 (TRW) .008-.010 (Venolia, etc.)
Piston-to-Pin	.0008-.0010
Piston Ring End Gap	.014-.016
Piston Ring-to-Groove	.002-.004 (.000 Top Ring W/Gas Ports)
Lifter-to-Bore	.0007-.0027

351 CLEVELANDS FOR THE CIRCLE TRACK

Since the 366 cubic inch limitation went into affect several years ago, there is little point discussing "stock car" 427 or 429 engines. If you are one of the few who are willing to go Grand National racing with a Ford (despite sanctioning body restrictions), your choice of a powerplant is probably going to be the 351 Cleveland. And since the factory no longer builds racing motors for you, this "stock" engine will have to be extensively modified to become competitive and strong enough to live 500 miles in the fast lane.

Several of the modification procedures applicable to a 351-C for circle-track racing have been covered already. Here we will point out some of the specific differences to consider when building a stock car Cleveland. Obviously, most of the procedures—apart from those limited by rules—will also apply to dirt trackers, flatbottom boats, and other endurance racing applications.

SHORT BLOCK

Ford may be officially out of racing, but the beefy Australian blocks are available and the front row Ford racers are getting them. Previously discussed in the Pro Stock section, this heavy duty casting is really suited for the Grand National circuit. One look at the big thick main bearing webs and one-inch thick skirt (pan rail) around the bottom will tell you that. They also have heavier high nodular iron four-bolt main caps, highly-accurate machining tolerances, and .165-inch minimum thickness cylinder walls. Of course, these blocks are quite a bit heavier than the standard four-bolt Cleveland, but on the big ovals this is not as critical as it is on the dragstrip.

If you don't have enough clout and dollars (it takes plenty of both) to get the Australian block, the only other choice is a four-bolt Cleveland which has been carefully checked for core shift, bore alignment, and close tolerances of all machined surfaces. Naturally, no production block is going to be "right on," so any Cleveland expected to withstand three to five hundred miles of seven-grand racing must be taken through a time-consuming and expensive block blueprinting process. Especially critical is that cylinder bores be perpendicular to the crankshaft and parallel to each other. Some slight misalignment might be able to be corrected by boring on a machine that locates on the crank centerline instead of on the deck surface. If the cylinders are too far out of line, scrap the block and find another one. The bearing saddles, deck surfaces, and lifter bores must likewise be brought into close tolerances.

Fatigue failure is a major problem in such an engine. The entire block must be carefully deburred and stress areas neatly radiused or ground down. Pay particular attention to the area below the main bearing saddles, as mentioned previously. It should go

Although the Mustang II body has been superseded by a Fairmont, Lee Hunter's candy blue Ford is a fine example of the current art of making full-bodied, "street-legal" cars run the quarter mile in eight seconds.

The best starting point for a Ford Grand National racer is the "Australian" block. Externally, it looks like any Cleveland, but the casting is thicker in almost every area. Naturally they are very rare and very expensive.

A good bet for all endurance competition is to use screw-in core plugs to close the sand coring opening in the side of the block. This prevents inadvertent loss of cooling fluid because of heat and vibration stress developed during long races.

This particular block has been fitted with "Cooper ring" seals (similar to those used on Shotgun Hemi Fords) to ensure against blown gaskets during 500 mile races. Note that the head gasket has been trimmed away.

without saying that the entire block be carefully checked for imperfections by the Magnaflux Zy-glo process before any major machining is begun.

Oil control is obviously very important in an endurance racing Cleveland. Current methods for converting the 351-C to positive crank oiling have already been detailed, the most popular for Grand National cars seeming to be the HTC oil tube manifold which gets right to the main bearings. Some cars use the lifter bore sleeves instead, as shown in the Pro Stock engine chapter. The difference in a circle tracker is that a dry-sump oil pan replaces the conventional wet-sump. Ground clearance is usually a problem, so a relatively shallow pan must be used, with scrapers and screens which collect oil at the right side of the pan. These are made by several manufacturers, Aviad being one of the more popular. Normally a three-stage, belt-driven, external oil pump consisting of two scavenge sections and one pressure module is mounted near the front of the engine. When converting to such a system, don't forget to block off the stock oil pump passage, located in the left front pan rail, with a plate or plug. Otherwise all of your oil will be pumped right back into the pan.

Although nothing but cast crankshafts were available in production 351 Clevelands, a few steel forgings can be found at specialty crankshaft grinders. Hank the Crank offers a chrome-moly steel billet for the Cleveland which is fully counterweighted and can be internally balanced with a minimum of Mallory metal added to the throws. It sells for about $1400, but Grand National engine builders such as Mario Rossi figure that this investment is cheap in the long run, as the billet crank will last six or seven races whereas a fully prepped cast 351-C crank will generally have to be replaced after each race on a superspeedway. If the cast crank is used, it must be chamfered, polished, Tufftrided, and internally balanced such as for Pro Stock racing. With either crank, a large harmonic balancer such as the Boss 302 or 351-C is generally used, with the stock eccentric weight cut out if the crank is internally balanced.

Super trick custom steel connecting rods are made primarily for this sort of racing abuse. They are available from Carrillo, Crower, and from Hank the Crank for the Cleveland and not only are they extremely durable, but they feature a dowel method of locating the cap so that it cannot walk or become misaligned once it is tightened on the rod. This greatly helps rod bearing life in a long-distance engine, plus it takes side loads off the rod bolts. Since custom-made rods are usually used in these engines, the rod length can be altered to tailor torque advantage for given conditions. Mario Rossi originally used a 6.0-inch rod for the longer tracks (Daytona, Talladega) and a 5.8-inch rod for other ovals. Now he uses the 6.0-inch long rod for all but the very short track applications (half mile of less).

Pistons for a circle tracker don't look much different from other high performance varieties, but there are a few requisites. They must have wide, rounded skirts (unlike drag racing

Endurance racing calls for considerable reworking of the Cleveland oiling system, just as Pro Stock drag racing does. This is a Hank the Crank direct-feed setup similar to the one described in the Pro Stock section, but plumbed differently on top to clear the underside of a single four-barrel manifold.

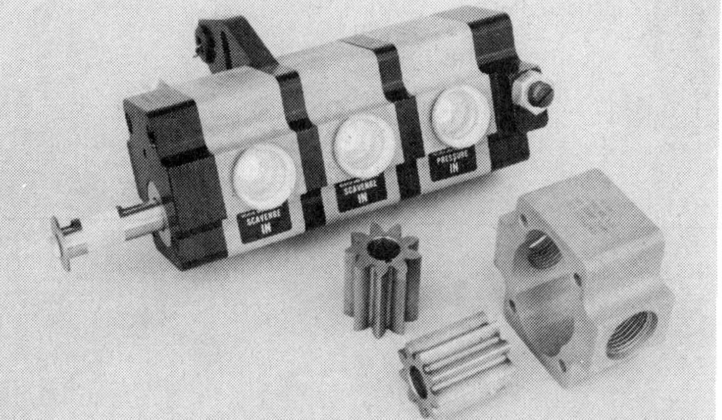

An absolute essential on any Grand National car, as well as most other circle racers (sprint cars, boats, etc.) is a dry-sump oil system. An external, belt-driven pump, such as this Weaver three-module unit, scavenges oil from the pan at two (or three) locations, then pumps it back to the engine.

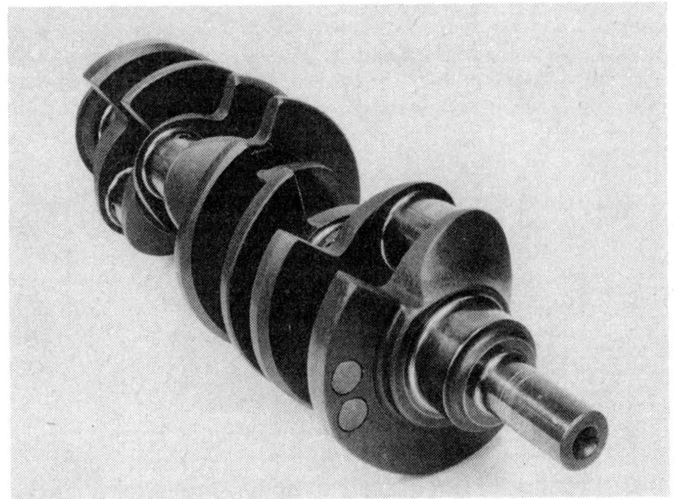

The cast Cleveland crank has been used successfully in Grand National racing, but a specialty steel billet such as this one from HTC will stand up to the pounding much better. This one has two extra counterweights in the center to reduce flexing and wide radii where the journals meet the cheeks to inhibit cracking. Mallory metal slugs are used for balancing.

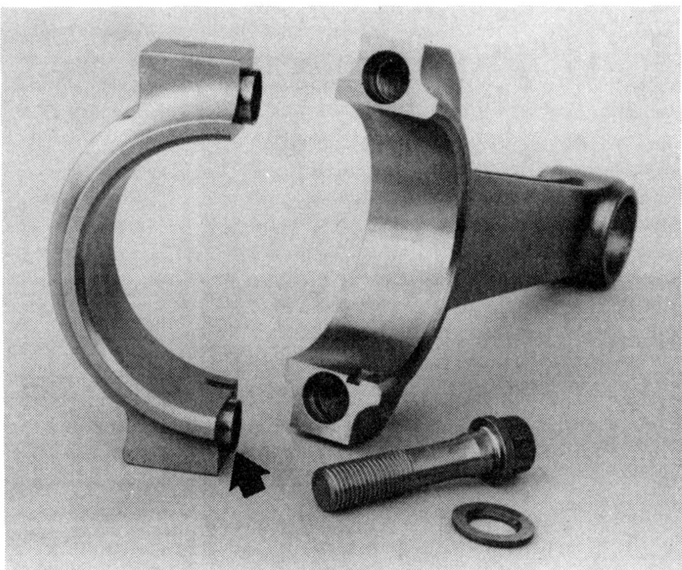

Billet steel rods, such as the famous Carrillo rods, also provide the ultimate in durability. Dowel sleeves eliminate shifting of the cap, and SPS bolts keep the cap and bearing shells firmly in place.

motors) to prevent the piston from rocking in the bore and to prevent the skirts from scoring the cylinder walls. The top ring should be placed fairly low on the piston (e.g., .425-inch down from the deck) so that the groove will not rob strength from the dome, which will be taking a real beating under the typical 12-12½:1 compression. Tough but lightweight full-floating pins ride in bronze bushings in the top of the rods, and the pin bosses of the pistons are drilled to feed extra oil to the pins. Double Spirolocs keep the pins in place. Like just about everybody else these days, GN racers generally use Sealed Power/Speed Pro rings, with a ductile iron, moly-filled type on top. After the crank/pistons/rods have been trial fitted in the block and the heads have been screwed on with all valve gear in place, take very careful measurements through a full cycle for minimum piston-to-valve clearance of .080-inch on the intake and .100-inch on the exhaust. With the new fast-action mushroom cams being used in these engines, some valve relief machining will usually have to be done to get these specs—you definitely do not want the valves kissing the pistons on the backstretch. The machined domes of the as-delivered pistons must at the same time be hand reworked to remove any sharp edges (which would promote preignition) and contoured to give good flow at low cam lifts and smooth flame propagation in the chamber (any good high compression piston for a Cleveland should have a fire slot machined in it from the manufacturer).

About the only other special considerations for the short block are the main and rod bearings, which turn out to be the usual TRW CL-77 type for both (fully-grooved mains). The only alterations are to chamfer the edges of the main bearing if a large-radius is ground between the throws and crank cheeks by the crank prep shop. (This is common with custom shops like HTC.) Also, enlarge the oil slot in the upper main bearing half, if you wish. Finally, one trick adhered to by most long-distance racers is to make sure the freeze plugs don't pop out of the block during a race. The easiest way to do this is to make a small metal strap, which will cover the plug, and attach it to the block with a couple of small screws (drill and tap two holes on either side of the core hole). Some builders prefer to tap the core hole instead, and insert large pipe plugs.

HEADS

Nascar racers are not allowed to

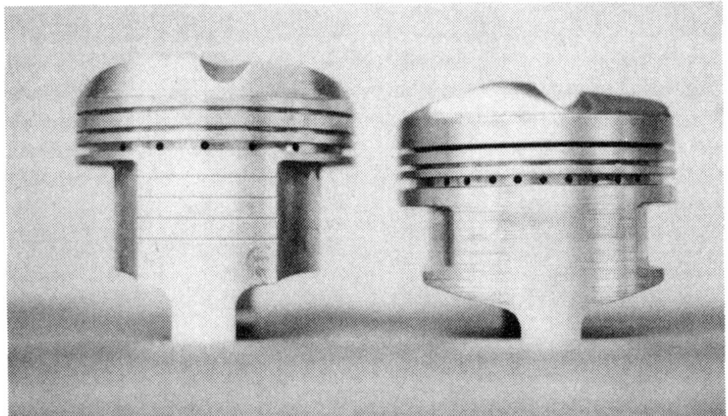

The differences between a circle track and drag racing piston are subtle but distinct. The endurance piston should have a wide skirt with smooth corners to minimize cylinder wear and to distribute shock loads. Also note, in contrast to a narrow-skirt drag piston, that the top ring groove is much further below the deck.

The dome configuration is very similar between a Pro Stock and a circle track piston for a Cleveland. The Pro Stocker, on the left (shown as it would arrive from the manufacturer) has gas ports drilled from the top to the first ring groove to help seal the ring. The circle track piston has been hand-contoured to fit a specific combustion chamber, it is not gas ported, and it has been plasma-coated on top to help reflect more heat.

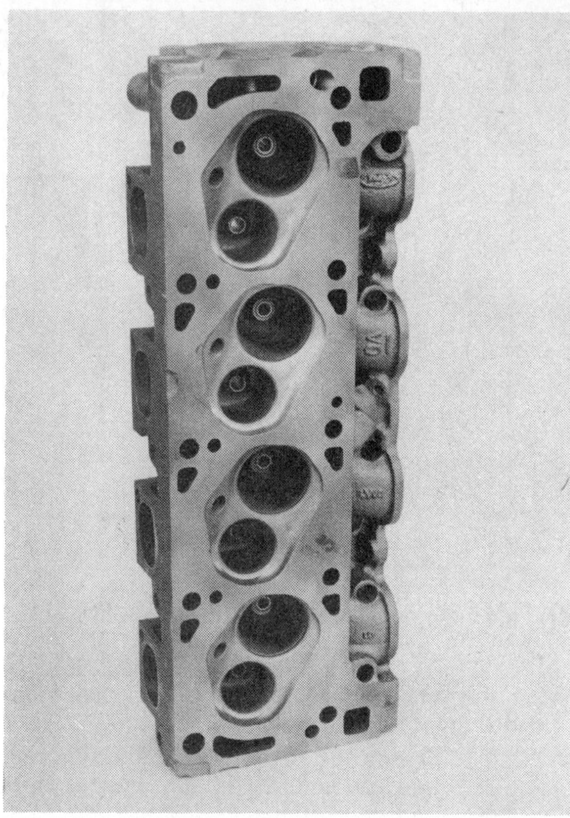

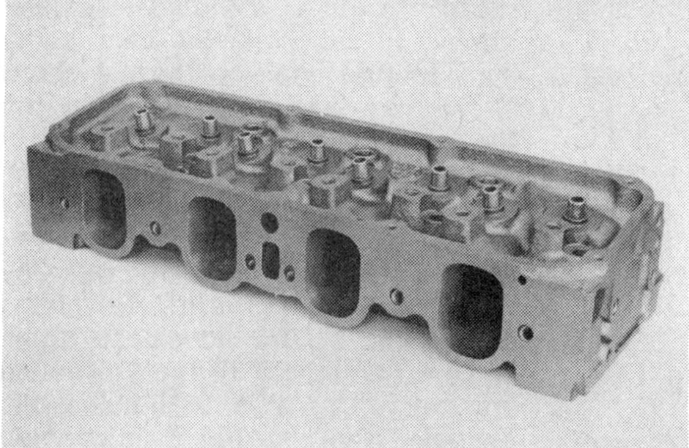

Durability and competition regulations severely restrict modification to a circle-track cylinder head. Intake porting is often restricted by the rules and radical surgery on the exhaust side will not withstand long-term racing abuse. However, extensive welding is often employed on the exhaust port floor to raise the flow activity higher in the port. The roof is also ground away as much as possible to maintain an adequate cross section. This is not as effective as the port-plate method used in Pro Stock drag racing, but any reduction in exhaust restriction will greatly improve cylinder head performance.

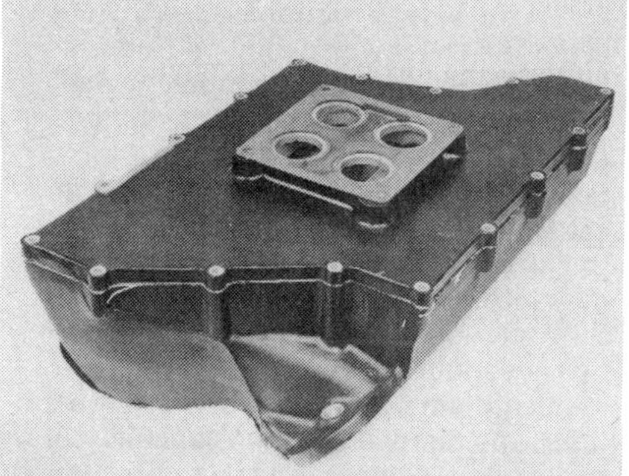

One of the most popular inductions for circle-track Clevelands is "The Box" manifold built and sold by Bud Moore. It utilizes long direct passages (much like a tunnel ram) across the bottom of the manifold and a huge plenum directly below the carb. This provides a large volume of fuel-air to feed the engine but a tremendous amount of accelerator pump fuel is required to gain adequate off-idle response. It is more suited for longer tracks and may require extensive "custom" modification to gain suitable mixture distribution. A Holley Dominator may be used but current Nascar required restrictor rings or plate considerably reduces the flow capability.

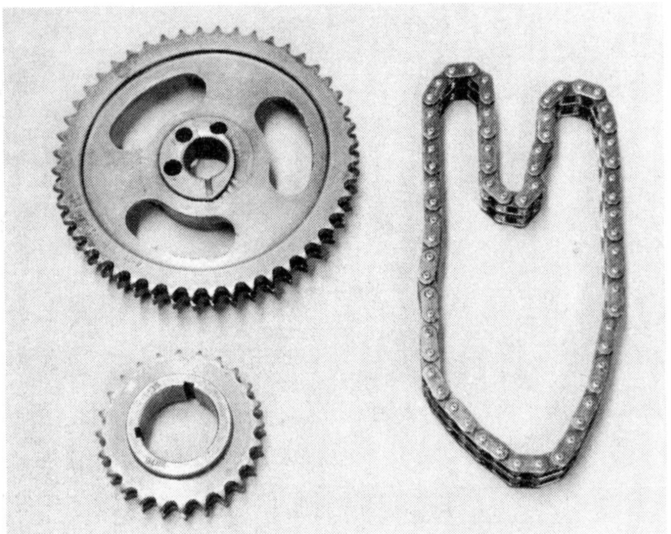

If local rules will allow, a gear drive should be used to turn the camshaft. In cases when a gear drive can not be used legally, a Cloyes Tru-roller double-row chain should be used to drive the cam. Very high lifter acceleration rates place a severe load on the cam and cam drive components. They should be checked and replaced often to prevent inopportune failure.

Stock cars are supposed to run stock ignitions, but somebody went to a lot of trouble to make this Accel distributor look just like a Ford. This gives you an indication of the amount of respect racers give stock Cleveland distributors.

run port plates on Clevelands. Some will raise exhaust ports by welding up the bottoms of the runners; others do not feel this is necessary. In either case the ports are enlarged (or recontoured) and fully polished. Standard valve selections are the 2.19-inch Ford/TRW titanium intakes and Manley 1.71-inch stainless steel exhausts.

The big difference in circle track Cleveland heads, however, is a process called "pinning" or "posting." Because of the thinwall casting, not only do the cylinders get pushed out of shape in the block, but even the combustion chambers and the sealing surface of the head can warp or even crack under the conditions of a three to four hour race. To help the heads keep their shape and help prevent head gasket failure, the heat riser passages are welded shut (not only is manifold heat unwanted, but the process strengthens the center of the head). Then, the head is drilled and tapped at several strategic locations and 3/8-inch threaded studs are screwed through the outside wall to butt up against the waterside of the combustion chamber or port passage wall. Typical pin locations would be from the end of the head against the side of the combustion chamber; through the exhaust rocker pedestal and against the back of the gasket surface; and through the gasket surface to butt against the intake runners. The heads of the pins screwed in through the gasket surface are cut off and machined flat during head surfacing operations. Such pinned heads are available for Nascar racing from Gapp and Roush and from Reed Cams.

Endurance racers should definitely drill the extra 3/16-inch hole in each head gasket as shown in the accompanying diagrams. Standard head gaskets, such as McCord #6850M (.035-inch thick), can be used, but it is a good idea to spray them with hi-temp (non-hardening) aluminum paint before installation. It wouldn't hurt to spray the surfaces of the head and block as well.

CAMSHAFT

When it comes to auto racing, rules are the mother of invention. You may think that the major advantage of a roller cam is less friction or wear. Actually, the roller was designed to allow steeper lobe ramps, faster opening and closing rates, and consequently longer effective duration. The problem with a flat lifter is that it must sit "flat" on the cam lobe at all times. If the lobe rises too sharply, the edge of the lifter face digs into the cam, causing immediate lifter and lobe wear. This is a simplistic description, however, given the relative diameter of the lobe and the lifter, and disregarding the capabilities of the other reciprocating components, the solid-lifter cam design can lift the valve only so quickly. And, as it turns out for any given duration, a roller-lifter cam can lift the valve faster.

Nascar rules do not allow roller-lifter cams. It took a while for the cam designers to find an alternative, but they have recently come up with the "mushroom tappet" cam, primarily for Nascar competition. It's called a mushroom lifter because what it gives the cam grinder is a larger diameter "head" with a standard diameter "stem" on the lifter—the head being the part that rides on the camshaft. The differences aren't great; in the Cleveland the stock lifter is .874-inch in diameter, and the extended head of the mushroom lifter can be as large as 1 inch across. But this small difference can increase valve lift rates by 13.3% (maximum valve lift rate with the stock lifter is .0075 inches per degree of cam rotation; with the 1.000-inch mushroom lifter it is .0085 inches per degree). What this means, in general, is that the valve can be opened at a faster rate, thereby allowing it to be fully opened for a longer time (given the same duration as other cam designs). In other words, you get more lift, faster, during the opening phase, even though maximum lift remains the same. This greatly improves the overall volumetric efficiency of the engine at lower engine speeds, which, for a Grand National racer, means a wider torque band and more power coming out of the corners. One of the major manufacturers of mushroom lifter cams for circle track Fords is Reed Cams of Decatur, Georgia.

To install the mushroom lifters in a Cleveland block, the bottom of the lifter bores must be spotfaced to a diameter larger than the head of the lifter and deep enough so that a minimum of .030- to .040-inch clearance will be maintained between the lifter head and the underside of the lifter bore at full lift. If you plan to run

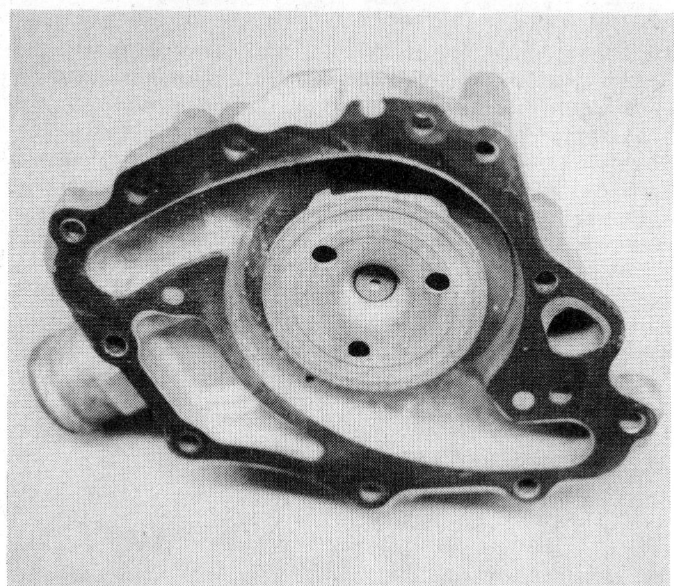

One of the last offerings in the Ford Muscle Parts program was an aluminum water pump housing for the Cleveland. This one has been fitted with a cut down, curved-blade impeller from a Boss 302—a trick that will supposedly eliminate cavitation in the pump at high rpm.

Since a Grand National race car will spend most of the day cruising at considerably faster speeds than city traffic, both a smaller crank pulley and a larger pump pulley are installed to turn the water pump more slowly and minimize wasted power.

more than one cam grind, take your measurements for this operation as well as for valve-to-piston clearance using the biggest cam you intend to run. Another major consideration with the mushroom design is fore-and-aft camshaft play. With the larger diameter heads, chances of a lifter contacting an adjacent lobe increase. On a Cleveland, camshaft end play can be controlled by machining either the cam sprocket or the thrust plate. Keep end play under .010-inch. And when you are ready to install all the good pieces in your engine, don't forget that the mushroom lifters must be inserted from the bottom, which means they go in before the crank and cam are installed.

Typical specs on a mushroom cam would read something like 274° intake and 280° exhaust (measured at .050-lift) with .675-inch intake lift and .685-inch exhaust lift for racing on the superspeedways. Slightly smaller numbers would apply to shorter tracks. Remember that these specs do not translate to non-mushroom lifter cam profiles.

Nascar also prohibits gear drives for cam timing. Mario Rossi says by all means use one if local rules allow it. The next best thing is the Cloyes Tru-roller double chain, and Rossi recommends installing it with the cam ½° advanced since just the load imposed by the valve springs and other components will usually retard the cam about half a degree (check it again once the heads are in place and the valve lash is set). The rest of the valve train would be similar to a Pro Stocker, except that parts are chosen for durability (e.g., titanium over aluminum).

OTHER PARTS

The hot induction setup for Nascar Cleveland Fords is the Bud Moore "box" intake plenum—generally modified to suit the particular builder's inclinations. A similarly much-modified Holley Dominator (4500 series) four-barrel is usually found on top, fitted with whatever size restrictor rings Nascar currently decides to impose on the Fords. Mechanical fuel pumps are also mandated, and the Clevelands have exhibited a tendency toward failure with the stock variety. Bud Moore has contracted with Carter to make a special fuel pump for the Nascar 351-C on a limited basis, but the price tag on one of these is a stout $225!

Another weak area on the 351-C is the distributor, but it must remain stock. The good "factory" ignition for racing is a Ford special magnetic impulse transistorized unit (not the current production type) which has a mechanical tach-drive in the housing. These are very rare and proportionately expensive. Another good possibility might be the marine distributor mentioned in the 429/460 engine section, since it will fit the 351. Some Nascar racers have been known to go to great lengths to disguise a specialty distributor to look like a stock Ford.

Mario Rossi recommends using the Boss 302 curved-blade impeller in the water pump housing, and also trimming it down ½-inch. Since the engine is running at such high speeds, you actually need to slow down the circulation rate somewhat to allow the water to remain in the radiator long enough to cool. Rossi says the modified pump is good for five horsepower.

And, finally, stock cars must run tailpipes as well as headers. Standard headers have 2-inch primaries, 34 inches long, with 3½-inch diameter collectors, and 3½-inch diameter tailpipes about 4 feet long. A cross-over "equalizer tube" between the tailpipes, about 18 inches behind the collectors, will help to increase torque.

351 CLEVELAND NASCAR/CIRCLE TRACK BLUEPRINT SPECIFICATIONS	
Bore	4.020
Stroke	3.50
Compression	12.5:1
Horsepower	560-570/7000-7200 rpm
Torque	445-450 ft-lbs/5600-5800 rpm
Piston to Bore Clearance	.0085-.0090
Cylinder Hone	8-13 microinches with Sunnen JHV-820 stones (400 grit)
Main Bearing Clearance	.0025-.00275
Rod Bearing Clearance	.0025
Rod Side Clearance	.017-.020
Piston Pin Clearance	.0008
Piston Ring End Gap	.014—#1 & 2
Piston Ring to Groove	.001
Piston to Deck Height	.010 down
Valve to Piston Clearance	.080—I .100—E
Crankshaft End Play	.004-.006
Valve Stem to Guide	.002—I .0025—E
Combustion Chamber Volume	64-65cc
Piston Dome Volume	8-10cc
Head Gasket Thickness	.035
Spark Plug Gap	.025
SPECIAL BOLT TORQUE SPECIFICATIONS	
Head Bolts	110 ft-lbs
SPS Rod Bolts	90-95 ft-lbs or .004-.0045 stretch

HOW TO BUILD A 351 CLEVELAND

The following is a step-by-step build-up of a four-bolt main 351-Cleveland by Doug "Cookie" Cook (previously of Stone-Woods-Cook renown) for use in a Pantera with a turbocharger. Some of the special parts were of the customer's choosing (Crower rods and Jackson gear drive), but the general configuration of the engine is very typical of a contemporary, hard-running, street-driving Cleveland. Doug's shop, Cook's High Performance, is located in Bell Gardens, CA, and specializes in Pantera mechanical up-dating.

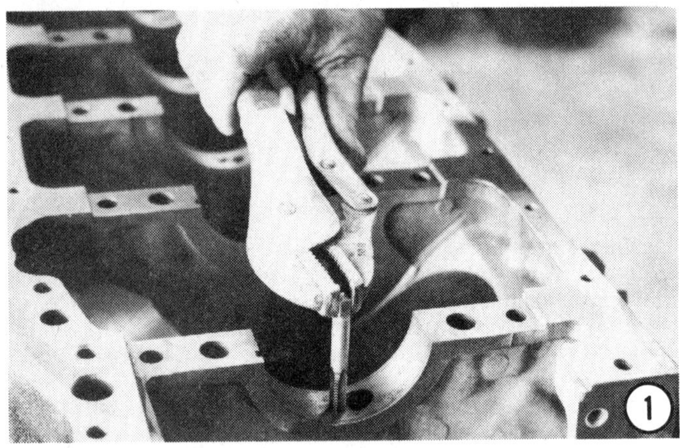

If you plan to turn very high crank speeds with your Cleveland, it would be very wise to install an oil system restrictor kit such as offered by Moroso. Its purpose is to limit oil travel to the cam bearings and to the left-side lifter gallery, leaving more for the main bearings; and it is very simple to install. First, tap the smaller hole in each main bearing saddle to a depth of about .500-inch.

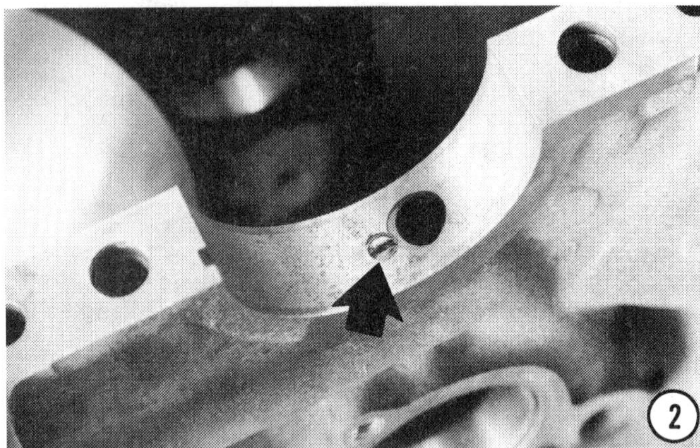

Add a drop of Loctite to each restrictor plug. And turn it with a screwdriver. Be sure the head of the plug is recessed sufficiently below the surface so the bearing will seat properly.

At the rear main, three passages come together. Restrictors should be installed in the center one leading to the cam bearing, and in the larger passage leading to the left-side lifter gallery (shown).

Installation of the oil restrictor kit takes only a few minutes and its cost is minimal. Now the block is ready for main bearings (Clevite 77 are preferable), and normal assembly.

With the main bearings in place and a shot of oil on each, Doug lays in the Velasco-prepped stock crank.

Bottom end torque specs vary on Cleveland (see blueprint chart). Doug runs the big main-cap bolts to 100 ft-lbs, the outer bolts to 40 ft-lbs for performance Pantera motors.

The finished assembly is admittedly not as beefy as a typical four-bolt bottom end, but Clevelands experience very little crank or main cap failure, even in a turbocharged engine like this one. Cook set the clearances at .003-inch on the mains and .002-inch on the rods.

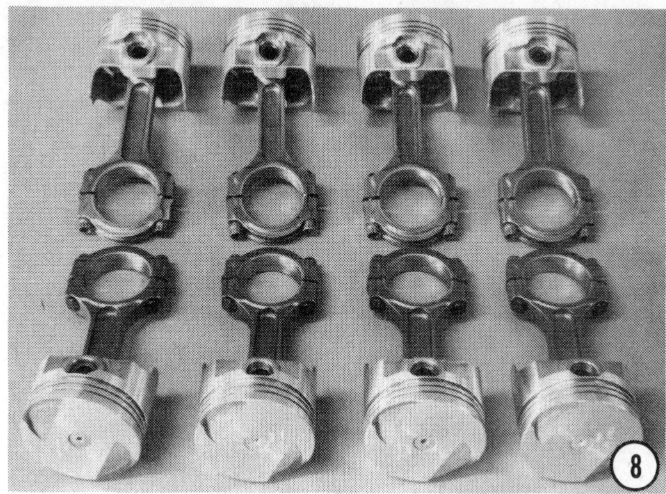

Having experienced previous rod failure, this customer ordered a set of bulletproof Crower steel connecting rods—an expensive but long-term investment. They are matched to TRW flat-top pistons, and the entire assembly including crank, flywheel, and dampener was balanced.

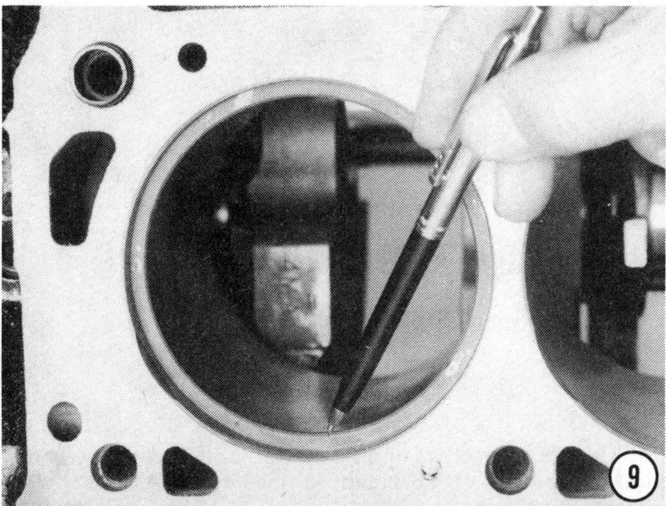

Doug uses TRW/Sealed Power standard ring sets, and it is imperative that each ring be hand-fitted in its repective bore before being installed on the piston. As you can see they are cut long enough as delivered so that the ends will butt.

Chuck each ring in a vise and file the end; then push the ring into the bore (with the top of a piston) so that it doesn't cock at an angle and measure the clearance with a feeler gauge.

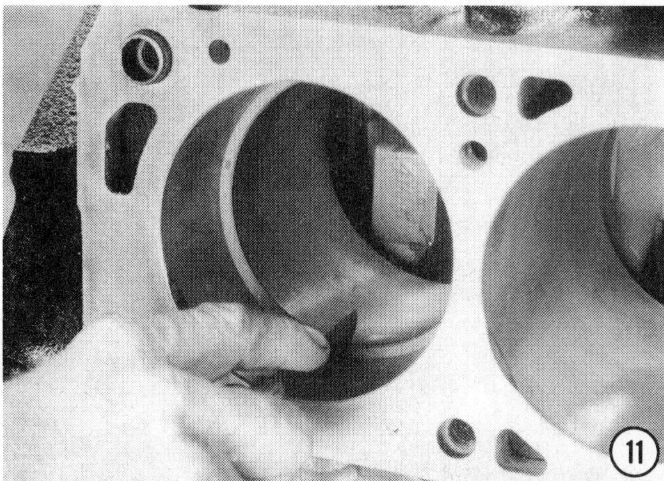

You will probably have to repeat the process a few times for each ring until you reach the desired clearance, which is .016-inch for top ring and .010-inch for the second ring in a street performance engine. This fitting takes time, but it is absolutely necessary.

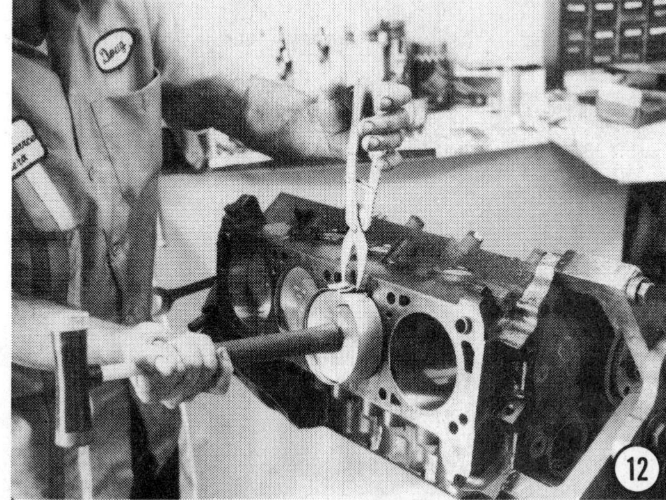

With the rings fitted on the pistons and rubber boots on the rod bolts, tap the pistons into the bores with a rubber or plastic handled hammer. The block has been honed for .004-inch piston skirt clearance.

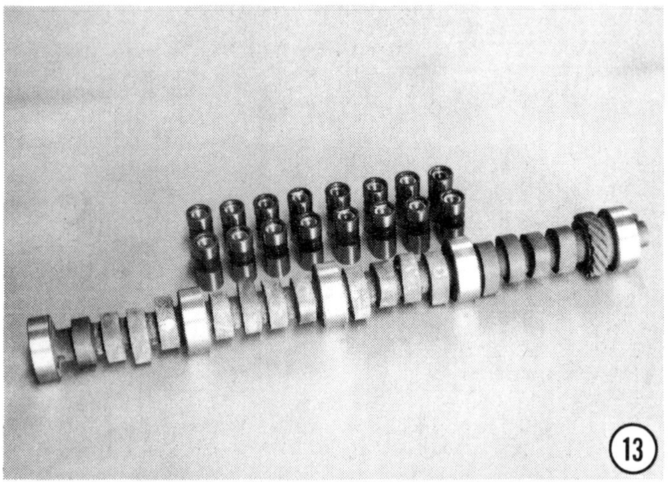

This engine will be driven primarily on the street, so Doug selected an Iskenderian hydraulic cam and anti-pumpup lifters. Coat each cam lobe with moly lube before installing it in the block.

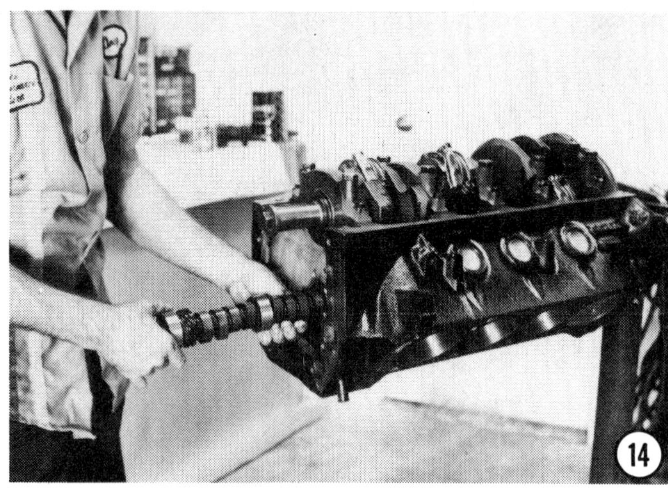

The cam should be slipped into the block with care. Modern cam bearings are not extremely fragile but due caution should be taken to prevent unnecessary damage.

The Pete Jackson gear drive is another expensive addition, especially on this sort of street performance engine, but some performance enthusiasts feel a gear drive increases reliability and cam timing accuracy.

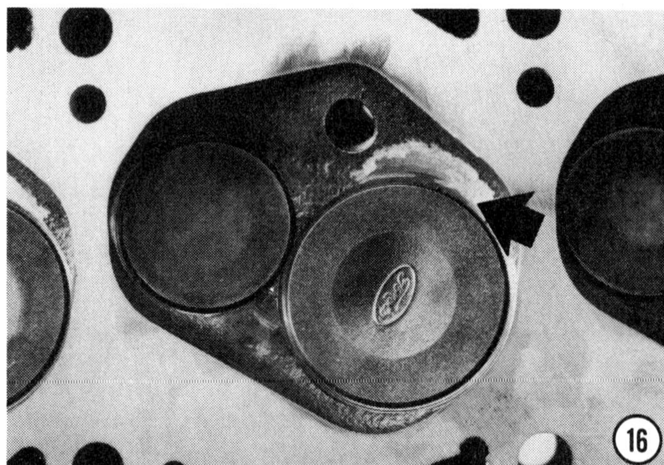

The heads are early quench-chamber four-barrel type and are left completely stock except for Isky #8005-A (inner/outer/damper) valve springs installed at 1-7/8-inch (140 lbs seat pressure), Isky chrome-moly retainers, and slight pass with a grinder (arrow) in the chamber to unshroud each intake valve.

The heads are installed with stock gaskets and torqued in four sequences to 110 ft-lbs.

Doug has special Cleveland pans made to his specifications for Pantera installations. Featuring an enlarged sump, a trap-door baffle, and a windage tray, they are available from Cook's High Peformance.

Use an extra dab of silicone sealant where the rubber and cork gaskets meet, since this area is prone to leak, then button up the bottom.

Bolting the pan in place is one of the easiest jobs but if you want the engine to be oil tight, take care. Tightening the pan bolts too much can easily warp the pan rail and lead to oil seepage. Pull them "snug" and work evenly from the center toward the end bolts.

Standard nonadjustable rockers are used with the hydraulic cam, so the slotted pedestals did not have to be altered. However, the spring seats had to be cut for Boss-type spring cups and the guides turned down for thinner P.C. valve stem seals. The intake manifold is an Edelbrock aluminum (painted black), dual-plane, four-barrel model, and Doug prefers four-piece specialty intake gaskets for better sealing.

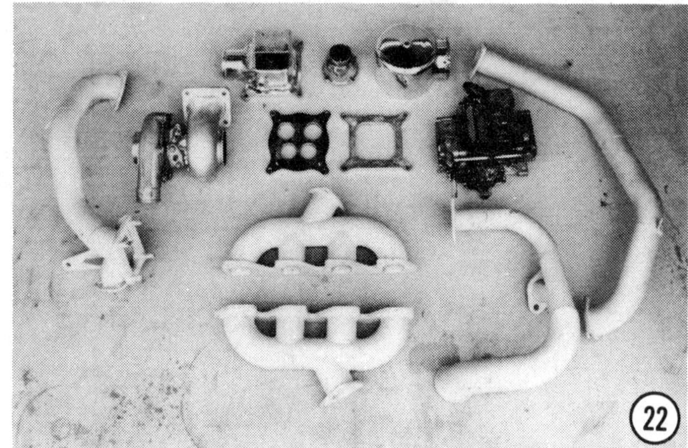

Turbocharging is relatively popular among the Pantera set. This particular system is designed and marketed by Ak Miller specifically for Panteras (it mounts the turbo behind the engine, which wouldn't work in a front-engined car). The turbo module is a Rajay, and the carburetor for this application is a 780 Holley.

Once the characteristic valve covers are in place, any Cleveland assumes singular good looks.

The completed package, with five-speed transaxle behind, is finally ready to shoehorn into the DeTomaso chassis. The ignition is stock Cleveland single-diaphragm with a Motorcraft breakerless kit installed. Wrinkle finish Pantera valve covers and air cleaner are products of Hall Panteras.

THE "385" FAMILY
429,429-BOSS and 460 ENGINES

429/460 "POLY ANGLE" BIG BLOCKS THE 385 ENGINE FAMILY

Do not confuse the 429 Ford big block with the 427/428 FE big block. They are totally different engines. In fact the 429, first introduced as the "Thunder Jet" in '68 T-Birds, is the predecessor of, and very similar to, the Cleveland series (335 family) of engines. The 429/460 is bigger, of course, with wider bore spacing and a beefier block (though still of thinwall design, like the Cleveland); it has a "skirtless" block, canted valve heads, and an identical oiling system to the Cleveland. Very few components will interchange between 385 and 335 family engines. Distributor bodies and rockerarms are about the only parts that can be swapped.

The 385 big block is certainly a more modern design than the old FE. Although Ford admits that "...the foremost design criteria during development was a complete 'induction-combustion-exhaust' process that would yield low emissions,"[1] what they came up with was a cylinder head designed for maximum flow. Valve inclination angles on the 429/460 are a little steeper, 5°/9°30' on the intakes and 4°30' on the exhausts, than those on the Boss 302 and Cleveland. All of these engines use a quench-type combustion chamber, and the intake ports are big ovals while the exhausts are more rectangular with rounded corners. What is really surprising is that the new Ford big block hasn't given the Chevy "Rat" more competition in popularity. The two big blocks are quite similar in design, displacement sizes, and weights (though no aluminum blocks or heads are commercially available for the Ford 385). One of the bigger differences between the two engines is the equally-spaced intake ports, allowing for more even intake distribution in the Ford engine.

Perhaps one of the major reasons why more 429 Fords aren't seen these days is because not too many were ever built. The 429 lasted in the Ford line-up only six years. The base 2V or 4V engines were used in T-Birds or large passenger cars and the performance CJ and SCJ 429 versions went into a select few Fairlanes, Montegos, and Mustangs. Much more abundant is the big 460 engine, which has been in continuous production since late '68 as an option in the large luxury cars (Lincoln, T-Bird, Mercury), Police units, and pickup trucks. The 460 has also become very popular lately as an inboard boat powerplant, and many of these engines are sold through Ford Industrial and Marine dealers. The "Marine" 460 comes with several heavy duty or performance oriented components not seen in other versions. Since the ski boat application appears to be one of the most popular for the 385-family Fords, we will demonstrate a typical jet-boat 460 buildup.

But, first let's go back and sort out the various components and combinations used in the 429/460. If you are shopping around for a complete engine the '70-71 Super Cobra Jet 429 gives you the best package with a four-bolt block, bigger valves and ports, forged pistons, and a solid-lifter cam with Boss 302-type valve train. Next in line is the '71 CJ which had the four-bolt block, big heads, hydraulic cam, cast pistons, and nonadjustable valve train. The '70 CJ used the standard two-bolt block, and early models came with adjustable rockers even though the engine had a juice cam. Of course, there was also the Boss 429 Hemi, which was actually built in a street version and sold in "a few hundred" Mustangs, as well as in a couple of racing versions. But don't expect to find one of these engines in the junkyard. They have become exceedingly scarce. Primarily for historical purposes, we will devote a special section to the "Shotgun" immediately following this one.

If you are beginning with used parts, rather than buying a complete engine such as from a marine dealer, it makes little difference whether you start with a 429 or a 460. The only difference between these two engines, dimensionally, is the stroke of the crankshaft and the pin height of the piston. Blocks, rods, heads, and all other parts will interchange.

CYLINDER BLOCK

Obviously the "good" block is the four-bolt SCJ ('70-71) or CJ ('71), which

385 SERIES SPECIFICATIONS

Displacement (Cu. In.)	429	429 CJ & SCJ	429 BOSS	460
Carburetor Horespower (Bhp/rpm) (72 specs SAE "net")	2V & 4V 320/4400—2V 360/4600—4V 212/4400—72	4V 370/5400 375/5600—Drag Pack	4V 375/5200	4V 365/4600 212/4400—72
Torque (lb.-ft./rpm) (72 specs SAE "net")	480/2800—4V 327/2600—72			342/2800—72
Compression Ratio (Maximum)	10.5:1—2V 11.0:1—4V 8.5:1—72	11.3:1 10.7 Nominal	10.5:1 Nominal 10.7:1 Nominal	10.5:1 10.7:1 Nominal 8.5:1—72
Head Volume (c.c.)	74.2-77.2 89.9-92.9—72	71.5-75.5 89.9-92.9—72	83-87 89.9-92.9—72	74.2-77.2 89.9-92.9—72
Bore	4.36	4.36	4.36	4.36
Stroke	3.59	3.59	3.59	3.85
Bore Spacing	4.90	4.90	4.90	4.90
Crankshaft Material Journal Dia-Main -Rod	Nodular Iron 3.00 2.50	Nodular Iron 3.00 2.50	Steel 3.00 2.50	Nodular Iron 3.00 2.50
Cam Journal Dia.	2.124	2.124	2.124	2.124
Centerline of Crankshaft to Top of Block (Block Deck Height)	10.300—68-70 10.310—70½ 10.322—72	10.300 10.310—70½ 10.322—72	10.300 10.310—70½ 10.322—72	10.300—68-70 10.310—70½ 10.322—72
Top of Piston to Top of Block (Deck Height Clearance)	0.010 0.020—70½ 0.032—72	0.010 0.020—70½ 0.032—72	0.010 (T) 0.020—70½ 0.032—72	0.010—68-72 0.020—70½ 0.032—72
Head Gasket Thickness	0.041—72			0.041—72
Head Gasket Volume	10.7—72			10.7—72
Total Clearance Volume	112.0—72			121.0—72
Compression Height	1.888-1.892	1.888-1.892	1.870 (T) 1.926 (S)	1.785-1.762
Con Ron Center (Center-to-Center)	6.605	6.605	6.605 (T) 6.549 (S)	6.605 6.549 (S)
Valve Head Dia.-Intake -Exhaust	2.075-2.090 1.646-1.661	2.242-2.248 1.722-1.728	2.275-2.285 1.895-1.905	2.075-2.090 1.646-1.661
Valve Stem Dia.	0.342	0.342	0.342	0.342
Valve Spring Load-Closed (lbs./installed height) -Open	76-84/1.81 218-240/1.33—72 240-266/1.33	85-93/1.82 294-318/1.36	88-96/1.82 300-330/1.32	76-84/1.81 218-240/1.33—72 240-266/1.33
Valve Lifters Lash (Mech.)	Hydraulic	Hyd-CJ Mech SCJ 0.019 Hot	Mech 0.013 Cold, 0.024 Hot	Hydraulic
Rocker Arm-Ratio -Type	1.75:1 Positive Stop Stud Non Adjustable	1.73:1 Threaded Stud-Adj-SCJ Positive Stop Stud Non Adj-CJ	Int-1.65, Exh-1.75 Individual-Shaft Adj	1.75:1 Positive Stop Stud Non Adj
External Balance	No			
Firing Order	1-5-4-2-6-3-7-8	1-5-4-2-6-3-7-8	1-5-4-2-6-3-7-8	1-5-4-2-6-3-7-8

1. Muscle Parts Story, Supplement No. 2; pg. 26.

This is actually a street Boss block, denoted by smaller four-bolt cap at number one journal, but it clearly demonstrates the ruggedness of the CJ/SCJ four-bolt main block (the CJ/SCJ blocks have a two-bolt cap at #1). Also notice thicker webbing above the main journals.

The standard 429/460 block has hardy two-bolt mains at all five positions. They will hold up fine unless you are running a supercharger or at Daytona. Modern thinwall casting (note pan rail thickness) is obvious, as is "skirtless" bottom end.

bears part number D10Z-6010-A—but don't expect to pick one up at your local Ford dealer. The only difference between this block and other 385 castings is that the main saddles on number two, three and four are machined for the four-bolt caps. We have never heard of a two-bolt block being converted to four-bolt caps (probably because of the scarcity of four-bolt caps). If you want to add strength to the bottom end of either a two-bolt or a four-bolt 429 or 460, you could add a Gapp and Roush Main Support Kit (GR8T-63A33C), consisting of reinforcing bars which fit against the (milled) heads of the center three main caps. The four-bolt block would be nice insurance for sustained high rpm racing, but there aren't too many instances anymore in which big blocks are used at such high engine speeds. For most purposes the two-bolt block works fine, which means you can use a newer and more readily available 460 block. Again, the thinwall casting calls for a recommendation of .030-inch maximum overbore on these blocks.

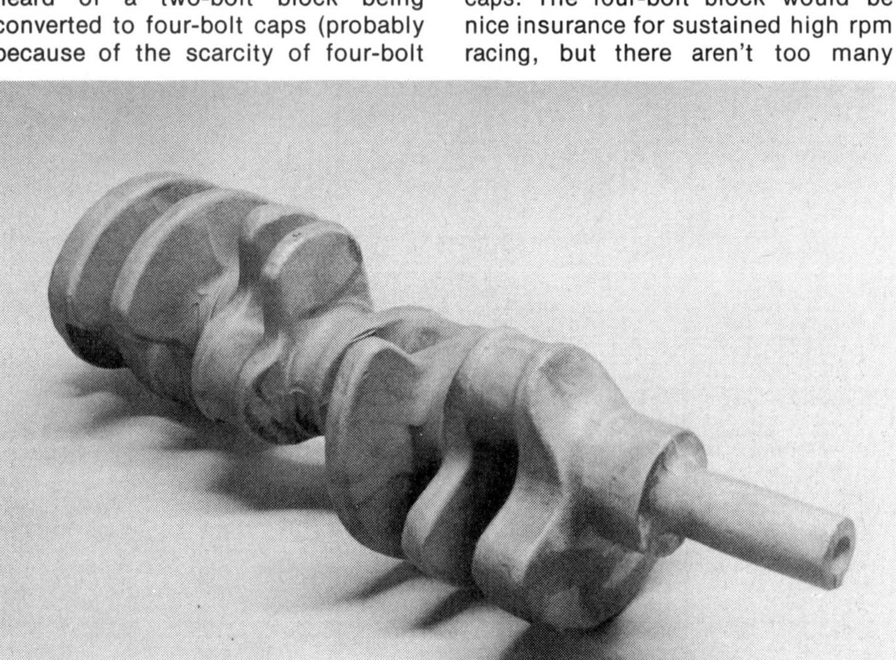

The only steel cranks made by Ford for the 385 series engines were a few billets intended for the 494-inch all aluminum Can Am Hemi engines. Hank the Crank obtained some left-over raw billets from Holman-Moody a few years back. Who knows how many others exist?

CRANKSHAFT

The 429 engines have a stroke of 3.59 inches and the 460 has a stroke of 3.85 inches. Journal diameters are the same on all 385 family engines (including the Boss), so all cranks will interchange. Some Ford literature claims that the CJ and SCJ engines had cranks "chosen for higher nodularity," but this isn't a big deal. Basically the cranks are all of the same durability, including the marine 460 crank, all being made of cast iron and all being internally balanced. The only steel cranks made for these engines came in the Boss 429. These were cross-drilled billet cranks with grooved main journals, and they came under two part numbers, because different piston/rod weights in the engines required slightly different crank balancing. If you are lucky, you might be able to find one of these cranks, which were listed as part C9AZ-6303-A for the "S" engine, C9AZ-6303-C for the "T" engine, or C9AZ-6303-E for an unbalanced ver-

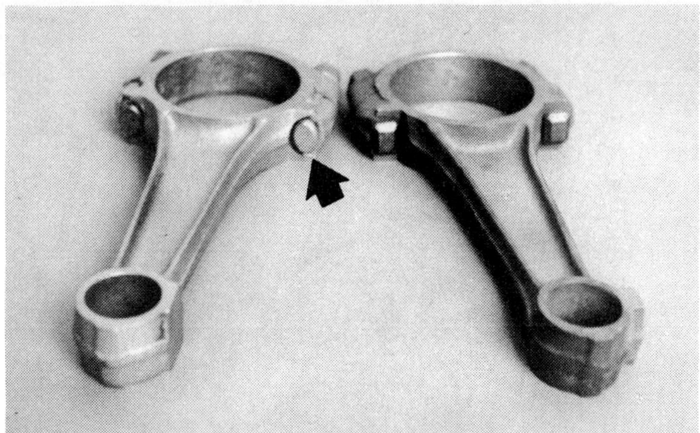

Other than the rod bolts, standard 429/460 rods and CJ/SCJ rods are the same. The semi-circular spot facing for the CJ/SCJ "football-head" bolt (left) lends greater strength to the rod shoulder than does the straight cut for the standard rod (right).

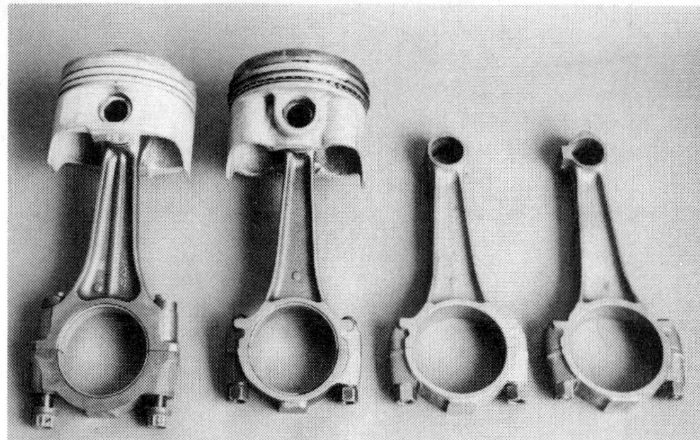

This line-up of 429 rods includes the rare Boss 429 Nascar rod on the left with an oil hole in the middle of the beam; a Super Cobra Jet rod with flat-top piston; a street Boss 429 "T" engine rod; and a stock rod (note the angular cut in shoulder for square-head bolt).

sion for special applications.

If you want a steel crank for a 460 you have two possibilities. Ford made a few aluminum-block 494 cubic inch Shotgun motors during a brief stint at Can Am racing. These engines had the same stroke as the 460 (3.850 inches) and used a forged steel crank. Holmon-Moody got the leftover billets for these cranks when Ford quit racing, and we saw a couple of these very rare forgings at Hank the Crank's shop in California. If you can't locate one of the factory pieces, the other possibility is a custom-machined steel billet (expensive!), available from specialty shops like Hank the Crank's.

For the majority of applications, however, the cast cranks hold up nicely. As in the case of other Ford engines, the recommendation for performance use is to chamfer the oil holes, micro-polish the journals, have the crank Tufftrided, and then realigned. Ford offered special-order fully-grooved main bearings for this engine under three part numbers: C9AZ-6333-G for 1, 2, 4, and 5 uppers; D00Z-6333-A for 1, 2, 4, and 5 lowers; and C9AZ-6337-G for the number 3 saddle upper and lower thrust bearings. For most applications these days a set of TRW/Clevite-77 bearings is all you need.

RODS

The fact that the 429 and 460 use the same length and size connecting rods really simplifies things. Base engines and CJ/SCJ engines used the same rods, except that the Cobra Jets have a semi-circular spot-faced bolt shoulder and an oval "football-head" bolt rather than the broached, straight-cut shoulder and rectangular-head bolt used on other engines. The spot-faced cut gives more strength to the CJ/SCJ

CRANKSHAFT I.D. AND APPLICATIONS

Part Number	Application		Journal Diameters		Stroke	Material	Remarks
	Engine	Year	Main	Rod			
D0OZ-6303-A	429 except Boss	68/71	3.00"	2.50"	3.59"	High Nod Iron	"U" #4 Counterweight
C9AZ-6303-A	429 Boss	69	3.00"	2.50"	3.59"	STEEL	"820-S" Engine only—balanced for 1145 gram rod
C9AZ-6303-C	429 Boss	69/70	3.00"	2.50"	3.59"	STEEL	"820-T" and later engines
C9AZ-6303-E	429 Boss	OHO	3.00"	2.50"	3.59"	STEEL	820-S Unbalanced
D2OZ-6303-A	429	72	3.00"	2.50"	3.59"	High Nod Iron	"H" #1 Counterweight
C8VY-6303-A	460	68/70	3.00"	2.50"	3.85"	IRON	"ZYA" #3 Counterweight

CON ROD I.D. AND APPLICATION

Part Number	Application		Weight	CTR-TO-CTR Distance	Bolt Seat	Bolt Size	Remarks
	Engine	Year	(Grams)	(Inches)	Finish	(Inches)	
C8SZ-6200-A	429/460	68/72	779-791	6.6050	Broached	3/8"	
D0OZ-6200-A	429 CJ/SCJ	70/71	779-791	6.6050	Spot-Faced	3/8"	
C9AZ-6200-B	429 BOSS	69/70	808-820	6.6050	Spot-Faced	3/8"	"820-T" Engines
C9AZ-6200-A	429 BOSS	69	1145	6.5490	Spot-Faced	1/2"	"820-S" Engines

For drag racing, aluminum con rods can easily be made to order for the 429/460; but for endurance applications such as in this jet boat big block, the wise choice is a custom steel rod, such as these Carrillo rods from Warren Machine.

SCJ's came with forged aluminum flat-top pistons with single valve reliefs; standard 429 pistons were similar but had two (smaller) reliefs per piston so that the same part could be installed in either the right or left bank. Also note the "figure eight" skirt on this stock Ford piston, plus the polished and shot-peened SCJ rod.

The current 460 stock piston looks like this. The Grand Canyon in the top is not designed to make compression!

rod (D00Z-6200-A). Installing the 3/8-inch football-head bolts in the standard rods, which also use 3/8-inch bolts, would be of no advantage.

Only one version of the Boss 429 rod can be used in the standard 429 or 460. The "T" street Boss rod (C9AZ-6200-B) is slightly beefier than the regular or CJ rod. It uses a similar football-head 3/8-inch bolt, and is the same length as 429/460 rods. The "S" Boss rod is .056-inch shorter than standard. The Nascar Boss 429 rod is .180-inch longer than standard. If you wanted to play around with rod-length-to-crank-stroke ratios (and if you could find either of these rare con rods), you could have special pistons made with the proper pin height to run the longer or shorter rods. Of course, it is pretty simple to have one of the several rod manufacturers make up either aluminum or steel (Carrillo, Crower) rods to fit the 429/460.

PISTONS

The base 429 came with a cast aluminum flat-top piston which gave 10½:1 compression with the regular heads. All 429/460 pistons use a pin offset of .0625-inch to the right; therefore, to make the same piston fit both right and left banks, Ford added an intake valve "eyebrow" to either side of the piston top. The CJ engines also use a cast aluminum piston, but to help boost compression to 11.3:1 (along with slightly smaller combustion chambers) it has only one valve relief per piston; therefore a different part is needed for each side of the engine. These pistons were never available separately from complete engines. The SCJ used an identical piston, except that it was forged aluminum. They were listed as the "service" parts for all CJ and SCJ engines (D1OZ-6109-B, right; D10Z-6108-B, left). These pistons, like many of the other Ford early high performance pistons, used the fully-rounded "figure-8" skirt design which has been known to have a tendency to crack. Ford also noted in their performance books that the forged SCJ pistons expand more than normal, so they give the following clearance specifications:

APPLICATION	CLEARANCE
Street	.004"
Street/Strip	.006"
Strip Only	.008—.010"

Original 460 engines came with a cast aluminum piston with a dished

New TRW forged pop-up, L-2442-F, (left) boosts compression in late model 460 Fords to a healthy 10:1. Flat-top with single eyebrow, L2366-F, (right) gives 11:1 in the CJ 429. Note difference in skirts on these two pistons, the 429 type having "figure-8" design.

For this 494-incher, George Streagle had J.E. Pistons make a set of forged flat-tops (part 70745) with 1/16-inch, 1/16-inch, 3/16-inch ring lands (big-block Chevy size), and a .990-inch diameter pin (again Chevy big block—a lighter pin). With standard bore and deck height, this piston gives 11:1 compression with a 98cc combustion chamber (460 head).

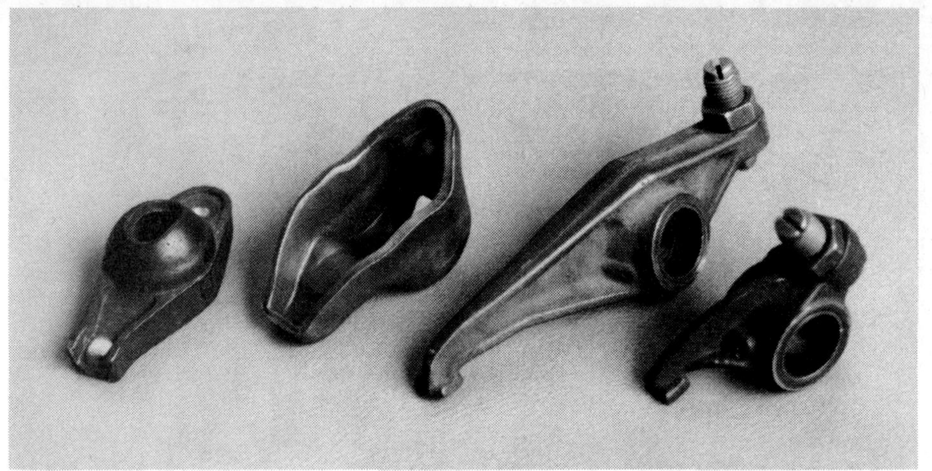

Early 429 and 460 engines used the cast rail rockerarms (left) which are not recommended for any sort of performance application. Later versions came with stamped steel rockers identical to 351 Clevelands, using either positive-stop or adjustable sled fulcrums. At right are the big-n-little exhaust and intake rockers used on the Boss 429 Hemi heads.

Rocker design on Boss 302's, 351-Clevelands, and 385-series Fords is the same—which happens to be very similar to big-block Chevy. So trick valvetrain components such as aluminum roller-tip rockerarms, heavy-duty studs, and adjustment locks are plentiful. These pieces are from Clay Smith.

top, but it yielded the same compression as the 429 (10½:1) because of the larger cylinder volume. In '72 the 460 compression dropped to 8.5:1, and the next year it fell to 8.0:1, where it has remained since. These later 460 pistons are *very* dished, as are all current Ford replacement pistons for the 460. Back in the Muscle Parts days, Ford offered a "stroker kit" for the 429, which consisted of the long-stroke 460 crank and a set of forged aluminum pistons (D10Z-6108-A). These pistons had a half-dished top which produced a nominal compression of 11:1. They would fit right into a 460, but, unfortunately there is no part number to indicate that these pistons could be purchased separately.

Just recently TRW introduced a new domed piston (L-2443-F) for the 460 to replace the dished type. It gives 10:1 compression with the stock 95cc late model cylinder heads, which would make a great combination for street or river running on currently available pump gas. With the early 77cc chamber heads, the .400-inch (12cc) dome can be machined flat to give a streetable 10.2:1 ratio. Of course, any of several excellent custom piston makers such as J.E., Venolia, Forgedtrue, Arias, etc., can make flat-top or other custom varieties of pistons to fit the 460 or 429. Follow the piston manufacturer's clearance recommendations when using a specialty part.

One of the excellent characteristics of the 460 engine, compared to the Chevy big block, is that the slightly open, yet small, combustion chamber can run on pump gas at about 11:1 compression; while the Chevy, which must use pop-up pistons to get this kind of compression, will tend to detonate. According to George Streagle of Clay Smith Cams (Buena Park, CA), who has built numerous 460 and stroker 494 engines for boats, the Ford can run an 11:1 compression ratio comfortably where the Chevy could only stand 10½:1 on the same gas.

George has also found a unique piston/ring combination for the 460. Since the desirable moly-type rings are not currently available in Ford widths (5/64-inch, 5/64-inch, 3/16-inch) and bore size, George bores the block .015-inch oversize to give the same bore as a .125-inch oversize 454 Chevy. Then, he has the pistons machined with Chevy ring grooves (1/16-inch, 1/16-inch, 3/16-inch) and uses TRW #T-9031-MM + .125 Chevy rings. He strongly recommends these rings over the stock Ford type in any heavy duty racing or high performance application, such as in a jet boat, which puts tremendous sustained loads on the engine.

HEADS/ROCKERS

There aren't too many variations to confuse you here. Boss hemi heads aside, there are three basic types of heads for 385 series engines, all of which are similar. Let's begin with valve train differences, however. Early base 429 and early 460 assemblies came with cast 1.75:1 ratio "rail" rockers which align themselves on the tops of the valvestems with a pair of

The difference in valve sizes, though not drastic, is apparent between the CJ/SCJ head (bottom) and the early standard head (top). The combustion chamber is sort of an open-quench design affording free breathing plus a squish area on the intake side of the chamber. Early heads have smaller 75cc (nominal) chambers for higher compression.

small rails at the tip of the rocker. These rockers are not recommended for any sort of high performance use because they will not allow adjustment, they can chafe or chew the valvestems, or when a high lift cam is installed they can hit on the retainer, popping the keepers out and allowing the valve to drop. Fortunately, heads using these rockers also had screw-in rocker studs, so they can very easily be converted to other types of rockers.

Early CJ (made before 1 November '69) and all SCJ engines came with stamped steel rockers, screw-in studs, and guide plates like those on the Boss 302 and 351 (the rockers are identical, the guide plates are a different part number). All CJ 429 engines made after November '69 had similar rockers, but used a "positive stop" shouldered screw-in stud, which did not allow for lash adjustment. Ford stamped steel rockers and sled fulcrums are readily available (1.73:1 ratio—same for Boss 302, 351-C and 429), as are screw-in rocker studs, making the conversion to adjustable rockers quite easy on these early heads. Pushrod guide plates are available from Ford (D00Z-6A564-A), from Manley, or from Gapp and Roush (GR-6A564-B). If you use guide plates you must also install hardened pushrods. The stock Ford type are 3/8-inch in diameter and 8.55 inches long (D00Z-6565-B).

As we mentioned in the Cleveland engine section, you might also consider Chevy big block rockers (with ball rather than sled fulcrums) and Chevy heat-treated 7/16-inch screw-in studs. If you want to use specialty needle-bearing roller rockers, big block Chevy type is what you will get. Steve Strange discovered that with the Chevy studs and Clay Smith roller rockers, plus guide plates under the studs, on his 460 he had to install .250-inch (approximately) longer pushrods to keep the rocker angles correct and to keep the rockers from hitting on the studs. Clay Smith made the pushrods, which are 5/16-inch in diameter, 8.875 inches long.

Now, let's look at the difference between the two basic varieties of 429 heads. It's interesting. The CJ and SCJ engines both came with substantially bigger ports than the base 429 or 460. Intake ports on the smaller heads measure approximately 1.85 inches by 2.56 inches while the ports on the CJ/SCJ are 2.12 inches by 2.86 inches. The valves are also bigger, measuring 2.42 inches (in.) and 1.72 inches (ex.) on the CJ; 2.07 inches/ 1.64 inches on the base engines. CJ and SCJ heads have the smallest combustion chamber size of all 385 series

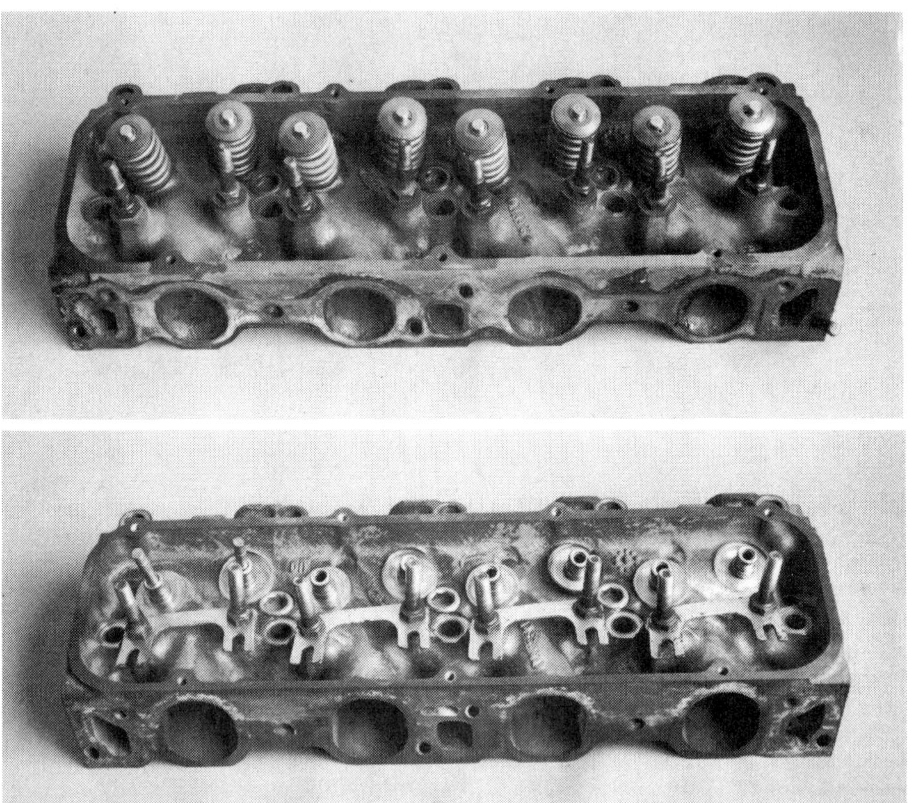

Intake ports on the CJ/SCJ heads (lower) are about .250-inch bigger than those on the standard 429 or 460 (top). Cobra Jets came with screw-in studs and pushrod guide plates, as shown; the standard head, also with screw-in studs, is an early version—the current variety has slotted pedestals for nonadjustable rockers.

The difference in exhaust port size is even more readily apparent between the CJ/SCJ (lower) and the standard head (top). Also apparent is the canted angle of the valves and rocker studs (which is slightly different than on the 351-C, so different guide plates must be used). Also notice that the CJ head uses smaller diameter spark plugs to provide clearance for bigger ports.

A CJ intake manifold can be bolted onto a standard head and will reportedly yield about 15 horsepower despite an obvious port mismatch (as shown by gasket line on lower port). Common practice these days is to grind out the stock port to match CJ gasket, as shown at top.

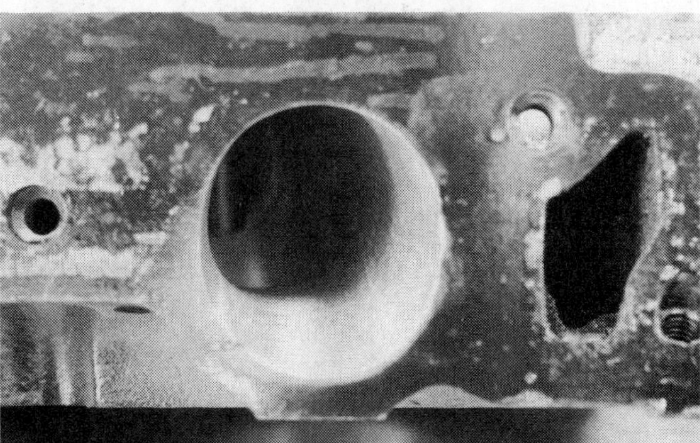

The intake passages are clean. Enlarge the opening to match the manifold, but there is no need to grind the passage itself larger.

The one downfall of 385-series heads is the exhaust port passage. Though the valve pocket and port are healthy, the passage is full of strange bumps and turns; some contouring will help greatly.

heads at 71-75cc. Early base 429 and 460 heads weren't much larger at 74-77cc, but then in '72 they went to big 90cc chambers (base 429 and 460 use the same heads). Obviously, the high compression, big port, big valve Cobra Jet or Super Cobra Jet heads are the ones to get, right? Simply bolting them on a base 429 will supposedly give you about 35 horsepower at 5200 rpm over the "small" heads. They are readily available from Ford, competitively priced at about $130 each, bare. But, the extra expense may not be worth the price. A good port and polish job on the base heads, along with installing the larger CJ valves, can give you a 65 horsepower increase over stock. In the unblushing words of the Ford Muscle Parts Book (Supplement Number 2): "These smaller ports when smoothed out flow better than the big CJ/SCJ sewer pipes." Those are Ford's words, not ours.

You might reckon that the larger heads with a good port and polish job might, in turn, flow better than the smaller ones with similar work. This may be true for some high-rpm racing applications (above 6000 rpm), especially on a 460, but there doesn't seem to be conclusive evidence. The fact appears to be that nobody has spent much time developing these heads on a flow bench, so opinions vary somewhat. One early publication states that bolting a CJ intake manifold on the base heads, despite a giant port mismatch, yields 15 horsepower; then they tested the same heads completely ported to match the intake manifold, and polished, and they state that not a single horsepower was gained. We would rather not draw conclusions from a single instance such as this, but we would say that in light of past evidence and recommendations, trying to find a set of CJ or SCJ heads for your 429 or 460 is probably not worth the effort. If you have a post-'72 engine, you might want to scare up a set of inexpensive pre-'72 base heads for a quick increase in compression (although installing higher compression pistons would be the better method.)

But considering you have a good set of heads with your 429/460 already, you'll save time and money and probably make just as much horsepower by reworking what you have. The exhaust ports are the real problem. They are more congested than the Los Angeles freeways at five PM. The inlet and outlet sizes aren't too bad, but the passage inside is full of big bumps and bad curves. Try to get your finger through it, and you'll see what we mean. You can pick up a quick 20 horses just by knocking down the bumps and blending them in—you don't have to be a professional head grinder to make a big improvement. Then, assuming you will be using a Cobra Jet intake manifold, or a specialty performance type that has the CJ-size ports, port-match the head to the CJ intake gaskets. You don't have to open up the entire runner, just "shoulder" the end of the port so that it blends smoothly into the smaller passage. While you are working with the Du-more, you would be wise to go ahead and polish the combustion chambers if you are planning to run some compression in the engine (to minimize the chance of preignition from hot spots). Finally, you might want to consider installing the CJ **valves (D00Z-6507-A, intake; D00Z-6505-A, exhaust), which are substantially bigger than the base valves**—especially the intakes. Any competent head shop will have the necessary

The 429/460 combustion chamber will allow hefty compression ratios even with current gasoline, and polishing the surfaces as shown will help further. This late 460 head retains stock valves, which are adequate for most high-performance applications and which give better unshrouding than the giant 2.25-inch CJ/SCJ intakes.

If you want a super light and big intake for your 429/460 you can install a set of the 2.250-inch hollow-stem 427 Tunnel-Port intakes (shown on right; CJ 429 intake on left). The FE valve stem is slightly longer, plus the diameter is 0.371-inch as opposed to 0.342-inch, so the guides would have to be enlarged.

equipment to enlarge the valve pockets and cut new seats. For the street, use a two-angle valve cut, as shown in the diagram, with a seat width of .070- to .080-inch. For competition, go to a three-angle job with a seat width of .050-inch. One word of caution: if you are going to install the larger valves in a base head, or if you are going to swap CJ/SCJ heads onto a base 429 engine with the early single eyebrow flat-top pistons, you must enlarge the valve relief or the big valves will hit the pistons. So "just bolting on" the CJ heads isn't as simple as it may at first appear.

INTAKE SYSTEMS

There isn't a great selection of intake equipment for the 385 series Fords. As far as factory equipment goes, there was a cast iron dual-plane, single four-barrel induction (D00Z-9424-C) which came on the CJ and had a flange for a Rochester Quadra-Jet carb. Preferable is the identical cast iron SCJ intake (D00Z-9424-B) which has a flange for the popular Holley four-barrels. The SCJ came with a vacuum-secondary 780-cfm; and an 850 will bolt right on, and would be a wise choice for top performance in a single four-barrel setup. For specialty induction systems Ford concentrated on the Boss 429 engine, but these manifolds will not fit on the wedge heads since the Boss has large round intake ports instead of ovals. Supposedly, Ford did make a few dual four-barrel aluminum manifolds to fit the CJ 429, but these are extremely rare. Shelby also made a four-barrel aluminum intake for the 429, but it, too, is a collector's piece today.

In the specialty market the choices aren't much better. For healthy ski boat or racing applications there are tunnel ram manifolds available from Offenhauser or Weiand, either of which can be fitted with single or dual four-barrel tops. The Offy tunnel ram has a larger plenum than the Weiand, and is preferable for jet-boat or low-rpm power applications. For good street or ski boat performance, Offy offers their Port-O-Sonic, X-type intake for the 460/base 429 with either a Quadra-Jet flange (#6158) or with a Holley flange (#6157). Edelbrock makes a Torker (#2795) for the same application. Both of these intakes have the smaller port sizes, but have plenty of meat around the runners so you can open them up to match CJ heads. If you are planning to pull your boat with a 460-equipped pickup or if you plan to use your 460 to make power and economy in the street-driving rpm ranges, try the Edelbrock Streetmaster (#3190).

CAMS/VALVE SPRINGS

Cobra Jet 429 engines came with a hydraulic camshaft (C9AZ-6250-A) which measured 282° intake and 296° exhaust duration and .496-inch lift with

CYLINDER HEAD I.D. AND APPLICATION CHART (Service Parts Only)

Part Number	Engine	Year	Chamber Volume (c.c.)	Valve Sizes		Port Sizes			
				Exh.	Int.	Intake WXH		Exhaust WXH	
D0VZ-6049-D	429/460	68/71	74.2-77.2	1.65	2.08	1.85	2.56	1.43	2.00
D0OZ-6049-H	429CJ/SCJ	70-71	71.5-75.5	1.72	2.24	2.12	2.86	1.32	2.24
D0AZ-6049-C	429 BOSS	69/70	83.0-87.0	1.90	2.28	2.36	2.36	1.68	2.04
D2OZ-6049-A	429 P.C.	72	87.4-90.4	1.72	2.25	2.12	2.86	1.32	2.24
D2VZ-6049-B	429	72	89.9-92.9	1.65	2.08	1.85	2.56	1.43	2.00

INTAKE MANIFOLD I.D. AND APPLICATION (Service Parts Only)

Part Number	Application		Type	Material	Bore Diameter		Port Sizes		Notes
	Engine	Year			Primary	Secondary	Width	Height	
C9AZ-9424-D	429 BOSS	69/70	4V Dual	Alum	1.72	1.72	2.24 Round		
D0AZ-9424-A	429	68/70	2V Dual	Iron	1.70	N.A.	1.76 Round		2V Version of D0VY-A
D0VY-9424-A	429/460	68/70	4V Dual	Iron	1.70	1.58	1.76 Round		
D1AZ-9424-B	429 CJ/PC	70	4V Dual	Iron	1.40	2.27	2.02	2.38	Uses Rochester Carburetor
D0OZ-9424-B	429 SCJ	70	4V Dual	Iron	1.70	1.70	2.02	2.38	Uses Holley Carburetor
D2VY-9424-A	429	72	2V Dual	Iron	1.70	—	1.76 Round		

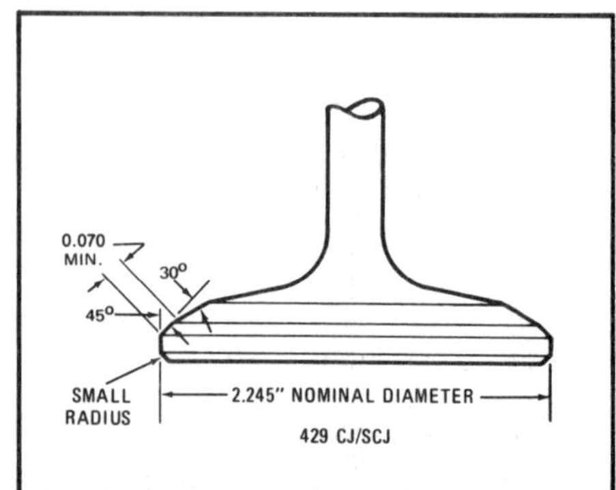

Valve seat and face preparation is the single most important aspect of cylinder head preparation. For best all around performance stick to the factory recommended specs.

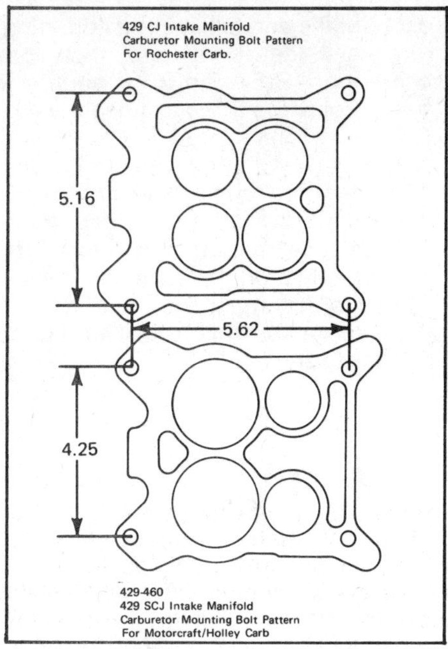

The Cobra Jet manifolds came with a Quadra-Jet mounting pad but the nearly identical Super Cobra Jet manifold had a mounting pad for the equi-bore spacing and bolt pattern for the Holley 4150 and 4160 carbs.

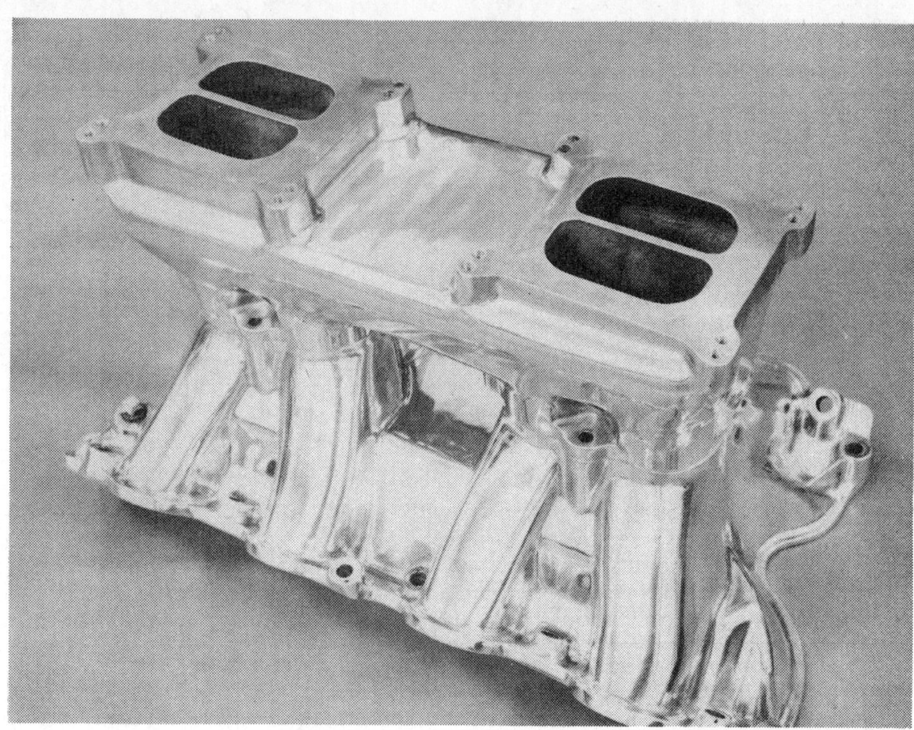

Both Offenhauser and Weiand make tunnel ram intake manifolds for 385-series Fords. Shown is a polished Offy 360° for two four-barrels; an alternate top is available for a single four.

1.73:1 rockerarms. Super Cobra Jets used a mechanical-lifter cam (D0AZ-6250-D), which was also used in the street version (solid-lifter) Boss 429. It is rated at 300° duration and .509-inch lift. As of this writing, both of these camshafts are still available from Ford. Another readily-available, good Ford hydraulic grind is the marine cam (D3JE-6250-AA) which measures 286° duration, .438-inch lift intake and .481-inch lift exhaust. You can get these from any Ford industrial/marine dealer.

With the SCJ solid-lifter cam, Ford recommends valve springs which will give 93 pounds pressure at the seat and 315 pounds with the valve open. On the SCJ engine, Ford used a single coil spring with an inner damper (D0ZZ-6513-A) and a hardened spring seat (D00Z-6514-A). To install these springs and seats on nonSCJ heads, you will have to machine the base of the valve guide boss to a smaller diameter. The same spring is used on the CJ engine with the hydraulic cam, but the seats are not used. On the CJ head the base of the valve guide is slightly smaller than on the standard 429/460 head, so installing the SCJ/CJ spring on the small heads causes the damper to ride on the edge of the valve guide boss, leading to wear, binding, or chafing. To eliminate this problem Ford offers an easy solution. If you install the CJ hydraulic cam in a base 429/460 use the 428 CJ/SCJ spring assembly (C90Z-6513-E) which is slightly wider and fits the stock head perfectly. Of course, it might be easier for you to order springs to fit from your favorite cam grinder—each has a wide selection and his own particular recommendations. The 428 CJ springs are rated at 90 pounds at the seat at an installed height of 1.82 inch and 281 pounds open to 1.32 inch.

If you are going to install a solid-lifter cam in a later 460, you will find that the stock heads have slotted rockerarm pedestals. Follow exactly the same procedure outlined in the 351-Cleveland section for cutting these pedestals and drilling and tapping them to accept regular screw-in studs, guide plates, and the necessary adjustable rockerarms. If you are going to use a hotter-than-stock hydraulic cam, you do not have to change the rockers, but it is still recommended. Ford originally offered anti-pumpup lifters (C90Z-6500-A) as

There is a limited selection of specialty/performance manifolds available for the 429-460 big block engine. One of the most popular is the readily-available Edelbrock single-plane Streetmaster manifold.

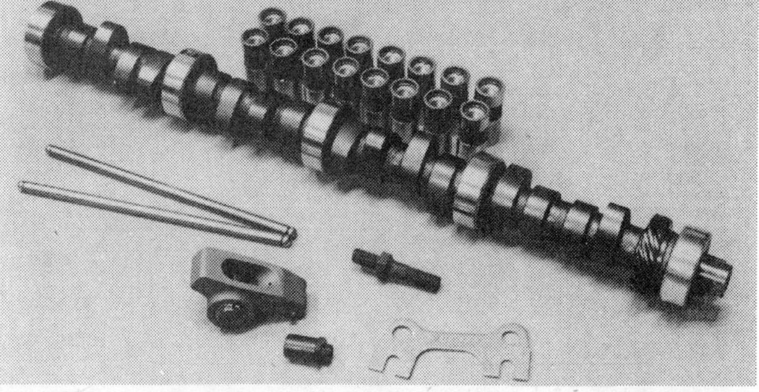

There is no shortage of camshafts and related components for 429 or 460. For the street or a pleasure ski boat you would probably want a hydraulic stick, but for snappier performance a solid-lifter combination requires screw-in rocker studs, guide plates, and hardened pushrods.

CAMSHAFT I.D. AND APPLICATION (Service Parts Only)

Part Number	Application		Type	Lash	Valve Events										
					Intake		Exhaust		Duration		Lift		Overlap	Identification	
	Engine	Year			Open	Close	Open	Close	Intake	Exhaust	Lobe	Valve		Mark	Location
C8SZ-6250-A	429-460	68/72	HYD		16°BTC	60°ABC	70°BBC	20°ATC	256°	270°	.278"	.487"	36°	8 B	Between Dist. and 1st Journal
					21°ATC	19°BBC	25°BBC	27°BTC							
C9AZ-6250-A	429 Boss & CJ	69 70	HYD		32°BTC	70°ABC	90°BBC	26°ATC	282°	296°	.289"	.506"	58°	8 J	
					15°ATC	21°BBC	41°BBC	27°BTC							
D0AZ-6250-D	429 Boss & SCJ	70 70/71	Mech.	.013*	41°BTC	79°ABC	89°BBC	31°ATC	300°	300°	.298"	.509"	72°	8 J	2 Grooves on Dist. Gear
					5°ATC	21°BBC	43°BBC	27°BTC							
D2OZ-6250-A	429 P.C.	72	HYD		35°BTC	73°ABC	86°BBC	26°ATC	288°	292°	.285"I .290"E	.493"I .501"E	61°		
					18°ATC	20°BBC	33°BBC	27°BTC							
D1ZX-6250-EA	429	OHO	Mech.	.013*	66°BTC	92°ABC	89°BBC	69°ATC	338°	338°	.368"	.620"	135°	D1ZX-EA	Stamped on end
					19°BTC	39°ABC	42°BBC	16°ATC							

* BOSS engine (0.013" cold, 0.024" hot—aluminum heads), 429SCJ (0.024" hot & cold).
NOTE: 429 OHO camshaft uses conventional tappets with 0.050" spherical radius seats.

an option for use with the CJ cam. Most specialty hydraulic cams also come with suitable anti-pumpup lifters. To set such lifters for best performance, turn the engine to TDC on the compression stroke on number one cylinder. Adjust both valves to zero clearance (rotate the pushrod as you tighten the rocker; stop when you feel drag on the pushrod). Then, tighten the rocker nuts an additional 1/16th turn. Rotate the crankshaft one-quarter turn, repeat the process at number five cylinder, and then continue in firing order (1-5-4-2-6-3-7-8). Obviously this process cannot be accomplished with nonadjustable rockers

There are some peculiarities about valve timing in the 385 series engines. The '73 vintage 429 and '73 and later 460 came with cam timing retarded eight degrees (measured at the crank). This is not unusual, since it is a common method for meeting pollution requirements without making new parts. On such an engine you will notice a marked difference if you simply pull the front cover and install an early "straight up" timing gear. If you can't find an early stocker, Gapp and Roush (GRST-6306-A) as well as others sell a multi-index crank sprocket which fits the 429/460 as well as the 351-C/400. The peculiar part is that Ford engineers recommended retarding the SCJ solid-lifter cam: "...to get the maximum power from it, you must install it differently. Instead of dialing it in at zero degrees, the cam should be retarded six cam degrees (equivalent to 12 crank degrees). This produces a peak gain of 50 horsepower at 6000 rpm over the stock 429-4V cam and 18 horsepower over the hydraulic 429 CJ stick."[1] They acknowledge that this setting does reduce mid-range torque somewhat; but the system still doesn't sound quite right. To further complicate the issue, Ford installed exactly the same camshaft in the "T" Boss 429 street engines using 1.65:1 intake rockers and 1.75:1 exhaust rockers; in the SCJ the rocker ratio was 1.73:1.

One person who knows what he is talking about when it comes to timing valve events in a 385 series Ford big block is George Streagle of Clay Smith Cams. After considerable testing, George has found that the most sensitive area in camming the 429/460 is the intake opening point. And that point, for best all around performance, should fall between 40-50° before top dead center. (Since the SCJ number DOAZ-6250-D cam opens the intake at 41° BTDC, it seems appropriate to install it "straight up" rather than retarded as Ford suggested.) Other valve events are not as critical, according to George, but he has found that this engine likes an equal-profile cam (intake and exhaust lift, duration, etc., are identical), and that lobe centers of 108° seem to be about the best. For Steve Strange's healthy 460, George recommended a Clay Smith #C-304-8-B, a solid-lifter profile with 304° duration and .615-inch lift. Of course, most of the other major performance cam manufacturers offer a wide selection of cams and related valve train components, and any of them should be able to deliver a grind similar to this.

1. Muscle Parts Story, Supplement No. 2. pg 33.

EXHAUST

You aren't going to find $39.95 headers for a 429/460 Ford. If you are running the engine in a boat, you have plenty of choices of dry or wet stacks—check your local high performance marine dealer. If you are running the engine in a '69-70 Mustang, Hooker makes a set to fit (#6115) which might be coaxed into other engine compartments as well. General recommendations for headers for this engine are 2-1/8-inch i.d. primaries, 34 inches long, running into 10- to 12-inch long collectors.

If you cannot find a set of headers to fit your particular application, or if the engine compartment doesn't allow the room, you might try to find a set of the CJ cast iron exhaust manifolds. They are big and nicely formed into a relatively free-flowing exhaust—as cast iron manifolds go.

OTHER PARTS

We will not cover ignition systems for the 385 series engines here, since the choices are the same as for the 351 Cleveland. Since hardly any 429/460 will be used in any sort of competition where ignition type is stipulated, one

Highly recommended for any acceleration-performance Ford engine application is a rear-sump and rear pickup oil pan. Dooley Enterprises of Anaheim, CA, make this unit primarily for boat applications where clearance problems are minimal.

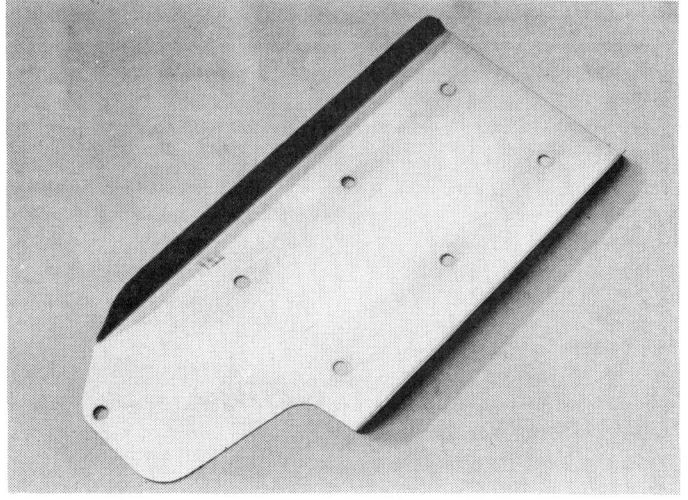

Also included in the Dooley package is this simple windage tray, which attaches to extensions on special main cap bolts.

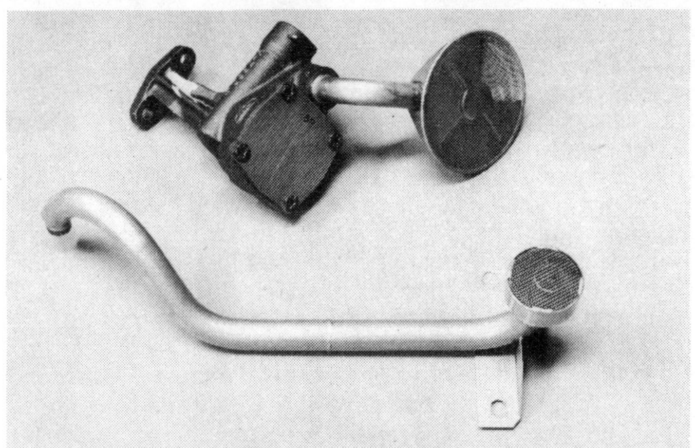

The standard 429/460 oil pump is fine for most applications. It uses a press-in pickup tube. The stock pickup tube is shown in the pump; a rear pickup extension tube is shown below it.

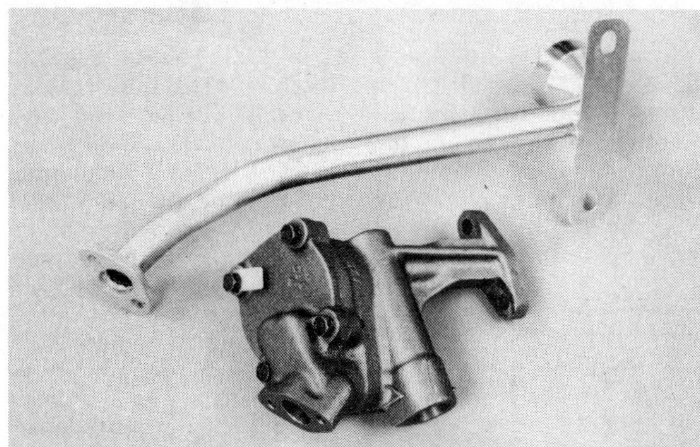

A better dual-entry high volume oil pump came on the Cobra Jets and is currently available from TRW. It uses a bolt-on pickup tube, and may also be used with a rear pickup extension as illustrated.

of the specialty/performance breakerless electronic systems are your best choice.

Another part that will fit both the 429 and the 351-C is the timing chain and gear set, and it is strongly recommended that you install a Cloyes "Tru-Roller" double chain and steel sprockets for accurate cam timing and durability under performance conditions. Gapp and Roush offers the Cloyes set for this engine (GRST-6306-A) with the crank sprocket modified for multi-indexing—a big plus for the later 460 if you want to set cam timing back to zero.

Finally, like most engines, the 429/460 needs some attention given to the oil system. Since this engine uses exactly the same system as the Cleveland motors, you might think that the hot tip is to install one of the restrictor kits or a direct crank oiling kit (as made for the 351-C). Most builders of the big engines, especially the 460, feel this is unnecessary. The Cleveland requires this special attention to main bearing and crank oiling because it is used in extreme high-rpm racing. The big motor just doesn't spin that fast—7000-7500 rpm being about the most any boat or drag racer is going to wind out of it.

Oiling is still critical in a 460; the approach is just a little different (fortunately it is simpler). George Streagle and Steve Strange both insist that the most important addition to a 460 in a jet boat or in a drag car (if you can make room in the chassis) is a rear-sump or rear-pickup oil pan. According to George the major mortality factor for the 460 is burned or spun main and rod bearings created by a lack of oil. This is primarily caused by starvation from a front-mounted pump pickup in an unbaffled pan. The problem is further complicated in jet boats because the engine is mounted on and angle (the same being true for some drag cars). George has found an excellent rear-pickup pan and windage tray combination to be the one made by Dooley Enterprises (Anaheim, CA). Also highly recommended for the oil system is an SCJ-type dual-entry, high-volume oil pump. This was offered by Ford in the CJ/SCJ engines and is listed as part C9AZ-6600-A; it is currently available from TRW under part number 50083. Not only does it pump more oil, but it has a bolt-on pickup tube rather than the push-in type. Before bolting the pump to the block, you should drill the oil passage from pump to filter to about 5/8-inch and flare the ends slightly with a grinder. Other than that, and using the good quality Clevite 77 bearings, you need take no further precautions to insure the life of your 429 or 460.

There is one more piece of unique and excellent oil system apparatus that you should consider for your 429/460, especially if the engine is mounted in a big pickup that will be pulling loads. It is an oil cooler system, which came on the SCJ 429 and which was also mounted on the Police Interceptor 429/460. One of your best sources for this complete setup might be a junked

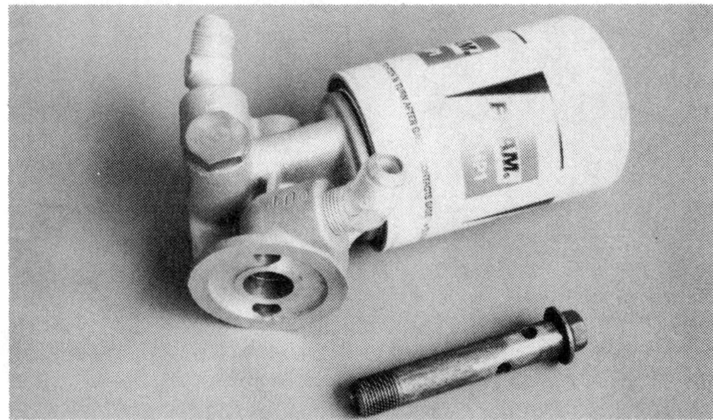

Super Cobra Jets and Police Interceptor 429 engines had the added protection of an add-on oil cooler radiator. The inlet/outlet adapter for this setup is still available, and can be bolted onto any 385-series, Cleveland, smallblock, or even a six cylinder Ford. Oil cooler radiators are available from several sources (such as suppliers of A-N fittings and steel braided hoses), so you could fashion your own system.

Don't let the Chevy valve covers fool you—this big block is a Ford. It's also the world's first 7-second Pro Stock engine, Don Nicholson's killer match-race motor. Using a rare aluminum block from a 494-inch Can Am Boss 429 and even rarer prototype aluminum CJ heads (which Don has modified with high-port exhaust plates), this is still basically a 385-series Ford big block.

Ford or Merc police car. Otherwise, you can order the special oil filter adapter (DOOZ-6881-B) and hollow attaching bolt (C4GY-6894-A) from Ford and hook it to any of the several oil-cooler radiators on the market these days. This same oil filter adapter will also fit all small block engines and Clevelands—a good tip.

PARTS LIST

Part Number	Part Name
1. C9OZ-6A642-A	Cooler Assy—Crankcase Oil
2. D0OZ-6B633-B	Bracket Assy—Oil Cooler Upper
3. 359662-S7-8	Screw & Wash Assy—5/16—1 BX 75 HEX HD
4. 55736-S	Locknut—5/16—18 Hex
5. D0OZ-6B634-B	Bracket Assy—Oil Cooler Lower
6. 57140-S	Bolt—5/16—18 x .88
7. D0OZ-6A715-A	Hose Assy—Engine Oil Cooler—Inlet
8. D0OZ-6A715-B	Hose Assy—Engine Oil Cooler—Outlet
9. NOT SERVICED	Clip—5/8 x 5/8
10. 55914-S2	Screw—1/4—14 x .75 Tapping
11. D0OZ-6881-B	Adapter—Oil Cooler

BOLT TORQUE SPECIFICATIONS

Cylinder Head	Step 1 75 Step 2 105 Step 3 130-140
Intake Manifold	25-30
Main Bearing Caps	95-105
4-Bolt Main Outer Bolts	70-80 (3/8 bolts) 35-40 (7/16 bolts)
Connecting Rod Caps	40-45
Rockerarm Stud	65-75
Rockerarm Nut (positive stop)	18-20

429-460
BLUEPRINT SPECIFICATIONS

Main Bearing Clearance	.0025—.0030
Rod Bearing Clearance	.0025-.0030
Rod Side Clearance	.025
Piston to Bore Clearance	cast: .007 forged: .004 street .006 street/strip .008-.010 comp
Piston Ring End Gap	.017-.023 #1 & 2
Piston Ring-to-Groove	.002-.004 #1 & 2
Piston Pin Clearance	.0007-.0009
Crankshaft End Play	.004-.008
Piston-to-Deck Height	.010-.020
Piston-to-Valve Clearance	auto: .070 I .100 E stick: .100 I .100 E
Valve Stem-to-Guide Clearance	.0008-.0018 I .0011-.0021 E
Lifter-to-Bore Clearance	.0007-.0027

THE BOSS 429

There is little point in discussing how to build or modify a Shotgun 429 Hemi, since the vast majority of you will never see one in person, let alone own one. But the engine is certainly of historical interest to anyone who loves Ford engines. These engines were never available to the general public, outside of the few hundred that were installed in '69 and '70 Boss 429 Mustangs and Mercury Cougars. Supposedly, a few were installed in Ford Talladegas, and at least one witness has seen a couple in '71 Boss 429 Mustangs. Then Ford quit building high performance machinery. Who knows where the Boss 429 has gone—relatively few exist today (compared to SOHC engines, for instance).

In the short career of the Boss 429 it was built in several versions. The two that were available in production, dealer-sold cars were labeled the "820-S" and the "820-T," or simply the S and T versions. The S engine came in early '69 model cars. It featured a hydraulic camshaft, and consequently a block drilled for hydraulic-lifter oiling. The T engine, which was the most toned-down version of the Boss 429, started out with a hydraulic cam, but switched to the SCJ solid grind in late '69 and '70. Besides the two street versions of the Shotgun, there were a few variations of the Nascar 429 Hemi, and then there was the big all-aluminum 494 cubic inch Can Am Shotgun Hemi. We will try to sort out the differences.

STREET BOSS 429

It's the heads that make the engine. Cast of aluminum, they feature what have been called "crescent" combustion chambers. These are actually the same as hemi heads except that the edges of the chamber have been squared off to provide a small "squish" area on either side. This provides slightly better bottom and midrange torque for street driving (and shorter circle tracks), plus it helps inhibit detonation. These heads use 2.280-inch intake valves and 1.90-inch exhausts, having the same stem diameter (0.342-inch) as the wedge 429. Different length rockerarms are mounted on short individual .784-inch diameter shafts supported by stands which bolt to the head. On both the S and T engines the rocker ratios are 1.76:1 for exhausts and 1.65:1 for the intakes.

None of the Boss 429 engines use conventional head gaskets; instead they have copper "Cooper Rings" to seal the cylinders and neoprene O-rings around water passages. In early engines the O-ring grooves were machined in the block deck surfaces; in later street Boss motors the grooves were in the heads (don't put grooved heads on a grooved block). In case you have one of these engines, Gapp and Roush have replacement O-rings: GR6X-6051-A for cylinder seals; GR6X-6051-B and -C for the water passage seals). A sealant was also necessary between head and block (such as hi-temp silicone) to keep valley chamber oil from leaking out. Both the S and T street 429 used large, round, intake ports and a matching aluminum, dual-plane intake manifold with a single 735-cfm Holley four-barrel.

The Boss 429 cylinder block is very similar to the wedge block, but is a different casting featuring slightly beefier main bearing webs and different oil passages. The bottom end has a four-bolt main bearing cap at number one, in addition to those on numbers two through four. A Boss block can be distinguished from the top by machined-round water passages in the deck (plus machined O-ring grooves on earlier models), as well as two oil passage "pedestals" in the middle of the valley chamber, and three screw-in oil passage plugs between the lifter bosses on the right side. If you are going to install a solid-lifter cam in a Boss 429 which originally came with a

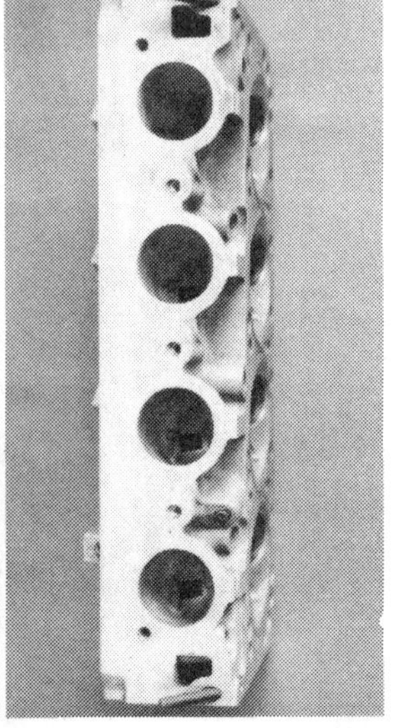

Street Boss 429 heads were aluminum, used O-rings instead of gaskets (this is a later head, with O-ring grooves machined in the head surface), and had "quench-hemi" combustion chambers. Intake ports were circular, exhausts were oval, and rockerarms were mounted on individual shafts which bolted to cast pedestals.

hydraulic, these plugs should be removed and substituted for a block-off kit (Gapp and Roush GR7H-65A01-A) which halts oil flow to the lifters. The street Boss blocks also have small machined pushrod reliefs at the edge of the deck surface to allow clearance for the angled pushrods.

Both S and T street Boss engines have cross-drilled steel cranks, but they are balanced differently to match separate piston/rod combinations. The S engine has the stronger rod, featuring huge ½-inch bolts with 12-point heads and nuts, plus this rod is shorter than all other 429 rods, at 6.549 inches (C9AZ-6200-A). It must be used with the matching piston (C9AZ-6108-A) which is forged aluminum with a full-floating on-center pin, rated at 10½:1 compression. The T engine uses a rod of the same length as the wedge 429/460 (6.605 inches), with a 3/8-inch "football-head" bolt (C9AZ-6200-B). This is a sturdier piece than the CJ/SCJ rod, but Ford still did not recommend it for use over 7000 rpm. The T piston (C9AZ-6108-G) was similar to the S except in weight and pin height.

THE NASCAR 429

Originally, the S engine was listed as the racing version of the Boss 429, toned down slightly for street use. But the all-out Nascar engine is a bit different. The block has a much bigger number one four-bolt main cap and the grooves for head sealing O-rings are in the block. It can also be quickly identified by much deeper pushrod relief grooves in the sides of the cylinder banks. The steel crank is essentially the same as S and T versions except that it was left unbalanced by the factory so that the particular engine builder could match it to a specific piston/rod combination. Two types of rods were used. One, known as the Nascar rod (C9AX-6200-B) is fully polished, uses a peculiar round-head, tri-lobe thread bolt (tighten this type by measuring bolt stretch, not by torquing), and it is really heavy and stout. At 6.785 inches, it is also longer than any other 429 rods. Another version of the Nascar rod, which is quite rare these days is similar except that it has a cast rib up the middle of the beam with a drilled oil passage inside to feed lubrication to the pin. Two Nascar pistons were also made by Ford to go with these rods, each rated at a nominal 13:1 compression. One (C9AX-6110-B), matched the partial-quench Boss head and was preferred for shorter tracks. The other (C9AX-6110-BH) was a full hemi design which produced ultimate top end power for the banked Daytona and Talladega race tracks. To use this latter piston the Boss heads had to be opened up to full hemispherical chambers and matched to the piston domes.

Most Nascar heads were the same as the street Boss 429 except that they used slightly smaller diameter (0.704-inch) rocker shafts and 1.75:1 ratio intake rockers instead of the 1.65:1 ratio used on the street motors. They also came with larger intake valves (2.37-inch diameter) which were hollow stem stainless steel (C9AX-6507-B), plus sodium-filled standard-diameter exhausts (C9AX-6505-D). These valves are .050-inch shorter than other Boss 429 valves because they were recessed this amount in the heads. Both are currently available under the original Ford part numbers from Gapp and Roush.

When these engines were being used for drag racing back in '69-70, some builders found that the Boss heads worked better with raised and slightly smaller diameter intake ports. Supposedly, Ford actually produced a few "D-port" Boss heads, but only a few have been seen. These have D-shaped intake ports with the bottom part of the runners filled in. The only specialty intake manifold available for the Boss 429 is a Weiand tunnel ram (#1990) for dual four-barrels. This manifold has D-shaped runners, and it is not recommended that they be ground out to match round intake ports in Boss heads. A big single four-barrel (Holley Dominator carb) "box" type manifold was made by Ford for the Nascar 429, but these are very hard to find today.

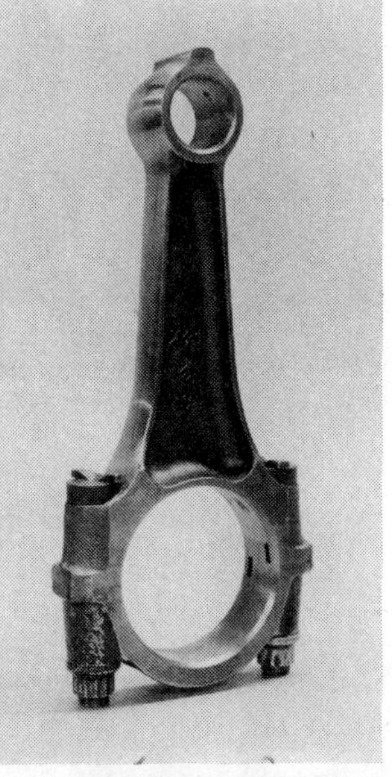

All components in the Boss 429 were built for action. The Boss blocks have machined reliefs (arrow) for exhaust pushrods. (Note this is a street Boss block with smaller reliefs than the racing blocks.) Possibly a case of overkill the Boss "S" connecting rod was huge and came with ½-inch bolts. The production intake was an aluminum single four-barrel manifold. Standard 429 manifolds will not fit the Boss heads.

THE CAN-AM BOSS 494

Boss 429 engines are rare, but this one is even a rarity within the family. Ford made a brief, relatively unsuccessful stab at Can-Am racing just before all of their racing activities were shut down. The engine they chose was the Boss 429, but they cast a brand new cylinder block for it—from aluminum. Using siamesed steel insert cylinder liners, it had a 4.52-inch bore compared to 4.36 inches for all other 385 series engines. The stroke was the same as the 460 at 3.850 inches but, of course, the Can Am engine used a special steel forging (some of which are still available for possible use in the 460—see prior section). It used a dry-sump oiling system with a specially cast two-piece aluminum pan, housing a belt-driven scavenge pump in the front with a pressure pump mounted to the stock location on the block. Induction was handled by a set of Hilborn injectors. More than this we can't tell you—very few of these one-off specials were built and virtually none remain alive today.

HOW TO BUILD A 460 BIG BLOCK

The beefy 429-460 big block has a reputation among RV and boat enthusiasts for building huge bundles of torque. It is one of the most popular powerplants for Southern California "river runners." The buildup shown here was completed by river enthusiast Steve Strange. The individual components were professionally prepared and modified but Steve saved a lot of money by doing the final assembly in his own workshop.

The average backyard hot rodder can take an engine apart and put it back together again, but few have the machinery or equipment needed to rebuild, balance, and blueprint a performance engine. On the other hand a complete custom-built engine from a pro shop can be very expensive. You can save money by doing the final assembly yourself. A clean, well lit, well organized work area is, however, mandatory.

The stock 460 block has received no special preparation other than a good cleaning and painting of inside and outside surfaces. The cylinders have been bored .015-inch oversize.

The stock cast 460 crank was sent to Velasco's for chamfering of oil holes, micro-polishing, and checking for straightness and tolerances.

Both the main and rod bearings are TRW Clevite-77 type. Note that both the journals and the bearings are liberally coated with moly assembly lube.

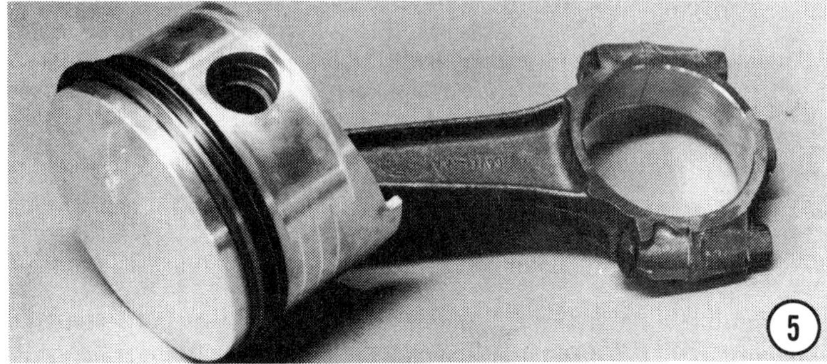

The reason for the .150-inch overbore on the block is to allow the use of .125-inch oversize Chevy 454 moly-faced rings. Venolia made the forged aluminum pistons for this application with flat tops and single eyebrows. Steve is using the stock 460 rods.

Main cap bolts torque to 105 ft-lb. Rod caps go 40-45 ft-lb with stock type rods. See blueprint table for other clearances (crank end play, rod side clearance) which must be checked before you can feel secure about the bottom end. Always double check all important measurements.

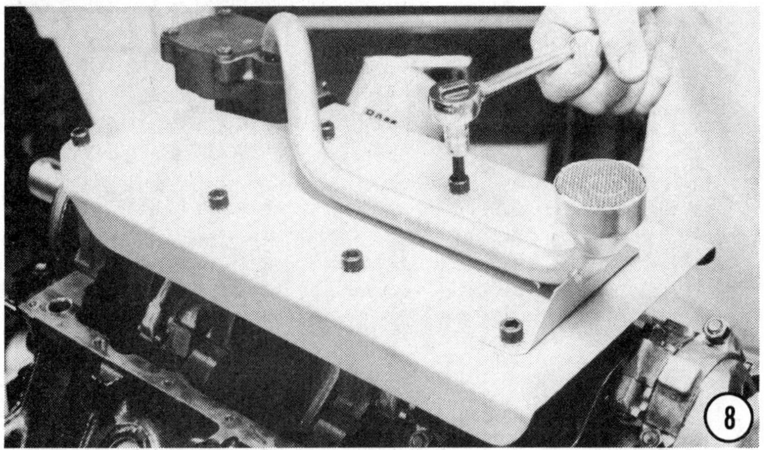

However, Steve strongly recommends the Dooley windage tray, rear oil pump pickup, and rear sump pan. Special main cap bolts have screw-on extensions which accept cap screws to hold both pan and pickup in place.

Clay Smith Engineering also prepared the stock 460 heads for Steve. The intake ports were enlarged to match the CJ-size intake manifold, the passages were smoothed and lightly polished, combustion chambers were polished, and the exhaust passages were cleaned up and enlarged. Stock valves were retained, but Clay Smith dual springs (140 lb at seat) and steel retainers were added.

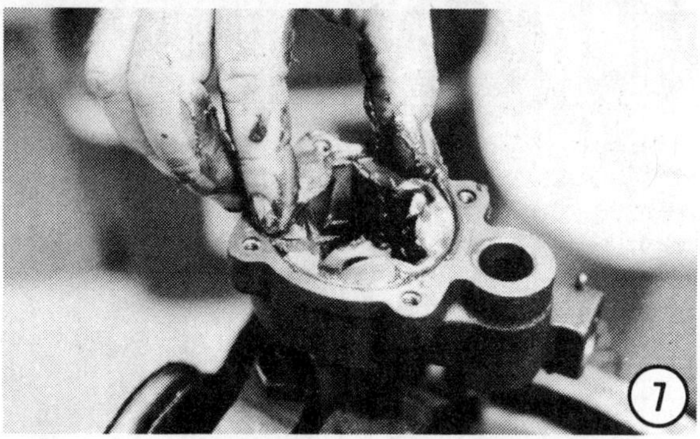

An unusual building tip preferred by Steve is to liberally coat the oil pump rotor with moly lube so that it will be well-greased even before you prime the engine. He feels the stock pump is adequate.

Although the 460 oil system is identical to a 351-C, elaborate oil system modification is unnecessary since the big engine will not rev into the 10,000 rpm range. Both Steve and George Streagle of Clay Smith Engineering insist on full oiling to the engine at all times as the best measure of insurance against breakage.

Steve installed a Clay Smith C-304-8-B solid-lifter cam in his 460, which measures 304° duration and .615-inch lift. He is also using the standard timing chain, with an early "straight up" crank gear and a steel (rather than fiber) cam gear. Since the 460 and the Cleveland use identical timing gear components, a very good alternative would be the Cloyes Tru-Roller setup (see Cleveland section).

Ford Industrial and Marine dealers carry a head gasket for the 460 that is far superior to the standard type. It is made of a stainless steel sandwich, and should be installed without any sort of sealer. Ask for part number D1JE-6051-BA.

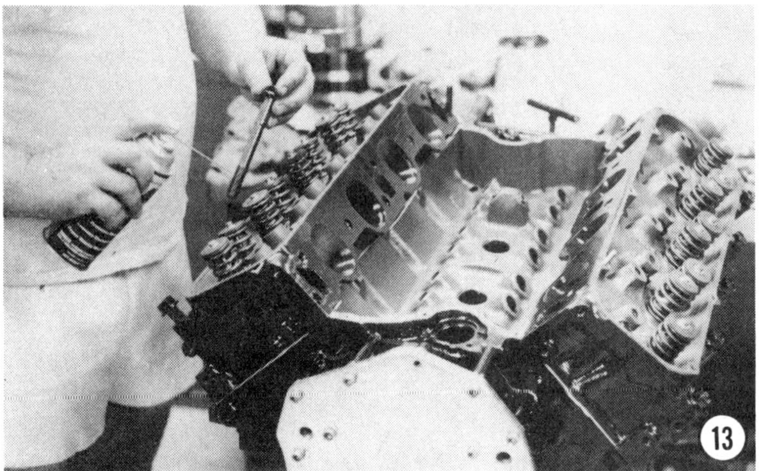

Before cinching down the heads, it is a good idea to spray the bolts with an anti-seize compound or a good lubricant such as WD-40 to insure accurate torque readings. Torque the bolts to 130-140 ft-lb in 25-lb increments beginning at 75 ft-lb.

Steve uses an Offy 360° tunnel intake with a single Holley 850 double-pumper.

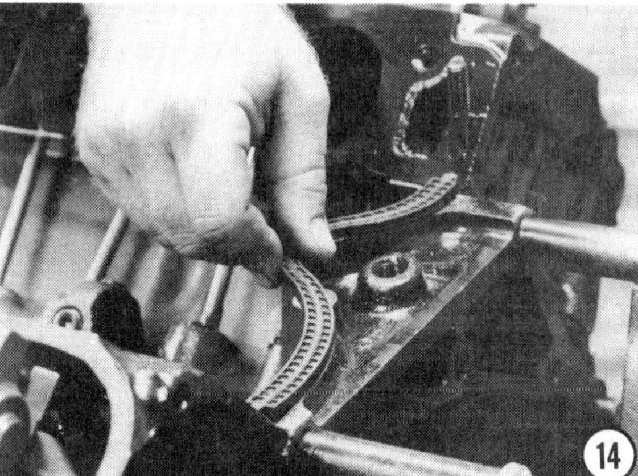

Another good tip from the Ford Marine supplier is this 4-piece intake manifold gasket set featuring rubber end seals. It's part number D00Z-9433-A.

Be sure to use a good high-temp silicone sealant around the front and rear water passages in the heads, since these sometimes cause leaks.

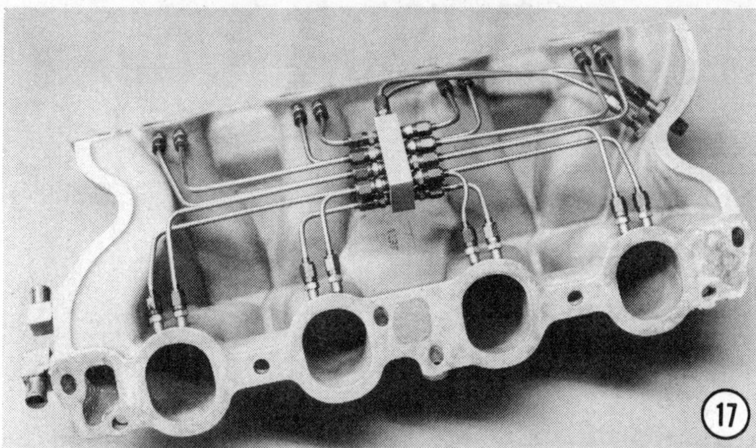

But what most river hot doggers fail to notice are the pair of unobtrusive braided steel lines feeding the Marvin Miller 150-hp nitrous-oxide injection system plumbed on the bottom side of the manifold. The Ford big block responds very well to the laughing gas.

With the manifold in place on the engine, the majority of the nitrous system is concealed. Harmon Marine makes the aluminum water pump block off plate.

The finished piece, with Lightning water-injected headers and a Harwood bug catcher in place, looks healthy enough but still belies the ultimate potential. First weekend out on the Colorado River it showed a rooster's backside to every rat motor on the water.

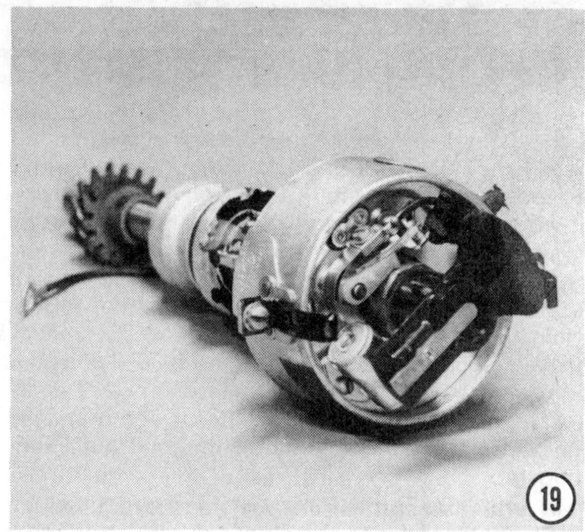

429/460 engines will also accept the same ignitions as Clevelands, so specialty varieties abound. However, Steve has found that this simple Marine single-point distributor (D3JL-12100-G) made by Prestolite is perfectly adequate to 8000 rpm—which is beyond the capacity of most 460's. The distributor has been recurved to give 15° advance by 1250 rpm, with 38-40° total timing in the engine.

Wouldn't this look sweet between the gunwales of a flatbottom or between the fenders of a hot street machine? A professionally-prepped 460 could cost $2000 but by shopping around and doing as much of the assembly work as possible himself Steve Strange was able to cut his costs almost in half. Don't waste money on unneeded frills but don't cut corners on basic necessities.

HOW TO READ FORD PART NUMBERS

They may look confusing and complicated, but there is a logic to the Ford parts numbering system that goes beyond simple counting. Each number is comprised of three groups of characters. The first group always contains a letter, a number, and two letters. For example, the number for the Muscle Parts hydraulic camshaft for 390 and 428 engines is C8AX-6250-C. The first group of this part number is C8AX. The first two characters of this group tell when the part was originally released. C stands for the decade 1960 (D is 1970; E will be the 1980's, and so on). The number following it is the specific year in that decade. The next letter, in this case "A," denotes the body style for which the part was made. A partial listing of this code system follows:

A = full-size Fords (Galaxies)	R = Capri
F = Pinto, Maverick, Falcon	S = Thunderbird
L = Lincoln Mark IV	T = Truck
M = Mercury	V = Lincoln
O = Fairlane	Z = Mustang, Mustang II

The final letter of the first group is a code telling where the part is warehoused. Special performance parts sold through the Ford Muscle Parts Program had an "X" designation. So the first group of characters—C8AX—tells us this part was released in 1968, it was ostensibly made for full-size Fords, and it was a Muscle Part.

The second set of digits, usually four numbers (though it can be more, and may contain letters), identifies the type of part. The number 6250 indicates this is a camshaft. All Ford camshafts are identified by this number. 9510 denotes a carburetor; 12127 is a distributor, and so on.

The final "group" of the part number is usually a single letter (though it can sometimes be more than one), signifying how many times the part has been revised since the original release. The suffix "C" means that the big block hydraulic camshaft is the third revision (A is the first, B the second, etc.) of the design.

SELECTED FORD PARTS BUYER'S GUIDE

All American Racers, Inc. **(Dan Gurney)** **2334 S. Broadway** **Santa Ana, CA 92700**	**Gurney-Eagle head conversion kits for smallblocks**
Babric Enterprises **P.O. Box 278** **M.t Eden, CA 94577**	**Some used Shelby and Cobra hard parts; emblems, trim, Mustang restoration parts**
Bud Moore Engineering **400 N. Fairview** **Spratenburg, SC 29303**	**Grand National racing components; "box" plenum intake manifold for Clevelands**
California Mustang Sales and Parts Co. **1249 E. Holt Ave.** **Pomona, CA 91767**	**Comprehensive line of Mustang restoration parts (Chassis, upholstery, trim, emblems), some engine parts**
Cobra Performance Parts **3523 LaGrande Blvd.** **Sacramento, CA 95823**	**Shelby Mustang and Cobra parts (body, chassis, trim, engine components)**
Ford Power Parts **(Ron Miller)** **12200 E. Washington Blvd., Unit C** **Whittier, CA 90606**	**Good selection of new and used Ford high performance and Muscle Parts (blocks, heads, valves, pistons, rods, cams, etc.)**
Gapp and Roush **12319 Leban Rd.** **Livonia, MI 48150**	**Complete engines, high-port heads, new Ford specialty performance parts for drag racing and circle track**
Hank the Crank **7523 Lankershim Blvd.** **North Hollywood, CA 91605**	**Performance crankshafts, Cleveland oiling systems, pistons, rods, etc.**
Holman Moody, Inc. **P.O. Box 27065** **Charlotte, NC 38219**	**Grand National and Baby Grand racing equipment; limited supply of Ford specialty racing parts**
Maier Racing Enterprises **(Bill Maier)** **235 Laurel Ave.** **Hayward, CA 94541**	**Mustang and Cobra engine, body, and chassis parts; good selection of engine hard parts and sports racing equipment**
Muscle Parts, Inc. **(Tom Tlusty)** **P.O. Box 724** **Dearborn, MI 48121**	**New smallblock and Cleveland engine parts; Mustang restoration parts**
Super Ford Parts Exchange **(John Paradise)** **T-110 Ovid St.** **Senca Falls, NY 13148**	**Monthly Ford performance magazine with extensive classified advertising section of Ford engine parts; also carry some exotic Ford parts (Boss, SOHC, Shelby) for sale**
Total Performance **(John Vermeersch)** **40631 Irwin** **Mt. Clemens, MI 48045**	**Excellent selection of new and used high-performance, Muscle Parts, and exotic racing parts for all Ford engines**
Valley Ford Parts **11604 Vanowen St.** **North Hollywood, CA 91605**	**Mustang and Shelby restoration parts (body, trim, chassis); some smallblock engine parts**
Vintage Shelby Mustang Sales **1942 Bluebell Dr.** **Livermore, CA 94550**	**Mustang parts; new smallblock speed equipment for street use**

KEY ENGINE DIMENSIONS

A Bore
B Stroke
C Bore Spacing
D Crankshaft Main Journal Dia.
E Crankshaft Rod Journal Dia.
F Cam Journal Dia.
G Centerline of Crank to Top of Block (Head Face)
H Block Deck Height Clearance
I Piston Compression Height
J Con Rod center-to-center length
K Intake and Exhaust Valve Head Dia.
L Valve Spring Installed Height

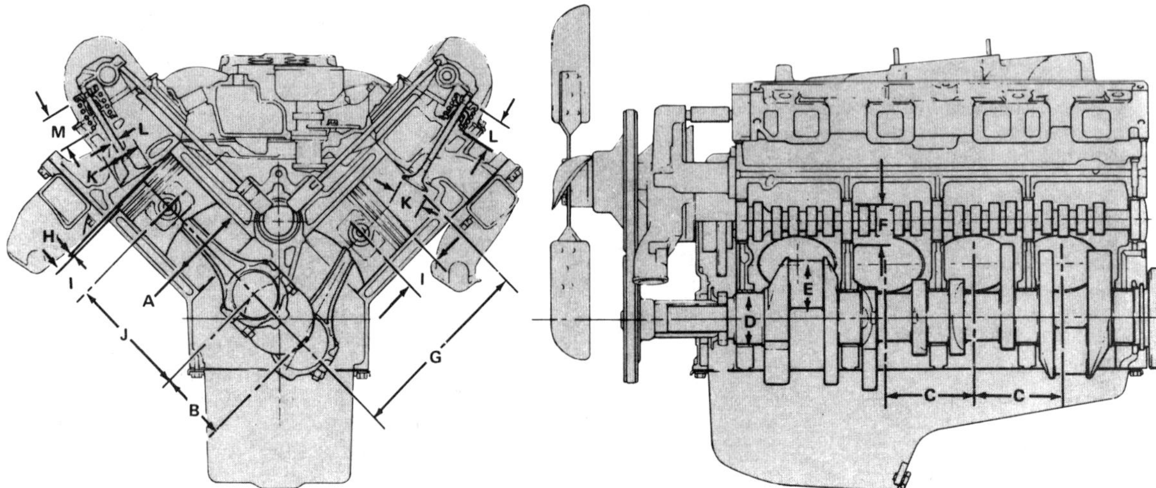

ADDITIONAL PARTS SUPPLIERS

A

ACCEL
P.O.Box 142
Branford, CT 06405
Ignitions

Addco Industries, Inc.
Watertower Rd.
Lake Park, FL 33403
Sway Bars

Advance Adapters
P.O.Box 2767
Santa Fe Springs, CA 90670
Engine/Trans Adapters

Appliance Industries
18747 Laurel Pk. Rd.
Compton, CA 90221
Headers & Wheels

Autohaus
1338 W. 6th St.
Corona, CA 91720
Accessories

Auto Meter Products
413 W. Elm St.
Sycamore, IL 60178
Instruments

Autotronic Controls Corp.
6908 Commerce St.
El Paso, TX 79915
Ignitions

B

B & B Performance Sales, Inc.
23190 Del Lago Dr.
Laguna Hills, CA 92653
Accessories

B & M Automotive Products
9152 Independence
Chatsworth, CA91311
Auto Transmissions

C

Cal Custom Hawk
23011 S. Wilmington
Carson, CA 90745
Accessories

Cam Dynamics
3926 Runway Rd.
Memphis, TN 38118
Cams

Carrera Racing Shocks
5412 New Peach Tree Rd.
Atlanta, GA 30341
Suspensions

Carter Carburetor, Div. ACF Ind.
9666 Olive St.
St. Louis, MO 63132
Carbs, Fuel Systems

Casler Performance Products
1032 W. Brooks St.
Ontario, CA 91761
Headers

Champion Spark Plug Co.
P.O.Box 910
Toledo, OH 43661
Spark Plugs

Cheshire Manufacturing Co., Inc.
312 E. Johnson Ave.
Cheshire, CT 06410
Coolers

Chrysler Corp.-Direct Connection
Box 1718 CIMS 423-13-06
Detroit, MI 48288
Cams, Headers, Ignitions

Clifford Research
1670 Sunflower Ave.
Costa Mesa, CA92626
Manifolds, Headers, Accessories

Competition Cams
2806 Hangar Rd.
Memphis, TN 28118
Cams

Cragar Industries
19007 S. Reyes Ave.
Compton, CA 90221
Headers, Ignitions

Crane Cams, Inc.
P.O. Box 160
Hallandale, FL 33009
Cams, Valvetrains

Crower Cams & Equipment Co.
3333 Main St.
Chula Vista, CA 92011
Cams, Valvetrains

Cyclone Automotive Products
7040 N. Lankershim Blvd.
N. Hollywood, CA 91605
Headers, Exhaust Systems

E

Eagle Specialty Products, Inc.
8341 Canoga Ave.
Canoga Park, CA 91304
Headers

Earl's Supply Co.
825 E. Sepulveda Blvd.
Carson, CA 90745
Plumbing

Edelbrock Equipment Co.
411 Coral Circle
El Segundo, CA 90245
Manifolds

Engle Cams
1621 12th St.
Santa Monica, CA 90404
Cams

Sig Erson Racing Cams
15881 Chemical Lane
Huntington Beach, CA 92649
Cams, Valvetrains

H

Harbor Industries
13025 Halldale Ave.
Gardena, CA 90249
Accessories

Hayden Trans Coolers
1531 Pomona Rd.
Corona, CA 91720
Trans Coolers

Hays Sales
15116 Adams St.
Midway City, CA 92655
Ignitions

Hedman Mfg. Co.
9599 W. Jefferson
Culver City, CA 90230
Headers

Hobrecht Enterprises
15662 Commerce Lane
Huntington Beach, CA 92649
Roll Bars

Holley Replacement Parts
11955 E. Nine Mile Rd.
Warren, MI 48090
Carbs, Fuel Systems

Hooker Headers
1009 W. Brooks St.
Ontario, CA 91761
Headers

Howard Cams
19122 S. Main St.
Los Angeles, CA 90003
Cams

Hurst Performance, Inc.
50 W. Street Rd.
Warminster, PA 18974
Shifters

I

Interpart Corp.
230 W. Rosecrans Ave.
Gardena, CA 90248
Cams, Headers, Accessories

Iskenderian Racing Cams
16020 S. Broadway
Gardena, CA 90248
Cams, Valvetrains

J

Pete Jackson Gear Drives
1905 Victory Bl.
Glendale, CA 91201
Gear Drives

Jones Instrument Corp.
432 Fairfield Ave.
Stamford, CT 06904
Instruments

K

K & N Engineering
561 Iowa Ave.
Riverside, CA 92507
Air Filters

Koni America, Inc.
111 W. Lover's Lane
Culpeper, VA 22701
Koni Shock Absorbers

L

Lakewood Industries
4566 Spring Rd.
Cleveland, OH 44131
Accessories

Lamb Components
1259 W. 9th St.
Upland, CA 91786
Specialty Brake Systems

M

Maier Racing Enterprises
235 Laurel Ave.
Hayward, CA 94541
Ford Specialties

Mallory Electric Corp.
1801 Oregon St.
Carson City, NV 89701
Ignitions

Manley Performance Products
13 Race St.
Bloomfield, NJ07003
Cams, Accessories

McCleod Industries
1125 N. Armando St.
Anaheim, CA 92806
Clutches

Milodon Engineering
7711 Ventura Canyon
Van Nuys, CA 91402
Accessories

Moroso Performance Products, Inc.
Carter Dr.
Guilford, CT 06437
Accessories

Moon Equipment
10820 S. Norwalk Blvd.
Santa Fe Springs, CA 90670
Cams, Accessories

Mullen & Co.
340-C East Carson St.
Carson, CA 90745
Valves, Head Preparation

N

Nelson-Dunn, Inc.
940 S. Vail Ave.
Montebello, CA90640
Aeroquip Hose, Fittings

Norris Performance Products
14762 Calvert St.
Van Nuys, CA 91401
Cams, Valvetrains

O

Offenhauser Sales Corp.
5232 Alhambra Ave.
Los Angeles, CA 90032
Manifolds

R

Race Car Parts
22628 S. Normandie
Torrance, CA 90502
Plumbing, Accessories

Racer Brown, Inc.
9270 Borden Ave.
Sun Valley, CA 91352
Cams, Valvetrains

Racer Walsh
11 Washington Ave.
Suffern, NY 10901
Cams, Accessories

Reed Cams
114 New St.
Decatur, GA 30030
Cams

Rocket Industries, Inc.
9935 Beverly Blvd.
Pico Rivera, CA 90660
Accessories

Ro-Lan Sales
1031 S. Laramie St.
Anaheim, CA 92806
Electrical Supplies

Rotiform Corporation
5140 W. 106th St.
Inglewood, CA 90304
Instruments

S

Schneider Racing Cams
1235 Cushman Ave.
San Diego, CA 92110
Cams

Sorenson Mfg. Co.
1115 Cleveland Ave.
Glasgow, KY 42141
Ignition Wiring

Spearco Performance Products
10936 S. La Cienega Bl.
Inglewood, CA 90304
Accessories

Speed Pro/Sealed Power Corp.
100 Terrace Plaza
Muskegon, MI 49443
Cams, Engine Parts

Stahl Headers
1515 Mt. Rose Ave.
York, PA 17403
Headers

Stewart-Warner Corp.
1826 Diversey Pkwy.
Chicago, IL 60614
Instruments

Sun Electric Corp., Consumer Products
1105 N. Fair Oaks Dr.
Sunnyvale, CA 94086
Instruments

T

Taylor Cable Products
301 Highgrove Rd.
Grandview, MO 64030
Ignition Wiring

Thermo-Chem
10516 E. Pine
Tulsa, OK 74116
Coolers

Doug Thorley Headers
7403 Telegraph Rd.
Los Angeles, CA 90040
Headers, Exhaust Systems

Thrush, Inc.
172 Bethridge Rd.
Rexdale, Ontario, Canada M9W 1N3
Exhaust Systems

Tom's Differentials
15547 Paramount Blvd.
Paramount, CA 90723
Custom Rear End Assembly

Trans-Dapt of California
16410 Manning Way
Cerritos, CA 90701
Trans/Engine Adapters

Trans-Go
2621 Merced Ave.
El Monte, CA 91733
Auto Trans Shift Kits

TRW Replacement Division
8001 E. Pleasant Valley Rd.
Cleveland, OH 44131
Cams, Engine Parts

Turbo Action, Inc.
Box 5581
Jacksonville, FL 32207
Auto Trans Shift Kits

VDO-ARGO Instruments, Inc.
980 Brooke Rd.
Winchester, VA 22601
Instruments

W

Weiand Automotive Industries
2316 San Fernando Rd.
Los Angeles, CA 90065
Manifolds